M000268395

World of Rhetoric

Volume II

Kendall Hunt

publishing company

Sam Perry • Sarah Walden

Cover image © Shutterstock, Inc.

Kendall Hunt
p u b l i s h i n g   c o m p a n y

www.kendallhunt.com
Send all inquiries to:
4050 Westmark Drive
Dubuque, IA 52004-1840

Copyright © 2017 by Kendall Hunt Publishing Company

ISBN 978-1-5249-0312-1

All rights reserved. No part of this publication may be reproduced,
stored in a retrieval system, or transmitted, in any form or by any means,
electronic, mechanical, photocopying, recording, or otherwise,
without the prior written permission of the copyright owner.

Published in the United States of America

Contents

Unit 3: Placing Texts in Contexts 151

Unit 1: Building Texts

The "Ideograph":
A Link Between Rhetoric and Ideology

Michael Calvin McGee

Mr. McGee is Associate Professor, Department of Speech and Dramatic Art, University of Iowa. Portions of this essay were presented at the Central States Communication Association convention, Detroit, Michigan, 1976. The author wishes to thank Herbert Simons for use of an unpublished paper and for exceptionally helpful criticism.

In 1950, Kenneth Burke, apparently following Dewey, Mead, and Lippmann, announced his preference for the notion "philosophy of myth" to explain the phenomenon of "public" or "mass consciousness" rather than the then-prevalent concept "ideology."[1] As contemporary writers have pushed on toward developing this "symbolic" or "dramatistic" alternative, the concept "ideology" has atrophied. Many use the term innocently, almost as a synonym for "doctrine" or "dogma" in political organizations[2]; and others use the word in a hypostatized sense that obscures or flatly denies the fundamental connection between the concept and descriptions of mass consciousness.[3] The concept seems to have gone the way of the dodo and of the neo-Aristotelian critic: As Bormann has suggested, the very word is widely perceived as being encrusted with the "intellectual baggage" of orthodox Marxism.[4]

Objecting to the use or abuse of any technical term would, ordinarily, be a sign of excessive crabbiness. But in this instance conceptualizations of "philosophy of myth," "fantasy visions," and "political scenarios," coupled with continued eccentric and/or narrow usages of "ideology," cosmetically camouflage significant and unresolved problems. We are presented with a brute, undeniable phenomenon: Human beings in collectivity behave and think differently than human beings in isolation. The collectivity is said to "have a mind of its own" distinct from the individual qua individual. Writers in the tradition of Marx and Mannheim explain this difference by observing that the only possibility of "mind" lies in the individual qua individual, in the human organism itself. When one appears to "think" and "behave" collectively, therefore, one has been tricked, self-deluded, or manipulated into accepting the brute existence of such fantasies as "public mind" or "public opinion" or "public philosophy." Symbolists generally want to say that this trick is a "transcendence," a voluntary agreement to believe in and to participate in a "myth." Materialists maintain that the trick is an insidious, reified form of "lie," a self-perpetuating system of beliefs and interpretations foisted on all members of the community by the ruling class. Burke, with his emphasis on the individuals who are tricked, con-

From *The Quarterly Journal of Speech,* Volume 66, Number 1, February 1980 by Michael Calvin McGee. Copyright © 1980 by Routledge. Reprinted by permission.

cerns himself more with the structure of "motive" than with the objective conditions that impinge on and restrict the individual's freedom to develop a political consciousness. Neo-Marxians, with focus on tricksters and the machinery of trickery, say that the essential question posed by the fact of society is one of locating precise descriptions of the dialectical tension between a "true" and a "false" consciousness, between reality and ideology.[5]

Though some on both sides of the controversy would have it otherwise, there is no *error* in either position. Both "myth" and "ideology" presuppose a fundamental falsity in the common metaphor which alleges the existence of a "social organism." "Ideology," however, assumes that the exposure of falsity is a moral act: Though we have never experienced a "true consciousness," it is nonetheless theoretically accessible to us, and, because of such accessibility, we are morally remiss if we do not discard the false and approach the true. The falsity presupposed by "myth," on the other hand, is amoral because it is a purely poetic phenomenon, legitimized by rule of the poet's license, a "suspension of disbelief." A symbolist who speaks of "myth" is typically at great pains to argue for a value-free approach to the object of study, an approach in which one denies that "myth" is a synonym for "lie" and treats it as a falsehood of a peculiarly redemptive nature. Materialists, on the other hand, seem to use the concept "ideology" expressly to warrant normative claims regarding the exploitation of the "proletarian class" by self-serving plunderers. No error is involved in the apparently contradictory conceptions because, fundamentally, materialists and symbolists pursue two different studies: The Marxian asks how the "givens" of a human environment impinge on the development of political consciousness; the symbolist asks how the human symbol-using, reality-creating potential impinges on material reality, ordering it normatively, "mythically."

Errors arise when one conceives "myth" and "ideology" to be contraries, alternative and incompatible theoretical descriptions of the same phenomenon. The materialists' neglect of language studies and the consequent inability of Marxian theory to explain socially constructed realities is well-publicized.[6] Less well described is the symbolists' neglect of the nonsymbolic environment and the consequent inability of symbolist theory to account for the impact of material phenomena on the construction of social reality.[7] I do not mean to denigrate in any way the research of scholars attempting to develop Burke's philosophy of myth; indeed, I have on occasion joined that endeavor. I do believe, however, that each of us has erred to the extent that we have conceived the rubrics of symbolism as an *alternative* rather than *supplemental* description of political consciousness. The assertion that "philosophy of myth" is an alternative to "ideology" begs the question Marx intended to pose. Marx was concerned with "power," with the capacity of an elite class to control the state's political, economic, and military establishment, to dominate the state's information systems and determine even the consciousness of large masses of people. He was politically committed to the cause of the proletariat: If a norm was preached by the upper classes, it was by virtue of that fact a baneful seduction; and if a member of the proletarian class was persuaded by such an argument, that person was possessed of an "ideology," victimized and exploited. Not surprisingly, symbolists criticize Marx for his politics, suggesting that his is a wonderfully convenient formula which mistakes commitment for "historically scientific truth." By conceiving poetic falsity, we rid ourselves of the delusion that interpretation is scientific, but we also bury the probability that the myths we study as an alternative are thrust upon us by the brute force of "power." While Marx overestimated "power" as a variable in describing political consciousness, Burke, Cassirer, Polanyi, and others do not want to discuss the capacity even of a "free" state to determine political consciousness.[8]

If we are to describe the trick-of-the-mind which deludes us into believing that we "think" with/through/ for a "society" to which we "belong," we need a theoretical model which accounts for both "ideology" and "myth," a model which neither denies human capacity to control "power" through the manipulation of symbols nor begs Marx's essential questions regarding the influence of "power" on creating and maintaining political consciousness. I will argue here that such a model must begin with the concept "ideology" and proceed to link that notion directly with the interests of symbolism.

I will elaborate the following commitments and hypotheses: If a mass consciousness exists at all, it must be empirically "present," itself a thing obvious to those who participate in it, or, at least, empirically manifested in the language which communicates it. I agree with Marx that the problem of consciousness is fundamentally practical and normative, that it is concerned essentially with describing and evaluating the legitimacy of public motives. Such consciousness, I believe, is always false, not because we are programmed automatons and not because we have a propensity to structure political perceptions in poetically false "dramas" or "scenarios," but because "truth" in politics, no matter how firmly we believe, is always an illusion. The falsity of an ideology is specifically rhetorical, for the illusion of truth and falsity with regard to normative commitments is the product of persuasion.[9] Since the clearest access to persuasion (and hence to ideology) is through the discourse used to produce it, I will suggest that ideology in practice is a political language, preserved in rhetorical documents, with the capacity to dictate decision and control public belief and behavior. Further, the political language which manifests ideology seems characterized by slogans, a vocabulary of "ideographs" easily mistaken for the technical terminology of political philosophy. An analysis of ideographic usages in political rhetoric, I believe, reveals interpenetrating systems or "structures" of public motives. Such structures appear to be "diachronic" and "synchronic" patterns of political consciousness which have the capacity both to control "power" and to influence (if not determine) the shape and texture of each individual's "reality."

HYPOTHETICAL CHARACTERISTICS OF "IDEOGRAPHS"

Marx's thesis suggests that an ideology determines mass belief and thus restricts the free emergence of political opinion. By this logic, the "freest" members of a community are those who belong to the "power" elite; yet the image of hooded puppeteers twisting and turning the masses at will is unconvincing if only because the elite seems itself imprisoned by the same false consciousness communicated to the polity at large. When we consider the impact of ideology on freedom, and of power on consciousness, we must be clear that ideology is transcendent, as much an influence on the belief and behavior of the ruler as on the ruled. Nothing *necessarily* restricts persons who wield the might of the state. Roosevelts and Carters are as free to indulge personal vanity with capricious uses of power as was Idi Amin, regardless of formal "checks and balances." The polity can punish tyrants and maniacs after the fact of their lunacy or tyranny (if the polity survives it), but, in practical terms, the only way to shape or soften power at the moment of its exercise is prior persuasion. Similarly, no matter what punishment we might imagine "power" visiting upon an ordinary citizen, nothing *necessarily* determines individual behavior and belief. A citizen may be punished for eccentricity or disobedience after the fact of a crime, but, at the moment when defiance is contemplated, the only way to combat the impulse to criminal behavior is prior persuasion. I am suggesting, in other words, that social control in its essence is control over consciousness, the a priori influence that learned predispositions hold over human agents who play the roles of "power" and "people" in a given transaction.[10]

Because there is a lack of necessity in social control, it seems inappropriate to characterize agencies of control as "socializing" or "conditioning" media. No individual (least of all the elite who control the power of the state) is *forced* to submit in the same way that a conditioned dog is obliged to salivate or socialized children are required to speak English. Human beings are "conditioned," not directly to belief and behavior, but to a vocabulary of concepts that function as guides, warrants, reasons, or excuses for behavior and belief. When a claim is warranted by such terms as "law," "liberty," "tyranny," or "trial by jury," in other words, it is presumed that human beings will react predictably and autonomically. So it was that a majority of Americans were surprised, not when allegedly sane young men agreed to go halfway around the world to kill for God, country, apple pie, and no other particularly good reason, but, rather, when other young men displayed good common sense by moving to Montreal instead, thereby refusing to be conspicuous in a civil war which was none of their business. The end product of the state's insistence on some degree of conformity in behavior and belief, I suggest, is a *rhetoric* of control, a system of persuasion presumed to be effective on the whole community. We make a rhetoric of war to persuade us of war's necessity, but then forget that it is a rhetoric—and regard negative popular judgments of it as unpatriotic cowardice.

It is not remarkable to conceive social control as fundamentally rhetorical. In the past, however, rhetorical scholarship has regarded the rhetoric of control as a species of argumentation and thereby assumed that the fundamental unit of analysis in such rhetoric is an integrated set-series of propositions. This is, I believe, a mistake, an unwarranted abstraction: To argue is to test an affirmation or denial of claims; argument is the means of proving the truth of grammatical units, declarative sentences, that purport to be reliable signal representations of reality. Within the vocabulary of argumentation, the term "rule of law" makes no sense until it is made the subject or predicable of a proposition. If I say "The rule of law is a primary cultural value in the United States" or "Charles I was a cruel and capricious tyrant," I have asserted a testable claim that may be criticized with logically coordinated observations. When I say simply "the rule of law," however, my utterance cannot qualify logically as a claim. Yet I am conditioned to believe that "liberty" and "property" have an obvious meaning, a behaviorally directive self-evidence. Because I am taught to set such terms apart from my usual vocabulary, words used as agencies of social control may have an intrinsic force—and, if so, I may very well distort the key terms of social conflict, commitment, and control if I think of them as parts of a proposition rather than as basic units of analysis.

Though words only (and not claims), such terms as "property," "religion," "right of privacy," "freedom of speech," "rule of law," and "liberty" are more pregnant than propositions ever could be. They are the basic structural elements, the building blocks, of ideology. Thus they may be thought of as "ideographs," for, like Chinese symbols, they signify and "contain" a unique ideological commitment; further, they presumptuously suggest that each member of a community will see as a gestalt every complex nuance in them. What "rule of law" means is the series of propositions, all of them, that could be manufactured to justify a Whig/Liberal order. Ideographs are one-term sums of an orientation, the species of "God" or "Ultimate" term that will be used to symbolize the line of argument the meanest sort of individual *would* pursue, if that individual had the dialectical skills of philosophers, as a defense of a personal stake in and commitment to the society. Nor is one permitted to question the fundamental logic of ideographs: Everyone is conditioned to think of "the rule of law" as a *logical* commitment just as one is taught to think that "186,000 miles per second" is an accurate empirical description of the speed of light even though few can work the experiments or do the mathematics; to prove it.[11]

The important fact about ideographs is that they exist in real discourse, functioning clearly and evidently as agents of political consciousness. They are not invented by observers; they come to be as a part of the real lives of the people whose motives they articulate. So, for example, "rule of law" is a more precise, objective motive than such observer-invented terms as "neurotic" or "paranoid style" or *"petit bourgeois."*

Ideographs pose a methodological problem *because* of their very specificity: How do we generalize from a "rule of law" to a description of consciousness that comprehends not only "rule of law" but all other like motives as well? What do we describe with the concept "ideograph," and how do we actually go about doing the specific cultural analysis promised by conceptually linking rhetoric and ideology?

Though both come to virtually the same conclusion, the essential argument seems more careful and useful in Ortega's notion of "the etymological man" than in Burke's poetically hidden concept of "the symbol-using animal" and "logology":

Man, when he sets himself to speak, does so *because* he believes that he will be able to say what he thinks. Now, this is an illusion. Language is not up to that. It says, more or less, a part of what we think, and raises an impenetrable obstacle to the transmission of the rest. It serves quite well for mathematical statements and proofs. . . . But in proportion as conversation treats of more important, more human, more "real" subjects than these, its vagueness, clumsiness, and confusion steadily increase. Obedient to the inveterate prejudice that "talking leads to understanding," we speak and listen in such good faith that we end by misunderstanding one another far more than we would if we remained mute and set ourselves to divine each other. Nay, more: since our thought is in large measure dependent upon our language . . . it follows that thinking is talking with oneself and hence misunderstanding oneself at the imminent risk of getting oneself into a complete quandary.[12]

All this "talk" generates a series of "usages" which unite us, since we speak the same language, but, more significantly, such "talk" *separates* us from other human beings who do not accept our meanings, our intentions.[13] So, Ortega claims, the essential demarcation of whole nations is language usage: "This gigantic architecture of usages is, precisely, society."[14] And it is through usages that a particular citizen's sociality exists:

A language, *speech*, is "what people say," it is the vast system of verbal usages established in a collectivity. The individual, the person, is from his birth submitted to the linguistic coercion that these usages represent. Hence the mother tongue is perhaps the most typical and clearest social phenomenon. With it "people" enter us, set up residence in us, making each an example of "people." Our mother tongue socializes our inmost being, and because of this fact every individual belongs, in the strongest sense of the word, to a society. He can flee from the society in which he was born and brought up, but in his flight the society inexorably accompanies him because he carries it within him. This is the true meaning that the statement "man is a social animal" can have.[15]

Ortega's reference, of course, is to language generally and not to a particular vocabulary within language. So he worked with the vocabulary of greeting to demonstrate the definitive quality of linguistic usages when conceiving "society."[16] His reasoning, however, invites specification, attention to the components of the "architecture" supposedly created by usages.

Insofar as usages both unite and separate human beings, it seems reasonable to suggest that the functions of uniting and separating would be represented by specific vocabularies, actual words or terms. With regard to political union and separation, such vocabularies would consist of ideographs. Such usages as "liberty" define a collectivity, i.e., the outer parameters of a society, because such terms either do not exist in other societies or do not have precisely similar meanings. So, in the United States, we claim a common belief in "equality," as do citizens of the Union of Soviet Socialist Republics; but "equality" is not the same word in its meaning or its usage. One can therefore precisely define the difference between the two communities, in part, by comparing the usage of definitive ideographs. We are, of course, still able to interact with the Soviets despite barriers of language and usage. The interaction is possible because of higher-order ideographs—"world peace," "detente," "spheres of influence," etc.—that permit temporary union.[17] And, in the other direction, it is also true that there are special interests within the United States separated from one another precisely by disagreements regarding the identity, legitimacy, or definition of ideographs. So we are divided by usages into subgroups: Business and labor, Democrats and Republicans, Yankees and Southerners are *united* by the ideographs that represent the political entity "United States" and *separated* by a disagreement as to the practical meaning of such ideographs.

The concept "ideograph" is meant to be purely descriptive of an essentially social human condition. Unlike more general conceptions of "Ultimate" or "God" terms, attention is called to the social, rather than rational or ethical, functions of a particular vocabulary. This vocabulary is precisely a group of *words* and not a series of symbols representing ideas. Ortega clearly, methodically, distinguishes a usage (what we might call "social" or "material" thought) from an *idea* (what Ortega would call "pure thought"). He suggests, properly, that *language gets in the way of thinking*, separates us from "ideas" we may have which cannot be surely expressed, even to ourselves, in the usages which imprison us. So my "pure thought" about liberty, religion, and property is clouded, hindered, made irrelevant by the existence in history of the ideographs "Liberty, Religion, and Property."[18] Because these terms are definitive of the society we have inherited, they are *conditions* of the society into which each of us is born, material ideas which we must accept to "belong." They penalize us, in a sense, as much as they protect us, for they prohibit our appreciation of an alternative pattern of meaning in, for example, the Soviet Union or Brazil.

In effect, ideographs—language imperatives which hinder and perhaps make impossible "pure thought"—are bound within the culture which they define. We can *characterize* an ideograph, say what it has meant and does mean as a usage, and some of us may be able to achieve an imaginary state of withdrawal from community long enough to speculate as to what ideographs *ought* to mean in the best of possible worlds; but the very nature of language forces us to keep the two operations separate: So, for example, the "idea" of "liberty" may be the subject of philosophical speculation, but philosophers can never be *certain* that they themselves or their readers understand a "pure" meaning unpolluted by historical, ideographic usages.[19] Should we look strictly at material notions of "liberty," on the other hand, we distort our thinking by believing that a rationalization of a particular historical meaning is "pure," the truth of the matter.[20] Ideographs can *not* be used to establish or test truth, and vice versa, the truth, in ideal metaphysical senses, is a consideration irrelevant to accurate characterizations of such ideographs as "liberty." Indeed, if examples from recent history are a guide, attempts to infuse usages with metaphysical meanings, or to confuse ideographs with the "pure" thought of philosophy, have resulted in the "nightmares" which Polanyi, for one, deplores.[21] The significance of ideographs is in their concrete history as usages, not in their alleged idea-content.

The Analysis of Ideographs

No one has ever seen an "equality" strutting up the driveway, so, if "equality" exists at all, it has meaning through its specific applications. In other words, we establish a meaning for "equality" by using the word as a description of a certain phenomenon; it has meaning only insofar as our description is acceptable, believable. If asked to make a case for "equality," that is to define the term, we are forced to make reference to its history by detailing the situations for which the word has been an appropriate description. Then, by comparisons over time, we establish an analog for the proposed present usage of the term. Earlier usages become precedent, touchstones for judging the propriety of the ideograph in a current circumstance. The meaning of "equality" does not rigidify because situations seeming to require its usage are never perfectly similar: As the situations vary, so the meaning of "equality" expands and contracts. The variations in meaning of "equality" are much less important, however, than the fundamental, categorical meaning, the "common denominator" of all situations for which "equality" has been the best and most descriptive term. The dynamism of "equality" is thus paramorphic, for even when the term changes its signification in particular circumstances, it retains a formal, categorical meaning, a constant reference to its history as an ideograph.

These earlier usages are vertically structured, related to each other in a formal way, every time the society is called upon to judge whether a particular circumstance should be defined ideographically. So, for example, to protect ourselves from abuses of power, we have built into our political system an ideograph that is said to justify "impeaching" an errant leader: If the President has engaged in behaviors which can be described as "high crimes and misdemeanors," even that highest officer must be removed.

But what is meant by "high crimes and misdemeanors"? If Peter Rodino wishes to justify impeachment procedures against Richard Nixon in the Committee on the Judiciary of the House of Representatives, he must mine history for touchstones, precedents which give substance and an aura of precision to the ideograph "high crimes and misdemeanors." His search of the past concentrates on situations analogous to that which he is facing, situations involving actual or proposed "impeachment." The "rule of law" emerged as a contrary ideograph, and Rodino developed from the tension between "law" and "high crimes" an argument indicting Nixon. His proofs were historical, ranging from Magna Carta to Edmund Burke's impeachment of Warren Hastings. He was able to make the argument, therefore, only because he could organize a series of events, situationally similar, with an ideograph as the structuring principle. The structuring is "vertical" because of the element of *time*; that is, the deep meanings of "law" and "high crime" derive from knowledge of the way in which meanings have evolved over a period of time—awareness of the way an ideograph can be meaningful *now* is controlled in large part by what it meant *then*.[22]

All communities take pains to record and preserve the vertical structure of their ideographs. Formally, the body of nonstatutory "law" is little more than a literature recording ideographic usages in the "common law" and "case law."[23] So, too, historical dictionaries, such as the *O. E. D.*, detail etymologies for most of the Anglo-American ideographs. And any so-called "professional" history provides a record in detail of the events surrounding earlier usages of ideographs—indeed, the historian's eye is most usually attracted precisely to those situations involving ideographic applications.[24] The more significant record of vertical structures, however, lies in what might be called "popular" history. Such history consists in part of novels, films, plays, even songs; but the truly influential manifestation is grammar school history, the very first contact most have with their existence and experience as a part of a community.

To learn the meanings of the ideographs "freedom" and "patriotism," for example, most of us swallowed the tale of Patrick Henry's defiant speech to the Virginia House of Burgesses: "I know not what course others may take, but as for me, give me liberty or give me death!" These specific words, of course, were concocted by the historian William Wirt and not by Governor Henry. Wirt's intention was to provide a model for "the young men of Virginia," asking them to copy Henry's virtues and avoid his vices.[25] Fabricated events and words meant little, not because Wirt was uninterested in the truth of what really happened to Henry, but rather because what he wrote about was the definition of essential ideographs. His was a task of socialization, an exercise in epideictic rhetoric, providing the youth of his age (and of our own) with general knowledge of ideographic touchstones so that they might be able to make, or comprehend, judgments of public motives and of their own civic duty.

Though such labor tires the mind simply in imagining it, there is no trick in gleaning from public documents the entire vocabulary of ideographs that define a particular collectivity. The terms do not hide in discourse, nor is their "meaning" or function within an argument obscure: We might disagree metaphysically about "equality," and we might use the term differently in practical discourse, but I believe we can nearly always discover the functional meaning of the term by measure of its grammatic and pragmatic context.[26] Yet even a complete description of vertical ideographic structures leaves little but an exhaustive lexicon understood etymologically and diachronically—and no ideally precise explanation of how ideographs function *presently*.

If we find forty rhetorical situations in which "rule of law" has been an organizing term, we are left with little but the simple chronology of the situations as a device to structure the lot: Case One is distinct from Case Forty, and the meaning of the ideograph thus has contracted or expanded in the intervening time. But time is an irrelevant matter in *practice*. Chronological sequences are provided by analysts, and they properly reflect the concerns of theorists who try to describe what "rule of law" *may* mean, potentially, by laying out the history of what the term *has* meant. Such advocates as Rodino are not so scrupulous in research; they choose eight or nine of those forty cases to use as evidence in argument, ignore the rest, and impose a pattern of organization on the cases recommended (or forced) by the demands of a current situation. As Ortega argues with reference to language generally, key usages considered historically and diachronically are purely formal; yet in real discourse, and in public consciousness, they are *forces*:

"[A]ll that diachronism accomplishes is to reconstruct other comparative "presents" of the language as they existed in the past. All that it shows us, then, is changes; it enables us to witness one present being replaced by another, the succession of the static figures of the language, as the "film," with its motionless images, engenders the visual fiction of a movement. At best, it offers us a cinematic view of language, but not a *dynamic* understanding of how the changes were, and came to be, *made*. The changes are merely results of the making and unmaking process, they are the externality of language, and there is need for an internal conception of it in which we discover not resultant *forms* but the operating *forces* themselves."[27]

In Burke's terminology, describing a vertical ideographic structure yields a culture-specific and relatively precise "grammar" of one public motive. That motive is not captured, however, without attention to its "rhetoric."

Considered rhetorically, as *forces*, ideographs seem structured horizontally, for when people actually make use of them presently, such terms as "rule of law" clash with other ideographs ("principle of confidentiality" or "national security," for example), and in the conflict come to mean with reference to synchronic confrontations. So, for example, one would not ordinarily think of an inconsistency between "rule of law" and "principle of confidentiality." Vertical analysis of the two ideographs would probably reveal a consonant relationship based on genus and species: "Confidentiality" of certain conversations is a control on the behavior of government, a control that functions to maintain a "rule of law" and prevents "tyranny" by preserving a realm of privacy for the individual.

The "Watergate" conflict between Nixon and Congress, however, illustrates how that consonant relationship can be restructured, perhaps broken, in the context of a particular controversy: Congress asked, formally and legally, for certain of Nixon's documents. He refused, thereby creating the appearance of frustrating the imperative value "rule of law." He attempted to excuse himself by matching a second ideograph, "principle of confidentiality," against normal and usual meanings of "rule of law." Before a mass television audience Nixon argued that a President's conversations with advisers were entitled to the same privilege constitutionally accorded exchanges between priest and penitent, husband and wife, lawyer and client. No direct vertical precedent was available to support Nixon's usage. The argument asked public (and later jurisprudential) permission to expand the meaning of "confidentiality" and thereby to alter its relationship with the "rule of law," making what appeared to be an illegal act acceptable. Nixon's claims were epideictic and not deliberative or forensic; he magnified "confidentiality" by praising the ideograph as if it were a person, attempting to alter its "standing" among other ideographs, even as an individual's "standing" in the community changes through praise and blame.[28]

Synchronic structural changes in the relative standing of an ideograph are "horizontal" because of the presumed consonance of an ideology; that is, ideographs such as "rule of law" are meant to be taken together, as a working unit, with "public trust," "freedom of speech," "trial by jury," and any other slogan characteristic of the collective life. If all the ideographs used to justify a Whig/Liberal government were placed on a chart, they would form groups or clusters of words radiating from the slogans originally used to rationalize "popular sovereignty"—"religion," "liberty," and "property." Each term would be a connector, modifier, specifier, or contrary for those fundamental historical commitments, giving them a meaning and a unity easily mistaken for logic. Some terms would be enshrined in the Constitution, some in law, some merely in conventional usage; but all would be constitutive of "the people." Though new usages can enter the equation, the ideographs remain essentialy unchanged. But when we engage ideological argument, when we cause ideographs to *do work* in explaining, justifying, or guiding policy in specific situations, the relationship of ideographs changes. A "rule of law," for example, is taken for granted, a simple connector between "property" and "liberty," until a constitutional crisis inclines us to make it "come first." In Burke's vocabulary, it becomes the "title" or "god-term" of all ideographs, the center-sun about which every ideograph orbits. Sometimes circumstance forces us to sense that the structure is not consonant, as when awareness of racism exposes contradiction between "property" and "right to life" in the context of "open-housing" legislation. Sometimes officers of state, in the process of justifying particular uses of power, manufacture seeming inconsistency, as when Nixon pitted "confidentiality" against "rule of law." And sometimes an alien force frontally assaults the structure, as when Hitler campaigned against "decadent democracies." Such instances have the potential to change the structure of ideographs and hence the "present" ideology—in this sense, an ideology is dynamic and a *force*, always resilient, always keeping itself in some consonance and unity, but not always the *same* consonance and unity.[29]

In appearance, of course, characterizing ideological conflicts as synchronic *structural* dislocations is an unwarranted abstraction: An ideological argument could result simply from multiple usages of an ideograph. Superficially, for example, one might be inclined to describe the "bussing" controversy as a disagreement over the "best" meaning for "equality," one side opting for "equality" defined with reference to "access" to education and the other with reference to the goal, "being educated." An ideograph, however, is always understood in its relation to another; it is defined tautologically by using other terms in its cluster. If we accept that there are three or four or however many possible meanings for "equality," each with a currency and legitimacy, we distort the nature of the ideological dispute by ignoring the fact that "equality" is made meaningful, not within the clash of multiple usages, but rather in its relationship with "freedom." That is, "equality" defined by "access" alters the nature of "liberty" from the relationship of "equality" and "liberty" thought to exist when "equality" is defined as "being educated." One would not want to rule out the possibility that ideological disagreements, however rarely, could be simply semantic; but we are more likely to err if we assume the dispute to be semantic than if we look for the deeper structural dislocation which likely produced multiple usages as a disease produces symptoms. When an ideograph is at the center of a semantic dispute, I would suggest, the multiple usages will be either metaphysical or diachronic, purely speculative or historical, and in either event devoid of the force and currency of a synchronic ideological conflict.[30]

In the terms of this argument, two recognizable "ideologies" exist in any specific culture at one "moment." One "ideology" is a "grammar," a historically defined diachronic structure of ideograph-meanings expanding and contracting from the birth of the society to its "present." Another "ideology" is a "rhetoric," a situationally defined synchronic structure of ideograph clusters constantly reorganizing itself to accommodate specific circumstances while maintaining its fundamental consonance and unity. A division of this sort, of course, is but an analytic convenience for talking about two *dimensions* (vertical and horizontal) of a single phenomenon: No present ideology can be divorced from past commitments if only because the very words used to express present dislocations have a history that establishes the category of their meaning. And no diachronic ideology can be divorced from the "here and now" if only because its entire *raison d'être* consists in justifying the form and direction of collective behavior. Both of these structures must be understood and described before one can claim to have constructed a theoretically precise explanation of a society's ideology, of its repertoire of public motives.

Conclusion

One of the casualties of the current "pluralist" fad in social and political theory has been the old Marxian thesis that governing elites control the masses by creating, maintaining, and manipulating a mass consciousness suited to perpetuation of the existing order.[31] Though I agree that Marx probably overestimated the influence of an elite, it is difficult *not* to see a "dominant ideology" which seems to exercise decisive influence in political life. The question, of course, turns on finding a way accurately to define and to describe a dominant ideology. Theorists writing in the tradition of Dewey, Burke, and Cassirer have, in my judgment, come close to the mark, but because they are bothered by poetic metaphors, these symbolists never conceive their work as description of a mass consciousness. Even these writers, therefore, beg Marx's inescapable question regarding the impact of "power" on the way we think. I have argued here that the concepts "rhetoric" and "ideology" may be linked without poetic metaphors, and that the linkage should produce a description and an explanation of dominant ideology, of the relationship between the "power" of a state and the consciousness of its people.

The importance of symbolist constructs is their focus on *media* of consciousness, on the discourse that articulates and propagates common beliefs. "Rhetoric," "sociodrama," "myth," "fantasy vision," and "political scenario" are not important because of their *fiction*, their connection to poetic, but because of their *truth*, their links with the trick-of-the-mind that deludes individuals into believing that they "think" with/for/ through a social organism. The truth of symbolist constructs, I have suggested, appears to lie in our claim to see a legitimate social reality in a vocabulary of complex, high-order abstractions that refer to and invoke a sense of "the people." By learning the meaning of ideographs, I have argued, everyone in society, even the "freest" of us, those who control the state, seem predisposed to structured mass responses. Such terms as "liberty," in other words, constitute by our very use of them in political discourse an ideology that governs or "dominates" our consciousness. In practice, therefore, ideology is a political language composed of slogan-like terms signifying collective commitment.

Such terms I have called "ideographs." A formal definition of "ideograph," derived from arguments made throughout this essay, would list the following characteristics: An ideograph is an ordinary-language term found in political discourse. It is a high-order abstraction representing collective commitment to a particular but equivocal and ill-defined normative goal. It warrants the use of power, excuses behavior and belief which might otherwise be perceived as eccentric or antisocial, and guides behavior and belief into channels easily recognized by a community as acceptable and laudable. Ideographs such as "slavery" and "tyranny," however, may guide behavior and belief negatively by branding unacceptable behavior. And many ideographs ("liberty," for example) have a non-ideographic usage, as in the sentence, "Since I resigned my position, I am at liberty to accept your offer." Ideographs are culture-bound, though some terms are used in different signification across cultures. Each member of the community is socialized, conditioned, to the vocabulary of ideographs as a prerequisite for "belonging" to the society. A degree of tolerance is usual, but people are expected to understand ideographs within a range of usage thought to be acceptable: The society will inflict penalties on those who use ideographs in heretical ways and on those who refuse to respond appropriately to claims on their behavior warranted through the agency of ideographs.

Though ideographs such as "liberty," "religion," and "property" often appear as technical terms in social philosophy, I have argued here that the ideology of a community is established by the usage of such terms in specifically rhetorical discourse, for such usages constitute excuses for specific beliefs and behaviors made by those who executed the history of which they were a part. The ideographs used in rhetorical discourse seem structured in two ways: In isolation, each ideograph has a history, an etymology, such that current meanings of the term are linked to past usages of it diachronically. The diachronic structure of an ideograph establishes the parameters, the category, of its meaning. All ideographs taken together, I suggest, are thought at any specific "moment" to be consonant, related to one another in such a way as to produce unity of commitment in a particular historical context. Each ideograph is thus connected to all others as brain cells are linked by synapses, synchronically in one context at one specific moment.

A complete description of an ideology, I have suggested, will consist of (1) the isolation of a society's ideographs, (2) the exposure and analysis of the diachronic structure of every ideograph, and (3) characterization of synchronic relationships among all the ideographs in a particular context. Such a description, I believe, would yield a theoretical framework with which to describe interpenetrating material and symbolic environments: Insofar as we can explain the diachronic and synchronic tensions among ideographs, I suggest, we can also explain the tension between *any* "given" human environment ("objective reality") and any "projected" environments ("symbolic" or "social reality") latent in rhetorical discourse.

ENDNOTES

[1]   Kenneth Burke, *A Rhetoric of Motives* (New York: Prentice-Hall, 1950), pp. 197-203; John Dewey, *The Public and Its Problems* (New York: Henry Holt, 1927); George H. Mead, *Mind, Self, and Society* (Chicago: Univ. of Chicago Press, 1934); and Walter Lippmann, *Public Opinion* (1922; rpt. New York: Free Press, 1965). Duncan groups the American symbolists by observing that European social theorists using "ideology" were concerned with "consciousness" (questions about the *apprehension* of society) while symbolists using poetic metaphors were concerned with a "philosophy of action" (questions about the way we do or ought *behave* in society). In rejecting the concept and theory of "ideology," Burke refused to consider the relationship between consciousness and action except as that relationship can be characterized with the agency of an a priori poetic metaphor, "dramatism." His thought and writing, like that of a poet, is

therefore freed from truth criteria: Supposing his *form*, no "motive" outside the dramatistic terminology need be recognized or accounted for *in its particularity*. Though Burkeans are more guilty than Burke, I think even he tends to redefine motives rather than account for them, to cast self-confessions in "scenarios" rather than deal with them in specific. One might say of "dramatism" what Bacon alleged regarding the Aristotelian syllogism, that it is but a form which chases its tail, presuming in its metaphoric conception the truth of its descriptions. See Hugh Dalziel Duncan, *Symbols in Society* (New York: Oxford Univ. Press, 1968), pp. 12-14; Richard Dewey, "The Theatrical Analogy Reconsidered," *The American Sociologist*, 4 (1969), 307-11; and R. S. Perinbanayagam; "The Definition of the Situation: An Analysis of the Ethnomethodological and Dramaturgical View," *Sociological Quarterly*, 15 (1974), 521-41.

2 See, e.g., Arthur M. Schlesinger, Jr., "Ideology and Foreign Policy: The American Experience," in George Schwab, ed., *Ideology and Foreign Policy* (New York: Cyrco, 1978), pp. 124-32; and Randall L. Bytwerk, "Rhetorical Aspects of the Nazi Meeting: 1926-1933," Quarterly Journal of Speech, 61 (1975), 307-18.

3 See, e.g., William R. Brown, "Ideology as Communication Process," *Quarterly Journal of Speech*, 64 (1978), 123-40; and Jürgen Habermas, "Technology and Science as 'Ideology,'" in *Toward a Rational Society*, trans. Jeremy J. Shapiro (1968; Boston: Beacon, 1970), pp. 81-122.

4 Bormann's distrust of "ideology" was expressed in the context of an evaluation of his "fantasy theme" technique at the 1978 convention of the Speech Communication Association. See "Fantasy Theme Analysis: An Exploration and Assessment," S. C. A. 1978 Seminar Series, Audio-Tape Cassettes. For authoritative accounts of the various "encrustations," see George Lichtheim, "The Concept of Ideology," *History and Theory*, 4 (1964-65), 164-95; and Hans Barth, Truth and Ideology, trans. Frederic Lilge, 2nd ed. 1961 (Berkeley: Univ. of California Press, 1976).

5 See Kenneth Burke, *Permanence & Change*, 2nd ed. rev. (1954; rpt. Indianapolis: Bobbs-Merrill, 1965), pp. 19-36, 216-36; Karl Marx and Frederick Engels, *The German Ideology* (1847), trans. and ed. Clemens Dutt, W. Lough, and C. P. Magill, in *The Collected Works of Karl Marx and Frederick Engels*, 9+ vols. (Moscow: Progress Publishers, 1975-77+), 5:3-5, 23-93; Karl Mannheim, *Ideology* and Utopia, trans. Louis Wirth and Edward Shils (1929; rpt. New York: Harvest Books, 1952); and Martin Seliger, *The Marxist Conception of Ideology: A Critical Essay* (Cambridge: Cambridge Univ. Press, 1977).
My purpose here is to expose the issue between symbolists (generally) and materialists (particularly Marxians). This of course results in some oversimplification: With regard to the brute problem of describing "consciousness," at least two schools of thought are not here accounted for, Freudian psychiatry and American empirical psychology. Freudians are generally connected with the symbolist position I describe here, while most of the operational conceptions of American empirical psychology (especially social psychology) may fairly be associated with Marxian or neo-Marxian description. Moreover, I treat the terms "ideology" and "myth" as less ambiguous than their history as concepts would suggest. My usage of the terms, and the technical usefulness I portray, reflects my own conviction more than the sure and noncontroversial meaning of either "myth" or "ideology."

6 See, e.g., Willard A. Mullins, "Truth and Ideology: Reflections on Mannheim's Paradox," *History and Theory*, 18 (1979), 142-54; William H. Shaw, "'The Handmill Gives You the Feudal Lord': Marx's Technological Determinism," *History and Theory*, 18 (1979), 155-76; Jean-Paul Sartre, *Critique of Dialectical Reason*, trans. Alan Sheridan-Smith (1960; Eng. trans. London: NLB, 1976), pp. 95-121; and Jean-Paul Sartre, *Search for a Method*, trans. Hazel E. Barnes (1958; Eng. trans. New York: Vintage, 1968), pp. 35-84.

7 See W. G. Runciman, "Describing," Mind, 81 (1972), 372-88; Perinbanayagam; and Herbert W. Simons, Elizabeth Mechling, and Howard N. Schreier, "Mobilizing for Collective Action From the Bottom Up:

The Rhetoric of Social Movements," unpub. MS., Temple Univ., pp. 48-59, forthcoming in Carroll C. Arnold and John Waite Bowers, eds., *Handbook of Rhetorical and Communication Theory.*

8   Adolph Hitler, this century's archetype of absolute power—as well as absolute immorality—rose to dominance and maintained himself by putting into practice symbolist theories of social process. Hitler's mere existence forces one to question symbolist theories, asking whether "sociodramas" and "rhetorics" and "myths" are things to be studied scientifically or wild imaginings conjured up from the ether, devil-tools playing upon human weakness and superstition, and therefore things to be politically eradicated. In the face of Hitler, most symbolists adopted a high moral stance of righteous wrath, concentrating on the evil of the man while underplaying the tools he used to gain and keep power. But subtly they modified their logics: Burke is most sensitive to the problem, but in the end he does little more than demonstrate the moral polemical power of dramatistic methods of criticism, becoming the "critic" of his early and later years rather than the "historian" and "theorist" of his middle years. Cassirer's reaction is more extreme, backing away from the logical implications of the symbolist epistemology he argued for before Hitler, begging the problem of power by characterizing the state itself as nothing but a "myth" to be transcended. Hitler was an inspiration to Polanyi, causing him to take up epistemology as a vehicle to discredit social philosophy generally. In the process Polanyi became an unabashed ideological chauvinist of his adopted culture. See, resp., Kenneth Burke, "The Rhetoric of Hitler's 'Battle,'" in *The Philosophy of Literary Form*, 3rd ed. (Berkeley: Univ. of California Press, 1973), pp. 191-220, and cf. Kenneth Burke, *Attitudes toward History* (1937; 2nd ed. rev. rpt. Boston: Beacon, 1961), pp. 92-107; Ernst Cassirer, *The Philosophy of Symbolic Forms*, trans. Ralph Manheim (1923-29; Eng. trans. New Haven: Yale Univ. Press, 1953), 1:105-14; Ernst Cassirer, *The Myth of the State* (New Haven: Yale Univ. Press, 1946); Michael Polanyi, *The Logic of Liberty* (Chicago: Univ. of Chicago Press, 1951), pp. 93-110, 138-53; and Michael Polanyi, *Personal Knowledge: Towards a Post-Critical Philosophy* (1958; rpt. Chicago: Univ. of Chicago Press, 1962), pp. 69-131, 203-48, 299-324.

9   I am suggesting that the topic of "falsity" is necessary whenever one's conception of consciousness transcends the mind of a single individual. This is so because the transcendent consciousness, by its very conception, is a legitimizing agency, a means to warrant moral judgments (as in Perelman) or a means to create the fiction of verification when verification is logically impossible (as in Ziman and Brown). To fail to acknowledge the undeniable falsity of any description of mass or group consciousness is to create the illusion that one or another series of normative claims have an independent "facticity" about them. In my view Brown and Ziman are reckless with hypostatized "descriptions" of the consciousness of an intellectual elite, a "scientific community," which itself is in fact a creature of convention, in the specific terms of "description" a fiction of Ziman's and Brown's mind and a rhetorical vision for their readers. See Brown; Ch. Perelman and L. Olbrechts-Tyteca, *The New Rhetoric: A Treatise on Argumentation*, trans. John Wilkinson and Purcell Weaver (1958; Eng. trans. Notre Dame: Univ. of Notre Dame Press, 1969), pp. 31-35, 61-74; J. M. Ziman, *Public Knowledge: An Essay Concerning the Social Dimension of Science* (Cambridge: Cambridge Univ. Press, 1968), pp. 102-42; and contrast George Edward Moore, *Principia Ethica* (1903; rpt. Cambridge: Cambridge Univ. Press, 1965), esp. pp. 142-80; and Bruce E. Gronbeck, "From 'Is' to 'Ought': Alternative Strategies," *Central States Speech Journal*, 19 (1968), 31-39.

10 See Kenneth Burke, "A Dramatistic View of the Origins of Language and Postscripts on the Negative" in *Language as Symbolic Action* (Berkeley: Univ. of California Press, 1966), pp. 418-79, esp. pp. 453-63; Hannah Arendt, "What Is Authority?" in *Between Past and Future* (New York: Viking, 1968), pp. 91-141; Hannah Arendt, "Lying in Politics: Reflections on the Pentagon Papers," in *Crises of the Republic* (New York: Harcourt Brace Jovanovich, 1972), pp. 1-47; Jürgen Habermas, "Hannah Arendt's Communica-

tions Concept of Power," *Social Research*, 44 (1977), 3-24; J. G. A. Pocock, *Politics, Language and Time* (New York: Atheneum, 1973), pp. 17-25, 202-32; and Robert E. Goodwin, "Laying Linguistic Traps," *Political Theory*, 5 (1977), 491-504.

[11] See Kenneth Burke, *A Grammar of Motives* (New York: Prentice-Hall, 1945), pp. 43-46, 415-18; Burke, *Rhetoric*, pp. 275-76, 298-301; Ernst Cassirer, *Language and Myth*, trans. Susanne K. Langer (1946; Eng. trans. 1946; rpt. New York: Dover, 1953), pp. 62-83; Richard M. Weaver, *The Ethics of Rhetoric* (1953; rpt. Chicago: Gateway, 1970), pp. 211-32; and Rosalind Coward and John Ellis, Language and Materialism (London: Routledge & Kegan Paul, 1977), pp. 61-152.

[12] José Ortega y Gasset, *Man and People*, trans. Willard R. Trask (New York: Norton, 1957), p. 245.

[13] Ibid., pp. 192-221, 258-72.

[14] Ibid., p. 221.

[15] Ibid., p. 251.

[16] Ibid., pp. 176-91.

[17] See Murray Edelman, *Political Language* (New York: Academic Press, 1977), pp. 43-49, 141-55; Schwab, pp. 143-57; and Thomas M. Franck and Edward Weisband, *Word Politics: Verbal Strategy Among the Superpowers* (New York: Oxford Univ. Press, 1972), pp. 3-10, 96-113, 137-69.

[18] Ortega y Gasset, *Man and People*, pp. 243-52. Further, contrast Ortega and Marx on the nature of "idea": José Ortega y Gasset, *The Modern Theme*, trans. James Cleugh (1931; rpt. New York: Harper, 1961), pp. 11-27; and Marx and Engels, pp. 27-37. See, also, Coward and Ellis, pp. 84-92, 122-35.

[19] Ortega y Gasset, *Man and People*, pp. 57-71, 94-111, 139-91. Husserl's recognition of *praxis* and contradiction in his doctrine of "self-evidence" confirms Ortega's critique: Edmund Husserl, *Ideas: General Introduction to Pure Phenomenology*, trans. W. R. Boyce Gibson (1913; Eng. trans. 1931; rpt. London: Collier Macmillan, 1962), pp. 353-67. See, also, Schutz's and Luckmann's elaboration of the bases of Carneadean skepticism: Alfred Schutz and Thomas Luckmann, *The Structures of the Life-World*, trans. Richard M. Zaner and H. Tristram Engelhardt, Jr. (Evanston: Northwestern Univ. Press, 1973), pp. 182-229.

[20] Michel Foucault, *The Archaeology of Knowledge*, trans. A. M. Sheridan Smith (1969; Eng. trans. New York: Pantheon, 1972), pp. 178-95; H. T. Wilson, *The American Ideology: Science, Technology and Organization as Modes of Rationality in Advanced Industrial Societies* (London: Routledge & Kegan Paul, 1977), pp. 231-53; and Roger Poole, *Towards Deep Subjectivity* (New York: Harper & Row, 1972), pp. 78-112.

[21] Michael Polanyi and Harry Prosch, *Meaning* (Chicago: Univ. of Chicago Press, 1975), pp. 9, 22: "We have all learned to trace the collapse of freedom in the twentieth century to the writings of certain philosophers, particularly Marx, Nietzsche, and their common ancestors, Fichte and Hegel. But the story has yet to be told how we came to welcome as liberators the philosophies that were to destroy liberty. . . . We in the Anglo-American sphere have so far escaped the totalitarian nightmares of the right and left. But we are far from home safe. For we have done little, in our free intellectual endeavors, to uphold thought as an independent, self-governing force." Contrast this "personal knowledge" explanation with Max Horkheimer and Theodor W. Adorno, *Dialectic of Enlightenment*, trans. John Cumming (1944; Eng. trans. New York: Herder and Herder, 1972), pp. 255-56; and Jacques Ellul, *Propaganda: The Formation of Men's Attitudes*, trans. Konrad Kellen and Jean Lerner (1962; Eng. trans. New York: Vintage, 1973), pp. 52-61, 232-57.

[22] See Peter Rodino's opening remarks in "Debate on Articles of Impeachment," U.S., Congress, House of Representatives, Committee on the Judiciary, 93rd Cong., 2nd sess., July 24, 1974, pp. 1-4.

The "vertical/horizontal" metaphor used here to describe the evident structure of ideographs should not be confused with Ellul's idea (pp. 79-84) of the structural effects of "Propaganda." Lasky's analysis of "the English ideology" represents the "vertical" description I have in mind: Melvin J. Lasky, *Utopia and Revolution* (Chicago: Univ. of Chicago Press, 1976), pp. 496-575.

23   See Edward H. Levi, *An Introduction to Legal Reasoning* (Chicago: Univ. of Chicago Press, 1948), esp. pp. 6-19, 41-74; Perelman and Tyteca, pp. 70-74, 101-02, 350-57; and Duncan, pp. 110-23, 130-40.

24   Collingwood suggests that the content or ultimate subject matter of history should consist of explaining such recurrent usages ("ideographs") as "freedom" and "progress": R. G. Collingwood, *The Idea of History* (1946; rpt. London: Oxford Univ. Press, 1972), pp. 302-34. See, also, Herbert J. Muller, *The Uses of the Past* (New York: Oxford Univ. Press, 1952), pp. 37-38.

25   See William Wirt, *Sketches of the Life and Character of Patrick Henry*, 9th ed. (Philadelphia: Thomas Cowperthwait, 1839) dedication and pp. 417-43; Judy Hample, "The Textual and Cultural Authenticity of Patrick Henry's 'Liberty or Death' Speech," *Quarterly Journal of Speech*, 63 (1977), 298-310; and Robert D. Meade, *Patrick Henry: Portrait in the Making* (New York: Lippincott, 1957), pp. 49-58.

26   At least two strategies (that is, two theoretical mechanisms) have the capacity to yield fairly precise descriptions of functional "meaning" within situational and textual contexts: See Hans-Georg Gadamer, *Philosophical Hermeneutics*, trans. David E. Linge (Berkeley: Univ. of California Press, 1976), pp. 59-94; and Umberto Eco, *A Theory of Semiotics* (Bloomington: Indiana Univ. Press, 1976), pp. 48-150, 276-313.

27   Ortega y Gasset, *Man and People*, p. 247. Cf. Ferdinand de Saussure, *Course in General Linguistics*, trans. Wade Baskin, ed. Charles Bally and Albert Sechehaye in collaboration with Albert Riedlinger (1915; Eng. trans. 1959; rpt. New York: McGraw-Hill, 1966), pp. 140-90, 218-21.

28   See Richard M. Nixon, "Address to the Nation on the Watergate Investigation," *Public Papers of the Presidents of the United States* (Washington, D.C.: U.S. Government Printing Office, 1975), Richard Nixon, 1973, pp. 691-98, 710-25. Lucas' analysis of "rhetoric and revolution" (though it is more "idea" than "terministically' conscious) represents the "horizontal" description I have in mind: Stephen E. Lucas, *Portents of Rebellion: Rhetoric and Revolution in Philadelphia, 1765-76* (Philadelphia: Temple Univ. Press, 1976).

29   See Jürgen Habermas, *Communication and the Evolution of Society*, trans. Thomas McCarthy (1976; Eng. trans. Boston: Beacon, 1979), pp. 1-68, 130-205.

30   See Foucault, pp. 149-65.

31   See Nicholas Abercrombie and Bryan S. Turner, "The Dominant Ideology Thesis," *British Journal of Sociology*, 29 (1978), 149-70.

Constitutive Rhetoric:
The Case of the Peuple Québécois

Maurice Charland

IN THE *Rhetoric of Motives,* Kenneth Burke proposes "identification" as an alternative to "persuasion" as the key term of the rhetorical process. Burke's project is a rewriting of rhetorical theory that considers rhetoric and motives in formal terms, as consequences of the nature of language and its enactment. Burke's stress on identification permits a rethinking of judgment and the working of the rhetorical effect, for he does not posit a transcendent subject as audience member, who would exist prior to and apart from the speech to be judged, but considers audience members to participate in the very discourse by which they would be "persuaded." Audiences would embody a discourse. A consequence of this theoretical move is that it permits an understanding within rhetorical theory of ideological discourse, of the discourse that presents itself as always only pointing to the given, the natural, the already agreed upon.[1] In particular, it permits us to examine how rhetoric effects what Louis Althusser identifies as the key process in the production of ideology: the constitution of the subject, where the subject is precisely he or she who simultaneously speaks and initiates action in discourse (a subject to a verb) and in the world (a speaker and social agent).[2]

As Burke recognizes, "persuasion," as rhetoric's key term, implies the existence of an agent who is free to be persuaded.[3] However, rhetorical theory's privileging of an audience's freedom to judge is problematic, for it assumes that audiences, with their prejudices, interests, and motives, are *given* and so extra-rhetorical. Rhetorical criticism, as Grossberg points out, posits the existence of transcendental subjects whom discourse would mediate.[4] In other words, rhetorical theory usually refuses to consider the possibility that the very existence of social subjects (who would become audience members) is already a rhetorical effect. Nevertheless, much of what we as rhetorical critics consider to be a product or consequence of discourse, including social identity, religious faith, sexuality, and ideology is beyond the realm of rational or even free choice, beyond the realm of persuasion. As Burke notes, the identifications of social identity can occur "spontaneously, intuitively, even unconsciously."[5] Such identifications are rhetorical, for they are discursive effects that induce human cooperation. They are also, however, logically prior to persuasion. Indeed, humans are constituted in these characteristics; they are essential to the "nature" of a subject and form the basis for persuasive appeals. Consequently, attempts to elucidate ideological or identity-forming discourses as persuasive are trapped in a contradiction: persuasive discourse requires a subject-as-audience who is already constituted with an identity and within an ideology.

Ultimately then, theories of rhetoric as persuasion cannot account for the audiences that rhetoric addresses. However, such an account is critical to the development of a theoretical understanding of the power of discourse. If it is easier to praise Athens before Athenians than before Laecedemonians, we should ask how those in Athens come to experience themselves as Athenians. Indeed, a rhetoric to Athenians in praise of Athens would be relatively insignificant compared to a rhetoric that constitutes Athenians as such. What I propose to develop in this essay is a theory of constitutive rhetoric that would account for this process. I will elaborate this theory of constitutive rhetoric through an examination of a case where the identity of the audience is clearly problematic: the independence movement in Quebec, Canada's French-speaking province. There, supporters of Quebec's political sovereignty addressed and so attempted to call into being a *peuple québécois* that would legitimate the constitution of a sovereign Quebec state.

From *The Quarterly Journal of Speech,* Volume 73, Number 2, May 1987 by Maurice Charland. Copyright © 1987 by Routledge. Reprinted by permission.

Central to my analysis of the constitutive rhetoric of Quebec sovereignty will be Althusser's category of the subject. Examining what Michael McGee would term Quebec's rhetoric of a "people," I will show how claims for Quebec sovereignty base themselves upon the asserted existence of a particular type of subject, the "Québécois." That subject and the collectivized "peuple québécois" are, in Althusser's language, "interpellated" as political subjects through a process of identification in rhetorical narratives that "always already" presume the constitution of subjects. From this perspective, a subject is not "persuaded" to support sovereignty. Support for sovereignty is inherent in the subject position addressed by *souverainiste* (pro-sovereignty) rhetoric because of what we will see to be a series of narrative *ideological effects*.

THE QUEST FOR QUEBEC SOVEREIGNTY

In 1967, the year of Canada's centennial, a new political association was formed in Quebec. This organization, the *Mouvement Souveraineté-Association (MSA)*, dedicated itself to Quebec's political sovereignty as it proclaimed the existence of an essence uniting social actors in the province. In French, Quebec's majority language, the *MSA* declared: "Nous sommes des Québécois" ("We are *Québécois*") and called for Quebec's independence from Canada.[6] This declaration marked the entry of the term "Québécois" into the mainstream of Quebec political discourse. Until that time, members of the French-speaking society of Quebec were usually termed "Canadiens français" ("French-Canadians"). With the *MSA*, a national identity for a new type of political subject was born, a subject whose existence would be presented as justification for the constitution of a new state. Thus, the *MSA's* declaration is an instance of constitutive rhetoric, for it calls its audience into being. Furthermore, as an instance of constitutive rhetoric, it was particularly effective, for within a decade of the creation of that *mouvement*, the term "Québécois" had gained currency even among certain supporters of the Canadian federal system, and Quebec voters had brought the *MSA's* successor, the *Parti Québécois* (PQ), to power.

Quebec voters gave the *PQ* control of the Quebec government on November 15, 1976. The party obtained 41.4% of the popular vote and won 71 of 110 seats in the *Assemblé nationale,* Quebec's legislature.[7] This election marked a major transformation in Canada's political life, for the *PQ* asserted that those in Quebec constituted a distinct *peuple* with the right and duty to political sovereignty, and was committed to leading Quebec, Canada's largest and second most populous province, out of Canada.

The *PQ's* major campaign promise was to hold a referendum on Quebec's political sovereignty during its first term of office. In preparation of this plebiscite, the Quebec government issued, on November 1, 1979, a formal policy statement, a "white paper," that outlined a proposed new political order in which Quebec would be a sovereign state associated economically with Canada.[8] While the Quebec-Canada economic association would include free trade, a customs union, a shared currency and central bank as negotiated, and the free movement of persons across the Quebec-Canada border, each government would have the full sovereignty of a nation-state.[9] The White Paper asserted that those in Quebec constituted a *peuple* and called upon them to support this project by voting OUI in a forthcoming referendum. Such a positive vote by the Quebec electorate would mandate their provincial government to negotiate for the envisioned new constitutional status with the federal government in Ottawa.[10]

The White Paper, as it articulated the reasons for Quebec's political independence, was a rhetorical document. It offered a variety of arguments demonstrating that *Québécois* were an oppressed *peuple* within the confines of Canada's constitution who would be better off with their own country. These arguments were presented in the context of the constitutive rhetoric of the "peuple québécois." This constitutive rhetoric took the form of a narrative account of Quebec history in which *Québécois* were identified with their forebears who explored New France, who suffered under the British conquest, and who struggled to erect the Quebec provincial state apparatus.

The Referendum on sovereignty-association was held on May 20, 1980. Although a majority of the populace voted against the measure, over 45% of the French-speaking population assented to their provincial government's interpretation of Quebec society.[11] Those voting OUI granted the legitimacy of the constitutional claims the White Paper asserted. Clearly, even if a majority of *Québécois* were not ready to seek sovereignty, a *malaise* powerful enough to dominate political debate and government priorities existed in the province. There was a strong sense in which "Québécois" was a term antithetical to "Canadien."

The election of the *PQ* and the strength of its *souverainiste* option in the Referendum reveals the significance of the constitutive rhetoric of a "people québécois." While some might consider the White Paper to be a rhetorical failure because less than half of Quebec's French-speaking population opted for independence, the outcome of the Referendum reveals that its constitutive rhetoric was particularly powerful. This rhetoric, which presents those in Quebec as *Québécois* requiring and deserving their own state, constituted at least close to half of Quebec voters such that they, as an audience, were not *really* Canadians.

What the debate in Quebec reveals is that the very character of a collective identity, and the nature of its boundary, of who is a member of the collectivity, were problematic. In other words, in Quebec there existed a struggle over the constitution of political subjects. In Quebec, the possibility of an alternative *peuple* and history was entertained. Thus, the movement for sovereignty permits us to see how peoples are rhetorically constituted.

"Peuple" as Legitimating Principle

As Michael McGee has noted, the term "people" can rhetorically legitimate constitutions.[12] Not surprisingly then, the independence debate in Quebec, as it developed since the formation of the *MSA*, centered upon whether a *peuple québécois* exists, and more importantly, on whether that *peuple* is the kind of "people" that legitimates a sovereign state. In Quebec, competing claims were made as to the nature of the *peuple*. Consider, for example, Claude Morin's polemical history of Quebec-Ottawa constitutional disputes from 1960 to 1972, where he distinguishes the emergent Quebec collectivity from its predecessor, French-Canada, as he identifies the perspective of the Quebec government: "Like many other peoples, Quebeckers have experienced an awakening of self-consciousness. They want to assert themselves, not as French-speaking Canadians, but as Québécois, citizens who, for the moment, suffer the want of a country that is their own."[13] In Morin's view, not only are those in Quebec *Québécois,* but they constitute the kind of *peuple* that warrants a sovereign state. Morin's observation confirms that populations can at different historical moments gain different identities that warrant different forms of collective life. Furthermore, if we consider that Morin's observation is contentious and partisan,[14] and that many in Quebec would contest his assessment of their collective identity, we find confirmation of McGee's further assertion that the identity of a "people," as a rhetorical construct, is not even agreed upon by those who would address it.[15] Rather, supporters and opponents of Quebec sovereignty both seek to justify their position on the basis of what they assert is a will intrinsic to their version of the *peuple's* very being. Their rhetoric is grounded in the constitution of *Québécois* as political subjects.

The debate over sovereignty in Quebec clearly reveals the degree to which peoples are constituted in discourse. Those in Quebec could be "Québécois"; they could also be "Canadiens français." The distinction is crucial, for only the former type of "peuple" can claim the right to a sovereign state. Indeed, the debate in Quebec permits us to see the radical implication of McGee's argument, for not only is the character or identity of the "peuple" open to rhetorical revision, but the very *boundary* of whom the term "peuple" includes and excludes is rhetorically constructed: as the "peuple" is variously characterized, the persons who make up the "peuple" can change. Thus, consider the rather extreme counter-argument to Morin's claim that a *peuple Québécois* exists and is gaining self-awareness, as articulated by William Shaw and Lionel Albert, two Quebec opponents of sovereignty, who conversely assert that no Quebec *peuple* exists, that the term "Québécois" properly only applies to residents of the City of Quebec, and that the term as used by Quebec nationalists constitutes a "semantic fraud":

> Separatists measure the degree of their penetration of the public consciousness by the extent to which the people are willing to call themselves *Québécois*. The more they can persuade the French Canadians in Quebec to call themselves *Québécois,* the easier the task of insinuating the idea that those French Canadians who happen to live in eastern or northern Ontario or in northern New Brunswick are somehow "different" from those living in Quebec. Once that idea has been established, then the idea that Quebec's borders, which are criss-crossed daily by tens of thousands of French Canadians, could somehow be thought of, not as casual signposts along the highway, but as a full-fledged international boundary, can also be established.[16]

Shaw and Albert display a keen sensitivity to the workings of the *péquiste* rhetoric of collective identity, even if as advocates, these opponents of Quebec independence assert that a French-Canadian *peuple* "really" exists outside of rhetorical construction. What Shaw and Albert ignore, of course, is that the French-speaking *peuple* or nation that they assert exists also becomes real only through rhetoric. Indeed, the possibility of political action requires that political actors be within a "fictive" discourse. More precisely, as Althusser asserts: "there is no practice except by and in an ideology."[17] Political identity must be an ideological fiction, even though, as McGee correctly notes, this fiction becomes historically material and of consequence as persons live it.

The Rhetoric of Interpellation

As we have seen, rhetorical claims for a sovereign Quebec are predicated upon the existence of an ideological subject, the "Québécois," so constituted that sovereignty is a natural and necessary way of life. Furthermore, and hardly surprisingly, the ultimate justification for these claims is the subject's character, nature, or essence. This is so because this identity defines inherent motives and interests that a rhetoric can appeal to. The ideological "trick" of such a rhetoric is that it presents that which is most rhetorical, the existence of a *peuple,* or of a subject, as extrarhetorical. These members of the *peuple* whose supposed essence demands action do not exist in nature, but only within a discursively constituted history. Thus, this rhetoric paradoxically must constitute the identity "Québécois" as it simultaneously presumes it to be pregiven and natural, existing outside of rhetoric and forming the basis for a rhetorical address.

We find a treatment of this constitutive phenomenon in Edwin Black's discussion of the "second persona."[18] As Michael McGuire observes, Black's process of transforming an audience occurs through *identification,* in Burke's sense.[19] However, to simply accept such an account of this process would be inadequate. It would not fully explain the significance of becoming one with a persona, of entering into and embodying it. In particular, to simply state that audiences identify with a persona explains neither (1) the ontological status of those in the audience before their identification nor (2) the ontological status of the persona, and the nature of identifying with it. In order to clarify these ontological issues, we must consider carefully the radical edge of Burke's identificatory principle. Burke asserts that, as "symbol using" animals, our being is significantly constituted in our symbolicity. As Burke puts it, "so much of the 'we' that is separated from the nonverbal by the verbal would not even exist were it not for the verbal (or for our symbolicity in general[)]."[20] In this, Burke moves toward collapsing the distinction between the realm of the symbolic and that of human conceptual consciousness. From such a perspective, we cannot accept the "givenness" of "audience," "person," or "subject," but must consider their very textuality, their very constitution in rhetoric as a structured articulation of signs. We must, in other words, consider the textual nature of social being.

The symbolically based critique of humanist ontology implicit in Burke has been developed in a tradition sharing much with him, that of structuralism.[21] Structuralist semiotics and narrative theory have deconstructed the concept of the unitary and transcendent subject. And, with rhetorical theory, they share an appreciation of the power of discourse, of its effects. Thus, in order to develop the radical implications of Burke's lead, it is to this tradition that I will turn.

Althusser describes the process of inscribing subjects into ideology as "interpellation":[22]

> I shall then suggest that ideology "acts" or "functions" in such a way that it "recruits" subjects among the individuals (it recruits them all), or "transforms" the individuals into subjects (it transforms them all) by that very precise operation which I have called *interpellation* or hailing, and which can be imagined along the lines of the most commonplace everyday police (or other) hailing: "Hey, you there!"[23]

Interpellation occurs at the very moment one enters into a rhetorical situation, that is, as soon as an individual recognizes and acknowledges being addressed. An interpellated subject participates in the discourse that addresses him. Thus, to be interpellated is to become one of Black's personae and be a position in a discourse. In consequence, interpellation has a significance to rhetoric, for the acknowledgment of an address entails an acceptance of an imputed self-understanding which can form the basis for an appeal. Furthermore, interpellation occurs rhetorically, through the effect of the addressed discourse. Note, however, that interpellation does not occur through persuasion in the usual sense, for the very act of *addressing* is rhetorical. It is logically prior to the rhetorical *narratio*. In addition, this rhetoric of identification is ongoing, not restricted to one hailing, but usually part of a rhetoric of socialization. Thus, one must already be an interpellated subject and exist as a discursive position in order to be part of the audience of a rhetorical situation in which persuasion could occur.

The "Peuple" as Narrative Ideological Effect

Events in Quebec demonstrate that the "peuple" is a persona, existing in rhetoric, and not in some neutral history devoid of human interpretation. But note, personae are not persons; they remain in the realm of words. As McGee observes, a "people" is a fiction which comes to be when individuals accept living within a political myth.[24] This myth would be ontological, constitutive of those "seduced" by it. In Quebec, what McGee terms the myth of the "people" is articulated in the Quebec government's White Paper. This document, speaking in the name of the independence movement, as institutionalized in a party and a government, offers a narrative of Quebec history that renders demands for sovereignty intelligible and reasonable.

The White Paper's narrative of the *peuple* since the founding of New France, through the British Conquest, the development of Canada into a federated state, and the setting up of the Referendum on Quebec sovereignty is, in McGee's sense, a myth. It paradoxically both reveals the *peuple* and makes it real. This making real is part of the ontological function of narratives. Indeed, as Jameson points out, "history . . . is inaccessible to us except in textual form, and . . . our approach to it and the Real itself necessarily passes through its prior textualization, its narrativization in the political unconscious."[25] Because the *peuple* exists as a subject in history, it is only intelligible within a narrative representation of history. In other words, this *peupie*, and the individual subject, the *Québécois*, exist as positions in a text.

Narratives "make real" coherent subjects. They constitute subjects as they present a particular textual position, such as the noun-term "peuple québécois" as the locus for action and experience. Roland Barthes well expresses this ultimate textuality of narratives when he asserts that: "Narrative does not show, does not imitate; the passion which may excite us . . . is not that of a 'vision' (in actual fact, we do not 'see' anything)."[26] In other words, narratives work through a representational *effect*. Texts are but surfaces; characters are, in a sense, but "paper beings," to use Barthes' phrase. These paper beings *seem* real through textual operations. The distinct acts and events in a narrative become linked through identification arising from the narrative form. Narratives lead us to construct and fill in coherent unified subjects out of temporally and spatially separate events. This renders the site of action and experience stable. The locus of yesterday's acts becomes that of today's. Consequently, narratives offer a world in which human agency is possible and acts can be meaningful.

All narratives, as they create the illusion of merely revealing a unified and unproblematic subjectivity, are ideological, because they occult the importance of discourse, culture, and history in giving rise to subjectivity, and because, as G. H. Mead and Freud have made clear, subjectivity is always social, constituted in language, and exists in a delicate balance of contradictory drives and impulses. Narratives suppress the fact that, in a very real sense, no person is the same as he or she was a decade ago, or last year, or indeed yesterday. In raising the ultimate "falsity" of narratives, my intention is not, however, to decry them and hold out for some unmediated consciousness. Nor am I here concerned with a philosophical critique of the subject in Western civilization. My intention is to show the degree to which collective identities forming the basis of rhetorical appeals themselves depend upon rhetoric; the "peuple québécois," and "peoples" in general, exist only through an ideological discourse that constitutes them. Furthermore, if the subject in all narratives is ideological, a "peuple" is triply so, for it does not even have a unitary body corresponding to its imputed unitary agency and consciousness. The persona or subject "peuple québécois" exists only as a series of narrative ideological effects.

In the rhetoric of Quebec sovereignty, the "Québécois" is a collective subject. It offers, in Burke's language, an "ultimate" identification permitting an overcoming or going beyond of divisive individual or class interests and concerns.[27] This identity transcends the limitations of the individual body and will. This process of constituting a collective subject is the *first ideological effect* of constitutive rhetoric. If a *peuple* exists, it is only in ideology, as McGee makes clear. That ideology arises in the very nature of narrative history. To tell the story of the *Québécois* is implicitly to assert the existence of a collective subject, the protagonist of the historical drama, who experiences, suffers, and acts. Such a narrative renders the world of events understandable with respect to a transcendental collective interest that negates individual interest. Consider the following passage from the White Paper's account of early French North America:

Our ancestors put down their roots in American soil at the beginning of the 17th century, at the time the first English settlers were landing on the East coast of the United States. As they were clearing the land of the St. Lawrence valley, they explored the vast continent in all directions, from the Atlantic to the Rocky Mountains, and from Hudson Bay to the Gulf of Mexico. Through discovering, claiming, and occupying the land, *Québécois* came to consider themselves North-Americans.

In 1760, our community was already an established society along the St. Lawrence. North American by geography, French by language, culture, and politics, this society had a soul, a way of life, traditions, that were its very own. Its struggles, its successes, and its ordeals had given it an awareness of its collective destiny, and it was with some impatience that it tolerated the colonial tie.[28]

In a radically empiricist mood, I could assert that a society *qua* society has no soul, no struggles, no successes. Clearly, history proceeds by the acts of individuals. But, of course, individuals can act in concert or as a mass, they can respond to apersonal historical forces, and we can interpret the sum total of their individual actions with respect to a collective agent. Historical narratives offer such interpretations. In the telling of the story of a *peuple*, a *peuple* comes to be. It is within the formal structure of a narrative history that it is possible to conceive of a set of individuals as if they were but one. Thus, the "struggles" and "ordeals" of settlers, as a set of individual acts and experiences, become identified with "community," a term that here masks or negates tensions and differences between members of any society. The community of *Québécois* is the master agent of a narratized history.

In the above passage, note also how the past is presented as an extension of the present through the use of the pronoun "our" and the term "Québécois" as signifiers of both eighteenth-century settlers who termed themselves "Canadiens" and those living in Quebec today. The White Paper, and histories of peoples in general, offer a "consubstantiality," to use Burke's expression, between the dead and the living. This positing of a transhistorical subject is the *second ideological effect* of constitutive rhetoric. Here, ancestry is offered as the concrete link between the French settlers of North America, those in Quebec today, and a collectivity. Time is collapsed as narrative identification occurs: Today's Quebec residents constitute a *peuple* and have a right to their own state because members of their community have discovered, claimed, and occupied the land. This interpretive stance is perfectly reasonable. It is also perfectly tautological, for it is a making sense that depends upon the a priori acceptance of that which it attempts to prove the existence of, a collective agent, the *peuple Québécois,* that transcends the limitations of individuality at any historical moment and transcends the death of individuals across history.

Form renders the "Québécois" a real subject within the historical narrative. The "Québécois" does not, however, become a free subject. Subjects within narratives are not free; they are *positioned* and so constrained. All narratives have power over the subjects they present. The endings of narratives are fixed before the telling. The freedom of the character in a narrative is an illusion, for narratives move inexorably toward their *telos.* The characters in a story are obviously not free. Only in Woody Allen's *The Purple Rose of Cairo* can characters abandon their script and walk off the screen. What Allen's film and Barthes' analysis of narratives so clearly illustrate is that narratives are but texts that offer the illusion of agency. The subject is constituted at the nodes of a narrative's surface. What Walter Fisher terms "narrative probability" is a formal and ideological constraint upon the subject's possibilities of being.[29] To be constituted as a subject in a narrative is to be constituted with a history, motives, and a *telos.* Thus, in the rhetoric of Quebec sovereignty, "Québécois" is not merely a descriptive term, but identifies and positions the Quebec voter with respect to his or her future.

The White Paper presents *Québécois* as agents, capable of acting freely in the world. However, the narrative's existence as a text is predicated upon *Québécois* asserting their existence as a collective subject through a politics of independence. In the White Paper on sovereignty, *Québécois* are constituted in the choice of national solidarity. As Burke observes is the case in ideological narratives, the White Paper effects an identification of the temporal sequence of its plot with the logical development of an ultimate principle.[30] In the resultant hierarchy, *Québécois* are free to choose only one course of action:

> **The Will to Survive**
>
> Sooner or later, this society would have shaken off the colonial yoke and acquired its independence, as was the case, in 1776, for the United States of America. But in 1763 the hazards of war placed it under British control. . . . Faced with this defeat, francophones spontaneously chose to be faithful. There could be no question of passing over to the winner's camp to reap the benefits that awaited them. They would adapt to the new situation, come to terms with the new masters, but above all preserve the essential of that which characterized our *peuple*: its language, its customs, its religion. At all costs, they would survive.[31]

The freedom of the protagonist of this narrative is but an illusion. This illusion of freedom is the *third ideological effect* of constitutive rhetoric. Freedom is illusory because the narrative is already spoken or written. Furthermore, because the narrative is a structure of understanding that produces totalizing interpretations,[32] the subject is constrained to *follow through*, to act so as to maintain the narrative's consistency. A narrative, once written, offers a logic of meaningful totality. *Québécois,* precisely because they are the subjects within a text, within a narrative rhetoric, must follow the logic of the narrative. They must be true to the motives through which the narrative constitutes them, and thus which presents characters as freely acting toward a predetermined and fixed ending.

THE EFFECTIVE POWER OF CONSTITUTIVE RHETORIC

The ideological effects of constitutive rhetoric that I have outlined are not merely formal effects inscribed within the bracketed experience of interpreting a text. In other words, these do not only permit a disinterested understanding of a fictive world. What is significant in constitutive rhetoric is that it positions the reader toward political, social, and economic action in the material world and it is in this positioning that its ideological character becomes significant. For the purpose of analysis, this positioning of subjects as historical actors can be understood as a two-step process. First, audience members must be successfully interpellated; not all constitutive rhetorics succeed. Second, the tautological logic of constitutive rhetoric must necessitate action in the material world; constitutive rhetoric must require that its embodied subjects act freely in the social world to affirm their subject position.

Audiences are, to use Althusser's famous phrase, "always already" subjects. This is to say that if we disregard the point at which a child enters language, but restrict ourselves to "competent" speakers within a culture, we can observe that one cannot exist but as a subject within a narrative. The necessity is ontological: One must already be a subject in order to be addressed or to speak. We therefore cannot say that one is persuaded to be a subject; one is "always already" a subject. This does not imply, however, that one's subject position is fixed at the moment one enters language. Indeed, the development of new subject positions, of new constitutive rhetorics, is possible at particular historical moments. The subject is a position within a text. To be an embodied subject is to experience and act in a textualized world. However, this world is not seamless and a subject position's world view can be laced with contradictions. We can, as Burke puts it, encounter "recalcitrance."[33] In addition, as Stuart Hall observes, various contradictory subject positions can simultaneously exist within a culture:[34] We can live within many texts. These contradictions place a strain upon identification with a given subject position and render possible a subject's rearticulation. Successful new constitutive rhetorics offer new subject positions that resolve, or at least contain, experienced contradictions. They serve to overcome or define away the recalcitrance the world presents by providing the subject with new perspectives and motives.

Thus, for example, the subject position "Québécois" arises from a rearticulation of two positions, that of "Canadien français," and that of the Quebec resident and voter with a collective will ostensibly represented by the Quebec government. Because some French-Canadians live outside of Quebec and not all those in Quebec are French-speaking, the identity "Canadien français" cannot permit the articulation of a French-speaking nation-state in North America. As the White Paper never fails to remind its audience, to be "Canadien français" is to be a member of an impotent minority without a proper homeland. The White Paper, penned by the Quebec government, invokes the contradiction of being a member of a French-speaking collectivity, or *nation,* that does not have a sovereign state apparatus, for the Quebec government remains subject to Canada's Federal government in Ottawa, and French-Canadians are subjects of the Federal state, a state that can be represented as ultimately foreign.

French-Canadians in Quebec had to live the contradiction of not being exclusively subjects of the state they collectively controlled. "Québécois" resolves this contradiction at the discursive level, by identifying the populace with a territory and a francophone state, rather than with an ethnic group. Constitutive rhetorics of new subject positions can be understood, therefore, as working upon previous discourses, upon previous constitutive rhetorics. They capture alienated subjects by rearticulating existing subject positions so as to contain or resolve experienced dialectical contradictions between the world and its discourses. The process by which an audience member enters into a new subject position is therefore not one of persuasion. It is akin more to one of conversion that ultimately results in an act of recognition of the "rightness" of a discourse and of one's identity with its reconfigured subject position.

The White Paper's constitutive rhetoric, as it articulates the meaning of being "Québécois," is not a mere fiction. It inscribes real social actors within its textualized structure of motives, and then inserts them into the world of practice. The White Paper offers a collectivized subject position that constitutes those in Quebec as members of a *peuple* which is transcendent of the limits of their biological individuality. This position thus opens the possibility for them to participate in a collective political project. The White Paper's narrative is characterized by a set of formal ideological effects that permit it to be intelligible as one accepts and enters into the collective consciousness it articulates. The White Paper offers, therefore, a particular instance of narrative rhetoric that, in Fisher's language, "give[s] order to human experience and . . . induce[s] others to *dwell in [it]* to establish ways of living in common, in communion in which there is sanction for the story that constitutes one's life" (italics added).[35] This dwelling place is, of course, prerequisite to the power of the rhetoric of Quebec sovereignty. To be *Québécois* as configured by the White Paper is to embody in the world the narrative and the motives it ascribes to members of the *peuple.*

To enter into the White Paper's rhetorical narrative is to identify with Black's second persona. It is the process of recognizing oneself as the subject in a text. It is to exist at the nodal point of a series of identifications and to be captured in its structure and in its production of meaning. It is to be a subject which exists beyond one's body and life span. It is to have and experience the dangerous memories of British conquest and rule. It is to live toward national independence. Then, the power of the text is the power of an embodied ideology. The form of an ideological rhetoric is effective because it is within the bodies of those it constitutes as subjects. These subjects owe their existence to the discourse that articulates them. As Burke puts it: "An 'ideology' is like a god coming down to earth, where it will inhabit a place pervaded by its presence. An 'ideology' is like a spirit taking up its abode in a body: it makes that body hop around in certain ways; and that same body would have hopped around in different ways had a different ideology happened to inhabit it."[36] Thus, from the subjectivity or point of view of the embodied *souverainiste* discourse, not only would there exist "good reasons" for supporting sovereignty, but good *motives* as well, motives arising from the very essence of the *Québécois'* being. Within the White Paper's account is embedded a "logic," a way of understanding the world, that offers those in Quebec a position from which to understand and act.

IDENTIFICATION WITH A CONSTITUTIVE RHETORIC

If the White Paper and historical narratives were but dead history, mere stories, their significance to ideology could easily be dismissed. However, constitutive rhetorics, as they identify, have power because they are oriented toward action. As Althusser and McGee both stress, ideology is material, existing not in the realm of ideas, but in that of *material practices*. Ideology is material because subjects enact their ideology and reconstitute their material world in its image.[37] Constitutive rhetorics are ideological not merely because they provide individuals with narratives to inhabit as subjects and motives to experience, but because they insert "narratized" subjects-as-agents into the world.

The insertion of subjects into the world is a product of both the identificatory and referential functions of the White Paper's historical narrative and its ideological effects. In particular, it is the third ideological effect, the constitution in action of a motivated subject, that orients those addressed toward particular future acts. Since narratives offer totalizing interpretations that ascribe transcendent meanings to individual acts, the maintenance of narrative consistency demands that a certain set of acts be chosen. This is amplified in the White Paper because it offers a narrative without closure. The White Paper offers an unfinished history: The *peuple Québécois* has yet to obtain its independence. Thus, the *Québécois* addressed by the White Paper must bring to a close the saga begun by the subjects of the White Paper's history. In other words, while classical narratives have an ending, constitutive rhetorics leave the task of narrative closure to their constituted subjects. It is up to the *Québécois* of 1980 to conclude the story to which they are identified. The story the White Paper offers is of a besieged *peuple* that has always continued to struggle in order to survive and to assert its right to self-determination. Nevertheless, in this account, each advance is blocked by the colonial power. The story proceeds through the recounting of a series of episodes, each exhibiting the same pattern.

As we have already seen, the White Paper asserts that the new *peuple's* aspirations were blocked by British conquest. This act of conquest recurs in other guises at other moments in the *peuple's* saga. Thus, in the rhetoric of Quebec sovereignty, for example, the victims of the conquest of 1760 become the protagonists in the parliamentary wrangles of 1837. Individual subjects, the *Québécois,* and their collective subject, the *peuple,* are somehow the same, even though the actual personages, institutions, material conditions, and struggles have changed. *Québécois* as explorers become political subjects. Thus, the White Paper asserts:

> The Parliament of Lower Canada, where the language was French, proposed laws and a budget that were submitted for approval to the Governor, who exercised executive power on behalf of London.

The *peuple's* will was often blocked by the veto of the Governor, particularly sensitive to the interests of the English minority of Lower Canada and those of the imperial power. The consequent tension was leading, by 1830, to exasperation. The representatives drew up a set of resolutions in which they expressed their demands: control by the Assembly of taxes and spending, and the adoption of urgent social and economic measures. The Governor refused and dissolved the House. In the elections that followed, the *Patriotes,* headed by Papineau, won 77 out of 88 seats with 90% of the vote. To the same demands, the Governor responded by dissolving the House once again.[38]

The rhetorical significance of this passage is twofold. First, it typifies the text's constitution of a subject subjugated by Britain. Note how it confronts victory with power. In doing so, it highlights what can be presented as an inherent contradiction of "French-Canadian" as a subject position that interpellates French-Canadians both as French ethnic subjects and Canadian political subjects. Second, this passage, again typically, rearticulates this subject position: It articulates "Québécois" as a *political* subject battling on the terrain of parliament. In doing so, it dissolves any possible contradiction between loyalty to an (ethnic) nation and the federal state and it articulates both a site for and an object of struggle: the Quebec state apparatus and its legitimated institutions.

The White Paper offers a narrative characterized by a teleological movement toward emancipation. If the root cause of the struggle of the *peuple* is the natural impossibility of the *peuple* to exist without self-determination, control of the state machinery becomes the point of resolution of a drama that began while *Québécois* were still under the rule of the French king. The narrative offers sovereignty as the ultimate point that must be reached in order to attain narrative closure and liberate its subjects. The White Paper offers no alternative but for *Québécois* to struggle against annihilation. To offer but one example among many, the recounting of the 1837 uprising by a nationalist party known as the *Patriotes* and their speedy defeat makes clear that *Québécois* are constituted in a struggle for life itself, a struggle, furthermore, that cannot be won militarily:

> After their lone victory at Saint-Denis, the *Patriotes* were crushed at Saint-Charles and Saint-Eustache. The repression was cruel: hundreds of *Patriotes* were imprisoned and twelve were hanged; here and there, farms were ablaze.[39]

Within the context of contemporary attempts to secure Quebec's independence, the White Paper offers a condensed historical narrative of the *people québécois* as teleologically moving toward emancipation. The historical account of the White Paper is decidedly presentist and rhetorical, for a society of the seventeenth century is identified with a society today: the seventeenth-century colonists who termed themselves "Canadiens" are termed "Québécois"; past struggles are presented as warranting action in the present. The particular issues over which nineteenth-century parliamentarians battled are rendered in ideological terms that are then applied to current battles between Quebec and Canada's Federal government. Each episode in the history moves the *peuple* as subject toward the Quebec Referendum on sovereignty-association. The narrative form provides a continuity across time in which the practices of the past are increasingly identified with the present-day order. Thus, the British Conquest, parliamentary wrangles, and the rebellions of 1837, find their counterpart in the "imposition" of a Canadian constitution:

> At the constitutional conferences of 1864 and 1866, the Quebec delegates and those of the other provinces were pursuing very different goals. Upper Canada in particular wanted a supraprovincial parliament, endowed with as many and as important powers as possible, that would have presided over the fates of the new country; Quebec, on the other hand, wanted to grant itself a

responsible government, enjoying a large degree of autonomy, that would guarantee once and for all the existence and progress of the Quebec *peuple*—and that would have been its *real* government. The opposition between a centralized federalism and a decentralized confederation was already making itself felt. The first idea finally won out. Granted, *Québécois* acquired an autonomous responsible government, but with its autonomy limited to jurisdictions seen then as being primarily of local interest.[40]

The *peuple québécois* is presented as preceding the Canadian state. Confederation, like the Conquest, the defeat of the *Patriotes,* and the unification in 1849 of the predominantly English-speaking colony of Upper Canada with the predominantly French-speaking colony of Lower Canada disrupted the movement of the *peuple* toward the "natural" ideal of its own constitution, responsible government, and a state. The implicit presumption that political structures should provide a means for the articulation and execution of a *peuple's* aspirations, as connoted by the term "peuple" itself, is set in opposition to this account of Canada's formation. The government in Ottawa is not a *real* government. Ottawa's power is represented as illegitimate. The Quebec *peuple* is frustrated, denied progress and its very existence. This narrative's movement toward closure is frustrated by the English presence. The emancipation of the *peuple* is blocked by the pattern of conquest and resistance *(narratio interrupta)*. The conquerors stand against narrative teleology as well as history's grand laws.

In the rhetoric of Quebec sovereignty then, the Government of Canada does not arise from the Quebec *peuple* and hence disrupts the teleological flow of history that the narrative form provides. Canada is an antagonist in this life-drama of a *peuple*. As such, Canada must be overcome so that the tensions in the mythic narrative and in history can be resolved. The "natural" principle that *peuples* attain control of their future is denied because Ottawa will preside over destiny. Within the context of the repression of the *Patriotes,* this new order does not arise from the *peuple québécois* but from external constraints. Confederation is but another manifestation of the Conquest to which, in this account, the *peuple* never assented: *Québécois* never acquiesce, but always struggle within the constraints of the possible. The change heralded by Confederation was but a small gain within the British system. Confederation is not the end of the struggle, only a new battleground. On this terrain, the *peuple* is threatened by a political reality that denies its very being.

The White Paper, having constituted *Québécois* in a struggle for survival, moves them and the narrative into the present. The current constitution that the independence movement opposes is represented as forming the basis for the continued subjugation of the *peuple*:

> The institution of the Canadian federal regime thus sanctioned, and favored as well, the hegemony of a Canada become English. It is quite natural that in such a regime the interests and aspirations of *Québécois* and Francophones in other provinces should take second place. In 1885, for example, all Quebec took the side of Louis Riel, who was fighting for the survival of francophone communities in the West. On the other hand, the federal government fought him and Louis Riel died on the scaffold.[41]

Any possibility that Confederation was advantageous for Quebec is denied. The will of the *peuple*, as instantiated in historical practice, is shown to be undermined in the federal regime. The White Paper describes various defeats of the will of the *peuple* in Confederation: Louis Riel fought for "survival" and climbed the scaffold; rights to French language education outside Quebec were denied; *Québécois* were forced to participate in British wars.[42] The accounts form a tragic tale; the francophones in Canada including the *peuple québécois* are without control of their circumstances.

The narrative concludes by identifying a threat to its very existence as a narrative. Canadian Confederation would deny that Québécois exist and so would deny the very possibility of this constitutive rhetoric and so of an audience inhabiting it. As the White Paper puts it: "The very balance of the system, as the Canadian majority wants it, requires that Quebec remain a province—or perhaps a territory—among ten others, and forbids the formal and concrete recognition of a Quebec nation."[43] This version of Quebec would require a revision of the meaning of "Québécois" such that it no longer positioned its subjects as members of both a nation and state. The "Québécois" would be but the Quebec resident, who might also be a French-Canadian defined in ethnic terms. Thus, in its concluding summary exhorting *Québécois* to vote OUI in the Referendum on sovereignty-association, the White Paper characterizes a NON vote as constituting:

> Only a brutal ending to the healthiest form of progress, one that leads an entire *peuple*, as naturally as an individual, to its maturity. We would simply fall back into line, remain in the state of oblivion kindly granted us by those outsiders who have been keeping a close eye on our progress.

> On the contrary, we believe that we are mature enough, and big enough, and strong enough, to come to terms with our destiny. Because that is what is true.[44]

To be constituted as a *Québécois* in the terms of this narrative is to be constituted such that sovereignty is not only possible, but necessary. Without sovereignty, this constitutive rhetoric would ultimately die and those it has constituted would cease to be subjects, or at least would remain, like children, partial and stunted subjects, lacking maturity, responsibility, and autonomy. In consequence, true *Québécois* could not vote NON. Only a OUI vote would be in harmony with their being and their collective destiny: "Indeed, the choice should be easy, for the heart as well as the mind. We need only give a little thought to how faithful we have been in the past and how strong we are at present; we must think also of those who will follow us, whose futures depend so utterly on that moment."[45]

In sum, the White Paper calls on those it has addressed to follow narrative consistency and the motives through which they are constituted as audience members. Its rhetorical effect derives from their interpellation as subjects and on their identification with a transhistorical and transindividual subject position. It is in this sense of textualizing audiences, therefore, that we can understand the process Black treats in his discussion of the second persona and McGee discusses in his study of the "people." From this perspective, we can see that audiences do not exist outside rhetoric, merely addressed by it, but live inside rhetoric. Indeed, from the moment they enter into the world of language, they are subjects; the very moment of recognition of an address constitutes an entry into a subject position to which inheres a set of motives that render a rhetorical discourse intelligible. These subject positions are bequeathed by the past, by yesterday's discourses. Furthermore, the contradictions between discourses as well as the dialectic between discourse and a changing concrete world open a space for new subject positions. Tensions in the realm of the symbolic render possible the rhetorical repositioning or rearticulation of subjects.

CONCLUSION

Early in this essay, I identified two problems deserving examination: the first regarding the ontological status of those addressed by discourse before their successful interpellation; the second regarding the ontological status of the persona and the process by which one is identified with it. I have treated the latter problem by introducing the concept of the subject and by showing that audiences are constituted as subjects through a process of identification with a textual position. This identification occurs through a series of ideological effects arising from the narrative structure of constitutive rhetoric. As for the first problem I posed, I have in a sense circumvented it through my analysis. Persons are subjects from the moment they acquire language and the capacity to speak and to be spoken to. As such, constitutive rhetoric is part of the discursive background of social life. It is always there, usually implicitly, and sometimes explicitly articulated. It is more than a set of common-places, but is the con-text, the pre-rhetoric that is necessary to any successful interpellation.

Our first subject positions are modest, linked to our name, our family, and our sex. As we enter the adult world, they become more complex, as different constitutive rhetorics reposition us with respect to such formal and informal institutions as the state, the economy, the church, and the school. Thus, though we are subjects through language, and indeed can only speak as subjects, our subjectivity and ideological commitments are not fixed at our first utterance. As Quebec public address illustrates, particular subject positions can undergo transformation: "Canadien français" can become "Québécois," an identity permitting claims for a new political order. At particular historical moments, political rhetorics can reposition or rearticulate subjects by performing ideological work upon the texts in which social actors are inscribed.

In this essay, I have suggested that Burke's privileging of the term "identification" and an understanding of rhetoric's constitutive and ontological effect, as suggested by structuralist discourse theory, have certain consequences for the theory and practice of rhetoric. A theory of constitutive rhetoric leads us to call into question the concept, usually implicit in rhetoric's humanist tradition, of an audience composed of unified and transcendent subjects. If we are left with a subject, that subject is partial and decentered. History, and indeed discourse itself, form the ground for subjectivity. Consequently, even what Fisher terms "narrative fidelity" has an ideological character, for the experiential ground to which narratives would be faithful are always already ideologically framed within the very being of the experiencing subject.[46]

Because ideology forms the ground for any rhetorical situation, a theory of ideological rhetoric must be mindful not only of arguments and ideographs, but of the very nature of the subjects that rhetoric both addresses and leads to come to be. Indeed, because the constitutive nature of rhetoric establishes the boundary of a subject's motives and experience, a truly ideological rhetoric must rework or transform subjects. A transformed ideology would require a transformed subject (not a dissolving of subjectivity). Such a transformation requires ideological and rhetorical work. This can proceed at two levels: (1) it can proceed at the level of the constitutive narrative itself, providing stories that through the identificatory principle shift and rework the subject and its motives; (2) it can also proceed at the aesthetic level of what Williams terms the "structure of feeling" and Grossberg describes as the "affective apparatus."[47] Since, as Fisher observes, the truth of a narrative resides in its "fidelity," which is an aesthetic quality, new true narratives become possible as new modes of aesthetic experience emerge and gain social meaning. Ideological rhetorical practice is not restricted to explicitly political public address, but can include a range of aesthetic practices, including music, drama, architecture, and fashion, that elicit new modes of experience and being.

The significance of the rhetorical tradition is that it has long realized that discourse has eminently political and practical effects. In recognizing the contingency of the social, it offers the possibility of social critique and the development of *praxis*. However, in order to overcome the constraints of ideology, rhetorical theory must see through the "givenness" of what appears to be the delimitable rhetorical situation, where the ontological status of speaker, speech, audience, topic, and occasion offer themselves as unproblematic. It must recognize that ultimately, the position one embodies as a subject is a rhetorical effect.

NOTES

Maurice Charland is Assistant Professor of Communication Studies at Concordia University, Montreal. This essay is in part derived from his dissertation (University of Iowa, 1983), directed, by Michael Calvin McGee. Portions of an early draft of this essay were presented at the Second Summer Conference on Argumentation (1981) and were published in its proceedings.

1. By ideology I mean a symbolic system, the discourse of which (1) is "false" in the sense that it is based on the presuppositions of some "terministie screen," (2) denies its historicity and linguisticality—pretending to bat present a naturally or self-evidently meaningful world, (3) denies or transforms contradictions, and (4) legitimates and structures power relations. As such, my usage is much like the one suggested in, Anthony Giddens, *Central Problems in Social Theory: Action, Structure and Contradiction in Social Analysis* (Berkeley: University of California Press. 1979), 165–197.

2. For a discussion of discourse-based theories of the subject, see, Kaja Silverman, *The Subject of Semiotics* (New York: Oxford University Press, 1983), 43–53, 126–131.

3. Kenneth Burke, *A Rhetoric of Motives* (1950; rpt, Berkeley: University of California Press, 1969), 50.

4. Lawrence Grossberg, "Marxist Dialectics and Rhetorical Criticism," *Quarterly Journal of Speech* 65 (1979): 249.

5. Kenneth Burke, *Language as Symbolic Action: Essays on Life, Literature, and Method* (Berkeley: University of California Press, 1966), 301.

6. Mouvement Souveraineté-Association, founding political manifesto, 1968, in *Le manuel de la parole: Manifestes québécois,* ed. Daniel Latouche and Diane Poliquin-Bourassa (Siilery, Quebec: Editions du boreal express, 1977) vol. 3, 97.

7. André Bernard and Bernard Descrôteaux *Québec: élections 1981* (Ville LaSalle, Québec: Editions Hurtibise HMH, Limitée, 1981), 15, 23.

8. Quebec (Prov.), Conseil exécutif. *La nouvelle entente Québec-Canada: Proposition du Gouvernement du Québec pour une entente d'égal à égal: La souveraineté-association.* Quebec: 1979. This document, a softcover book sold in bookstores, consists of a foreword, six chapters which explain the Quebec government's reasons for seeking sovereignty, and a concluding direct address by Quebec's premier, René Levesque, calling for a OUI vote in the forthcoming referendum. The significance of the document arises from its clear articulation of Quebec's rhetoric of sovereignty as it had developed for over a decade in Quebec public address, and from its institutional status, offering the official rhetoric of the government's pro-sovereignty position.

9. *Quebec, La nouvelle entente, 62–64.*

10. As adopted by the Quebec *Assemblé nationale,* March 20, 1980, the following question appeared on the ballot: "Le Gouvernement du Québec a fait connaitre sa proposition d'en arriver. avec le reste du Canada, à une nouvelle entente fondée sur le principe de l'égalité des peuples; cette entente permettrait au Québec d'acquérir le pouvoir exclusif de faire ses lois, de percevoir ses impôts et d'établir ses relations extérieurs, ce qul est la souveraineté—et, en même temps, de maintenir avec le Canada une association economique comportant l'utilisauon de la même monnaie; aucun changement de statut politique resultant de ces négociations ne sera réalisé sans l'accord de la population lors d'un autre référendum; en consequence, accordez-vous au Gouvernement du Québec le mandat de négocier l'entente proposée entre le Québec et le Canada?

OUI   NON

The Government of Québec has made public its proposal to negotiate a new agreement with the rest of Canada, based on the equality of nations; this agreement would enable Québec to acquire the exclusive power to make its laws, levy its taxes and establish relations abroad—in other words, sovereignty—and at the same time, to maintain with Canada an economic association including a common currency; no change in political status resulting from these negotiations will be effected without approval by the people through another referendum; on these terms, do you give the Government of Québec the mandate to negotiate the proposed agreement between Quebec and Canada?

YES   NO."

Quebec (Prov.), Directeur Général des élections, Rapport des résultats officiels du scrutin, référendum du 20 mai 1980, 9.

[11] In the May 1980 referendum on "sovereignty-assoriatipn," 85.6% of eligible voters cast valid ballots. Of these, 40.4% voted OUI. See, *Rapport des résulidls.* 19. Among francophones, the vote was slightly higher and is estimated at 46%. See. Jean-Claude Picard, "Le gouvernement et le Parti Québécois analysent l'échec référendaire de mardi," *Le Devoir,* Thursday, May 22, 1980.

[12] Michael C. McGee, "In Search of 'The People': A Rhetorical Alternative." *Quarterly Journal of Speech* 61 (October 1975): 239.

[13] Claude Morin, *Quebec versus Ottawa: The Struggle for Self-Government, 1960–1972,* trans. Richard Howard (Toronto: University of Toronto Press, 1976), 5.

[14] Claude Morin's text was written as a reflection on his experience of federal-provincial relations as a high-ranking civil servant. He was also an early and active proponent of sovereignty and member of the *PQ* who became a cabinet minister in the *PQ* government.

[15] McGee, 246.

[16] William F. Shaw and Lionel Albert, *Partition* (Montreal: Thornhill Publishing, 1980), 143–144.

[17] Louis Althusser. *Lenin and Philosophy and other Essays,* trans. Ben Brewster (New York: Monthly Review Press, 1971), 170.

[18] Edwin Black, "The Second Persona," *Quarterly Journal of Speech* 56 (April 1970): 109–119.

[19] Miehaei D. McGuire, "Rhetoric. Philosophy and the *Volk:* Johann Gottlieb Fichte's *Addresses to the German Nation. " Quarterly Journal of Speech* 62 (April 1976): 135–136.

[20] *Burke, Symbolic Action, 5.*

[21] Burke reveals a structuralist tendency in his discussions of the formal interplay between the elements of his "pentad," which, are constitutive of motives. While Burke differs with the French structuralist tradition, particularly in holding on to the concept of "act," his denial of a foundational character for any of his pentadic terms and his sensitivity to unresolvable ambiguities do lead him, just like the French structuralists, to consider the agent's constitution in symbolic structures. See Frank Lentricehia, *Criticism and Social Change* (Chicago: University of Chicago Press, 1983), 66–83.

[22] "Interpeller" is a rather commonly used French verb which designates the act of calling upon someone by name and demanding an answer. It is not surprising that Althusser, in the quote that follows, uses the example of a policeman's hailing, since a person who is *interpellé* is usually under some constraint to respond. Thus, the term is used to refer to the questioning of ministers by members of parliament and to the formal address of a judge or bailiff as part of a legal act. *Petit Larousse illustré,* 1979. s. v. "interpeller," "interpellation."

[23] Althusser, 174.

[24] McGee, 244.

25 Fredrie Jameson, *The Political Unconscious: Narrative as a Socially Symbolic Act* (Ithaca: Cornell University Press, 1981), 35.

26 Roland Barthes, *Image, Music, Text,* trans. by Stephen Heath (New York: Hill & Wang, 1977), 124.

27 Burke, *Rhetoric of Motives,* 194.

28 Québec, *La nouvelle entente,* 3. The primary language of Quebec public discourse is French. As such, political life proceeds through a French "terministie screen." To be true to the political consciousness of that society, this essay is based on the analysis of the French primary texts. It is for this reason that I continue to use the terms "peuple" and "Québécois" throughout this essay. Note specifically that "peuple," the French term for "people," is a singular noun; in French, one would write "the people is." Note also that there is no adequate translation of "Québécois." The closest equivalent, "Quebecker," lacks all of the French term's nationalist connotations. While analyzed in French, cited passages are presented in English translation for the reader's convenience. My translation is in large measure based on the simultaneously published official English version of the White Paper: *Québec-Canada a New Deal: The Québec Government Proposal for a New Partnership between Equals: Sovereignty-Association* (Quebec: 1979).

29 Walter Fisher, "Narration as a Human Communication Paradigm: The Case of Public Moral Argument," *Communication Monographs* 51 (March 1984): 8.

30 *Burke, Rhetoric of Motives, 197.*

31 *Quebec, La nouvelle entente, 3–4.*

32 Paul Ricoeur, *Hermeneutics and the Human Sciences,* ed. and trans. John B. Thompson (New York: Cambridge University Press, 1981), 278–279.

33 Kenneth Burke, *Permanence and Change: An Anaiomy of Purpose,* 2nd rev. ed. (Indianapolis: The Bobbs-Merrill Company, Inc., 1954), 255.

34 Stuart Hall, "Signification, Representation, Ideology: Althusser and the Post-Structuralist Debates," *Critical Studies in Mass Communication* 2 (June 1985): 107–113.

35 Fisher, 6.

36 *Burke, Symbolic Action, 6.*

37 McGee and Althusser adopt a similar strategy in order to assert the materiality of meaning. Althusser argues that, "Ideology . . . prescribe[es] material practices governed by a material ritual, which practices exist in the material actions of a subject in all consciousness according to his belief" (Althusser, 170), Similarly, McGee, after tracing out the relationship of myth to ideology, asserts: "Though [myths] technically represent 'false consciousness,' they nonetheless function as a means of providing social unity and collective unity. Indeed, 'the people' are the social and political myths they accept" (McGee, 247).

38 *Quebec, La nouvelle entente, 5.*

39 *Quebec, La nouvelle entente, 6.*

40 *Quebec, La nouvelle entente, 7–8.*

41 *Quebec, La nouvelle entente, 11.*

42 *Quebec, La nouvelle entente, 11–12.*

43 *Quebec, La nouvelle entente, 44–45.*

44 *Quebec, La nouvelle entente, 109–110.*

45 *Quebec, La nouvelle entente, 118.*

46 Fisher, 8.

47 Raymond Williams, *Marxism and Literature* (New York: Oxford University Press, 1977), 128–135; Lawrence Grossberg, "Is There Rock after Punk," *Critical Studies in Mass Communications* 3 (March 1986): 69–70.

What is the Meaning of
The Medium is the Message?

by Mark Federman, Former Chief Strategist
McLuhan Program in Culture and Technology

"In a culture like ours, long accustomed to splitting and dividing all things as a means of control, it is sometimes a bit of a shock to be reminded that, in operational and practical fact, the medium is the message. This is merely to say that the personal and social consequences of any medium—that is, of any extension of ourselves—result from the new scale that is introduced into our affairs by each extension of ourselves, or by any new technology." (McLuhan, 1964, p. 7). Thus begins the classic work of Marshall McLuhan, *Understanding Media*, in which he introduced the world to his enigmatic paradox, "The medium is the message." But what does it mean? How can the medium be its own message?

Of all the Internet searches that end up at the McLuhan Program website and weblog, the search for the meaning of the famous "McLuhan Equation" is the most frequent. Many people presume the conventional meaning for "medium" that refers to the mass media of communications—radio, television, the press, the Internet. And most apply our conventional understanding of "message" as content or information. Putting the two together allows people to jump to the mistaken conclusion that, somehow, the channel supersedes the content in importance, or that McLuhan was saying that the information content should be ignored as inconsequential. Often people will triumphantly hail that the medium is "no longer the message," or flip it around to proclaim that the "message is the medium," or some other such nonsense. McLuhan meant what he said; unfortunately, his meaning is not at all obvious, and that is where we begin our journey to understanding.

Marshall McLuhan was concerned with the observation that we tend to focus on the obvious. In doing so, we largely miss the structural changes in our affairs that are introduced subtly, or over long periods of time. Whenever we create a new innovation—be it an invention or a new idea—many of its properties are fairly obvious to us. We generally know what it will nominally do, or at least what it is intended to do, and what it might replace. We often know what its advantages and disadvantages might be. But it is also often the case that, after a long period of time and experience with the new innovation, we look backward and realize that there were some effects of which we were entirely unaware at the outset. We sometimes call these effects "unintended consequences," although "unanticipated consequences" might be a more accurate description.

Many of the unanticipated consequences stem from the fact that there are conditions in our society and culture that we just don't take into consideration in our planning. These range from cultural or religious issues and historical precedents, through interplay with existing conditions, to the secondary or tertiary effects in a cascade of interactions. All of these dynamic processes that are entirely nonobvious comprise our ground or context. They all work silently to influence the way in which we interact with one another, and with our society at large. In a word (or four), ground comprises everything we don't notice.

Copyright © by Mark Federman. Reprinted by permission.

If one thinks about it, there are far more dynamic processes occurring in the ground than comprise the actions of the figures, or things that we do notice. But when something changes, it often becomes noticeable. And noticing change is the key.

McLuhan tells us that a "message" is, "the change of scale or pace or pattern" that a new invention or innovation "introduces into human affairs" (McLuhan 8). Note that it is not the content or use of the innovation, but the change in interpersonal dynamics that the innovation brings with it. Thus, the message of theatrical production is not the musical or the play being produced, but perhaps the change in tourism that the production may encourage. In the case of a specific theatrical production, its message may be a change in attitude or action on the part of the audience that results from the medium of the play itself, which is quite distinct from the medium of theatrical production in general. Similarly, the message of a newscast is not the news stories themselves, but a change in the public attitude toward crime, or the creation of a climate of fear. A McLuhan message always tells us to look beyond the obvious and seek the nonobvious changes or effects that are enabled, enhanced, accelerated, or extended by the new thing.

McLuhan defines medium for us as well. Right at the beginning of *Understanding Media*, he tells us that a medium is "any extension of ourselves." Classically, he suggests that a hammer extends our arm and that the wheel extends our legs and feet. Each enables us to do more than our bodies could do on their own. Similarly, the medium of language extends our thoughts from within our mind out to others. Indeed, since our thoughts are the result of our individual sensory experience, speech is an "outering" of our senses—we could consider it as a form of reversing senses—whereas usually our senses bring the world into our minds, speech takes our sensorially shaped minds out to the world.

But McLuhan always thought of a medium in the sense of a growing medium, like the fertile potting soil into which a seed is planted, or the agar in a Petri dish. In other words, a medium—this extension of our body or senses or mind—is anything from which a change emerges. And since some sort of change emerges from everything we conceive or create, all of our inventions, innovations, ideas, and ideals are McLuhan media.

Thus we have the meaning of "the medium is the message:" We can know the nature and characteristics of anything we conceive or create (medium) by virtue of the changes—often unnoticed and nonobvious changes—that they effect (message.) McLuhan warns us that we are often distracted by the content of a medium (which, in almost all cases, is another distinct medium in itself). He writes, "it is only too typical that the "content" of any medium blinds us to the character of the medium" (p. 9). And it is the character of the medium that is its potency or effect—its message. In other words, "This is merely to say that the personal and social consequences of any medium—that is, of any extension of ourselves—result from the new scale that is introduced into our affairs by each extension of ourselves, or by any new technology."

Why is this understanding of "the medium is the message" particularly useful? We tend to notice changes—even slight changes (that unfortunately we often tend to discount in significance). "The medium is the message" tells us that noticing change in our societal or cultural ground conditions indicates the presence of a new message, that is, the effects of a new medium. With this early warning, we can set out to characterize and identify the new medium before it becomes obvious to everyone—a process that often takes years or even decades. And if we discover that the new medium brings along effects that might be detrimental to our society or culture, we have the opportunity to influence the development and evolution of the new innovation before the effects becomes pervasive. As McLuhan reminds us, "Control over change would seem to consist in moving not with it but ahead of it. Anticipation gives the power to deflect and control force." (p. 199).

REFERENCE

McLuhan, Marshall. (1964) Understanding Media: The Extensions of Man. New York: McGraw Hill.

CITATION

Federman, M. (2004). What is the Meaning of the Medium is the Message? Retrieved <DATE> from http://individual.utoronto.ca/markfederman/MeaningTheMediumistheMessage.pdf.

Excerpts from Understanding Media

Marshall McLuhan

THE GADGET LOVER
Narcissus as Narcosis

The Greek myth of Narcissus is directly concerned with a fact of human experience, as the word *Narcissus* indicates. It is from the Greek word *narcosis* or numbness. The youth Narcissus mistook his own reflection in the water for another person. This extension of himself by mirror numbed his perceptions until he became the servomechanism of his own extended or repeated image. The nymph Echo tried to win his love with fragments of his own speech, but in vain. He was numb. He had adapted to his extension of himself and had become a closed system.

Now the point of this myth is the fact that men at once become fascinated by any extension of themselves in any material other than themselves. There have been cynics who insisted that men fall deepest in love with women who give them back their own image. Be that as it may, the wisdom of the Narcissus myth does not convey any idea that Narcissus fell in love with anything he regarded as himself. Obviously he would have had very different feelings about the image had he known it was an extension or repetition of himself. It is, perhaps, indicative of the bias of our intensely technological and, therefore, narcotic culture that we have long interpreted the Narcissus story to mean that he fell in love with himself, that he imagined the reflection to be Narcissus!

Physiologically there are abundant reasons for an extension of ourselves involving us in a state of numbness. Medical researchers like Hans Selye and Adolphe Jonas hold that all extensions of ourselves, in sickness or in health, are attempts to maintain equilibrium. Any extension of ourselves they regard as "autoamputation," and they find that the autoamputative power or strategy is resorted to by the body when the perceptual power cannot locate or avoid the cause of irritation. Our language has many expressions that indicate this self-amputation that is imposed by various pressures. We speak of "wanting to jump out of my skin" or of "going out of my mind," being "driven batty" or "flipping my lid." And we often create artificial situations that rival the irritations and stresses of real life under controlled conditions of sport and play.

While it was no part of the intention of Jonas and Selye to provide an explanation of human invention and technology, they have given us a theory of disease (discomfort) that goes far to explain why man is impelled to extend various parts of his body by a kind of autoamputation. In the physical stress of superstimulation of various kinds, the central nervous system acts to protect itself by a strategy of amputation or isolation of the offending organ, sense, or function. Thus, the stimulus to new invention is the stress of acceleration of pace and increase of load. For example, in the case of the wheel as an extension of the foot, the pressure of new burdens resulting from the acceleration of exchange by written and monetary media was the immediate occasion of the extension or "amputation" of this function from our bodies. The wheel as a counter-irritant to increased burdens, in turn, brings about a new intensity of action by its amplification of a separate or isolated function (the feet in rotation). Such amplification is bearable by the nervous system only through numbness or blocking of perception. This is the sense of the Narcissus myth. The young man's image is

McLuhan, Marshall. Introduction by Lewis H. Lapham, *Understanding Media: The Extensions of Man*, pp 41-55, © 1994 Massachusetts Institute of Technology, by permission of The MIT Press.

a self-amputation or extension induced by irritating pressures. As counter-irritant, the image produces a generalized numbness or shock that declines recognition. Self-amputation forbids self-recognition.

The principle of self-amputation as an immediate relief of strain on the central nervous system applies very readily to the origin of the media of communication from speech to computer.

Physiologically, the central nervous system, that electric network that coordinates the various media of our senses, plays the chief role. Whatever threatens its function must be contained, localized, or cut off, even to the total removal of the offending organ. The function of the body, as a group of sustaining and protective organs for the central nervous system, is to act as buffers against sudden variations of stimulus in the physical and social environment. Sudden social failure or shame is a shock that some may "take to heart" or that may cause muscular disturbance in general, signaling for the person to withdraw from the threatening situation.

Therapy, whether physical or social, is a counter-irritant that aids in that equilibrium of the physical organs which protect the central nervous system. Whereas pleasure is a counter-irritant (e.g., sports, entertainment, and alcohol), comfort is the removal of irritants. Both pleasure and comfort are strategies of equilibrium for the central nervous system.

With the arrival of electric technology, man extended, or set outside himself, a live model of the central nervous system itself. To the degree that this is so, it is a development that suggests a desperate and suicidal autoamputation, as if the central nervous system could no longer depend on the physical organs to be protective buffers against the slings and arrows of an outrageous mechanism. It could well be that successive mechanizations of various physical organs since the invention of printing have made too violent and superstimulated a social experience for the central nervous system to endure.

In relation to that only too plausible cause of such development, we can return to the Narcissus theme. For if Narcissus is numbed by his self-amputated image, there is a very good reason for the numbness. There is a close parallel of response between the patterns of physical and psychic trauma or shock. A person suddenly deprived of loved ones and a person who drops a few feet unexpectedly will both register shock. Both the loss of family and a physical fall are extreme instances of amputations of the self. Shock induces a generalized numbness or an increased threshold to all types of perception. The victim seems immune to pain or sense.

Battle shock created by violent noise has been adapted for dental use in the device known as *audiac*. The patient puts on headphones and turns a dial raising the noise level to the point that he feels no pain from the drill. The selection of a *single* sense for intense stimulus, or of a single extended, isolated, or "amputated" sense in technology, is in part the reason for the numbing effect that technology as such has on its makers and users. For the central nervous system rallies a response of general numbness to the challenge of specialized irritation.

The person who falls suddenly experiences immunity to all pain or sensory stimuli because the central nervous system has to be protected from any intense thrust of sensation. Only gradually does he regain normal sensitivity to sights and sounds, at which time he may begin to tremble and perspire and to react as he would have done if the central nervous system had been prepared in advance for the fall that occurred unexpectedly.

Depending on which sense or faculty is extended technologically, or "autoamputated," the "closure" or equilibrium-seeking among the other senses is fairly predictable. It is with the senses as it is with color. Sensation is always 100 per cent, and a color is always 100 per cent color. But the ratio among the components in the sensation or the color can differ infinitely. Yet if sound, for example, is intensified, touch and taste and sight are affected at once. The effect of radio on literate or visual man was to reawaken his tribal memories, and the effect of sound added to motion pictures was to diminish the role of mime, tactility, and kinesthesis. Similarly, when nomadic man turned to sedentary and specialist ways, the senses specialized too. The development of writing and the visual organization of life made possible the discovery of individualism, introspection, and so on.

Any invention or technology is an extension or self-amputation of our physical bodies, and such extension also demands new ratios or new equilibriums among the other organs and extensions of the body. There is, for example, no way of refusing to comply with the new sense ratios or sense "closure" evoked by the TV image. But the effect of the entry of the TV image will vary from culture to culture in accordance with the existing sense ratios in each culture. In audile-tactile Europe, TV has intensified the visual sense, spurring them toward American styles of packaging and dressing. In America, the intensely visual culture, TV has opened the doors of audile-tactile perception to the nonvisual world of spoken languages and food and the plastic arts. As an extension and expediter of the sense life, any medium at once affects the entire field of the senses, as the Psalmist explained long ago in the 115th Psalm:

> Their idols are silver and gold,
> The work of men's hands.
> They have mouths, but they speak not;
> Eyes they have, but they see not;
> They have ears, but they hear not;
> Noses have they, but they smell not;
> They have hands, but they handle not;
> Feet have they, but they walk not;
> Neither speak they through their throat.
> They that make them shall be like unto them;
> Yea, every one that trusteth in them.

The concept of "idol" for the Hebrew Psalmist is much like that of Narcissus for the Greek mythmaker. And the Psalmist insists that the *beholding* of idols, or the use of technology, conforms men to them. "They that make them shall be like unto them." This is a simple fact of sense "closure." The poet Blake developed the Psalmist's ideas into an entire theory of communication and social change. It is in his long poem of *Jerusalem* that he explains why men have become what they have beheld. What they have, says Blake, is "the spectre of the Reasoning Power in Man" that has become fragmented and "separated from Imagination and enclosing itself as in steel." Blake, in a word, sees man as fragmented by his technologies. But he insists that these technologies are self-amputations of our own organs. When so amputated, each organ becomes a closed system of great new intensity that hurls man into "martyrdoms and wars." Moreover, Blake announces as his theme in *Jerusalem* the organs of perception:

> If Perceptive Organs vary, Objects of Perception seem to vary:
> If Perceptive Organs close, their Objects seem to close also.

To behold, use, or perceive any extension of ourselves in technological form is necessarily to embrace it. To listen to radio or to read the printed page is to accept these extensions of ourselves into our personal system and to undergo the "closure" or displacement of perception that follows automatically. It is this continuous embrace of our own technology in daily use that puts us in the Narcissus role of subliminal awareness and numbness in relation to these images of ourselves. By continuously embracing technologies, we relate ourselves to them as servomechanisms. That is why we must, to use them at all, serve these objects, these extensions of ourselves, as gods or minor religions. An Indian is the servomechanism of his canoe, as the cowboy of his horse or the executive of his clock.

Physiologically, man in the normal use of technology (or in variously extended body) is perpetually modified by it and in turn finds ever new ways of modifying his technology. Man becomes, as it were, the sex organs of the machine world, as the bee of the plant world, enabling it to fecundate and to evolve ever new forms. The machine world reciprocates man's love by expediting his wishes and desires, namely, in providing him with wealth. One of the merits of motivation research has been the revelation of man's sex relation to the motorcar.

Socially, it is the accumulation of group pressures and irritations that prompt invention and innovation as counter-irritants. War and the fear of war have always been considered the main incentives to technological extension of our bodies. Indeed, Lewis Mumford, in his *The City in History*, considers the walled city itself an extension of our skins, as much as housing and clothing. More even than the preparation for war, the aftermath of invasion is a rich technological period; because the subject culture has to adjust all its sense ratios to accommodate the impact of the invading culture. It is from such intensive hybrid exchange and strife of ideas and forms that the greatest social energies are released, and from which arise the greatest technologies. Buckminster Fuller estimates that since 1910 the governments of the world have spent 3½ trillion dollars on airplanes. That is 62 times the existing gold supply of the world.

The principle of numbness comes into play with electric technology, as with any other. We have to numb our central nervous system when it is extended and exposed, or we will die. Thus the age of anxiety and of electric media is also the age of the unconscious and of apathy. But it is strikingly the age of consciousness of the unconscious, in addition. With our central nervous system strategically numbed, the tasks of conscious awareness and order are transferred to the physical life of man, so that for the first time he has become aware of technology as an extension of his physical body. Apparently this could not have happened before the electric age gave us the means of instant, total field awareness. With such awareness, the subliminal life, private and social, has been hoicked up into full view, with the result that we have "social consciousness" presented to us as a cause of guilt feelings. Existentialism offers a philosophy of structures, rather than categories, and of total social involvement instead of the bourgeois spirit of individual separateness or points of view. In the electric age we wear all mankind as our skin.

Hybrid Energy
Les Liaisons Dangereuses

"For most of our lifetime civil war has been raging in the world of art and entertainment. . . . Moving pictures, gramophone records, radio, talking pictures..." This is the view of Donald McWhinnie, analyst of the radio medium. "Most of this civil war affects us in the depths of our psychic lives, as well, since the war is conducted by forces that are extensions and amplifications of our own beings. Indeed, the interplay among media is only another name for this civil war" that rages in our society and our psyches alike. "To the blind all things are sudden," it has been said. The crossings or hybridizations of the media release great new force and energy as by fission or fusion. There need be no blindness in these matters once we have been notified that there is anything to observe.

It has now been explained that media, or the extensions of man, are "make happen" agents, but not "make aware" agents. The hybridizing or compounding of these agents offers an especially favorable opportunity to notice their structural components and properties. "As the silent film cried out for sound, so does the sound film cry out for color," wrote Sergei Eisenstein in his *Notes of a Film Director*. This type of observation can be extended systematically to all media: "As the printing press cried out for nationalism, so did the radio cry out for tribalism." These media, being extensions of ourselves, also depend upon us for their interplay and their evolution. The fact that they do interact and spawn new progeny has been a source of wonder over the ages. It need baffle us no longer if we trouble to scrutinize their action. We can, if we choose, think things out before we put them out.

Plato, in all his striving to imagine an ideal training school, failed to notice that Athens was a greater school than any university even he could dream up. In other words, the greatest school had been put out for human use before it has been thought out. Now, this is especially true of our media. They are put out long before they are thought out. In fact, their being put outside us tends to cancel the possibility of their being thought of at all.

Everybody notices how coal and steel and cars affect the arrangements of daily existence. In our time, study has finally turned to the medium of language itself as shaping the arrangements of daily life, so that society begins to look like a linguistic echo or repeat of language norms, a fact that has disturbed the Russian Communist party very deeply. Wedded as they are to nineteenth-century industrial technology as the basis of class liberation, nothing could be more subversive of the Marxian dialectic than the idea that linguistic media shape social development, as much as do the means of production.

In fact, of all the great hybrid unions that breed furious release of energy and change, there is none to surpass the meeting of literate and oral cultures. The giving to man of an eye for an ear by phonetic literacy is, socially and politically, probably the most radical explosion that can occur in any social structure. This explosion of the eye, frequently repeated in "backward areas," we call Westernization. With literacy now about to hybridize the cultures of the Chinese, the Indians, and the Africans, we are about to experience such a release of human power and aggressive violence as makes the previous history of phonetic alphabet technology seem quite tame.

That is only the East side story, for the electric implosion now brings oral and tribal ear-culture to the literate West. Not only does the visual, specialist, and fragmented Westerner have now to live in closest daily association with all the ancient oral cultures of the earth, but his own electric technology now begins to translate the visual or eye man back into the tribal and oral pattern with its seamless web of kinship and interdependence.

We know from our own past the kind of energy that is released, as by fission, when literacy explodes the tribal or family unit. What do we know about the social and psychic energies that develop by electric fusion or implosion when literate individuals are suddenly gripped by an electromagnetic field, such as occurs in the new Common Market pressure in Europe? Make no mistake, the fusion of people who have known individualism and nationalism is not the same process as the fission of "backward" and oral cultures that are just coming to individualism and nationalism. It is the difference between the "A" bomb and the "H" bomb. The latter is more violent, by far. Moreover, the products of electric fusion are immensely complex, while the products of fission are simple. Literacy creates very much simpler kinds of people than those that develop in the complex web of ordinary tribal and oral societies. For the fragmented man creates the homogenized Western world, while oral societies are made up of people differentiated, not by their specialist skills or visible marks, but by their unique emotional mixes. The oral man's inner world is a tangle of complex emotions and feelings that the Western practical man has long ago eroded or suppressed within himself in the interest of efficiency and practicality.

The immediate prospect for literate, fragmented Western man encountering the electric implosion within his own culture is his steady and rapid transformation into a complex and depth-structured person emotionally aware of his total interdependence with the rest of human society. Representatives of the older Western individualism are even now assuming the appearance, for good or ill, of Al Capp's General Bull Moose or of the John Birchers, tribally dedicated to opposing the tribal. Fragmented, literate, and visual individualism is not possible in an electrically patterned and imploded society. So what is to be done? Do we dare to confront such facts at the conscious level, or is it best to becloud and repress such matters until some violence releases us from the entire burden? For the fate of implosion and interdependence is more terrible for Western man than the fate of explosion and independence for tribal man. It may be merely temperament in my own case, but I find some easing of the burden in just understanding and clarifying the issues. On the other hand, since consciousness and awareness seem to be a human privilege, may it not be desirable to extend this condition to our hidden conflicts, both private and social?

The present book, in seeking to understand many media, the conflicts from which they spring, and the even greater conflicts to which they give rise, holds out the promise of reducing these conflicts by an increase in human autonomy. Let us now note a few of the effects of media hybrids, or of the interpenetration of one medium by another.

Life at the Pentagon has been greatly complicated by jet travel, for example. Every few minutes an assembly gong rings to summon many specialists from their desks to hear a personal report from an expert from some remote part of the world. Meantime, the undone paper work mounts on each desk. And each department daily dispatches personnel by jet to remote areas for more data and reports. Such is the speed of this process of the meeting of the jet plane, the oral report, and the typewriter that those going forth to the ends of the earth often arrive unable to spell the name of the spot to which they have been sent as experts. Lewis Carroll pointed out that as large-scale maps got more and more detailed and extensive, they would tend to blanket agriculture and rouse the protest of farmers. So why not use the actual earth as a map of itself? We have reached a similar point of data gathering when each stick of chewing gum we reach for is acutely noted by some computer that translates our least gesture into a new probability curve or some parameter of social science. Our private and corporate lives have become information processes just because we have put our central nervous systems outside us in electric technology. That is the key to Professor Boorstin's bewilderment in *The Image, or What Happened to the American Dream*.

The electric light ended the regime of night and day, of indoors and out-of-doors. But it is when the light encounters already existing patterns of human organization that the hybrid energy is released. Cars can travel all night, ball players can play all night, and windows can be left out of buildings. In a word, the message of the electric light is total change. It is pure information without any content to restrict its transforming and informing power.

If the student of media will but meditate on the power of this medium of electric light to transform every structure of time and space and work and society that it penetrates or contacts, he will have the key to the form of the power that is in all media to reshape any lives that they touch. Except for light, all other media come in pairs, with one acting as the "content" of the other, obscuring the operation of both.

It is a peculiar bias of those who operate media for the owners that they be concerned about the program content of radio, or press, or film. The owners themselves are concerned more about the media as such, and are not inclined to go beyond "what the public wants" or some vague formula. Owners are aware of the media as power, and they know that this power has little to do with "content" or the media within the media.

When the press opened up the "human interest" keyboard after the telegraph had restructured the press medium, the newspaper killed the theater, just as TV hit the movies and the night clubs very hard. George Bernard Shaw had the wit and imagination to fight back. He put the press into the theater, taking over the controversies and the human interest world of the press for the stage, as Dickens had done for the novel. The movie took over the novel and the newspaper and the stage, all at once. Then TV pervaded the movie and gave the theater-in-the-round back to the public.

What I am saying is that media as extensions of our senses institute new ratios, not only among our private senses, but among themselves, when they interact among themselves. Radio changed the form of the news story as much as it altered the film image in the talkies. TV caused drastic changes in radio programming, and in the form of the *thing* or documentary novel.

It is the poets and painters who react instantly to a new medium like radio or TV. Radio and gramophone and tape recorder gave us back the poet's voice as an important dimension of the poetic experience. Words became a kind of painting with light, again. But TV, with its deep-partcipation mode, caused young poets suddenly to present their poems in cafés, in public parks, anywhere. After TV, they suddenly felt the need for personal contact with their public. (In print-oriented Toronto, poetry reading in the public parks is a public offense. Religion and politics are permitted, but not poetry, as many young poets recently discovered.)

John O'Hara, the novelist, wrote in *The New York Times Book Review* of November 27, 1955:

> You get a great satisfaction from a book. You know your reader is captive inside those covers, but as novelist you have to imagine the satisfaction he's getting. Now, in the theater-well, I used to drop in during both productions of *Pal Joey* and watch, not imagine, the people enjoy it. I'd willingly start my next novel—about a small town—right now, but I need the diversion of a play.

In our age artists are able to mix their media diet as easily as their book diet. A poet like Yeats made the fullest use of oral peasant culture in creating his literary effects. Quite early, Eliot made a great impact by the careful use of jazz and film form. *The Love Song of J. Alfred Prufrock* gets much of its power from an interpenetration of film form and jazz idiom. But this mix reached its greatest power in *The Waste Land* and *Sweeney Agonistes*. *Prufrock* uses not only film form but the film theme of Charlie Chaplin, as did James Joyce in *Ulysses*. Joyce's Bloom is a deliberate takeover from Chaplin ("Chorney Choplain," as he called him in *Finnegans Wake*). And Chaplin, just as Chopin had adapted the pianoforte to the style of the ballet, hit upon the wondrous media mix of ballet and film in developing his Pavlova-like alternation of ecstasy and waddle. He adopted the classical steps of ballet to a movie mime that converged exactly the right blend of the lyric and the ironic that is found also in *Prufrock* and *Ulysses*. Artists in various fields are always the first to discover how to enable one medium to use or to release the power of another. In a simpler form, it is the technique employed by Charles Boyer in his kind of French-English blend of urbane, throaty delirium.

The printed book had encouraged artists to reduce all forms of expression as much as possible to the single descriptive and narrative plane of the printed word. The advent of electric media released art from this straitjacket at once, creating the world of Paul Klee, Picasso, Braque, Eisenstein, the Marx Brothers, and James Joyce.

A headline in *The New York Times Book Review* (September 16, 1962) trills: There's Nothing Like a Best Seller to Set Hollywood a-Tingle.

Of course, nowadays, movie stars can only be lured from the beaches or science-fiction or some self-improvement course by the cultural lure of a role in a famous book. That is the way that the interplay of media now affects many in the movie colony. They have no more understanding of their media problems than does Madison Avenue. But from the point of view of the owners of the film and related media, the best seller is a form of insurance that some massive new *gestalt* or pattern has been isolated in the public psyche. It is an oil strike or a gold mine that can be depended on to yield a fair amount of boodle to the careful and canny processer. Hollywood bankers, that is, are smarter than literary historians, for the latter despise popular taste except when it has been filtered down from lecture course to literary handbook.

Lillian Ross in *Picture* wrote a snide account of the filming of *The Red Badge of Courage*. She got a good deal of easy kudos for a foolish book about a great film by simply *assuming* the superiority of the literary medium to the film medium. Her book got much attention as a hybrid.

Agatha Christie wrote far above her usual good level in a group of twelve short stories about Hercule Poirot, called *The Labours of Hercules*. By adjusting the classical themes to make reasonable modern parallels, she was able to lift the detective form to extraordinary intensity.

Such was, also, the method of James Joyce in *Dubliners* and *Ulysses*, when the precise classical parallels created the true hybrid energy. Baudelaire, said Mr. Eliot, "taught us how to raise the imagery of common life to first intensity." It is done, not by any direct heave-ho of poetic strength, but by a simple adjustment of situations from one culture in hybrid form with those of another. It is precisely in this way that during wars and migrations new cultural mix is the norm of ordinary daily life. Operations Research programs the hybrid principle as a technique of creative discovery.

When the movie scenario or picture story was applied to the *idea* article, the magazine world had discovered a hybrid that ended the supremacy of the short story. When wheels were put in tandem form, the wheel principle combined with the lineal typographic principle to create aerodynamic balance. The wheel crossed with industrial, lineal form released the new form of the airplane.

The hybrid or the meeting of two media is a moment of truth and revelation from which new form is born. For the parallel between two media holds us on the frontiers between forms that snap us out of the Narcissus-narcosis. The moment of the meeting of media is a moment of freedom and release from the ordinary trance and numbness imposed by them on our senses.

Showing Seeing:
A Critique of Visual Culture

W.J.T. Mitchell

ABSTRACT

This essay attempts to map out the main issues surrounding visual studies as an emergent academic formation, and as a theoretical concept or object of research and teaching. After a survey of some of the resistances encountered by visual studies in fields such as art history, aesthetics, and media studies, and a suggestion that visual studies is playing the role of "dangerous supplement" to these fields, the essay turns to a discussion of some of the major received ideas that have seemed foundational to both negative and positive accounts of visual studies. These received ideas or myths include notions of the de-materialization of the image, and the erasure of boundaries between art and nonart, or visual and verbal media. They also include notions such as the very idea that there are such things as distinctly "visual media." The political stakes of iconoclastic criticism (e.g., the overturning of "scopic regimes") are also questioned, and an alternative (Nietzschean) strategy of "sounding the idols" is proposed. The essay concludes with a description of pedagogical strategies in the teaching of visual culture, centered on an exercise the author calls "showing seeing."

KEY WORDS

aesthetics • art history • communication • cultural studies • discipline(s) and interdisciplinarity • image studies • media and media studies • pedagogy • poetics • rhetoric

What is visual culture or visual studies? Is it an emergent discipline, a passing moment of inter-disciplinary turbulence, a research topic, a field or subfield of cultural studies, media studies, rhetoric and communication, art history, or aesthetics? Does it have a specific object of research, or is it a grab bag of problems left over from respectable, well-established disciplines? If it is a field, what are its boundaries and limiting definitions? Should it be institutionalized as an academic structure, made into a department or given programmatic status, with all the appurtenances of syllabi, textbooks, prerequisites, requirements, and degrees? How should it be taught? What would it mean to profess visual culture in a way that is more than improvisatory?

I have to confess that, after almost 10 years of teaching a course called Visual Culture at the University of Chicago, I still do not have categorical answers to all these questions.[1] What I can offer is my own take on where the field of visual studies is going today, and how it might avoid a number of pitfalls along the way. What follows is based mainly on my own formation as a literary scholar who has been involved as a migrant worker in the fields of art history, aesthetics, and media studies. It is also based on my experience as a teacher attempting to awaken students to the wonders of visuality, practices of seeing the world and especially the seeing of other people. My aim in this course has been to overcome the veil of familiarity and self-evidence that surrounds

W.J.T. Mitchell, *Journal of Visual Culture*, Volume 1, Issue 2, pp. 165-181, Copyright © 2002 SAGE Publications, Ltd. Reprinted by permission of SAGE Publications, Ltd.

the experience of seeing, and to turn it into a problem for analysis, a mystery to be unraveled. In doing this, I suspect that I am rather typical of those that teach this subject, and that this is the common core of our interest, however different our methods or reading lists might be. The problem is one of staging a paradox that can be formulated in a number of ways: that vision is itself invisible; that we cannot see what seeing is; that the eyeball (pace Emerson) is never transparent. I take my task as a teacher to be to make seeing show itself, to put it on display, and make it accessible to analysis. I call this "showing seeing," a variation on the American elementary school ritual called "show and tell," and I return to it at the conclusion of this article.

THE DANGEROUS SUPPLEMENT

Let me begin, however, with the gray matters: the questions of disciplines, fields, and programs that are intersected by visual studies. I think it's useful at the outset to distinguish between visual studies and visual culture as, respectively, the field of study and the object or target of study. Visual studies is the study of visual culture. This avoids the ambiguity that plagues subjects like history, in which the field and the things covered by the field bear the same name. In practice, of course, we often confuse the two, and I prefer to let visual culture stand for both the field and its content, and to let the context clarify the meaning. I also prefer visual culture because it is less neutral than visual studies, and commits one at the outset to a set of hypotheses that need to be tested—for example, that vision is (as we say) a cultural construction, that it is learned and cultivated, not simply given by nature; that therefore it might have a history related in some yet to be determined way to the history of arts, technologies, media, and social practices of display and spectatorship; and (finally) that it is deeply involved with human societies, with the ethics and politics, aesthetics and epistemology of seeing and being seen. So far, I hope (possibly in vain) that we are all singing the same tune.[2]

The dissonance begins, as I see it, when we ask what the relation of visual studies is to existing disciplines such as art history and aesthetics (see Foster, 1987). At this point, certain disciplinary anxieties, not to mention territorial grumpiness and defensiveness, begin to emerge. If I were a representative of cinema and media studies, for instance, I would ask why the discipline that addresses the major new art forms of the twentieth century is so often marginalized in favor of fields that date to the eighteenth and nineteenth centuries.[3] If I were here to represent visual studies (which I am) I might see the triangulation of my field in relation to the venerable fields of art history and aesthetics as a classic pincers movement, designed to erase visual studies from the map. The logic of this operation is easy enough to describe. Aesthetics and art history are in a complementary and collaborative alliance. Aesthetics is the theoretical branch of the study of art. It raises fundamental questions about the nature of art, artistic value, and artistic perception within the general field of perceptual experience. Art history is the historical study of artists, artistic practices, styles, movements, and institutions. Together, then, art history and aesthetics provide a kind of completeness; they cover any conceivable question one might have about the visual arts. And if one conceives them in their most expansive manifestations, art history as a general iconology or hermeneutics of visual images, aesthetics as the study of sensation and perception, then it seems clear that they already take care of any issues that a discipline of visual studies might want to raise. The theory of visual experience would be dealt with in aesthetics; the history of images and visual forms would be dealt with in art history.

Visual studies, then, is from a certain familiar disciplinary point of view, quite unnecessary. We don't need it. It adds on a vague, ill-defined body of issues that are covered quite adequately within the existing academic structure of knowledge. And yet, here it is, cropping up as a kind of quasi-field or pseudo-discipline, complete with anthologies, courses, debates, conferences, and professors. The only question is: What is visual studies a symptom of? Why has this unnecessary thing appeared?

It should be clear by this point that the disciplinary anxiety provoked by visual studies is a classic instance of what Jacques Derrida called the "dangerous supplement." Visual studies stands in an ambiguous relation to art history and aesthetics. On the one hand, it functions as an internal complement to these fields, a way of filling in a gap. If art history is about visual images, and aesthetics about the senses, what could be more natural than a subdiscipline that would focus on visuality as such, linking aesthetics and art history around the problems of light, optics, visual apparatuses and experience, the eye as a perceptual organ, the scopic drive, etc.? But this complementary function of visual studies threatens to become supplementary as well: first, in that it indicates an incompleteness in the internal coherence of aesthetics and art history, as if these disciplines had somehow failed to pay attention to what was most central in their own domains; and second, in that it opens both disciplines to outside issues that threaten their boundaries. Visual studies threatens to make art history and aesthetics into subdisciplines within some expanded field of inquiry whose boundaries are anything but clear. What, after all, can fit inside the domain of visual studies? Not just art history and aesthetics, but scientific and technical imaging, film, television, and digital media, as well as philosophical inquiries into the epistemology of vision, semiotic studies of images and visual signs, psychoanalytic investigation of the scopic drive, phenomenological, physiological, and cognitive studies of the visual process, sociological studies of spectatorship and display, visual anthropology, physical optics and animal vision, and so forth and so on. If the object of visual studies is what Hal Foster (1987) calls visuality, it is a capacious topic indeed, one that may be impossible to delimit in a systematic way.

Can visual studies be an emergent field, a discipline, a coherent domain of research, even (*mirabile dictu*) an academic *department*? Should art history fold its tent and, in a new alliance with aesthetics and media studies, aim to build a larger edifice around the concept of visual culture? Should we just merge everything into cultural studies? We know very well, of course, that institutional efforts of this sort have already been underway for some time at places like Irvine, Rochester, Chicago, Wisconsin, and no doubt others of which I am unaware. I have been a small part of some of these efforts, and have generally been supportive of institution-building efforts. I am mindful, however, of the larger forces in academic politics which have, in some cases, exploited interdisciplinary efforts like cultural studies in order to downsize and eliminate traditional departments and disciplines, or to produce what Tom Crow has called a de-skilling of whole generations of scholars.[4] The erosion of the forensic skills of connoisseurship and authentication among art historians in favor of a generalized iconological interpretive expertise is a trade-off that ought to trouble us. I want both kinds of expertise to be available, so that the next generation of art historians will be skilled with *both* the concrete materiality of art objects and practices, *and* with the intricacies of the dazzling PowerPoint presentation that moves effortlessly across the audiovisual media in search of meaning. I want visual studies to attend *both* to the specificity of the things we see, *and* to the fact that most of traditional art history was already mediated by highly imperfect representations such as the lantern slide, and before that by engraving, lithographs, or verbal descriptions.[5]

So if visual studies is a dangerous supplement to art history and aesthetics, it seems to me important neither to romanticize nor to underestimate the danger, but also important not to let disciplinary anxieties lure us into a siege mentality, circling our wagons around straight art history, or narrow notions of tradition.[6] We might take some comfort from the precedent of Derrida's own canonical figure of the dangerous supplement, the phenomenon of *writing*, and its relation to speech, to the study of language, literature, and philosophical discourse. Derrida (1978) traces the way that writing, traditionally thought of as a merely instrumental tool for recording speech, invades the domain of speech once one understands the general condition of language to be its iterability, its foundation in repetition and re-citation. The authentic *presence* of the voice, of the phonocentric core of language, *immediately* connected to meaning in the speaker's mind, is lost in the traces of writing, which remain when the speaker is absent and ultimately even when he or she is present. The whole onto-theological domain of originary self-presence is undermined and restaged as an effect of writing, of an infinite series of substitutions, deferrals, and differentials. This was heady, intoxicating, and dangerous news in the 1970s when it hit the American academy. Could it be that not only linguistics, but all the human sciences, indeed all human knowledge, was about to be swallowed up in a new field called grammatology. Could it be that our own anxieties about the boundlessness of visual studies are a replay of an earlier panic brought on by the news that there is nothing outside the text?

One obvious connection between the two panic attacks is their common emphasis on *visuality* and *spacing*. Grammatology promoted the visible signs of written language, from pictographs to hieroglyphics to alphabetic scripts to the invention of printing and finally of digital media, from their status as parasitical supplements to an original, phonetic language-as-speech, to the position of primacy, as the general precondition for all notions of language, meaning, and presence. Grammatology challenged the primacy of language as invisible, authentic speech in the same way that iconology challenges the primacy of the unique, original artifact. A general condition of iterability or citationality—the repeatable acoustic image in one case, the visual image in the other—undermines the privilege of both visual art and literary language, placing them inside a larger field that, at first, seemed merely supplementary to them. Writing, not so accidentally, stands at the nexus of language and vision, epitomized in the figure of the rebus or hieroglyphic, the painted word or the visible language of a gesture-speech that precedes vocal expression.[7] Both grammatology and iconology, then, evoke the fear of the visual image, an iconoclastic panic that, in the one case, involves anxieties about rendering the invisible spirit of language in visible forms, in the other, the worry that the immediacy and concreteness of the visible image is in danger of being spirited away by the dematerialized, visual copy—a mere image of an image. It is no accident that Martin Jay's (1994) investigation of the history of philosophical optics is mainly a story of suspicion and anxiety about vision, or that my own explorations of iconology (Mitchell, 1987) tended to find a fear of imagery lurking beneath every theory of imagery.

Defensive postures and territorial anxieties may be inevitable in the bureaucratic battlegrounds of academic institutions, but they are notoriously bad for the purposes of clear, dispassionate thinking. My sense is that visual studies is not quite as dangerous as it has been made out to be (as, for instance, a training ground to prepare subjects for the next phase of global capitalism)[8] but that its own defenders have not been especially adroit in questioning the assumptions and impact of their own emergent field either. I want to turn, then, to a set of fallacies or myths about visual studies that are commonly accepted (with different value quotients) by both the opponents and proponents of this field. I will then offer a set of counter-theses which, in my view, emerge when the study of visual culture moves beyond these received ideas, and begins to define and analyze its object of investigation in some detail. I have summarized these fallacies and counter-theses in the following broadside (followed by a commentary). The broadside may be handy for nailing up on the doors of certain academic departments.

CRITIQUE: MYTHS AND COUNTER-THESES

Ten myths about visual culture

1. Visual culture entails the liquidation of art as we have known it.
2. Visual culture accepts without question the view that art is to be defined by its working exclusively through the optical faculties.

3. Visual culture transforms the history of art into a history of images.
4. Visual culture implies that the difference between a literary text and a painting is a nonproblem. Words and images dissolve into undifferentiated representation.
5. Visual culture implies a predilection for the disembodied, dematerialized image.
6. We live in a predominantly visual era. Modernity entails the hegemony of vision and visual media.
7. There is a coherent class of things called visual media.
8. Visual culture is fundamentally about the social construction of the visual field. What we see, and the manner in which we come to see it, is not simply part of a natural ability.
9. Visual culture entails an anthropological, and therefore unhistorical, approach to vision.
10. Visual culture consists of scopic regimes and mystifying images to be overthrown by political critique.

Eight counter-theses on visual culture

1. Visual culture encourages reflection on the differences between art and nonart, visual and verbal signs, and the ratios between different sensory and semiotic modes.
2. Visual culture entails a meditation on blindness, the invisible, the unseen, the unseeable, and the overlooked; also on deafness and the visible language of gesture; it also compels attention to the tactile, the auditory, the haptic, and the phenomenon of synesthesia.
3. Visual culture is not limited to the study of images or media, but extends to everyday practices of seeing and showing, especially those that we take to be immediate or unmediated. It is less concerned with the meaning of images than with their lives and loves.
4. There are no visual media. All media are mixed media, with varying ratios of senses and sign-types.
5. The disembodied image and the embodied artifact are permanent elements in the dialectics of visual culture. Images are to pictures and works of art as species are to specimens in biology.
6. We do not live in a uniquely visual era. The visual or pictorial turn is a recurrent trope that displaces moral and political panic onto images and so-called visual media. Images are convenient scapegoats, and the offensive eye is ritually plucked out by ruthless critique.
7. Visual culture is the visual construction of the social, not just the social construction of vision. The question of visual *nature* is therefore a central and unavoidable issue, along with the role of animals as images and spectators.
8. The political task of visual culture is to perform critique without the comforts of iconoclasm.

*Note: most of the fallacies above are quotations or close paraphrases of statements by well-known critics of visual culture. A prize will be awarded to anyone who can identify all of them.

COMMENTARY

If there is a defining moment in the concept of visual culture, I suppose it would be in that instant that the hoary concept of social construction made itself central to the field. We are all familiar with this Eureka! moment, when we reveal to our students and colleagues that vision and visual images, things that (to the novice) are apparently automatic, transparent, and natural, are actually symbolic constructions, like a language to be learned, a system of codes that interposes an ideological veil between us and the real world.[9] This overcoming of what has been called the natural attitude has been crucial to the elaboration of visual studies as an arena for political and ethical critique, and we should not underestimate its importance (see Byron, 1983). But if it becomes an unexamined dogma, it threatens to become a fallacy just as disabling as the naturalistic fallacy it sought to overturn. To what extent is vision *unlike* language, working (as Roland Barthes, 1982, observed of photography) like a message without a code? In what ways does it *transcend* specific or local forms of social construction to function like a universal language that is relatively free of textual or interpretive elements? (We should recall that Bishop Berkeley, 1709, who first claimed that vision was like a language, also insisted that it was a universal language, not a local or national language.) To what extent is vision *not* a learned activity, but a genetically determined capacity, and a programmed set of automatisms that has to be activated at the right time, but that are not learned in anything like the way that human languages are learned?

A dialectical concept of visual culture leaves itself open to these questions rather than foreclosing them with the received wisdom of social construction and linguistic models. It expects that the very notion of vision as a *cultural* activity necessarily entails an investigation of its *non*cultural dimensions, its pervasiveness as a sensory mechanism that operates in animal organisms all the way from the flea to the elephant. This version of visual culture understands itself as the opening of a dialogue with visual *nature*. It does not forget Lacan's (1978: 91) reminder that the eye goes back as far as the species that represent the appearance of life, and that oysters are seeing organisms. It does not content itself with victories over natural attitudes and naturalistic fallacies, but regards the seeming naturalness of vision and visual imagery as a problem to be explored, rather than a benighted prejudice to be overcome.[10] In short, a dialectical concept of visual culture cannot rest content with a definition of its object as the social construction of the visual field, but must insist on exploring the chiastic reversal of this proposition, *the visual construction of the social field*. It is not just that we see the way we do because we are social animals, but also that our social arrangements take the forms they do because we are seeing animals.

The fallacy of overcoming the naturalistic fallacy (we might call it the naturalistic fallacy fallacy, or naturalistic fallacy²)[11] is not the only received idea that has hamstrung the embryonic discipline of visual culture. The field has trapped itself inside of a whole set of related assumptions and commonplaces that, unfortunately, have become the common currency of both those who defend and attack visual studies as a dangerous supplement to art history and aesthetics. Here is a résumé of what might be called the constitutive fallacies or myths of visual culture, as outlined in my earlier broadside:

1. that visual culture means an end to the distinction between artistic and nonartistic images, a dissolving of the history of art into a history of images. This might be called the democratic or leveling fallacy, and it is greeted with alarm by unreconstructed high modernists and old-fashioned aesthetes, and heralded as a revolutionary breakthrough by the theorists of visual culture. It involves related worries (or elation) at the leveling of semiotic distinctions between words and images, digital and analog communication, between art and nonart, and between different kinds of media, or different concrete artifactual specimens.

2. that it is a reflex of, and consists in a visual turn or hegemony of the visible in modern culture, a dominance of visual media and spectacle over the verbal activities of speech, writing, textuality, and reading. It is often linked with the notion that other sensory modalities such as hearing and touch are likely to atrophy in the age of visuality. This might be called the fallacy of the pictorial turn, a development viewed with horror by iconophobes and opponents of mass culture, who see it is as the cause of a decline in literacy, and with delight by iconophiles who see new and higher forms of consciousness emerging from the plethora of visual images and media.

3. that the hegemony of the visible is a Western, modern invention, a product of new media technologies, and not a fundamental component of human cultures as such. Let's call this the fallacy of technical modernity,

a received idea which never fails to stir the ire of those who study non-Western and non-modern visual cultures, and which is generally taken as self-evident by those who believe that modern technical media (television, cinema, photography, the Internet) simply are the central content and determining instances of visual culture.

4. that there are such things as visual media, typically exemplified by film, photography, video, television, and the Internet. This, the fallacy of the visual media, is repeated by both sides as if it denoted something real. When media theorists object that it might be better to think of at least some of these as audiovisual media, or composite, mixed media that combine image and text, the fallback position is an assertion of the dominance of the visual in the technical, mass media. Thus it is claimed that we watch TV, we don't listen to it, an argument that is clinched by noting that the remote control has a mute button, but no control to blank out the picture.

5. that vision and visual images are expressions of power relations in which the spectator dominates the visual object and images and their producers exert power over viewers. This commonplace power fallacy is shared by opponents and proponents of visual culture who worry about the complicity of visual media with regimes of spectacle and surveillance, the use of advertising, propaganda, and snooping to control mass populations and erode democratic institutions. The split comes over the question of whether we need a discipline called visual culture to provide an oppositional critique of these scopic regimes, or whether this critique is better handled by sticking to aesthetics and art history, with their deep roots in human values, or media studies, with its emphasis on institutional and technical expertise.

It would take many pages to refute each of these received ideas in detail. Let me just outline the main theses of a counterposition that would treat them as I have treated the naturalistic fallacy fallacy, not as axioms of visual culture, but as invitations to question and investigate.

1. The democratic or leveling fallacy. There is no doubt that many people think the distinction between high art and mass culture is disappearing in our time, or that distinctions between media, or between verbal and visual images, are being undone. The question is: Is it true? Does the blockbuster exhibition mean that art museums are now mass media, indistinguishable from sporting events and circuses? Is it really that simple? I think not. The fact that some scholars want to open up the domain of images to consider both artistic and nonartistic images does not automatically abolish the differences between these domains.[12] One could as easily argue that, in fact, the boundaries of art/nonart only become clear when one looks at both sides of this ever-shifting border and traces the transactions and translations between them. Similarly, with semiotic distinctions between words and images, or between media types, the opening out of a general field of study does not abolish difference, but makes it available for investigation, as opposed to treating it as a barrier that must be policed and never crossed. I have been working between literature and visual arts, and between artistic and nonartistic images for the last three decades, and I have never found myself confused about which was which, though I have sometimes been confused about what made people so anxious about this work. As a practical matter, distinctions between the arts and media are ready-to-hand, a vernacular form of theorizing. The difficulty arises (as Lessing noted long ago in his *Laocoon*, see Mitchell, 1987), when we try to make these distinctions systematic and metaphysical.[13]

2. The fallacy of a pictorial turn. Since this is a phrase that I have coined (see Mitchell, 1994: ch. 1) I'll try to set the record straight on what I meant by it. First, I did not mean to make the claim that the modern era is unique or unprecedented in its obsession with vision and visual representation. My aim was to acknowledge

the perception of a turn to the visual or to the image as a *commonplace*, a thing that is said casually and unreflectively about our time, and is usually greeted with unreflective assent both by those who like the idea and those who hate it. But the pictorial turn is a *trope*, a figure of speech that has been repeated many times since antiquity. When the Israelites turn aside from the invisible god to a visible idol, they are engaged in a pictorial turn. When Plato warns against the domination of thought by images, semblances, and opinions in the allegory of the cave, he is urging a turn away from the pictures that hold humanity captive and toward the pure light of reason. When Lessing warns, in the Laocoon, about the tendency to imitate the effects of visual art in the literary arts, he is trying to combat a pictorial turn that he regards as a degradation of aesthetic and cultural proprieties. When Wittgenstein complains in the *Philosophical Investigations* that a picture held us captive, he is lamenting the rule of a certain metaphor for mental life that has held philosophy in its grip.

The pictorial or visual turn, then, is not unique to our time. It is a repeated narrative figure that takes on a very specific form in our time, but which seems to be available in its schematic form in an innumerable variety of circumstances. A critical and historical use of this figure would be as a diagnostic tool to analyze specific moments when a new medium, a technical invention, or a cultural practice erupts in symptoms of panic or euphoria (usually both) about the visual. The invention of photography, of oil painting, of artificial perspective, of sculptural casting, of the Internet, of writing, of mimesis itself are conspicuous occasions when a new way of making visual images seemed to mark a historical turning point for better or worse. The mistake is to construct a grand binary model of history centered on just one of these turning points, and to declare a single great divide between the age of literacy (for instance) and the age of visuality. These kinds of narratives are beguiling, handy for the purposes of presentist polemics, and useless for the purposes of genuine historical criticism.

3. It should be clear, then, that the supposed hegemony of the visible in our time (or in the ever-flexible period of modernity, or the equally flexible domain of the West) is a chimera that has outlived its usefulness. If visual culture is to mean anything, it has to be generalized as the study of all the social practices of human visuality, and not confined to modernity or the West. To live in any culture whatsoever is to live in a visual culture, except perhaps for those rare instances of societies of the blind, which for that very reason deserve special attention in any theory of visual culture.[14] As for the question of hegemony, what could be more archaic and traditional than the prejudice in favor of sight? Vision has played the role of the sovereign sense since God looked at his own creation and saw that it was good, or perhaps even earlier when he began the act of creation with the division of the light from the darkness. The notion of vision as hegemonic or non-hegemonic is simply too blunt an instrument to produce much in the way of historical or critical differentiation. The important task is to describe the specific relations of vision to the other senses, especially hearing and touch, as they are elaborated within particular cultural practices. Descartes regarded vision as simply an extended and highly sensitive form of touch, which is why (in his *Optics*) he compared eyesight to the sticks a blind man uses to grope his way about in real space. The history of cinema is in part the history of collaboration and conflict between technologies of visual and audio reproduction. The evolution of film is in no way aided by explaining it in terms of received ideas about the hegemony of the visible.

4. Which leads us to the fourth myth, the notion of visual media. I understand the use of this phrase as a shorthand figure to pick out the difference between (say) photographs and phonograph records, or paintings and novels, but I do object to the confident assertion that the visual media are really a distinct class of things, or that there is such a thing as an exclusively, purely visual medium.[15] Let us try out, as a counter-axiom, the notion that all media are mixed media, and see where that leads us. One place it will not

lead us is into misguided characterizations of audiovisual media like cinema and television as if they were exclusively or predominantly (echoes of the hegemonic fallacy) visual. The postulate of mixed, hybrid media leads us to the specificity of codes, materials, technologies, perceptual practices, sign-functions, and institutional conditions of production and consumption that go to make up a medium. It allows us to break up the reification of media around a single sensory organ (or a single sign-type, or material vehicle) and to pay attention to what is in front of us. Instead of the stunning redundancy of declaring literature to be a verbal and not a visual medium, for instance, we are allowed to say what is true: That literature, insofar as it is written or printed, has an unavoidable visual component which bears a specific relation to an auditory component, which is why it makes a difference whether a novel is read aloud or silently. We are also allowed to notice that literature, in techniques like ekphrasis and description, as well as in more subtle strategies of formal arrangement, involves virtual or imaginative experiences of space and vision that are no less real for being indirectly conveyed through language.

5. We come finally to the question of the power of visual images, their efficacy as instruments or agents of domination, seduction, persuasion, and deception. This topic is important because it exposes the motivation for the wildly varying political and ethical estimations of images, their celebration as gateways to new consciousness, their denigration as hegemonic forces, the need for policing and thus reifying the differences between the visual media and the others, or between the realm of art and the wider domain of images.

While there is no doubt that visual culture (like material, oral, or literary culture) can be an instrument of domination, I do not think it is productive to single out visuality or images or spectacle or surveillance as the exclusive vehicle of political tyranny. I wish not to be misunderstood here. I recognize that much of the interesting work in visual culture has come out of politically motivated scholarship, especially the study of the construction of racial and sexual difference in the field of the gaze. But the heady days when we were first discovering the male gaze or the feminine character of the image are now well behind us, and most scholars of visual culture who are invested in questions of identity are aware of this. Nevertheless, there is an unfortunate tendency to slide back into reductive treatments of visual images as all-powerful forces and to engage in a kind of iconoclastic critique which imagines that the destruction or exposure of false images amounts to a political victory. As I've said on other occasions, pictures are a popular political antagonist because one can take a tough stand on them and yet, at the end of the day, everything remains pretty much the same. Scopic regimes can be overturned repeatedly without any visible effect on either visual or political culture.

I propose what I hope is a more nuanced and balanced approach located in the equivocation between the visual image as instrument and agency, the image as a tool for manipulation, on the one hand, and as an apparently autonomous source of its own purposes and meanings on the other. This approach would treat visual culture and visual images as go-betweens in social transactions, as a repertoire of screen images or templates that structure our encounters with other human beings. Visual culture would find its primal scene, then, in what Emmanuel Levinas calls the face of the Other (beginning, I suppose, with the face of the Mother): the face-to-face encounter, the evidently hardwired disposition to recognize the eyes of another organism (what Lacan and Sartre call the gaze). Stereotypes, caricatures, classificatory figures, search images, mappings of the visible body, of the social spaces in which it appears would constitute the fundamental elaborations of visual culture on which the domain of the image—and of the Other—is constructed. As go-betweens or subaltern entities, these images are the filters through which we recognize and of course misrecognize other people. They are the paradoxical mediations which make possible what we call the unmediated or face-to-face relations that Raymond Williams postulates as the origin of society as such. And this means that the social construction of the visual field has to be continuously replayed as the visual construction of the social field, an invisible screen or latticework of apparently unmediated figures that makes the effects of mediated images possible.

Lacan, you will recall, diagrams the structure of the scopic field as a cat's cradle of dialectical intersections with a screened image at its center. The two hands that rock this cradle are the subject and the object, the observer and the observed. But between them, rocking in the cradle of the eye and the gaze, is this curious intermediary thing, the image and the screen or medium in which it appears. This phantasmatic thing was depicted in ancient optics as the eidolon, the projected template hurled outward by the probing, seeking eye, or the simulacrum of the seen object, cast off or propagated by the object like a snake shedding its skin in an infinite number of repetitions (see Lindbergh, 1981). Both the extramission and intramission theory of vision share the same picture of the visual process, differing only in the direction of the flow of energy and information. This ancient model, while no doubt incorrect as an account of the physical and physiological structure of vision, is still the best picture we have of vision as a psychosocial process. It provides an especially powerful tool for understanding why it is that images, works of art, media, figures, and metaphors have lives of their own, and cannot be explained simply as rhetorical, communicative instruments, or epistemological windows onto reality. The cat's cradle of intersubjective vision helps us to see why it is that objects and images look back at us; why the eidolon has a tendency to become an idol that talks back to us, gives orders, and demands sacrifices; why the propagated image of an object is so efficacious for propaganda, so fecund in reproducing an infinite number of copies of itself. It helps us to see why vision is never a one-way street, but a multiple intersection teeming with dialectical images, why the child's doll has a playful half-life on the borders of the animate and inanimate, and why the fossil traces of extinct life are resurrected in the beholder's imagination. It makes it clear why the questions to ask about images are not just what do they mean, or what do they do? But what is the secret of their vitality—and what do they want?

SHOWING SEEING

I want to conclude by reflecting on the disciplinary location of visual studies. I hope it's clear that I have no interest in rushing out to establish programs or departments. The interest of visual culture seems to me to reside precisely at the transitional points in the educational process at the introductory level (what we used to call art appreciation), at the passageway from undergraduate to graduate education, and at the frontiers of advanced research.[16] Visual studies belongs, then, in the freshman year in college, in the introduction to graduate studies in the humanities, and in the graduate workshop or seminar.

In all of these locations I have found it useful to return to one of the earliest pedagogical rituals in American elementary education, the show and tell exercise. In this case, however, the object of the show and tell performance is the process of seeing itself, and the exercise could be called showing seeing. I ask the students to frame their presentations by assuming that they are ethnographers who come from, and are reporting back to, a society that has no concept of visual culture. They cannot take for granted that their audience has any familiarity with everyday notions such as color, line, eye contact, cosmetics, clothing, facial expressions, mirrors, glasses, or voyeurism, much less with photography, painting, sculpture or other so-called visual media. Visual culture is thus made to seem strange, exotic, and in need of explanation.

The assignment is thoroughly paradoxical, of course. The audience does in fact live in a visible world, and yet has to accept the fiction that it does not, and that everything which seems transparent and self-evident is in need of explanation. I leave it to the students to construct an enabling fiction. Some choose to ask the audience to close their eyes and to take in the presentation solely with their ears and other senses. They work primarily by description and evocation of the visual through language and sound, telling *as*, rather than telling *and* showing. Another strategy is to pretend that the audience has just been provided with prosthetic visual organs, but does not yet know how to see with them. This is the favored strategy, since it allows for a visual presentation of objects and images. The audience has to pretend ignorance, and the presenter has to lead them toward the understanding of things they would ordinarily take for granted.

The range of examples and objects that students bring to class is quite broad and unpredictable. Some things routinely appear: eyeglasses are favorite objects of explanation, and someone almost always brings in a pair of mirror shades to illustrate the situation of seeing without being seen, and the masking of the eyes as a common strategy in a visual culture. Masks and disguises more generally are popular props. Windows, binoculars, kaleidoscopes, microscopes, and other pieces of optical apparatus are commonly adduced. Mirrors are frequently brought in, generally with no hint of an awareness of Lacan's mirror stage, but often with learned expositions of the optical laws of reflection, or discourses on vanity, narcissism, and self-fashioning. Cameras are often exhibited, not just to explain their workings, but to talk about the rituals and superstitions that accompany their use. One student elicited the familiar reflex of camera shyness by aggressively taking snapshots of other members of the class. Other presentations require even fewer props, and sometimes focus directly on the body image of the presenter, by way of attention to clothing, cosmetics, facial expressions, gestures, and other forms of body language. I have had students conduct rehearsals of a repertoire of facial expressions, change clothing in front of the class, perform tasteful (and limited) evocations of a striptease, put on makeup (one student put on white face paint, describing his own sensations as he entered into the mute world of the mime); another introduced himself as a twin, and asked us to ponder the possibility that he might be his brother impersonating himself; still another, a male student, did a cross-dressing performance with his girlfriend in which they asked the question of what the difference is between male and female transvestism. Other students who have gifts with performance have acted out things like blushing and crying, leading to discussions of shame and self-consciousness at being seen, involuntary visual responses, and the importance of the eye as an expressive as well as receptive organ. Perhaps the simplest gadget-free performance I have ever witnessed was by a student who led the class through an introduction to the experience of eye contact which culminated in that old first-grade game, the stare-down contest (the first to blink is the loser).

Without question, the funniest and weirdest show and tell performance that I have ever seen was by a young woman whose prop was her 9-month-old baby boy. She presented the baby as an object of visual culture whose specific visual attributes (small body, large head, pudgy face, bright eyes) added up, in her words, to a strange visual effect that human beings call "cuteness." She confessed her inability to explain cuteness, but argued that it must be an important aspect of visual culture, because all the other sensory signals given off by the baby—smell and noise in particular—would lead us to despise and probably kill the object producing them, if it were not for the countervailing effect of cuteness. The truly wondrous thing about this performance, however, was the behavior of the infant. While his mother was making her serious presentation, the baby was wiggling in her arms, mugging for the audience, and responding to their laughter at first with fright, but gradually (as he realized he was safe) with a kind of delighted and aggressive showmanship. He began showing off for the class while his mother tried, with frequent interruptions, to continue her telling of the visual characteristics of the human infant. The total effect was of a contrapuntal, mixed-media performance which stressed the dissonance or lack of suturing between vision and voice, showing and telling, while demonstrating something quite complex about the very nature of the show and tell ritual as such.

What do we learn from these presentations? The reports of my students suggest that the showing seeing performances are the thing that remains most memorable about the course, long after the details of perspective theory, optics, and the gaze have faded from memory. The performances have the effect of acting out the method and lessons of the curriculum, which is elaborated around a set of simple but extremely difficult questions: What is vision? What is a visual image? What is a medium? What is the relation of vision to the other senses? To language? Why is visual experience so fraught with anxiety and fantasy? Does vision have a history? How do visual encounters with other people (and with images and objects) inform the construction of social life? The performance of showing seeing assembles an archive of practical demonstrations that can be referenced within the sometimes abstract realm of visual theory. It is astonishing how much clearer the Sartrean and Lacanian paranoid theories of vision become after you have had a few performances that highlight the aggressivity of vision. Merleau-Ponty's abstruse discussions of the dialectics of seeing, the chiasmus of the eye and the gaze, and the entangling of vision with the flesh of the world, become much more down-to-earth when the spectator/spectacle has been visibly embodied and performed in the classroom.

A more ambitious aim of showing seeing is its potential as a reflection on theory and method in themselves. As should be evident, the approach is informed by a kind of pragmatism, but not (one hopes) of a kind that is closed off to speculation, experiment, and even metaphysics. At the most fundamental level, it is an invitation to rethink what theorizing is, to picture theory and perform theory as a visible, embodied, communal practice, not as the solitary introspection of a disembodied intelligence.

The simplest lesson of showing seeing is a kind of de-disciplinary exercise. We learn to get away from the notion that visual culture is covered by the materials or methods of art history, aesthetics, and media studies. Visual culture starts out in an area beneath the notice of these disciplines the realm of nonartistic, nonaesthetic, and unmediated or immediate visual images and experiences. It comprises a larger field of what I would call vernacular visuality or everyday seeing that is bracketed out by the disciplines addressed to visual arts and media. Like ordinary language philosophy and speech act theory, it looks at the strange things we do while looking, gazing, showing and showing off such as hiding, dissembling, and refusing to look. In particular, it helps us to see that even something as broad as the image does not exhaust the field of visuality; that visual studies is not the same thing as image studies, and that the study of the visual image is just one component of the larger field. Societies which ban images (like the Taliban) still have a rigorously policed visual culture in which the everyday practices of human display (especially of women's bodies) are subject to regulation. We might even go so far as to say that visual culture emerges in sharpest relief when the second commandment, the ban on the production and display of graven images, is observed most literally, when seeing is prohibited and invisibility is mandated.

One final thing the showing seeing exercise demonstrates is that visuality, not just the social construction of vision, but the visual construction of the social, is a problem in its own right that is approached, but never quite engaged by the traditional disciplines of aesthetics and art history, or even by the new disciplines of media studies. That is, visual studies is not merely an indiscipline or dangerous supplement to the traditional vision-oriented disciplines, but an interdiscipline that draws on their resources and those of other disciplines to construct a new and distinctive object of research. Visual culture is, then, a specific domain of research, one whose fundamental principles and problems are being articulated freshly in our time. The showing seeing exercise is one way to accomplish the first step in the formation of any new field, and that is to rend the veil of familiarity and awaken the sense of wonder, so that many of the things that are taken for granted about the visual arts and media (and perhaps the verbal ones as well) are put into question. If nothing else, it may send us back to the traditional disciplines of the humanities and social sciences with fresh eyes, new questions, and open minds.

ACKNOWLEDGMENTS

This article was first written for a conference on Art History, Aesthetics, and Visual Studies held at the Clark Institute in May 2001. I am grateful to Jonathan Bordo, James Elkins, Ellen Esrock, Joel Snyder, and Nicholas Mirzoeff for their valuable comments and advice.

NOTES

1. For anyone interested in my previous stabs at them, however, see Mitchell (1995a, 1995b).
2. If space permitted, I would insert here a rather lengthy footnote on the many kinds of work that have made it possible to even conceive of a field such as visual studies.
3. For a discussion of the peculiar distancing between visual studies and cinema studies, see Anu Koivunen and Astrid Soderbergh Widding (2002). Other institutional formations that seem notably excluded are visual anthropology (which now has its own journal with articles collected in Taylor, 1994); cognitive science (highly influential in contemporary film studies); and communications theory and rhetoric, which have ambitions to install visual studies as a component of introductory college-level writing programs.
4. See Crow's response to the questionnaire on visual culture in October (1996).
5. For a masterful study of art historical mediations, see Nelson (2000).
6. I am alluding here to a lecture entitled 'Straight Art History' given by O.K. Werckmeister at the Art Institute of Chicago several years ago. I have great respect for Werckmeister's work, and regard this lecture as a regrettable lapse from his usual rigor.
7. For further discussion of the convergence of painting and language in the written sign, see "Blake's Wondrous Art of Writing," in Mitchell (1994).
8. A phrase that appears in the *October* questionnaire on visual culture.
9. This defining moment had been rehearsed, of course, many times by art historians in their encounters with literary naïveté about pictures. One of the recurrent rituals in teaching interdisciplinary courses that draw students from both literature and art history is the moment when the art history students set straight the literary folks about the nontransparency of visual representation, the need to understand the languages of gesture, costume, compositional arrangement, and iconographic motifs. The second, more difficult, moment in this ritual is when the art historians have to explain why all these conventional meanings don't add up to a linguistic or semiotic decoding of pictures, why there is some non-verbalizable surplus in the image.
10. Bryson's (1983: 7) denunciation of the natural attitude which he sees as the common error of Pliny, Villani, Vasari, Berenson, and Francastel, and no doubt the entire history of image theory up to his time.
11. I owe this phrase to Michael Taussig, who developed the idea in our joint seminar, "Vital Signs: The Life of Representations," at Columbia University and New York University in the fall of 2000.
12. I am echoing here the title of Elkins (1999).

13. See the discussion of Lessing in Mitchell (1987: ch. 4).
14. See Jose Saramago's marvelous novel *Blindness* (1997), which explores the premise of a society suddenly plunged into an epidemic of blindness spread, appropriately enough, by eye contact.
15. See Mitchell (1994) for a fuller discussion of the claim that all media are mixed media, and especially the discussion of Clement Greenberg's search for optical purity in abstract painting. Indeed, unmediated vision itself is not a purely optical affair, but a coordination of optical and tactile information.
16. It may be worth mentioning here that the first course in Visual Culture ever offered at the University of Chicago was the "Art 101" course I gave in the fall of 1991 with the invaluable assistance of Tina Yarborough.

REFERENCES

Barthes, Roland (1982) *Camera Lucida*. New York: Hill and Wang.

Bishop Berkeley (1709) *A New Theory of Vision*.

Bryson, Norman (1983) 'The Natural Attitude', in *Vision and Painting: The Logic of the Gaze*, pp. 1–12. New Haven, CT: Yale University Press.

Derrida, Jacques (1978) 'The Dangerous Supplement', in *Of Grammatology*, trans. Gayatri Spivak, pp. 141–64. Baltimore, MD: Johns Hopkins University Press.

Elkins, James (1999) *The Domain of Images*. Ithaca, NY: Cornell University Press.

Foster, Hal (1987) *Vision and Visuality*. Seattle: Bay Press.

Jay, Martin (1994) *Downcast Eyes*. Berkeley: University of California Press.

Koivunen, Anu and Widding, Astrid Soderbergh (2002) 'Cinema Studies into Visual Theory?', in *Introdiction*, [http://www.utu.fi/hum/etvtiede/preview.html], consulted 21 April.

Lacan, Jacques (1978) 'The Split Between the Eye and the Gaze', in *Four Fundamental Concepts of Psychoanalysis*, pp. 67–78. New York: W.W. Norton.

Lindbergh, David C. (1981) *Theories of Vision from All-kindi to Kepler*. Chicago: University of Chicago Press.

Mitchell, W.J.T. (1987) *Iconology*. Chicago: University of Chicago Press.

Mitchell, W.J.T. (1994) *Picture Theory*. Chicago: University of Chicago Press.

Mitchell, W.J.T. (1995a) 'What Is Visual Culture?', in Irving Lavin (ed.) *Meaning in the Visual Arts: Views from the Outside: A Centennial Commemoration of Erwin Panofsky (1892–1968)*, pp. 207–17. Princeton, NJ: Princeton Institute for Advanced Study.

Mitchell, W.J.T. (1995b) 'Interdisciplinarity and Visual Culture', *Art Bulletin* 77(4), December.

Mitchell, W.J.T. (1996) 'What Do Pictures Want?', *October* 77 (Summer).

Nelson, Robert (2000) 'The Slide Lecture, or the Work of Art *History* in the Age of Mechanical Reproduction', *Critical Inquiry* 26(3), Spring. October 77 (1996) 'Visual Culture Questionnaire', Summer: 25–70.

Saramago, Jose (1997) *Blindness*. New York: Harcourt.

Taylor, Lucien (ed.) (1994) *Visualizing Theory*. New York: Routledge.

W.J.T. Mitchell is the Gaylord Donnelley Distinguished Service Professor of Art History and English Literature at the University of Chicago, and editor of Critical Inquiry. His books include *Iconology* (University of Chicago Press, 1987), *Picture Theory* (University of Chicago Press, 1994), *The Last Dinosaur Book* (University of Chicago Press, 1998), and *Landscape and Power* (University of Chicago Press, 2nd edn, 2002). The present essay is part of a forthcoming book, *What Do Pictures Want?*

Representative Form and the Visual Ideograph: The Iwo Jima Image in Editorial Cartoons

Janis L. Edwards and Carol K. Winkler

Much has been written about the iconic power of Joe Rosenthal's 1945 photograph of the flag-raising at Iwo Jima. This scholarship, however, insufficiently accounts for the rhetorical function of this image as it is appropriated in an unusual number of recent editorial cartoons. Building upon rhetorical theory addressing repetitive form and visual metaphor, we propose a concept of representative form. Exemplifying representative form, the parodied Iwo Jima image operates as an instance of depictive rhetoric that functions ideographically.

Key words: political cartoons, ideograph, Iwo Jima, icon, visual metaphor

On February 23, 1945, Joe Rosenthal, a photographer working for the Associated Press, climbed a rough volcanic hill on a Pacific island of Iwo Jima. He hoped the view from the summit would allow for some good shots of the military activity in the area, and he got one. Along with three other photographers and a film cameraman, Rosenthal snapped a picture of a large American flag being hoisted into place, a picture that would become one of the most famous and controversial American photographs ever made. The story of this photograph has invited scholarly attention among those interested in the visual artifacts of American culture. Our interest in the image, however, is not in its historical context, but in its appropriation by editorial cartoonists in the present day. The image of those five Marines and one Navy Corpsman raising the flag has appeared in recent editorial cartoons[1] so frequently that it was derided as a visual cliche by David Astor (1993) in the magazine of the American Association of Editorial Cartoonists.

While the term "cliche" may be pejorative, the repetitive use of the Iwo Jima image is what initially inspires investigation into its rhetorical aspects, for rhetorical analyses often involve a search for recurrent patterns. The cultural salience of the image also compels attention. Images used strategically in the public sphere reflect not only beliefs, attitudes, and values of their creators, but those of the society at large. Cartoonists must use cultural references that readers can easily understand or, as Roger Fischer predicts, "risk almost certain failure, for obscurity and snob humor are fatal to the medium" (1996, p. 122).[2] Yet, our sample of cartoons shows that in more than fifty instances, cartoonists have reached back half a century to appropriate Rosenthal's patriotic cultural icon in service of an art directed at iconoclasm rather than sanctification.[3]

The assumptions common to research in iconology raise more questions than they resolve regarding the rhetorical experience provoked by the parodied Iwo Jima image. The term "icon" proves problematic in this case because, despite its variant meanings and aspects,[4] the presumptive definition usually focuses on factors of representation by concrete resemblance. In describing visual studies as "iconology," Lester Olson (1987) defines icon as "a visual representation so as to designate a type of image that is palpable in manifest form and denotative in function" (p. 38). W.J.T. Mitchell (1986) and Ernst Gombrich (1996) similarly emphasize the quality of resemblance in iconographic study. Writings on the editorial cartoon, specifically those by

"Representative Form and the Visual Ideograph: The Iwo Jima Image in Editorial Cartoons" by Janis L. Edwards & Carol K. Winkler from *Quarterly Journal of Speech*, Vol. 83, No. 3, August 1, 1997. Copyright © 1997 The National Communication Association, reprinted by permission of Taylor & Francis Ltd., www.tandfonline.com on behalf of The National Communication Association

Gombrich (1963) and Sol Worth (1981), call attention to the importance of denotation in establishing recognizability and subsequent interpretation of a caricature's meaning.

If representation proceeds from resemblance, the cartoon parodies of Iwo Jima should denote and represent the historical moment of February 23, 1945, as it occurred on Mt. Suribachi.[5] This denotative reading of the Iwo Jima image, however, is incongruent with the nature of political cartoons. Cartoonists concern themselves with contemporary subjects; the Iwo Jima flag-raising is a fixed moment in past history. The historical reference to Iwo Jima in editorial cartoons does not provide a theme, in the manner of a motif, but serves as a reference point for other themes. The image functions as visual topos, a visual reference point that forms the basis of arguments about a variety of themes and subjects.

The rhetorical experience of the parodied Iwo Jima image is not defined so much, then, by the denotative function of the iconic image, but by the abstracted qualities of the image as symbol. Paul Messaris (1994) notes the presence of ambivalence in parodied images, which he calls an ineffability that pushes an image beyond its concrete, motivated constraints, allowing for elasticity in application and interpretation. The visual image thus becomes more of an abstraction, an available site for the attachment of multiple connotations serviceable in multiple contexts. We contend that the Iwo Jima image, as appropriated and parodied in recent editorial cartoons, is a special type of symbolic form that represents an essence of cultural beliefs and ideals at a high level of abstraction. As such, we will argue, the parodied image constitutes an instance of depictive rhetoric that functions ideographically.

Our argument proceeds in three stages. First, we review literature on visual form and repetitive form that provides suggestive, but limited, explanations for the power and rhetorical function of this recurring visual image. Then, we consider the metaphoric properties of the image and argue that metaphor is not sufficient to explain the image's use in the parodied context. Instead, we articulate a concept of *representative form* to more fully account for the rhetorical experience and function of the parodied Iwo Jima image in cartoons. Third, we isolate the ways in which the parodied image functions as visual ideograph in editorial cartoons, thus challenging the assumption that only verbal expressions can fulfill such a rhetorical function. In the process, we expand Michael C. McGee's (1980) definition of the ideograph, posit potential differences between verbal and visual ideographs, and explore how the context of cultural parodies functions to express ideographic forms.

THE IWO JIMA IMAGE AS VISUAL FORM

The power of the Iwo Jima image in editorial cartoons necessarily draws from the visual and symbolic power of Joe Rosenthal's photograph, which depicts the raising of an 8' by 4'8" American flag by five Marines and a Navy corpsman to mark the successful capture of Mt. Suribachi, an early moment in a protracted battle for the strategically located Pacific Island of Iwo Jima. This large flag replaced a smaller flag that had been planted earlier that day as Americans first reached the summit.[6] The second, more visible flag signaled the patriotic significance of the battle at this strategic place, an effort that would take weeks to complete and kill more than 20,000 Japanese and nearly 7,000 American soldiers, including three of the six men depicted in Rosenthal's picture and the Marine camera operator who made a motion picture record of the event.[7]

Previous scholars have identified meaningful compositional features of the photograph in an effort to account for its power and impact as a memorable image. Parker Albee & Keller Freeman (1995), Lance Bertelsen (1989), and Vicki Goldberg (1991) note the emphatic diagonal element of the flagpole and the vaulted perspective with the sky as backdrop as significant compositional elements. Kevin Leary & Carl Nolte (1995) suggest the strong, "sculptural" lighting makes some detail stand out in sharp relief, even as the men's faces are obscured in shadow. Following from Roland Barthes (1977) we might say the pose of the photograph connotes a sacred effort, as the bodies strain in unified action and the hands reach heavenward in lifting the flag, which is caught in a moment of unfurling. These interpretations of the image's visual form are consistent with theoretical propositions concerning a universal vocabulary of graphic or compositional features, summarized by Evelyn Hatcher (1974) and Paul Martin Lester (1995). They note that the elemental dynamic quality of the diagonal lines and the triangular form of the image are particularly vital, suggesting movement, energy, determination, virility, and strength. Directionality and placement are also significant, according to the grammar identified by Gunther Kress and Theo van Leeuwen (1996). The flag, symbolizing the American ideals of liberty, equality, and democracy, is moving toward the upper space in the frame-the space of the ideal, a place, as Goldberg (1991) suggests, that is "waiting to be filled" (p. 142).

Other compositional features signify more symbolic notions of communal effort, egalitarianism, and patriotism. Paul Fussell (1982) and George Roeder (1993) posit that the group effort and the obscured faces[8] speak to common cause and communal involvement. James Guimond (1991) asserts that photographs published in mass outlets at that time, as Rosenthal's was, function to embody common values and goals that would unite the public. The spontaneous photograph was embraced as an embodiment of a culturally preferred interpretation of war's heroism and valor.[9] Additional symbolic connotations derive from one feature of the image, the American flag. Bertelsen (1989) argues that military flag fetishism plays a role in the canonical reception of Rosenthal's photograph by inducing patriotic associations.

No doubt, the compositional and symbolic associations of Rosenthal's photograph contribute to its resonance with the American public. The flexibility of interpretation as cartoonists omit, distort, and add to the original composition without losing its recognizability attests to the image's visual power. But any number of images display dramatic compositional elements or possess historical and symbolic significance, yet have not emerged as recurrent visual topoi to the extent we have seen with the Iwo Jima image in recent cartoons.

The Iwo Jima Image as Recurring Form

Unsatisfied that the account of Rosenthal's photograph as a distinctive image fully accounts for the rhetorical import of the image as visual topos in political cartoons, we examined literature on repetitive form to search for an explanation for the image's modern-day resonance. Karlyn Campbell and Kathleen Jamieson's (1978) insights into form and genre appeared relevant, given that generic criticism "permit[s] the critic to generalize beyond the individual event which is constrained by time and place to affinities and traditions across time" (p. 27), and Fischer (1990, 1995) has previously recognized the generic features of political cartoons. But, as before, a generic interpretation of the Iwo Jima's recurrence in editorial cartoons was insufficient to explain the rhetorical application of the image. Unlike genre, which depends on recurrent situational elements that prompt recurrent substantive and stylistic elements, our sample displays the Iwo Jima image within a wide variety of contexts. While military settings predominate, more than a third of our sample uses the image in nonmilitary references.

Beyond the lack of situational constraint, the lack of a constellation of recurrent stylistic and substantive elements renders any interpretation of the parodied image as genre suspect. Campbell and Jamieson insist that a constellation of elements should be present for an artifact to meet the audience's expectations associated with a specified genre. Our sample reveals that the formal elements of the Iwo Jima image are frequently omitted, distorted, or substituted during the parody operation. The cartoonists substitute elephants, rats, veterans in wheelchairs, etc., for the Marines; gas tanks, George Bush, eating utensils, a baseball bat, a Christmas tree, and alternative flags for the American flag; and pedestals, a trash can, and Bosnian quicksand for the rubbled peak of Mt. Suribachi. In one cartoon, the only remaining formal feature of Rosenthal's image is the summit's terrain which, like many of our examples, lacks the fusion of dynamic elements necessary for a successful application of genre, but appears to still have utility for the cartoonist in providing a resonant image for the audience.

While the concept of genre has limited applicability to the Iwo Jima image in editorial cartoons, the repeated presentation of the image, as well as its concrete nature, signal its categorization as depictive rhetoric. Michael Osborn (1986) defines depictive rhetoric as "strategic pictures, verbal or nonverbal visualizations, that linger in the collective memory of audiences as representative of their subjects when rhetoric has been successful" (p. 79). In the functions of depictive rhetoric (to present, intensify, facilitate identification, implement, and reaffirm identity), we discover a close correlation with the function of the Iwo Jima image as it appears in cartoons. Osborn (1986) declares that, through repeated presentations, depictive rhetoric generates "pictures for sharing that can be transmitted quickly and precisely by the mass media" (p. 89). The Iwo Jima image as rhetorical depiction would appear to be an instance where cartoonists use graphic lessons from the past to identify solutions for present decisions.

Osborn (1986) further defines the particular symbols of depiction as culturetypes which, grounded in cultural specificity, "authorize arguments and social practices" (p. 89) through their status as shared, communal symbols. The Iwo Jima photographic image as national icon is recalled in the depictive function of reaffirmation of identity, where symbols serve as "moral markers [that] fill our minds again with their radiance and power, and coronates them as basic premises that ought to govern moral reasoning" (Osborn, 1986, p. 95).

Among forms of figuration known as culturetypes, Osborn (1994) lists icons, which he defines as concrete embodiments of an abstraction, implying that this is a suitable label for nonverbal rhetorical depictions. According to Osborn (1986), icons also acquire a "secular sacredness" among the public (p. 82). Certainly, the original photographic image of Iwo Jima inspired a reverential attitude, demonstrated by its widespread popularity and achievement of the Pulitzer Prize in the months following initial publication. But the parodied use of the image in cartoons is distinctly irreverent. Furthermore, the decontextualization and elasticity that characterizes the parodied image suggests that its meaning is not grounded in what it concretely represents or denotes, but in its more general and abstract function.

THE IWO JIMA IMAGE AS REPRESENTATION

When conceived as an abstraction, the parodied Iwo Jima image moves into the representational realm. It functions symbolically to represent events and subjects that expand beyond the historical constraints of the original battle at Iwo Jima. Specifically, the role of metaphor and representative form appear relevant to this broader conceptualization of image's resonance.

Metaphor

When a familiar figure is placed in a new, incongruent, context, it is not uncommon to assume that metaphor is the functional rhetorical operation. Messaris (1997) makes this assumption about the Iwo Jima image as parodied in a motion picture advertisement, and similar conclusions could be drawn regarding Iwo Jima parodies in editorial cartoons. Recent research into political cartoons, although subject-centered,[10] strongly suggests the potentials of metaphor as an explanatory framework for the functions of symbolic imagery in cartoons.[11] Through the use of subversive mimicry, which often involves a metaphorical transformation, cartoonists offer debunking parodies of their subjects.

Carl Hausman (1989) notes that "one of the marks of a metaphor is that its particular conjoining of terms is integral to its significance. This indispensability of the expression as it is initially articulated must be sustained if the expression is to be regarded as a metaphor" (p. 14). However, in many of these cartoons, the Iwo Jima image is not indispensable to meaning, but is replaceable. Frequently, the Iwo Jima image is used as a sign for the military, rather than a metaphor that creates a new conception through a transforming mutual adjustment between tenor and vehicle. This use of sign, rather than metaphoric adjustment, is evident in a group of cartoons about gays in the military. Dennis Renault of the *Sacramento Bee,* for example, draws the group of Iwo Jima Marines as a sign for a generic military organization being reviewed by the military establishment for homosexual infiltration. However, any relationship between yesterday's heroes and today's military policies and population is not metaphorically constructed as a matching and transformation process where qualities of one are mapped onto the other, and there is no specific and evident referral to the military of yesterday. The configuration of the soldiers into the familiar pose of the Iwo Jima image functions more as a sign, assisting the viewer in quickly identifying the military context.

Where Renault's soldiers in the Iwo Jima pose stand for the rank and file under review by the military establishment, Bill Schorr, in a 1993 cartoon, converts the flag-raising soldiers into representatives of the military establishment through their collective effort to keep the closet door closed on the gay issue. Any reference to the original Iwo Jima image is an implicit and vague contrast between the heroic accomplishments of yesterday's military and today's concern with the sexual orientation of its members. This contrast reflects a common rhetorical strategy used by editorial cartoonists, identified by Denise Bostdorff (1987), where cartoonists provide perspective by incongruity. But incongruity as a factor is neither consistent nor explicit. A metaphor, to be clear, should function explicitly. The cartoon plays off the familiarity of the military context of the Iwo Jima configuration more than it alludes to the metaphorical meaning of that image in relationship to the cartoon's subject—gays in today's military.

In some other cartoons that refer to the military, the comparison with the heroes at Iwo Jima is a strictly ironic one, indicative of the perceived weaknesses of today's military "antiheroes." For example, some of the more recently published cartoons in our study make reference to criminal sexual misconduct—the rape of an Okinawan girl by American soldiers or sexual harassment against female military members. In these cases, no indication exists that the group of soldiers patterned visually after the Iwo Jima Marines stands for anything other than themselves, but there is an implied contrast with the more positive values exhibited by "yesterday's" military. Similarly, two cartoons in our sample depict today's military members as self-absorbed, media-oriented, and cynically shallow in contrast to the selfless, dedicated heroes represented in by Rosenthal's 1945 photograph.

Some cartoons are structured more clearly as metaphors. If the heroism of Iwo Jima is only a dream, it is a daydream of Bill Clinton's, as envisioned by Wayne Stayskal (1995). In this cartoon, Clinton metaphorically transforms himself into the heroic World War II Marines who are raising a proud flag over Haiti. Several other cartoonists recall the heroism of the Iwo Jima soldiers as they convey laudatory comments about the U.S. military's role in providing famine relief to Somalia. While some parodied references to the Iwo Jima image are metaphoric, the relationship induced between the image and its referenced subjects is not consistent across our sample.

Representative Form

The limitations of compositional symbolism, visual metaphor, and genre theory in providing a comprehensive explanation for the Iwo Jima image's rhetorical significance in contemporary editorial cartoons and the suggestion that, as a cliched image, its representative qualities have transcended the denotative prompts us to consider the question of representation more directly. We propose that the Iwo Jima image is a special type of visual presentation that, through a combination of determined visual features and symbolic attributions, constitutes a representative form. A representative form transcends the specifics of its immediate visual references and, through a cumulative process of visual and symbolic meaning, rhetorically identifies and delineates the ideals of the body politic.

In proposing the idea of a representative form, we refer to two related constructs which inform the concept: Burke's "representative anecdote" (1969a) and S. Paige Baty's (1995) "representative character." Although an anecdote is a formal feature, the representative anecdote is not merely a reductive element featured in the text. Rather, as Barry Brummett (1984) notes, the representative anecdote may be a filter identified by the critic in the course of reconstructing discourse. In a sense, cartoonists function as cultural critics; some have chosen the Iwo Jima image, not because it is literally embedded in the discourse of the Gulf War, gays in the military, presidential campaigns, etc., but because it provides a perspective on the situation. Burke considers the representative anecdote to demonstrate the aspects of representation and reduction by fulfilling the requirements of an explanatory language of human motives. It serves as a discussion point or frame offering a prototype that Burke (1969a) argues, "sums up action" (p. 61) in accounting for the varieties of human nature or envisioning future conditions. Representative stories outline strategies for human responses to situations, or "equipments for living" (Burke, 1957, p. 262). Because they aim at collective understanding they are "sufficiently generalized to extend far beyond the particular combination of events named by them in any one instance" (Burke, 1957, p. 260). Burke (1969a) notes, "a given calculus must be supple and complex enough to be representative of the subject matter it is designed to calculate. It must have scope. Yet it must also possess simplicity, in that it is broadly a reduction of the subject matter" (p. 60).

The Iwo Jima image functions similarly in editorial cartoons. Visually, its compositional power can be likened to a kind of simplicity, which allows for recognizability of the abstract symbolic allusions we bring to the photograph from our understanding or knowledge of World War II. Yet the image also possesses sufficient complexity to be applicable to a wide variety of military and nonmilitary subjects and is supple enough to withstand and accommodate frequent visual distortions and alterations. The anecdotal nature of the Iwo Jima flag-raising is not predominantly represented in the cartoons. Even for those five in our sample that implicitly or directly recall the history of Iwo Jima, the formal image is paramount, for rather than depict a specific moment of heroic achievement, they coalesce a set of abstracted attitudes about communal effort, patriotism, and militarism that transcend the facts of the event. The Iwo Jima image functions representatively in cartoons, then, not as anecdote, but as visual form.

The transcendence of the particular to a representation of the general is also outlined in Baty's concept of the representative character, extended from work by Robert Bellah, Richard Madsen, William Sullivan, Ann Swidler, and Steven Tipton (1985). In their construct, a person (character) is abstracted and elevated to the status of a cultural figure, and becomes a surface for the articulation of the political character, embodying cultural ideals. As Bellah et al. (1985) have described the concept, a representative character is more than a collection of individual traits or personalities. It is rather a public image that helps define, for a given group of people, just what kinds of personality traits it is good and legitimate to develop. A representative character provides an ideal, a point of reference and focus, that gives living expression to a vision of life. (p. 39)

Like the Iwo Jima image, a representative character originates in actuality and specificity, but is abstracted into a symbol or concentrated image, and provides an explanatory model for human motive.

Baty further charts the process for how such a cultural figure comes to represent and articulate the political character. Rather than characterize these figures as static representations, Baty posits that they are "reconstructions that reveal the nature of conversations about the present even as they draw on materials from the past. . . . [They point] to inclusions and exclusions made in the greater construction of a national identity" (p. 49). For Baty, the representative character is a featured element of mass-mediated modes of remembering that reconstitute the space of politics each time they are invoked. Such representations help articulate the fast-paced space of politics, and "allow for building and expressing forms of community" (Baty, p. 41). At the same time, each invocation of a representative character adds to the definition of the character.

In a similar way, we would argue that each use of the Iwo Jima image, as parodied in editorial cartoons, contributes to the meaning of the image and to the way in which the image defines and constructs a political and ideological reality. Although the U.S. government singled out the surviving men depicted in Rosenthal's photograph as embodiments of heroic ideals, the specific individuals do not give the image its rhetorical force. For one thing, the personal stories of the flagmen are characterized by death and self-destruction as well as heroism. Moreover, their individual identities are obscured in the photograph in the cartoons. Again, the symbolic import of the total visual form is representative, not indicative of the individual characters who are present in the visual form. In this sense, the form becomes abstracted, creating a new perception or concept that is grounded in the original meaning, while trascending it.[12] As Chris Jenks (1995) describes the process, "To abstract implies a removal, a drawing out from an original location, and an enforced movement of elements from one level to another. Abstraction, then, involves the transposition of worlds. . . . The new world, the created level, the (re)presentation, provides the potential arena for the manipulation and control of images. Images become infinitely malleable once freed from their original context, whilst still retaining significations within that original context" (p. 9).

The abstraction that allows for the Iwo Jima image's flexibility and applicability to various contexts creates new worlds of signification in what the Iwo Jima image represents. It also recalls the original context in some indirect referential, and continuously reifying way, suggesting that the Iwo Jima image functions rhetorically as an ideograph, rather than an icon.

The Iwo Jima Image as Visual Ideograph

In 1980 Michael C. McGee formulated the concept of ideographs-culturally-grounded, summarizing, and authoritative terms that enact their meaning by expressing an association of cultural ideals and experiences in an ever-evolving and reifying form within the rhetorical environment. An ideograph's meaning develops through its usages and applications, operating as an abstraction and a fragment within the larger rhetorical environment. McGee identifies ideographs as a word or group of words, such as "liberty" or "patriotism," that serve to rhetorically create communities according to ideological constraints and beliefs.[13] By stressing the role of language, McGee specifically confines the notion of the ideograph to the linguistic realm.

McGee's assumption that ideographs must be "actual words or terms" lacks a clear rationale (p. 8). While maintaining that ideology by necessity is always false and thereby rhetorical, he insists that the "clearest access to persuasion (and hence to ideology) is through the discourse used to produce it" (p. 5). He presumes that the relevant discourse must be "political language preserved in rhetorical documents" (p. 5), never addressing the potential inclusion (or exclusion) of nondiscursive forms.[14] Further, he argues that ideographs should be restricted to words because he rejects propositional logic to explain incidents of "social conflict, commitment, and control" (p. 6). McGee distinguishes between the use of terms and the ideas that become clouded through the use of those terms. Defining the ideograph as "language imperatives which hinder and perhaps make impossible pure thought" (p. 9), he again disregards the rhetorical potential of visual images. In the process, he limits the ideograph to the verbal rather than the visual realm.

McGee outlines four characteristics that constitute his formal definition of an ideograph. Based on an application of these characteristics, we argue that the Iwo Jima image, originally disseminated by governmental sources, is a "non-ideographic use" (p. 15) of the image. A review of recent popular history as represented through editorial cartoon depictions, however, reveals modern-day usages of the Iwo Jima image do fall within the definitional and functional boundaries of the ideograph, the "language term" requirement notwithstanding. The image has become a discourse fragment that multiple publics appropriate for diverse purposes.

Ordinary Term in Political Discourse

McGee contends that the ideograph must be "an ordinary language term found in political discourse" (p. 15). He argues that ideographs in their ordinary sense garner much of their power precisely because they are not reserved for the political elite. They are "transcendent, as much an influence on the belief and behavior of the ruler as on the ruled" (p. 5). The artifacts which expose ideographs are not limited to academic treatises and documents recording the words of the nation's leadership. McGee suggests that critics examining a particular ideograph look to "popular history" (p. 11), such as novels, films, plays, songs, and grammar school history to trace the chronological expansions and contractions of such terms.

On one level, the Iwo Jima image does appear to qualify as "an ordinary image" (McGee, p. 15). Rosenthal's photograph was widely published within days of Suribachi's capture. Government officials subsequently used both the photographic image and the surviving men depicted in it to nurture Americans' personal involvement in the war effort. Although the Iwo Jima image's power arguably evokes a narrative about heroism, the rank and file Marines' obscured faces and diverse backgrounds form a representation of the common citizen/warrior, enhancing the "ordinary" quality of the image.

Unlike the present-day usage of the Iwo Jima, however, the first mass dissemination of Rosenthal's photograph was reserved for the nation's leadership. The original photograph was a product of a liberalized censorship policy ordered by Admiral Kelly Turner in response to a Washington directive that the Navy pursue a more aggressive policy of press coverage related to Pacific Ocean military activities. After negotiating with the Associated Press to use the photograph as the official image of the flag-raising without cost, the Marines subsequently used the visual symbol for war bond drives and Marine recruiting. The photograph appeared on 3,500,000 posters and 15,000 panels, as recorded by Joe Rosenthal and W.C. Heinz (1955). On July 11, 1945, the federal government issued an official postage stamp bearing the image of the Iwo Jima flag-raising. The flag itself was treated as a national relic during the Seventh War Loan Drive (Albee & Freeman, 1995). While the early uses of the photograph, and subsequent monument, undoubtedly qualify as ordinary visual images with high public recognizability, neither garnered the power commensurate with regular use in political discourse by both elite and nonelite sources.

The use of the Iwo Jima image as visual material within the context of editorial cartoons, however, disseminates the ordinary visual image into both elite and nonelite public discourse. With access to national audiences, editorial cartoonists arguably have "as much influence on the belief and behavior of the ruler as on the ruled" (McGee, p. 5). William Gamson and David Stuart (1992) propose that the wide syndication of cartoons provides their creators with a national forum for addressing the public, and a segment of scholarship argues that such a forum has public influence.[15]

All of the cartoons using the Iwo Jima image parody aspects of political decision-making to some degree. Nearly one-third (17 of 53) of the cartoons we surveyed directly address political campaigns or public opinion on political issues. In one, Mike Luckovich (1995) transforms the soldiers of Iwo Jima into the New Hampshire primary challengers for the 1996 Republican Presidential nomination to parody the lack of unity evident in the GOP leadership. Each candidate has an independent concern: Arlen Spector advocating a more centrist position, Pat Buchanan proclaiming even right-wing talk show hosts as liberal, Phil Gramm worried about his war record, and Bob Dole concerned about distancing himself from his past. In other cartoons by Doug Marlette (1994) and Bill Schorr (1995), the focus shifts to questioning the day-to-day decisions of the nation's chief executive. In these parodies, the cartoonists remove some soldiers from the image to signify military budget cutbacks. As these illustrations suggest, the Iwo Jima image has been appropriated from the exclusive control of the ruling elite to those who would parody the nation's leadership.

Abstraction Representing Collective Commitment

McGee's second characteristic of an ideograph is that it must be a "high-order abstraction representing collective commitment to a particular but equivocal and ill-defined normative goal" (p. 15). The abstraction is necessary to distinguish between those publics that fall within the social control motivated by the term and those that fall outside those parameters. The equivocal normative goal is necessary to ensure that the ideograph could never be empirically verifiable; the ambiguity allows the ideograph to be more inclusive of groups that might otherwise feel excluded.

As already argued, the compositional and symbolic representations of Rosenthal's original photograph constitute a visual abstraction reminiscent of the national unity required for success in war efforts. The use of a large amount of empty space in the background, the anonymity of the soldiers' faces, and the reliance on the flag as an icon for patriotism, all contribute to the Iwo Jima image as a form representing collective commitment to shared ideals.

The appeal to collective commitment embodied in Rosenthal's photograph also serves as an abstraction to "a particular but equivocal and ill-defined normative goal" (McGee, p. 15). Initially, the government used the photograph to serve as a public relations vehicle for celebrating the capture of the Japanese stronghold, and as the official symbol of the Seventh War Loan Drive. However, the symbolic interpretations of the image, as noted earlier, tapped into broader, inchoate notions of heroism, honor, and patriotism which proved transcendent, and permitted its force to expand beyond its utility for a given war effort, resulting in a broader public subscription to cultural ideals.

Within the context of editorial cartoons, the use of the Iwo Jima image retains the representative quality of collective commitment, while focusing that commitment toward equivocal and ill-defined normative goals. The use of the Iwo Jima image across our sample of editorial cartoons demonstrates the elasticity and abstractness of this image in its application. When applied to military contexts in editorial cartoons, the Iwo Jima image functions to comment on collective commitment required for a wide range of modern usages of the nation's armed forces. Where referring to humanitarian relief efforts such as Somalia, the U.S. flag is transformed into a bag of grain, a sack of food, or a spoon. When coupled with protracted ethnic struggles such as Bosnia, the rocky terrain of Mt. Suribachi is replaced with a swampy quicksand. In proposed military interventions that lack the full support of foreign citizenries, such as Haiti, the soldiers prop up Aristide rather than the Stars and Stripes.

The cartoons analyzed in our sample suggest that the image of Iwo Jima has come to represent collective commitment to normative goals that transcend the military environment. In a 1989 cartoon published in the *Los Angeles Times,* Paul Conrad replaces the terrain of Mt. Suribachi with the pinnacle of the U.S. Supreme Court Building, the soldiers with five of the nation's Supreme Court justices, and the intact U.S. flag with a half-burned U.S. flag. The caption on the cartoon reads: "Monument to the First Amendment." Here, Conrad uses the visual image of Iwo Jima to expose the irony of those who support a flag-burning amendment for patriotic reasons.

While the Iwo Jima image accommodates application to a wide array of political contexts, the precise normative goal being represented defies an easy explanation. Democracy, freedom, liberty, patriotism, military preparedness, and equality of opportunity are all components of the representation, but no single language term sums up the interpretations of the image. The Iwo Jima image, like its verbal counterparts, "liberty" and "patriotism," functions as "a high-order abstraction representing collective commitment to a particular but equivocal and ill-defined goal" (McGee, p. 15).

Warrants Power/Guides Behavior

McGee maintains that an ideograph also "warrants the use of power, excuses behavior and belief which might otherwise be perceived as eccentric or antisocial, and guides behavior and belief into channels easily recognized by a community as acceptable and laudable" (p. 15). He dispels the widely held notion that ideology is discussed as propositional logic in the public arena.

Even when Rosenthal's famous photograph first appeared in public forums, the use of the image was an attempt to warrant behavior that could be deemed as antisocial. Without an alternative frame in which to interpret the event, the public might have considered the large number of casualties that the military leadership was willing to sacrifice in the capture of Iwo Jima (6,281 dead; 19,217 wounded) to be unacceptable. Placed within the frame of collective, heroic effort embodied in Rosenthal's photograph, however, the battle of Iwo Jima—expressed metonymically through the Mt. Suribachi flag-raising—comes to represent the success that is achievable through collective sacrifice. Viewed from this perspective, the cost of military engagement becomes an indicator, if not evidence, for the acceptability of U.S. risk-taking during wartime.

In the context of contemporary editorial cartoons, the Iwo Jima image is used to parody governmental actions for the purpose of highlighting whether they are acceptable or antisocial in nature. Instead of guiding "behavior and belief into channels easily recognized by a community as acceptable and laudable," the parodied image functions to expose the "eccentric or antisocial" (McGee, p. 15). It further highlights unwarranted attempts by the government to call for collective sacrifice. Richard Morin (1990) provides an illustration in one of his cartoons printed during the Persian Gulf War. Rather than climb the hilly terrain of Mt. Suriba-chi, the soldiers struggle along the oil fields of Saudi Arabia, an ally of the United States. Raising an oversized gas pump in place of the Stars and Stripes, the cartoon belittles the motivation for U.S. involvement in the Gulf War to be one of economic self-interest.

Repeatedly, editorial cartoonists manipulate the flag in the Iwo Jima image to parody the less than noble moti-vations that govern American society. Our sample reveals that cartoonists transform the flag into a dollar sign to symbolize the greed of those in the drug trade, into a campaign banner to underscore the political agenda of Gulf War supporters, into a gas tank or gas gauge to reveal the oil interests motivating U.S. military defense of Saudi Arabia, into a poll indicator to signify the political agenda behind the invasion of Haiti, and into the figure of Aristide to expose the political motivations behind U.S. military intervention in Haiti. Rather than function as a subject of parody itself, in these cartoons the Iwo Jima image serves as a point of comparison for determining what is an "acceptable and laudable" use of governmental power (McGee, p. 15).

Culture-bound

The final characteristic McGee identifies for the ideograph is that it must be culture-bound. He insists that society's interactions with ideographs work to define and exclude groupings of the public. He claims that members who do not "respond appropriately to claims on their behavior warranted through the agency of ideographs" will experience societal penalties (pp. 15-16).

From the initial release of Rosenthal's photograph for public consumption, the Iwo Jima image came to rep-resent the ideals of American culture. Karal Ann Marling and John Wetenhall (1991) describe how the sol-diers themselves contribute to cultural definition embodied in the image: "That the group indeed included a son of immigrants, an Indian, boys from the Midwest, the plains, the East, only confirmed the representative character of the image" (p. 9). In addition to reinforcing the American heritage of a melting pot of diverse cultures, the image of Iwo Jima relies on the American flag, the cultural icon of patriotism.

The use of irony in editorial cartoons makes the medium particularly suited to society's infliction of penal-ties on individuals who might ignore or misuse the ideograph. The question of society's tolerance of cultural diversity serves as an example. Bill Schorr (1993) uses the Iwo Jima image to expose the military's own intolerance for gender diversity. Instead of raising the flag, the grouped Marines harass a female recruit by peering under her skirt. Schorr juxtaposes the military's current intolerance for diversity with the celebrated ideal of cultural heterogeneity embodied in the Iwo Jima image.

Perhaps the most obvious linkage of the Iwo Jima image to American culture involves a cartoon by Steve Benson for the *Arizona Republic* (1995). Above the visual image of the cartoon, a caption reads, "As the na-tion reflects, memories return of the opening day, the struggle in the sand, the deafening roar—and Amer-icans ponder the things that, to them, matter most." In this case, though, it isn't the sand and roar of the heroic battlefield, but the playing field that "matters most" as our soldiers join together to raise a dominant symbol of American culture—the baseball bat.[16]

CONCLUSIONS

As a representative form, the parodied Iwo Jima image transcends its historical referents, gains meaning from its subsequent symbolic associations, and helps create and reaffirm the identity of the body politic through its ideographic functions. Like representative anecdotes and representative characters, such forms provide instructive perspectives on varied, multiple situations by summing up the culturally defined essences of human motivations.

This conceptualization of representative form extends conventional interpretations of how visual images function within societal contexts. Rather than serve in an iconic relationship to a verbal referent, representative forms perform as visual ideographs. While our review of related literature uncovers no specific discussion of ideographs relative to visual forms, we do find implicit assumptions about the nature of the relationship. Like McGee, Osborn (1986, 1994) emphasizes the implicit verbal features of the ideograph by setting it apart from its companion construction—the icon. Osborn implicitly assigns a verbal quality to ideographs when he contrasts them with the concrete qualities of icons; ideographs and icons are positioned as rival terms, a view consistent with the commonplace definition of icon as picture representation.[17] Even though both the icon and the ideograph are culturetypes in Osborn's view, the terms are not interchangeable. To consider the icon as an embodiment of the ideograph is to establish a hierarchical relationship whereby the icon primarily illustrates that which is already linguistically manifested in the ideograph. The ideograph is more authoritative because it expresses a concept that an icon can only reconstruct through illustration.[18] Following this line of thought, the icon's relationship to the ideograph is circumvented; it can only redescribe and imitate the meaning of the ideograph, which *stands for* something. The ideograph, as a verbal expression, is privileged because language is often considered paradigmatic for meaning. Maria Mayenova (1981) typifies this view in saying, "I regard iconic signs in general as being of a derivative, lame character, requiring verbal intervention" (p. 134). In this view, the icon may refer to the ideograph, but ideographs do not refer to icons, and must be preceded by language to obtain meaning.[19]

Osborn may have foreseen a stronger symbolic potential for icons in asserting "the *combination* of ideograph and icon may be especially potent in popular discourse, because it offers the virtues of both abstract and concrete rhetorical expression" (1994, p. 93). In the cartooned Iwo Jima image, we find these virtues coexistent and transcendent. We do not deny the denotative aspects of these visual parodies. We do propose, however, that the function of denotative representation associated with icons is a secondary feature of the totalized rhetorical function of these images. More significantly, the images are symbols realized as representative forms that transcend univocal denotative reference. Similarly, metaphor may operate as a presentational mechanism in these cartoons, but it is transcended as the source of rhetorical invention by the more abstract symbolic aspect of representative form.

Confirmation that certain visual images can function as ideographs, rather than be confined to the more restricted representational territory of icons, emerges in light of previous scholarship on repetitive form. Unlike recurrent forms operative in rhetorical genres, representative forms such as the parodied image of the Iwo Jima flag-raising transcend particular groupings of symbolic or rhetorical contexts. The situations prompting the use of the parodied Iwo Jima image are not wholly recurrent; instead, they vary from military to political to entertainment contexts. Even the military-related themes span domestic and international arenas with subjects ranging from motives for war to questions of military policy and from actions by individual soldiers to the conduct of the media. Like McGee's example of equality, the parodied Iwo Jima image is "paramorphic, for even when the [image] changes its signification in particular circumstances, it retains a formal, categorical meaning, a constant reference to its history as an ideograph" (p. 10).

Our examination of the Iwo Jima image would readily concede that, in many cases, visual images bear an iconic relationship to the ideas they represent. If either the elite or the nonelite are influenced by the image exclusively, or the purposes of the image are clearly defined and unequivocal, or the image lacks the elasticity to accommodate meanings beyond its contextual specifics, the image fails to meet the requirements of the ideograph. Only in its appropriation does the influence of the image transcend the domain of the political elite to affect both the nation's leadership and its citizenry.

Appropriation and recontextualization appear to be central features of the transformation of visual images into representative forms. By choosing the situational context for the use of the image, the editorial cartoonist identifies the times and places that warrant ideological judgment. Like McGee's verbal ideographs, representative forms garner their meaning through the description they provide to situations.[20] Editorial cartoons present politicized contexts that, through satire, irony, and parody, motivate differing senses of community. The cartoonist can elevate actions through complementary comparison to the visual ideographs, i.e., equating humanitarian relief in Somalia to the valor of World War II by transforming the flag into a spoon feeding the hungry. Or, the parody can denigrate actions that fail to meet the moral standards established by the ideology, i.e., underscoring the economic rather than the moral justification for entering the Persian Gulf conflict by transforming the flag into a gas pump or gas gauge. By replacing the heroic Marines at Iwo Jima with distinctly unheroic businessmen or political operatives, or with wheelchair-bound soldiers suffering from war's less glorious effects, cartoonists provide an ironic counter-perspective that questions the boundaries of ideological concern.

Not only does the parodied context of a representative form identify the specific circumstances which inspire the ideology's application, it also draws attention to key elements of the ideology at issue. Cartoonists direct the audience's attention by the addition, omission, substitution, and/or distortion of visual elements. Changes made to the flag within the image, for example, can applaud or denounce the motivations used by the nation's leadership to call for collective effort. Manipulation of the Iwo Jima servicemen can focus attention on who constitutes (or does not constitute) the cultural membership of the ideology. Alterations in the terrain of the Iwo Jima image can prompt the audience to consider the degree of sacrifice called for in the ideological application.

The ability of cartoonists to alter visual images arguably distinguishes the verbal from the visual ideograph. Unlike the verbal version, visual ideographs can appear to members of the culture in a variety of forms through the addition, omission, and distortion of their component elements. For the audience to respond to an image manifested in an array of forms, they must have a prior memory or recognition of the original. By comparing the cartoonist's rendition of the image to the memory of the original form, the audience can participate in the reinforcement of the ideograph's categorical meaning, and the creation of the expansions and contractions that result from its parodied contexts. Since words have a limited capacity for manipulation before their recognizability is lost, the opportunity for potential audience participation in the linguistic realm is comparatively small.

The comparative potentials of visual and verbal ideographs also relate to the ability of the visual realm to embody iconic images. A single language term usually lacks an iconic relationship between the letters of its makeup and a situational referent. Visual ideographs like the Iwo Jima image can embody icons such as the American flag to bolster tenets of the ideology at work. The inclusion of these icons can both constrain and expand the meaning of representative forms. Representative forms in parodied contexts, then, would appear to have persuasive potentials unavailable to their linguistic counterparts.

At this point we are unprepared to identify definitively other visual images that function ideographically as representative forms. Messaris (1994) has identified a small number of widely parodied, resonant images (such as Grant Wood's *American Gothic* and Flagg's "I Want You" poster of Uncle Sam) that might serve as a basis for future study of images that serve as representative forms. To Messaris's list we might add Mt. Rushmore and specific photographic records of the Vietnam War.

Although we agree with Mitchell (1994) that "visual experience. . . . might not be fully explicable on the model of textuality" (p. 16) and that visual images and language resist conflation, this study illuminates the value of considering visual images in light of existing rhetorical constructs and emphasizes the importance of continued attention to visual forms of rhetorical experiences. Rather than marginalizing visual studies within the communication discipline, as Sonja Foss (1992) warns is inevitable when visual images are compared with the properties of discursive symbols, we believe the case for the visual ideograph affirms the value of multi-strategic inquiry into rhetorical acts and artifacts.

NOTES

Janis L. Edwards is Visiting Assistant Professor of Speech Communication at the University of Georgia. Carol K. Winkler is Associate Professor and Chair of the Department of Communication at Georgia State University. The authors wish to note that while coauthorship sometimes implies a differentiation between primary and secondary contributions to a research project, this essay is the result of a collaboration of mutual contribution. An earlier version of this essay was presented at the 1994 SCA Convention in New Orleans. The authors wish to thank Judy Butler and Cameron Murray for their research assistance on this project, as well as Janette Kenner-Muir and Celeste Condit for their helpful comments.

[1]   In this study, we define an editorial cartoon as a graphic presentation typically designed in a one-panel, non-continuing format to make an independent statement or observation on political events or social policy (as opposed to illustrating a written editorial). Such cartoons are a type of graphic art which regularly appear on newspaper editorial and op-ed pages, and which are typically created by a person employed on a newspaper staff, but may be distributed through syndication. We located fifty-eight editorial cartoons published between 1988 and 1996 which used the Iwo Jima image in reference to a current event or concern. Our sample consisted of cartoons collected from newspapers, from periodical and book collections of cartoons, and, in two cases, directly from a syndicate source, but all meet the above definitional criteria. In this essay, we use the terms "political cartoon" and "editorial cartoon" interchangeably.

[2]   In making the same point about the necessity of recognizable reference points, Medhurst and DeSousa (1981) identify literary/cultural allusions, political commonplaces, recognizable character traits, and situational factors as the "inventional storehouse" of cartoonists.

[3]   Despite the fame of Rosenthal's photograph, its contemporary recognition value is unclear, as those who would personally remember the events of World War II are replaced by those familiar only with collective memory. Messaris (1994), for example, in an informal survey of 29 college students, found that not quite half could accurately place the image in historical context. Similar results occurred in our own survey of 78 students responding to a cartoon version of the image, although we speculate recognition might be greater among an audience more representative of the general population in age distribution.

[4]   See, for example, a discussion of verbal icons in Leff and Sachs (1990), "Words the most like things: Iconicity and the rhetorical text;" and J.A. Campbell (1990), "Between the fragment and the icon: Prospect for a rhetorical house of the middle way" in *Western Journal of Communication* 54. In calling Rosenthal's photograph an "icon," we refer to the definition of icon as a highly symbolic, canonical, emblematic figure or object of uncritical devotion.

[5] For example, Olson's (1987, 1990, 1991) investigation of iconic images such as political cartoons focused on early visual representations of the American colonies in artifacts of the historical moment.

[6] The effort to claim the summit took four days, but by the time Rosenthal took his picture, the fighting was in hiatus. That Rosenthal photographed the *second* flag-raising is the crucial factor in controversies about the authenticity of the photograph. The facts of the two flag-raisings, and their photographic record, are recounted in detail in Albee and Freeman, (1995), *Shadow of Suribachi: Raising the Flags on Iwo Jima, and Thomey*, (1996), *Immortal Images: A Personal History of Two Photographs and the Flag Raising at Iwo Jima.* Additionally, we drew historical information from accounts in Bertelsen (1989), Dart (1995), Marling & Wetenhall (1991), Rosenthal (1995), Rosenthal & Heinz (1995), and Ross (1986).

[7] At least eleven photographs taken by six photographers, in addition to film shot by Bill Genaust, captured the two flag-raisings and the subsequent scene at Suribachi from a variety of perspectives. Rosenthal himself took two additional pictures at the summit that day.

[8] The exact identity of the men remained uncertain for some time after Rosenthal's picture was published.

[9] See, for example, Gregory and Lewis (1988) and Bertelsen (1989).

[10] These subject categories include presidential campaigns and candidates (DeSousa & Medhurst, 1982; Hill, 1984; Kenner-Muir, 1986; Sewell, 1993; Edwards, 1995, 1997); other political figures (DeSousa, 1984; Bostdorff, 1987; Templin, 1995); religion (Sewell, 1987; Edwards, 1988); and wartime enemies (Edwards, 1993).

[11] See, for example, Bostdorff (1987), DeSousa (1984), Edwards (1993, 1995, 1997), Hill (1984), Kenner-Muir, (1986), DeSousa and Medhurst (1982), Medhurst and DeSousa (1981), Sewell (1993), and Worth (1981).

[12] Fischer's (1995) analysis of the use of the Lincoln Monument in editorial cartoons also reflects the idea of a representative form, yet the centrality of Lincoln as an American figure retains aspects of the representative character, which would seem to impede the abstraction of the Lincoln Monument. In other respects, cartoonists' visual exploitation of the monument, as argued by Fischer, is conducted to ends similar to their use of the Iwo Jima image—it is held up as ideal against which lesser men are measured.

[13] In this sense, they are similar to Weaver's (1953) and Burke's (1969b) articulation of "ultimate terms" which embody propositions through their place in a constellation of terms that progress sequentially.

[14] Burke (1969b) provides a rationale for the potential of the visual ideograph in suggesting that nonverbal meanings take on the nature of words.

[15] See also Bohrmann, Koester, and Bennett (1978), Langeveld (1981), and Root (1996).

[16] The linkage between militarism and masculine sport may itself be revelatory of currents in American culture that substantiate the Iwo Jima image as a meaningful ideograph. For discussions of the intersections of masculine culture and paramilitarism, especially during the time frame when our sampled cartoons were published, see L.E. Boose (1993) and J.W. Gibson (1994).

[17] Argan (1980), J.A. Campbell (1990), Mitchell (1986), Olson (1983), and Steakley (1983) employ the term "icon" in this sense.

[18] Gombrich (1963) echoes Osborn's interpretation of the relationship between language and image when he specifically says of cartoons that they are "merely [the tangible expression] of what language has prepared" (p. 128).

[19] The view that pictures can only have meaning through their illustrations of words is common, particularly in the realm of photography theory, but it has been challenged by Barthes (1977), who maintained that an image may function as the principle message which is rationalized by words.

[20] J.A. Campbell (1990) maintains that we come to understand the rhetorical function of ideographs through their performances, as they "enact what they mean" (p. 367).

REFERENCES

Albee, P.B., Jr. & Freeman, K.C. (1995). *Shadow of Suribachi: Raising the flags on Iwo Jima.* Westport, CT: Praeger.

Argan, G.C. (1980). Ideology and iconology (R. West, Trans.) In W.J.T. Mitchell (Ed.), *The language of images* (pp.15–23). Chicago: University of Chicago Press.

Astor, D. (1993, Summer/Fall). Tack and Joel hack the hackneyed. *The Association of American Editorial Cartoonists Notebook,* 12–13.

Barthes, R. (1977). The photographic message. *Image, music, text* (S. Heath, Trans.). New York: Hill and Wang.

Baty, S.P. (1995). *American Monroe: The making of a body politic.* Berkeley, CA: University of California Press.

Bellah, R.N., Madsen, R., Sullivan, W.M., Swidler, A., & Tipton, S.M. (1985). *Habits of the heart: Individualism and commitment in American life.* Berkeley, CA: University of California Press.

Benson, S. (1995, February). [Cartoon]. *Arizona Republic.*

Bertelsen, L. (1989). Icons on Iwo. *Journal of Popular Culture, 2,* 79–95.

Bohrmann, E.G., Koester, J., & Bennett, J. (1978). Political cartoons and salient rhetorical fantasies: An empirical analysis of the '76 presidential campaign. *Communication Monographs, 45,* **317–329.**

Boose, L.E. (1993). Techno-muscularity and the boy eternal. In M. Cooke & A. Woollacott (Eds.), *Gendering war talk* (pp. 67–106). Princeton, NJ: Princeton University Press.

Bostdorff, D.M. (1987). Making light of James Watt: A Burkean approach to the form and attitude of political cartoons. *Quarterly Journal of Speech, 73,* 43–59.

Brummett, B. (1984). Burke's representative anecdote as a method in media criticism. *Critical Studies in Mass Communication, 1,* 161–176.

Burke, K. (1969a). *A grammar of motives.* Berkeley, CA: University of California Press.

Burke, K. (1969b). *A rhetoric of motives.* Berkeley, CA: University of California Press.

Burke, K. (1957). *The philosophy of literary firm: Studies in symbolic action* (Revised Edition). New York: Vintage Books. Campbell, J.A. (1990). Between the fragment and the icon: Prospect for a rhetorical house of the middle way. *Western Journal of Communication, 54,* 346–376.

Campbell, K.K. & Jamieson, K.H. (1978). *Form and genre: Shaping rhetorical action.* Falls Church, VA.: Speech Communication Association.

Conrad, P. (1989, June). [Cartoon]. *Los Angeles Times,* p. B7.

Dart, B. (1995, February 20). 'Grateful' nation thanks survivors of Iwo Jima. *Atlanta Journal-Constitution,* p. 16.

DeSousa, M.A. (1984). Symbolic action and pretended insight: The Ayatollah Khomeini in U.S. editorial cartoons. In M.J. Medhurst & T.W. Benson (Eds.), *Rhetorical dimensions in media: A critical casebook* (pp. 204–230). Dubuque, IA: Kendall/Hunt.

DeSousa, M.A. & Medhurst, MJ. (1982). Political cartoons and American culture: Significant symbols of campaign 1980. *Studies in Visual Communication, 8,* 84–97.

Edwards, J.L. (1988). Keepers of the flame: Rhetorical themes in recent editorial cartoons on religion. Paper presented at the Eastern Communication Association, Baltimore, MD.

Edwards, J.L. (1993). Metaphors of enmity in Gulf War political cartoons. *Ohio Speech Journal, 30,* 62–75.

Edwards, J.L. (May, 1995). Wee George and the seven dwarfs: Caricature and metaphor in campaign '88 cartoons. *INKS Cartoon and Comic Art Studies,* 26–34.

Edwards, J.L. (1997). *Political cartoons in the 1988 presidential campaign: Image, metaphor, and narrative.* New York: Garland Press [forthcoming].

Fischer, R.A. (1990). The Lucifer legacy: Boss Tweed and Richard Nixon as generic sleaze symbols in cartoon art. *Journal of American Culture, 13,* 1–19.

Fischer, R.A. (1995, February). The 'monumental' Lincoln as an American cartoon convention. *INKS Cartoon and Comic Art Studies,* 12–25.

Fischer, R.A. (1996). *Them damned pictures: Explorations in American political cartoon art.* North Haven, CT: Archon Books.

Forceville, C. (1996). *Pictorial metaphor in advertising.* London: Routledge.

Foss, S. (1992). Visual imagery as communication. *Text and Performance Quarterly, 12,* 85–96.

Fussell, P. (1982). *The boy scout handbook and other observations.* New York: Oxford University Press.

Gamson, W.A. & Stuart, D. (1992, March). Media discourse as a symbolic contest: The bomb in political cartoons. *Sociological Forum, 7,* 55–86.

Gibson, J.W. (1994). *Warrior dreams: Violence and manhood in post-Vietnam America.* New York: Hill & Wang.

Goldberg, V. (1991). *The power of photography.* New York: Abbeville Press.

Gombrich, E.H. (1963). *Meditations on a hobbyhorse.* Chicago: University of Chicago Press.

Gombrich, E.H. (1996). Aims and limits of iconology. In R. Woodfield (Ed.) *The essential Gombrich* (pp. 457–484). London: Phaidon Press Limited.

Gregory, S.W., Jr. & Lewis, J.M. (1988, Fall). Symbols of collective memory: The social process of memorializing May 4, 1970, at Kent State University. *Symbolic Interaction, 11,* 213–233.

Guimond, J. (1991). *American photography and the American dream.* Chapel Hill, NC: University of North Carolina Press.

Hatcher, E.P. (1974). *Visual metaphors: A methodological study in visual communication.* Albuquerque, NM: University of New Mexico Press.

Hausman, C.R. (1989). *Metaphor and art: Interactionism and reference in the verbal and nonverbal arts.* New York: Cambridge University Press.

Hill, A. (1984). The Carter campaign in retrospect: Decoding the cartoons. In M.J. Medhurst & T.W. Benson (Eds.), *Rhetorical dimensions in media: A critical casebook* (pp. 182–203). Dubuque, IA: Kendall/Hunt.

Jenks, C. (Ed.) (1995). *Visual culture.* London: Routledge.

Kaplan, S.J. (1990). Visual metaphor in the representation of communication technology. *Critical Studies in Mass Communication, 7,* 37–47.

Kaplan, S.J. (1992). A conceptual analysis of form and content in visual metaphors. *Communication, 13,* 197–209.

Kenner-Muir, J. (1986). *Political cartoons and synecdoche: A rhetorical analysis of the 1984 Presidential campaign.* Unpublished doctoral dissertation, University of Massachusetts, Amherst.

Kress, G. and van Leeuwen, T. (1996). *Reading images: The grammar of visual design.* London: Routledge.

Langeveld, W. (1981). Political cartoons as a medium of political communication. *International Journal of Political Education, 4,* 343–371.

Leary, K. and Nolte, C. (1995, February 19). The shot of a lifetime. *San Francisco Chronicle,* Sunday section, p. 3.

Leff, M. and Sachs, A. (1990). Words the most like things: Iconicity and the rhetorical text. *Western Journal of Speech Communication, 54,* 252–273.

Lester, P.M. (1995). *Visual communication: Images with messages.* Belmont, CA: Wadsworth Publishing Company.

Luckovitch, M. (1995). [Cartoon], *The Atlanta Constitution.*

Marlette, D. (1994, Winter). [Cartoon]. *Notebook of the AAEC,* **25.**

Marling, K.A. & Wetenhall, J. (1991). *Iwo Jima: Monuments, memories, and the American hero.* Cambridge, MA: Harvard University Press.

Mayenova, M.R. (1981). Verbal texts and iconic-visual texts. In W. Steiner (Ed.), *Image and code* (pp. 133–137). University of Michigan, Ann Arbor, MI.

McGee, M.C. (1980). The 'ideograph': A link between rhetoric and ideology. *Quarterly Journal of Speech, 66,* 1–16.

Medhurst, M.J. and DeSousa, M.A. (1981). Political cartoons as rhetorical form: A taxonomy of graphic discourse. *Communication Monographs, 48,* 197–236.

Messaris, P. (1994). *Visual "literacy": Image, mind, and reality.* Boulder, CO: West View Press.

Messaris, P. (1997). *Visual persuasion: The role of images in advertising.* Thousand Oaks: SAGE Publications.

Mitchell, W.J.T. (1986). *Iconology: Image, text, ideology.* Chicago: University of Chicago Press.

Mitchell, W.J.T. (1994). *Picture theory: Essays on verbal and visual representation.* Chicago: University of Chicago Press.

Morin, R. (1990, August 20). [Cartoon]. *Political Pix.*

Olson, L.C. (1983). Portraits in praise of a people: A rhetorical analysis of Norman Rockwell's icons in Franklin D. Roosevelt's 'Four Freedoms' campaign. *Quarterly Journal of Speech, 69,* 15–24

Olson, L.C. (1987). Benjamin Franklin's Pictorial Representations of the British Colonies in America: A study in rhetorical iconology. *Quarterly Journal of Speech, 73,* 18–42.

Olson, L.C. (1990). Benjamin Franklin's commemorative medal, *Libertas Americana*: A study in rhetorical iconology. *Quarterly Journal of Speech, 76,* 23–45.

Olson, L.C. (1991). *Emblems of American community in the revolutionary era: A study in rhetorical iconology.* Washington, D.C.: Smithsonian Institute Press.

Osborn, M. (1986). Rhetorical depiction. In H.W. Simons & A.A. Aghazian (Eds.), *Form, genre, and the study of political discourse* (pp. 79–107). Columbia, SC: University of South Carolina Press.

Osborn, M. (1994). The invention of rhetorical criticism in my work. In W.L. Nothstine, C. Blair, & G.C. Copeland (Eds.), *Critical questions: Invention, creativity, and the criticism of discourse and media* (pp. 82–94). New York: St. Martin's Press.

Renault, D. (1993, January 27). [Cartoon]. *Sacramento Bee,* p. B6.

Roeder, G., Jr. (1993). *The censored war: American visual experience during World War Two.* New Haven, CT: Yale University Press.

Root, J.R. (1996). *Is a picture worth a thousand words? A Q methodological study of political cartoons.* Unpublished doctoral dissertation, University of Houston, Texas.

Rosenthal, J. (1995, May 31). [Telephone interview with author].

Rosenthal, J. & Heinz, W.C. (1955). The picture that will live forever. *Collier's Magazine.* 18 Feb, pp. 62–67.

Ross, B.D. (1986). *Iwo Jima: Legacy of valor.* New York: Vintage Books.

Schorr, B. (1993, February 7). [Cartoon]. *The Sacramento Bee,* p. Forum 5.

Schorr, B. (1994). [Cartoon]. In C. Brooks (Ed.), *Best editorial cartoons of the year, 1994 edition* (p. 8). Gretna, LA: Pelican Publishing Company.

Schorr, B. (1995, July 23). [Cartoon]. *San Francisco Examiner & Chronicle,* p. 8.

Sewell, E.H. (1987). Exorcism of fools: Images of the televangelist in editorial cartoons. In M. Fishwick & R.B. Brown (Eds.), *The God pumpers: Religion in the electronic age* (pp. 46–59). Bowling Green, OH: Bowling Green State University Popular Press.

Sewell, E.H. (1993). Editorial cartoon images of Bill Clinton in the 1992 Presidential campaign. Paper presented at the meeting of the Speech Communication Association, Miami, FL.

Stayskal. (1995, March). [Cartoon]. *Tampa Tribune.*

Steakley, J.D. (1983). Iconography of a scandal: Political cartoons and the Eulenburg affair. *Studies in Visual Communication, 9,* 20–51.

Templin, C. (1995). The political cartoon and the President's wife: Bashing Hillary. Paper presented at the meeting of the International Society for Humor Studies, Birmingham, England.

Thomey, T. (1996). *Immortal images: A personal history of two photographers and the flag-raising on Iwo Jima.* Annapolis, MD: Naval Institute Press.

Weaver, R. (1953). *The ethics of rhetoric.* Chicago: Henry Regency.

Worth, S. (1981). *Studying visual communication.* L. Gross (Ed.). Philadelphia: University of Pennsylvania Press.

Unit 2: Building Contexts

Eichmann in Jerusalem: A Report on the Banality of Evil

Hannah Arendt

II: The Accused

Otto Adolf, son of Karl Adolf Eichmann and Maria née Schefferling, caught in a suburb of Buenos Aires on the evening of May 11, 1960, flown to Israel nine days later, brought to trial in the District Court in Jerusalem on April 11, 1961, stood accused on fifteen counts: "together with others" he had committed crimes against the Jewish people, crimes against humanity, and war crimes during the whole period of the Nazi regime and especially during the period of the Second World War. The Nazis and Nazi Collaborators (Punishment) Law of 1950, under which he was tried, provides that "a person who has committed one of these . . . offenses . . . is liable to the death penalty." To each count Eichmann pleaded: "Not guilty in the sense of the indictment."

In what sense then did he think he was guilty? In the long cross-examination of the accused, according to him "the longest ever known," neither the defense nor the prosecution nor, finally, any of the three judges ever bothered to ask him this obvious question. His lawyer, Robert Servatius of Cologne, hired by Eichmann and paid by the Israeli government (following the precedent set at the Nuremberg Trials, where all attorneys for the defense were paid by the Tribunal of the victorious powers), answered the question in a press interview: "Eichmann feels guilty before God, not before the law," but this answer remained without confirmation from the accused himself. The defense would apparently have preferred him to plead not guilty on the grounds that under the then existing Nazi legal system he had not done anything wrong, that what he was accused of were not crimes but "acts of state," over which no other state has jurisdiction (*par in parem imperium non habet*), that it had been his duty to obey and that, in Servatius' words, he had committed acts "for which you are decorated if you win and go to the gallows if you lose." (Thus Goebbels had declared in 1943: "We will go down in history as the greatest statesmen of all times or as their greatest criminals.") Outside Israel (at a meeting of the Catholic Academy in Bavaria, devoted to what the *Rheinischer Merkur* called "the ticklish problem" of the "possibilities and limits in the coping with historical and political guilt through criminal proceedings"), Servatius went a step farther, and declared that "the only legitimate criminal problem of the Eichmann trial lies in pronouncing judgment against his Israeli captors, which so far has not

"The Accused," from *Eichmann in Jerusalem: A Report on the Banality of Evil* by Hannah Arendt, Copyright © 1963, 1964 by Hannah Arendt; copyright renewed © 1991, 1992 by Lotte Kohler. Used by permission of Viking Books, an imprint of Penguin.

been done"—a statement, incidentally, that is somewhat difficult to reconcile with his repeated and widely publicized utterances in Israel, in which he called the conduct of the trial "a great spiritual achievement," comparing it favorably with the Nuremberg Trials.

Eichmann's own attitude was different. First of all, the indictment for murder was wrong: "With the killing of Jews I had nothing to do. I never killed a Jew, or a non-Jew, for that matter—I never killed any human being. I never gave an order to kill either a Jew or a non-Jew; I just did not do it," or, as he was later to qualify this statement, "It so happened . . . that I had not once to do it"—for he left no doubt that he would have killed his own father if he had received an order to that effect. Hence he repeated over and over (what he had already stated in the so-called Sassen documents, the interview that he had given in 1955 in Argentina to the Dutch journalist Sassen, a former S.S. man who was also a fugitive from justice, and that, after Eichmann's capture, had been published in part by *Life* in this country and by *Der Stern* in Germany) that he could be accused only of "aiding and abetting" the annihilation of the Jews, which he declared in Jerusalem to have been "one of the greatest crimes in the history of Humanity." The defense paid no attention to Eichmann's own theory, but the prosecution wasted much time in an unsuccessful effort to prove that Eichmann had once, at least, killed with his own hands (a Jewish boy in Hungary), and it spent even more time, and more successfully, on a note that Franz Rademacher, the Jewish expert in the German Foreign Office, had scribbled on one of the documents dealing with Yugoslavia during a telephone conversation, which read: "Eichmann proposes shooting." This turned out to be the only "order to kill," if that is what it was, for which there existed even a shred of evidence.

The evidence was more questionable than it appeared to be during the trial, at which the judges accepted the prosecutor's version against Eichmann's categorical denial—a denial that was very ineffective, since he had forgotten the "brief incident [a mere eight thousand people] which was not so striking," as Servatius put it. The incident took place in the autumn of 1941, six months after Germany had occupied the Serbian part of Yugoslavia. The Army had been plagued by partisan warfare ever since, and it was the military authorities who decided to solve two problems at a stroke by shooting a hundred Jews and Gypsies as hostages for every dead German soldier. To be sure, neither Jews nor Gypsies were partisans, but, in the words of the responsible civilian officer in the military government, a certain Staatsrat Harald Turner, "the Jews we had in the camps [anyhow]; after all, they too are Serb nationals, and besides, they have to disappear" (quoted by Raul Hilberg in *The Destruction of the European Jews*, 1961). The camps had been set up by General Franz Böhme, military governor of the region, and they housed Jewish males only. Neither General Böhme nor Staatsrat Turner waited for Eichmann's approval before starting to shoot Jews and Gypsies by the thousand. The trouble began when Böhme, without consulting the appropriate police and S.S. authorities, decided to *deport* all his Jews, probably in order to show that no special troops, operating under a different command, were required to make Serbia *judenrein*. Eichmann was informed, since it was a matter of deportation, and he refused approval because the move would interfere with other plans; but it was not Eichmann but Martin Luther, of the Foreign Office, who reminded General Böhme that "In other territories [meaning Russia] other military commanders have taken care of considerably greater numbers of Jews without even mentioning it." In any event, if Eichmann actually did "propose shooting," he told the military only that they should go on doing what they had done all along, and that the question of hostages was entirely in their own competence. Obviously, this was an Army affair, since only males were involved. The implementation of the Final Solution in Serbia started about six months later, when women and children were rounded up and disposed of in mobile gas vans. During cross-examination, Eichmann, as usual, chose the most complicated and least likely explanation: Rademacher had needed the support of the Head Office for Reich Security, Eichmann's outfit, for his own stand on the matter in the Foreign Office, and therefore had forged the document. (Rademacher himself explained the incident much more reasonably at his own trial, before a West German court in 1952: "The Army was responsible for order in Serbia and had to kill rebellious Jews by shooting." This sounded more plausible but was a lie, for we know—from Nazi sources—that the Jews were not "rebellious.") If it was difficult to interpret a remark made over the phone as an order, it was more difficult to believe that Eichmann had been in a position to give orders to the generals of the Army.

Would he then have pleaded guilty if he had been indicted as an accessory to murder? Perhaps, but he would have made important qualifications. What he had done was a crime only in retrospect, and he had always been a law-abiding citizen, because Hitler's orders, which he had certainly executed to the best of his ability, had possessed "the force of law" in the Third Reich. (The defense could have quoted in support of Eichmann's thesis the testimony of one of the best-known experts on constitutional law in the Third Reich, Theodor Maunz, currently Minister of Education and Culture in Bavaria, who stated in 1943 [in *Gestalt und Recht der Polizei*]: "The command of the Führer . . . is the absolute center of the present legal order.") Those who today told Eichmann that he could have acted differently simply did not know, or had forgotten, how things had been. He did not want to be one of those who now pretended that "they had always been against it," whereas in fact they had been very eager to do what they were told to do. However, times change, and he, like Professor Maunz, had "arrived at different insights." What he had done he had done, he did not want to deny it; rather, he proposed "to hang myself in public as a warning example for all anti-Semites on this earth." By this he did not mean to say that he regretted anything: "Repentance is for little children." (*Sic!*)

Even under considerable pressure from his lawyer, he did not change this position. In a discussion of Himmler's offer in 1944 to exchange a million Jews for ten thousand trucks, and his own role in this plan, Eichmann was asked: "Mr. Witness, in the negotiations with your superiors, did you express any pity for the Jews and did you say there was room to help them?" And he replied: "I am here under oath and must speak the truth. Not out of mercy did I launch this transaction"—which would have been fine, except that it was not Eichmann who "launched" it. But he then continued, quite truthfully: "My reasons I explained this morning," and they were as follows: Himmler had sent his own man to Budapest to deal with matters of Jewish emigration. (Which, incidentally, had become a flourishing business: for enormous amounts of money, Jews could buy their way out. Eichmann, however, did not mention this.) It was the fact that "here matters of emigration were dealt with by a man who did not belong to the Police Force" that made him indignant, "because I had to help and to implement deportation, and matters of emigration, on which I considered myself an expert, were assigned to a man who was new to the unit. . . . I was fed up. . . . I decided that I had to do something to take matters of emigration into my own hands."

Throughout the trial, Eichmann tried to clarify, mostly without success, this second point in his plea of "not guilty in the sense of the indictment." The indictment implied not only that he had acted on purpose, which he did not deny, but out of base motives and in full knowledge of the criminal nature of his deeds. As for the base motives, he was perfectly sure that he was not what he called an *innerer Schweinehund*, a dirty bastard in the depths of his heart; and as for his conscience, he remembered perfectly well that he would have had a bad conscience only if he had not done what he had been ordered to to—to ship millions of men, women, and children to their death with great zeal and the most meticulous care. This, admittedly, was hard to take. Half a dozen psychiatrists had certified him as "normal"—"More normal, at any rate, than I am after having examined him," one of them was said to have exclaimed, while another had found that his whole psychological outlook, his attitude toward his wife and children, mother and father, brothers, sisters, and friends, was "not only normal but most desirable"—and finally the minister who had paid regular visits to him in prison after the Supreme Court had finished hearing his appeal reassured everybody by declaring Eichmann to be "a man with very positive ideas." Behind the comedy of the soul experts lay the hard fact that his was obviously no case of moral, let alone legal insanity. (Mr. Hausner's recent revelations in the *Saturday Evening Post* of things he "could not bring out at the trial" have contradicted the information given informally in Jerusalem. Eichmann, we are now told, had been alleged by the psychiatrists to be "a man obsessed with a dangerous and insatiable urge to kill," "a perverted, sadistic personality." In which case he would have belonged in an insane asylum.) Worse, his was obviously also no case of insane hatred of Jews, of fanatical anti-Semitism or indoctrination of any kind. He "personally" never had anything whatever against Jews; on the contrary, he had plenty of "private reasons" for not being a Jew hater. To be sure, there were fanatic anti-Semites among his closest friends, for instance Lászlo Endre, State Secretary in Charge of Political (Jewish) Affairs in Hungary, who was hanged in Budapest in 1946; but this, according to Eichmann, was more or less in the spirit of "some of my best friends are anti-Semites."

Alas, nobody believed him. The prosecutor did not believe him, because that was not his job. Counsel for the defense paid no attention because he, unlike Eichmann, was, to all appearances, not interested in questions of conscience. And the judges did not believe him, because they were too good, and perhaps also too conscious of the very foundations of their profession, to admit that an average, "normal" person, neither feeble-minded nor indoctrinated nor cynical, could be perfectly incapable of telling right from wrong. They preferred to conclude from occasional lies that he was a liar—and missed the greatest moral and even legal challenge of the whole case. Their case rested on the assumption that the defendant, like all "normal persons," must have been aware of the criminal nature of his acts, and Eichmann was indeed normal insofar as he was "no exception within the Nazi regime." However, under the conditions of the Third Reich only "exceptions" could be expected to react "normally." This simple truth of the matter created a dilemma for the judges which they could neither resolve nor escape.

He was born on March 19, 1906, in Solingen, a German town in the Rhineland famous for its knives, scissors, and surgical instruments. Fifty-four years later, indulging in his favorite pastime of writing his memoirs, he described this memorable event as follows: "Today, fifteen years and a day after May 8, 1945, I begin to lead my thoughts back to that nineteenth of March of the year 1906, when at five o'clock in the morning I entered life on earth in the aspect of a human being." (The manuscript has not been released by the Israeli authorities. Harry Mulisch succeeded in studying this autobiography "for half an hour," and the German-Jewish weekly *Der Aufbau* was able to publish short excerpts from it.) According to his religious beliefs, which had not changed since the Nazi period (in Jerusalem Eichmann declared himself to be a *Gottgläubiger*, the Nazi term for those who had broken with Christianity, and he refused to take his oath on the Bible), this event was to be ascribed to "a higher Bearer of Meaning," an entity somehow identical with the "movement of the universe," to which human life, in itself devoid of "higher meaning," is subject. (The terminology is quite suggestive. To call God a *Höheren Sinnesträger* meant linguistically to give him some place in the military hierarchy, since the Nazis had changed the military "recipient of orders," the *Befehlsempfänger*, into a "bearer of orders," a Befehls*träger*, indicating, as in the ancient "bearer of ill tidings," the burden of responsibility and of importance that weighed supposedly upon those who had to execute orders. Moreover, Eichmann, like everyone connected with the Final Solution, was officially a "bearer of secrets," a *Geheimnisträger*, as well, which as far as self-importance went certainly was nothing to sneeze at.) But Eichmann, not very much interested in metaphysics, remained singularly silent on any more intimate relationship between the Bearer of Meaning and the bearer of orders, and proceeded to a consideration of the other possible cause of his existence, his parents: "They would hardly have been so overjoyed at the arrival of their first-born had they been able to watch how in the hour of my birth the Norn of misfortune, to spite the Norn of good fortune, was already spinning threads of grief and sorrow into my life. But a kind, impenetrable veil kept my parents from seeing into the future."

The misfortune started soon enough; it started in school. Eichmann's father, first an accountant for the Tramways and Electricity Company in Solingen and after 1913 an official of the same corporation in Austria, in Linz, had five children, four sons and a daughter, of whom only Adolf, the eldest, it seems, was unable to finish high school, or even to graduate from the vocational school for engineering into which he was then put. Throughout his life, Eichmann deceived people about his early "misfortunes" by hiding behind the more honorable financial misfortunes of his father. In Israel, however, during his first sessions with Captain Avner Less, the police examiner who was to spend approximately 35 days with him and who produced 3,564 typewritten pages from 76 recorder tapes, he was in an ebullient mood, full of enthusiasm about this unique opportunity "to pour forth everything . . . I know" and, by the same token, to advance to the rank of the most cooperative defendant ever. (His enthusiasm was soon dampened, though never quite extinguished, when he was confronted with concrete questions based on irrefutable documents.) The best proof of his initial boundless confidence, obviously wasted on Captain Less (who said to Harry Mulisch: "I was Mr. Eichmann's father confessor"), was that for the first time in his life he admitted his early disasters, although he must have been aware of the fact that he thus contradicted himself on several important entries in all his official Nazi records.

Well, the disasters were ordinary: since he "had not exactly been the most hard-working" pupil—or, one may add, the most gifted—his father had taken him first from high school and then from vocational school, long before graduation. Hence, the profession that appears on all his official documents: construction engineer, had about as much connection with reality as the statement that his birthplace was Palestine and that he was fluent in Hebrew and Yiddish—another outright lie Eichmann had loved to tell both to his S.S. comrades and to his Jewish victims. It was in the same vein that he had always pretended he had been dismissed from his job as salesman for the Vacuum Oil Company in Austria because of membership in the National Socialist Party. The version he confided to Captain Less was less dramatic, though probably not the truth either: he had been fired because it was a time of unemployment, when unmarried employees were the first to lose their jobs. (This explanation, which at first seems plausible, is not very satisfactory, because he lost his job in the spring of 1933, when he had been engaged for two full years to Veronika, or Vera, Liebl, who later became his wife. Why had he not married her before, when he still had a good job? He finally married in March, 1935, probably because bachelors in the S.S., as in the Vacuum Oil Company, were never sure of their jobs and could not be promoted.) Clearly, bragging had always been one of his cardinal vices.

While young Eichmann was doing poorly in school, his father left the Tramway and Electricity Company and went into business for himself. He bought a small mining enterprise and put his unpromising youngster to work in it as an ordinary mining laborer, but only until he found him a job in the sales department of the Oberösterreichischen Elektrobau Company, where Eichmann remained for over two years. He was now about twenty-two years old and without any prospects for a career; the only thing he had learned, perhaps, was how to sell. What then happened was what he himself called his first break, of which, again, we have two rather different versions. In a hand-written biographical record he submitted in 1939 to win a promotion in the S.S., he described it as follows: "I worked during the years of 1925 to 1927 as a salesman for the Austrian Elektrobau Company. I left this position of my own free will, as the Vacuum Oil Company of Vienna offered me the representation for Upper Austria." The key word here is "offered," since, according to the story he told Captain Less in Israel, nobody had offered him anything. His own mother had died when he was ten years old, and his father had married again. A cousin of his stepmother—a man he called "uncle"—who was president of the Austrian Automobile Club and was married to the daughter of a Jewish businessman in Czechoslovakia, had used his connection with the general director of the Austrian Vacuum Oil Company, a Jewish Mr. Weiss, to obtain for his unfortunate relation a job as traveling salesman. Eichmann was properly grateful; the Jews in his family were among his "private reasons" for not hating Jews. Even in 1943 or 1944, when the Final Solution was in full swing, he had not forgotten: "The daughter of this marriage, half-Jewish according to the Nuremberg Laws, . . . came to see me in order to obtain my permission for her emigration into Switzerland. Of course, I granted this request, and the same uncle came also to see me to ask me to intervene for some Viennese Jewish couple. I mention this only to show that I myself had no hatred for Jews, for my whole education through my mother and my father had been strictly Christian; my mother, because of her Jewish relatives, held different opinions from those current in S.S. circles."

He went to considerable lengths to prove his point: he had never harbored any ill feelings against his victims, and, what is more, he had never made a secret of that fact. "I explained this to Dr. Löwenherz [head of the Jewish Community in Vienna] as I explained it to Dr. Kastner [vice president of the Zionist Organization in Budapest]; I think I told it to everybody, each of my men knew it, they all heard it from me sometime. Even in elementary school, I had a classmate with whom I spent my free time, and he came to our house; a family in Linz by the name of Sebba. The last time we met we walked together through the streets of Linz, I already with the Party emblem of the N.S.D.A.P. [the Nazi Party] in my buttonhole, and he did not think anything of it." Had Eichmann been a bit less prim or the police examination (which refrained from cross-examination, presumably to remain assured of his cooperation) less discreet, his "lack of prejudice" might have shown itself in still another aspect. It seems that in Vienna, where he was so extraordinarily successful in arranging the "forced emigration" of Jews, he had a Jewish mistress, an "old flame" from Linz. *Rassenschande*, sexual intercourse with Jews, was probably the greatest crime a member of the S.S. could commit, and though during the war the raping of Jewish girls became a favorite pastime at the front, it was by no means common for a Higher S.S. officer to have an affair with a Jewish woman. Thus, Eichmann's repeated violent denunciations of Julius Streicher, the insane and obscene editor of *Der Stürmer*, and of his pornographic anti-Semitism, were perhaps personally motivated, and the expression of more than the routine contempt an "enlightened" S.S. man was supposed to show toward the vulgar passions of lesser Party luminaries.

The five and a half years with the Vacuum Oil Company must have been among the happier ones in Eichmann's life. He made a good living during a time of severe unemployment, and he was still living with his parents, except when he was out on the road. The date when this idyll came to an end—Pentecost, 1933—was among the few he always remembered. Actually, things had taken a turn for the worse somewhat earlier. At the end of 1932, he was unexpectedly transferred from Linz to Salzburg, very much against his inclinations: "I lost all joy in my work, I no longer liked to sell, to make calls." From such sudden losses of *Arbeitsfreude* Eichmann was to suffer throughout his life. The worst of them occurred when he was told of the Führer's order for the "physical extermination of the Jews," in which he was to play such an important role. This, too, came unexpectedly; he himself had "never thought of . . . such a solution through violence," and he described his reaction in the same words: "I now lost everything, all joy in my work, all initiative, all interest; I was, so to speak, blown out." A similar blowing out must have happened in 1932 in Salzburg, and from his own account it is clear that he cannot have been very surprised when he was fired, though one need not believe his saying that he had been "very happy" about his dismissal.

For whatever reasons, the year 1932 marked a turning point in his life. It was in April of this year that he joined the National Socialist Party and entered the S.S., upon an invitation of Ernst Kaltenbrunner, a young lawyer in Linz who later became chief of the Head Office for Reich Security (the *Reichssicherheitshauptamt* or R.S.H.A., as I shall call it henceforth), in one of whose six main departments—Bureau IV, under the command of Heinrich Müller—Eichmann was eventually employed as head of section B-4. In court, Eichmann gave the impression of a typical member of the lower middle classes, and this impression was more than borne out by every sentence he spoke or wrote while in prison. But this was misleading; he was rather the *déclassé* son of a solid middle-class family, and it was indicative of his comedown in social status that while his father was a good friend of Kaltenbrunner's father, who was also a Linz lawyer, the relationship of the two sons was rather cool: Eichmann was unmistakably treated by Kaltenbrunner as his social inferior. Before Eichmann entered the Party and the S.S., he had proved that he was a joiner, and May 8, 1945, the official date of Germany's defeat, was significant for him mainly because it then dawned upon him that thenceforward he would have to live without being a member of something or other. "I sensed I would have to live a leaderless and difficult individual life, I would receive no directives from anybody, no orders and commands would any longer be issued to me, no pertinent ordinances would be there to consult—in brief, a life never known before lay before me." When he was a child, his parents, uninterested in politics, had enrolled him in the Young Men's Christian Association, from which he later went into the German youth movement, the *Wandervogel*. During his four unsuccessful years in high school, he had joined the *Jungfront-kämpfe-verband*, the youth section of the German-Austrian organization of war veterans, which, though violently pro-German and anti-republican, was tolerated by the Austrian government. When Kaltenbrunner suggested that he enter the S.S., he was just on the point of becoming a member of an altogether different outfit, the Freemasons' Lodge Schlaraffia, "an association of businessmen, physicians, actors, civil servants, etc., who came together to cultivate merriment and gaiety. . . . Each member had to give a lecture from time to time whose tenor was to be humor, refined humor." Kaltenbrunner explained to Eichmann that he would have to give up this merry society because as a Nazi he could not be a Freemason—a word that at the time was unknown to him. The choice between the S.S. and Schlaraffia (the name derives from *Schlaraffenland*, the gluttons' Cloud-Cuckoo Land of German fairy tales) might have been hard to make, but he was "kicked out" of Schlaraffia anyhow; he had committed a sin that even now, as he told the story in the Israeli prison, made him blush with shame: "Contrary to my upbringing, I had tried, though I was the youngest, to invite my companions to a glass of wine."

A leaf in the whirlwind of time, he was blown from Schlaraffia, the Never-Never Land of tables set by magic and roast chickens that flew into your mouth—or, more accurately, from the company of respectable philistines with degrees and assured careers and "refined humor," whose worst vice was probably an irrepressible desire for practical jokes—into the marching columns of the Thousand-Year Reich, which lasted exactly twelve years and three months. At any rate, he did not enter the Party out of conviction, nor was he ever convinced by it—whenever he was asked to give his reasons, he repeated the same embarrassed clichés about the Treaty of Versailles and unemployment; rather, as he pointed out in court, "it was like being swallowed up by the Party against all expectations and without previous decision. It happened so quickly and suddenly." He had no time and less desire to be properly informed, he did not even know the Party program, he never read *Mein Kampf*. Kaltenbrunner had said to him: Why not join the S.S.? And he had replied, Why not? That was how it had happened, and that was about all there was to it.

Of course, that was not all there was to it. What Eichmann failed to tell the presiding judge in cross-examination was that he had been an ambitious young man who was fed up with his job as traveling salesman even before the Vacuum Oil Company was fed up with him. From a humdrum life without significance and consequence the wind had blown him into History, as he understood it, namely, into a Movement that always kept moving and in which somebody like him—already a failure in the eyes of his social class, of his family, and hence in his own eyes as well—could start from scratch and still make a career. And if he did not always like what he had to do (for example, dispatching people to their death by the trainload instead of forcing them to emigrate), if he guessed, rather early, that the whole business would come to a bad end, with Germany losing the war, if all his most cherished plans came to nothing (the evacuation of European Jewry to Madagascar, the establishment of a Jewish territory in the Nisko region of Poland, the experiment with carefully built defense installations around his Berlin office to repel Russian tanks), and if, to his greatest "grief and sorrow," he never advanced beyond the grade of S.S. *Obersturmbannführer* (a rank equivalent to lieutenant colonel)—in short, if, with the exception of the year in Vienna, his life was beset with frustrations, he never forgot what the alternative would have been. Not only in Argentina, leading the unhappy existence of a refugee, but also in the courtroom in Jerusalem, with his life as good as forfeited, he might still have preferred—if anybody had asked him—to be hanged as *Obersturmbannführer a.D.* (in retirement) rather than living out his life quietly and normally as a traveling salesman for the Vacuum Oil Company.

The beginnings of Eichmann's new career were not very promising. In the spring of 1933, while he was out of a job, the Nazi Party and all its affiliates were suspended in Austria, because of Hitler's rise to power. But even without this new calamity, a career in the Austrian Party would have been out of the question: even those who had enlisted in the S.S. were still working at their regular jobs; Kaltenbrunner was still a partner in his father's law firm. Eichmann therefore decided to go to Germany, which was all the more natural because his family had never given up German citizenship. (This fact was of some relevance during the trial. Dr. Servatius had asked the West German government to demand extradition of the accused and, failing this, to pay the expenses of the defense, and Bonn refused, on the grounds that Eichmann was not a German national, which was a patent untruth.) At Passau, on the German border, he was suddenly a traveling salesman again, and when he reported to the regional leader, he asked him eagerly "if he had perhaps some connection with the Bavarian Vacuum Oil Company." Well, this was one of his not infrequent relapses from one period of his life into another; whenever he was confronted with telltale signs of an unregenerate Nazi outlook, in his life in Argentina and even in the Jerusalem jail, he excused himself with "There I go again, the old song and dance [*die alte Tour*]." But his relapse in Passau was quickly cured; he was told that he had better enlist for some military training—"All right with me, I thought to myself, why not become a soldier?"—and he was sent in quick succession to two Bavarian S.S. camps, in Lechfeld and in Dachau (he had nothing to do with the concentration camp there), where the "Austrian Legion in exile" received its training. Thus he did become an Austrian after a fashion, despite his German passport. He remained in these military camps from August 1933, until September 1934, advanced to the rank of *Scharführer* (corporal) and had plenty of time to reconsider his willingness to embark upon the career of a soldier. According to his own account, there was but one thing in which he distinguished himself during these fourteen months, and that was punishment drill, which he performed with great obstinacy, in the wrathful spirit of "Serves my father right if my hands freeze, why doesn't he buy me gloves." But apart from such rather dubious pleasures, to which he owed his first promotion, he had a terrible time: "The humdrum of military service, that was something I couldn't stand, day after day always the same, over and over again the same." Thus bored to distraction, he heard that the Security Service of the Reichsführer S.S. (Himmler's *Sicherheitsdienst*, or S.D., as I shall call it henceforth) had jobs open, and applied immediately.

Excerpts from Theory of Moral Sentiments

Adam Smith

SECTION I: OF THE SENSE OF PROPRIETY

CHAPTER 1: *Of Sympathy.*

How selfish soever man may be supposed, there are evidently some principles in his nature, which interest him in the fortune of others, and render their happiness necessary to him, though he derives nothing from it, except the pleasure of seeing it. Of this kind is pity or compassion, the emotion which we feel for the misery of others, when we either see it, or are made to conceive it in a very lively manner. That we often derive sorrow from the sorrow of others is a matter of fact too obvious to require any instances to prove it; for this sentiment, like all the other original passions of human nature, is by no means confined to the virtuous and humane, though they perhaps may feel it with the most exquisite sensibility. The greatest ruffian, the most hardened violator of the laws of society, is not altogether without it.

As we have no immediate experience of what other men feel, we can form no idea of the manner in which they are affected, but by conceiving what we ourselves should feel in the like situation. Though our brother is upon the rack, as long as we ourselves are at our ease, our senses will never inform us of what he suffers. They never did, and never can, carry us beyond our own person, and it is by the imagination only that we can form any conception of what are his sensations. Neither can that faculty help us to this any other way, than by representing to us what would be our own, if we were in his case. It is the impressions of our own senses only, not those of his, which our imaginations copy. By the imagination we place ourselves in his situation, we conceive ourselves enduring all the same torments, we enter as it were into his body, and become in some measure the same person with him, and thence form some idea of his sensations, and even feel something which, though weaker in degree, is not altogether unlike them. His agonies, when they are thus brought home to ourselves, when we have thus adopted and made them our own, begin at last to affect us, and we then tremble and shudder at the thought of what he feels. For as to be in pain or distress of any kind excites the most excessive sorrow, so to conceive or to imagine that we are in it, excites some degree of the same emotion, in proportion to the vivacity or dulness of the conception.

That this is the source of our fellow feeling for the misery of others, that it is by changing places in fancy with the sufferer, that we come either to conceive or to be affected by what he feels, may be demonstrated by many obvious observations, if it should not be thought sufficiently evident of itself. When we see a stroke aimed, and just ready to fall upon the leg or arm of another person, we naturally shrink and draw back our own leg or our own arm; and when it does fall, we feel it in some measure, and are hurt by it as well as the sufferer. The mob, when they are gazing at a dancer on the slack rope, naturally writhe and twist and balance their own bodies as they see him do, and as they feel that they themselves must do if in his situation. Persons of delicate fibers and a weak constitution of body complain, that in looking on the sores and ulcers which are exposed by beggars in the streets, they are apt to feel an itching or uneasy sensation in the corresponding part of their own bodies. The horror which they conceive at the misery of those wretches affects that particular part in themselves more than any other; because that horror arises from conceiving what they

From *The Theory of Moral Sentiments* by Adam Smith, 1759.

themselves would suffer, if they really were the wretches whom they are looking upon, and if that particular part in themselves was actually affected in the same miserable manner. The very force of this conception is sufficient, in their feeble frames, to produce that itching or uneasy sensation complained of. Men of the most robust make, observe that in looking upon sore eyes they often feel a very sensible soreness in their own, which proceeds from the same reason; that organ being in the strongest man more delicate than any other part of the body is in the weakest.

Neither is it those circumstances only, which create pain or sorrow, that call forth our fellow feeling. Whatever is the passion which arises from any object in the person principally concerned, an analogous emotion springs up, at the thought of his situation, in the breast of every attentive spectator. Our joy for the deliverance of those heroes of tragedy or romance who interest us, is as sincere as our grief for their distress, and our fellow feeling with their misery is not more real than that with their happiness. We enter into their gratitude toward those faithful friends who did not desert them in their difficulties; and we heartily go along with their resentment against those perfidious traitors who injured, abandoned, or deceived them. In every passion of which the mind of man is susceptible, the emotions of the bystander always correspond to what, by bringing the case home to himself, he imagines should be the sentiments of the sufferer.

Pity and compassion are words appropriated to signify our fellow feeling with the sorrow of others. Sympathy, though its meaning was, perhaps, originally the same, may now, however, without much impropriety, be made use of to denote our fellow feeling with any passion whatever.

Upon some occasions sympathy may seem to arise merely from the view of a certain emotion in another person. The passions, upon some occasions, may seem to be transfused from one man to another, instantaneously, and antecedent to any knowledge of what excited them in the person principally concerned. Grief and joy, for example, strongly expressed in the look and gestures of any person, at once affect the spectator with some degree of a like painful or agreeable emotion. A smiling face is, to everybody that sees it, a cheerful object; as a sorrowful countenance, on the other hand, is a melancholy one.

This, however, does not hold universally, or with regard to every passion. There are some passions of which the expressions excite no sort of sympathy, but, before we are acquainted with what gave occasion to them, serve rather to disgust and provoke us against them. The furious behavior of an angry man is more likely to exasperate us against himself than against his enemies. As we are unacquainted with his provocation, we cannot bring his case home to ourselves, nor conceive anything like the passions which it excites. But we plainly see what is the situation of those with whom he is angry, and to what violence they may be exposed from so enraged an adversary. We readily, therefore, sympathize with their fear or resentment, and are immediately disposed to take part against the man from whom they appear to be in danger.

If the very appearances of grief and joy inspire us with some degree of the like emotions, it is because they suggest to us the general idea of some good or bad fortune that has befallen the person in whom we observe them: and in these passions this is sufficient to have some little influence upon us. The effects of grief and joy terminate in the person who feels those emotions, of which the expressions do not, like those of resentment, suggest to us the idea of any other person for whom we are concerned, and whose interests are opposite to his. The general idea of good or bad fortune, therefore, creates some concern for the person who has met with it; but the general idea of provocation excites no sympathy with the anger of the man who has received it. Nature, it seems, teaches us to be more averse to enter into this passion, and, till informed of its cause, to be disposed rather to take part against it.

Even our sympathy with the grief or joy of another, before we are informed of the cause of either, is always extremely imperfect. General lamentations, which express nothing but the anguish of the sufferer, create rather a curiosity to inquire into his situation, along with some disposition to sympathize with him, than any actual sympathy that is very sensible. The first question which we ask is, What has befallen you? Till this be answered, though we are uneasy both from the vague idea of his misfortune, and still more from torturing ourselves with conjectures about what it may be, yet our fellow feeling is not very considerable.

Sympathy, therefore, does not arise so much from the view of the passion, as from that of the situation which excites it. We sometimes feel for another, a passion of which he himself seems to be altogether incapable; because, when we put ourselves in his case, that passion arises in our breast from the imagination, though it does not in his from the reality. We blush for the impudence and rudeness of another, though he himself appears to have no sense of the impropriety of his own behavior; because we cannot help feeling with what confusion we ourselves should be covered, had we behaved in so absurd a manner.

Of all the calamities to which the condition of mortality exposes mankind, the loss of reason appears, to those who have the least spark of humanity, by far the most dreadful; and they behold that last stage of human wretchedness with deeper commiseration than any other. But the poor wretch, who is in it, laughs and sings, perhaps, and is altogether insensible to his own misery. The anguish which humanity feels, therefore, at the sight of such an object, cannot be the reflection of any sentiment of the sufferer. The compassion of the spectator must arise altogether from the consideration of what he himself would feel if he was reduced to the same unhappy situation, and, what perhaps is impossible, was at the same time able to regard it with his present reason and judgment.

What are the pangs of a mother, when she hears the moanings of her infant, that, during the agony of disease, cannot express what it feels? In her idea of what it suffers, she joins, to its real helplessness, her own consciousness of that helplessness, and her own terrors for the unknown consequences of its disorder; and out of all these, forms, for her own sorrow, the most complete image of misery and distress. The infant, however, feels only the uneasiness of the present instant, which can never be great. With regard to the future, it is perfectly secure, and in its thoughtlessness and want of foresight, possesses an antidote against fear and anxiety, the great tormentors of the human breast, from which reason and philosophy will in vain attempt to defend it, when it grows up to a man.

We sympathize even with the dead, and overlooking what is of real importance in their situation, that awful futurity which awaits them, we are chiefly affected by those circumstances which strike our senses, but can have no influence upon their happiness. It is miserable, we think, to be deprived of the light of the sun; to be shut out from life and conversation; to be laid in the cold grave, a prey to corruption and the reptiles of the earth; to be no more thought of in this world, but to be obliterated, in a little time, from the affections, and almost from the memory, of their dearest friends and relations. Surely, we imagine, we can never feel too much for those who have suffered so dreadful a calamity. The tribute of our fellow feeling seems doubly due to them now, when they are in danger of being forgotten by everybody; and, by the vain honors which we pay to their memory, we endeavor, for our own misery, artificially to keep alive our melancholy remembrance of their misfortune. That our sympathy can afford them no consolation seems to be an addition to their calamity; and to think that all we can do is unavailing, and that, what alleviates all other distress, the regret, the love, and the lamentations of their friends, can yield no comfort to them, serves only to exasperate our sense of their misery. The happiness of the dead, however, most assuredly is affected by none of these circumstances; nor is it the thought of these things which can ever disturb the profound security of their repose. The idea of that dreary and endless melancholy, which the fancy naturally ascribes to their condition, arises altogether from our joining to the change which has been produced upon them, our own consciousness of that change; from our putting ourselves in their situation, and from our lodging, if I may be allowed to say so, our own living souls in their inanimated bodies, and thence conceiving what would be our emotions in this case. It is from this very illusion of the imagination, that the foresight of our own dissolution is so terrible to us, and that the idea of those circumstances, which undoubtedly can give us no pain when we are dead, makes us miserable while we are alive. And from thence arises one of the most important principles in human nature, the dread of death—the great poison to the happiness, but the great restraint upon the injustice of mankind; which, while it afflicts and mortifies the individual, guards and protects the society.

CHAPTER 2: *Of the Pleasure of Mutual Sympathy.*

But whatever may be the cause of sympathy, or however it may be excited, nothing pleases us more than to observe in other men a fellow feeling with all the emotions of our own breast; nor are we ever so much shocked as by the appearance of the contrary. Those who are fond of deducing all our sentiments from certain refinements of self-love, think themselves at no loss to account, according to their own principles, both for this pleasure and this pain. Man, say they, conscious of his own weakness, and of the need which he has for the assistance of others, rejoices whenever he observes that they adopt his own passions, because he is then assured of that assistance; and grieves whenever he observes the contrary, because he is then assured of their opposition. But both the pleasure and the pain are always felt so instantaneously, and often upon such frivolous occasions, that it seems evident that neither of them can be derived from any such self-interested consideration. A man is mortified when, after having endeavored to divert the company, he looks around and sees that nobody laughs at his jests but himself. On the contrary, the mirth of the company is highly agreeable to him, and he regards this correspondence of their sentiments with his own as the greatest applause.

Neither does his pleasure seem to arise altogether from the additional vivacity which his mirth may receive from sympathy with theirs, nor his pain from the disappointment he meets with when he misses this pleasure; though both the one and the other, no doubt, do in some measure. When we have read a book or poem so often that we can no longer find any amusement in reading it by ourselves, we can still take pleasure in reading it to a companion. To him it has all the graces of novelty; we enter into the surprise and admiration which it naturally excites in him, but which it is no longer capable of exciting in us; we consider all the ideas which it presents, rather in light in which they appear to him, than in that in which they appear to ourselves, and we are amused by sympathy with his amusement, which thus enlivens our own. On the contrary, we should be vexed if he did not seem to be entertained with it, and we could no longer take any pleasure in reading it to him. It is the same case here. The mirth of the company, no doubt, enlivens our own mirth; and their silence, no doubt, disappoints us. But though this may contribute both to the pleasure which we derive from the one, and to the pain which we feel from the other, it is by no means the sole cause of either; and this correspondence of the sentiments of others with our own appears to be a cause of pleasure, and the want of it a cause of pain, which cannot be accounted for in this manner. The sympathy which my friends express with my joy, might indeed give me pleasure by enlivening that joy; but that which they express with my grief could give me none, if it served only to enliven that grief. Sympathy, however, enlivens joy and alleviates grief. It enlivens joy by presenting another source of satisfaction; and it alleviates grief by insinuating into the heart almost the only agreeable sensation which it is at that time capable of receiving.

It is to be observed accordingly, that we are still more anxious to communicate to our friends our disagreeable, than our agreeable, passions; that we derive still more satisfaction from their sympathy with the former, than from that with the latter, and that we are still more shocked by the want of it.

How are the unfortunate relieved when they have found out a person to whom they can communicate the cause of their sorrow! Upon his sympathy they seem to disburden themselves of a part of their distress: He is not improperly said to share it with them. He not only feels a sorrow of the same kind with that which they feel, but, as if he had derived a part of it to himself; what he feels seems to alleviate the weight of what they feel. Yet, by relating their misfortunes, they in some measure renew their grief. They awaken in their memory the remembrance of those circumstances which occasion their affliction. Their tears accordingly flow faster than before, and they are apt to abandon themselves to all the weakness of sorrow. They take pleasure, however, in all this, and it is evident are sensibly relieved by it; because the sweetness of this sympathy more than compensates the bitterness of that sorrow, which, in order to excite this sympathy, they had thus enlivened and renewed. The cruelest insult, on the contrary, which can be offered to the unfortunate, is to appear to make light of their calamities. To seem not to be affected with the joy of our companions is but want of politeness, but not to wear a serious countenance when they tell us their afflictions is real and gross inhumanity.

Love is an agreeable, resentment a disagreeable passion: and accordingly we are not half so anxious that our friends should adopt our friendships, as that they should enter into our resentments. We can forgive them, though they seem to be little affected with the favors which we may have received, but lose all patience if they seem indifferent about the injuries which may have been done to us; nor are we half so angry with them for not entering into our gratitude, as for not sympathizing with our resentment. They can easily avoid being friends to our friends, but can hardly avoid being enemies to those with whom we are at variance. We seldom resent their being at enmity with the first, though, upon that account, we may sometimes affect to make an awkward quarrel with them; but we quarrel with them in good earnest, if they live in friendship with the last. The agreeable passions of love and joy can satisfy and support the heart without any auxiliary pleasure. The bitter and painful emotions of grief and resentment more strongly require the healing consolation of sympathy.

As the person who is principally interested in any event is pleased with our sympathy, and hurt by the want of it, so we, too, seem to be pleased when we are able to sympathize with him, and to be hurt when we are unable to do so. We run not only to congratulate the successful, but to condole with the afflicted; and the pleasure which we find in the conversation of one, whom in all the passions of his heart we can entirely sympathize with, seems to do more than compensate the painfulness of that sorrow with which the view of his situation affects us. On the contrary, it is always disagreeable to feel that we cannot sympathize with him; and, instead of being pleased with this exemption from sympathetic pain, it hurts us to find that we cannot share his uneasiness. If we hear a person loudly lamenting his misfortunes, which, however, upon bringing the case home to ourselves, we feel, can produce no such violent effect upon us, we are shocked at his grief; and, because we cannot enter into it, call it pusillanimity and weakness. It gives us the spleen, on the other hand, to see another too happy, or too much elevated, as we call it, with any little piece of good fortune. We are disobliged even with his joy; and, because we cannot go along with it, call it levity and folly. We are even put out of humor if our companion laughs louder or longer at a joke than we think it deserves; that is, than we feel that we ourselves could laugh at it.

CHAPTER 3: *Of the manner in which we judge of the Propriety or Impropriety of the affections of other men, by their concord or dissonance with our own.*

When the original passions of the person principally concerned are in perfect concord with the sympathetic emotions of the spectator, they necessarily appear to this last just and proper, and suitable to their objects; and, on the contrary, when, upon bringing the case home to himself, he finds that they do not coincide with what he feels, they necessarily appear to him unjust and improper, and unsuitable to the causes which excite them. To approve of the passions of another, therefore, as suitable to their objects is the same thing as to observe that we entirely sympathize with them; and not to approve of them as such, is the same thing as to observe that we do not entirely sympathize with them. The man who resents the injuries that have been done to me, and observes that I resent them precisely as he does, necessarily approves of my resentment. The man whose sympathy keeps time to my grief, cannot but admit the reasonableness of my sorrow. He who admires the same poem or the same picture, and admires them exactly as I do, must surely allow the justness of my admiration. He who laughs at the same joke, and laughs along with me, cannot well deny the propriety of my laughter. On the contrary, the person who, upon these different occasions, either feels no such emotion as that which I feel, or feels none that bears any proportion to mine, cannot avoid disapproving my sentiments, on account of their dissonance with his own. If my animosity goes beyond what the indignation of my friend can correspond to; if my grief exceeds what his most tender compassion can go along with; if my admiration is either too high or too low to tally with his own; if I laugh loud and heartily when he only smiles, or, on the contrary, only smile when he laughs loud and heartily; in all these cases, as soon as he comes, from considering the object, to observe how I am affected by it, according as there is more or less disproportion between his sentiments and mine, I must incur a greater or less degree of his disapprobation: and, upon all occasions, his own sentiments are the standards and measures by which he judges of mine.

To approve of another man's opinions is to adopt those opinions, and to adopt them is to approve of them. If the same arguments which convince you, convince me likewise, I necessarily approve of your conviction; and if they do not, I necessarily disapprove of it; neither can I possibly conceive that I should do the one without the other. To approve or disapprove, therefore, of the opinions of others is acknowledged, by every body, to mean no more than to observe their agreement or disagreement with our own. But this is equally the case with regard to our approbation or disapprobation of the sentiments or passions of others.

There are, indeed, some cases in which we seem to approve, without any sympathy or correspondence of sentiments; and in which, consequently, the sentiment of approbation would seem to be different from the perception of this coincidence. A little attention, however, will convince us, that even in these cases our approbation is ultimately founded upon a sympathy or correspondence of this kind. I shall give an instance in things of a very frivolous nature, because in them the judgments of mankind are less apt to be perverted by wrong systems. We may often approve of a jest, and think the laughter of the company quite just and proper, though we ourselves do not laugh, because, perhaps, we are in a grave humor, or happen to have our attention engaged with other objects. We have learned, however, from experience, what sort of pleasantry is upon most occasions capable of making us laugh, and we observe that this is one of that kind. We approve, therefore, of the laughter of the company, and feel that it is natural and suitable to its object; because, though in our present mood we cannot easily enter into it, we are sensible that upon most occasions we should very heartily join in it.

The same thing often happens with regard to all the other passions. A stranger passes by us in the street with all the marks of the deepest affliction; and we are immediately told that he has just received the news of the death of his father. It is impossible that, in this case, we should not approve of his grief. Yet it may often happen, without any defect of humanity on our part, that, so far from entering into the violence of his sorrow, we should scarce conceive the first movements of concern upon his account. Both he and his father, perhaps, are entirely unknown to us, or we happen to be employed about other things, and do not take time to picture out in our imagination the different circumstances of distress which must occur to him. We have learned, however, from experience, that such a misfortune naturally excites such a degree of sorrow; and we know that if we took time to consider his situation fully, and in all its parts, we should without doubt most sincerely sympathize with him. It is upon the consciousness of this conditional sympathy, that our approbation of his sorrow is founded, even in those cases in which that sympathy does not actually take place; and the general rules derived from our preceding experience of what our sentiments would commonly correspond with, correct, upon this, as upon many other occasions, the impropriety of our present emotions.

- The sentiment or affection of the heart, from which any action proceeds, and upon which its whole virtue or vice must ultimately depend, may be considered under two different aspects, or in two different relations; first, in relation to the cause which excites it, or the motive which gives occasion to it; and, second, in relation to the end which it proposes, or the effect which it tends to produce.

In the suitableness or unsuitableness, in the proportion or disproportion, which the affection seems to bear to the cause or object which excites it, consists the propriety or impropriety, the decency or ungracefulness, of the consequent action.

In the beneficial or hurtful nature, of the effects which the affection aims at, or tends to produce, consists the merit or demerit of the action, the qualities by which it is entitled to reward, or is deserving of punishment.

Philosophers have, of late years, considered chiefly the tendency of affections, and have given little attention to the relation which they stand in to the cause which excites them. In common life, however, when we judge of any person's conduct, and of the sentiments which directed it, we constantly consider them under both these aspects. When we blame in another man the excesses of love, of grief, of resentment, we not only consider the ruinous effects which they tend to produce, but the little occasion which was given for them. The merit of his favourite, we say, is not so great, his misfortune is not so dreadful, his provocation is not so extraordinary, as to justify so violent a passion. We should have indulged, we say, perhaps have approved of the violence of his emotion, had the cause been in any respect proportioned to it.

When we judge in this manner of any affection, as proportioned or disproportioned to the cause which excites it, it is scarcely possible that we should make use of any other rule or canon but the correspondent affection in ourselves. If, upon bringing the case home to our own breast, we find that the sentiments which it gives occasion to coincide and tally with our own, we necessarily approve of them, as proportioned and suitable to their objects; if otherwise, we necessarily disapprove of them, as extravagant and out of proportion.

Every faculty in one man is the measure by which he judges of the like faculty in another. I judge of your sight by my sight, of your ear by my ear, of your reason by my reason, of your resentment by my resentment, of your love by my love. I neither have, nor can have, any other way of judging about them.

CHAPTER 4: *The same subject continued.*

We may judge of the propriety or impropriety of the sentiments of another person by their correspondence or disagreement with our own, upon two different occasions; either, first, when the objects which excite them are considered without any peculiar relation, either to ourselves or to the person whose sentiments we judge of; or, second, when they are considered as peculiarly affecting one or other of us.

1. With regard to those objects which are considered without any peculiar relation either to ourselves or to the person whose sentiments we judge of; wherever his sentiments entirely correspond with our own, we ascribe to him the qualities of taste and good judgment. The beauty of a plain, the greatness of a mountain, the ornaments of a building, the expression of a picture, the composition of a discourse, the conduct of a third person, the proportions of different quantities and numbers, the various appearances which the great machine of the universe is perpetually exhibiting, with the secret wheels and springs which produce them; all the general subjects of science and taste, are what we and our companions regard as having no peculiar relation to either of us. We both look at them from the same point of view, and we have no occasion for sympathy, or for that imaginary change of situations from which it arises, in order to produce, with regard to these, the most perfect harmony of sentiments and affections. If, notwithstanding, we are often differently affected, it arises either from the different degrees of attention which our different habits of life allow us to give easily to the several parts of those complex objects, or from the different degrees of natural acuteness in the faculty of the mind to which they are addressed.

When the sentiments of our companion coincide with our own in things of this kind, which are obvious and easy, and in which, perhaps, we never found a single person who differed from us, though we, no doubt, must approve of them, yet he seems to deserve no praise or admiration on account of them. But when they not only coincide with our own, but lead and direct our own; when, in forming them, he appears to have attended to many things which we had overlooked, and to have adjusted them to all the various circumstances of their objects; we not only approve of them, but wonder and are surprised at their uncommon and unexpected acuteness and comprehensiveness, and he appears to deserve a very high degree of admiration and applause. For approbation, heightened by wonder and surprise, constitutes the sentiment which is properly called admiration, and of which applause is the natural expression. The decision of the man who judges that exquisite beauty is preferable to the grossest deformity, or that twice two are equal to four, must certainly be approved of by all the world, but will not, surely, be much admired. It is the acute and delicate discernment of the man of taste, who distinguishes the minute, and scarce perceptible differences of beauty and deformity; it is the comprehensive accuracy of the experienced mathematician, who unravels with ease the most intricate and perplexed proportions; it is the great leader in science and taste, the man who directs and conducts our own sentiments, the extent and superior justness of whose talents astonish us with wonder and surprise, who excites our admiration, and seems to deserve our applause; and upon this foundation is grounded the greater part of the praise which is bestowed upon what are called the intellectual virtues.

The utility of these qualities, it may be thought, is what first recommends them to us; and, no doubt, the consideration of this, when we come to attend to it, gives them a new value. Originally, however, we approve of another man's judgment, not as something useful, but as right, as accurate, as agreeable to truth and reality; and it is evident we attribute those qualities to it for no other reason but because we find that it agrees with our own. Taste, in the same manner, is originally approved of, not as useful, but as just, as delicate, and as precisely suited to its object. The idea of the utility of all qualities of this kind is plainly an afterthought, and not what first recommends them to our approbation.

2. With regard to those objects, which affect in a particular manner either ourselves or the person whose sentiments we judge of, it is at once more difficult to preserve this harmony and correspondence, and, at the

same time, vastly more important. My companion does not naturally look upon the misfortune that has befallen me, or the injury that has been done me, from the same point of view in which I consider them. They affect me much more nearly. We do not view them from the same station, as we do a picture, or a poem, or a system of philosophy; and are therefore apt to be very differently affected by them. But I can much more easily overlook the want of this correspondence of sentiments with regard to such indifferent objects as concern neither me nor my companion, than with regard to what interests me so much as the misfortune that has befallen me, or the injury that has been done me. Though you despise that picture, or that poem, or even that system of philosophy which I admire, there is little danger of our quarrelling upon that account. Neither of us can reasonably be much interested about them. They ought, all of them, to be matters of great indifference to us both; so that, though our opinions may be opposite, our affections may still be very nearly the same. But it is quite otherwise with regard to those objects by which either you or I are particularly affected. Though your judgments in matters of speculation, though your sentiments in matters of taste, are quite opposite to mine, I can easily overlook this opposition; and if I have any degree of temper, I may still find some entertainment in your conversation, even upon those very subjects. But if you have either no fellow feeling for the misfortunes I have met with, or none that bears any proportion to the grief which distracts me; or if you have either no indignation at the injuries I have suffered, or none that bears any proportion to the resentment which transports me, we can no longer converse upon these subjects. We become intolerable to one another. I can neither support your company, nor you mine. You are confounded at my violence and passion, and I am enraged at your cold insensibility and want of feeling.

In all such cases, that there may be some correspondence of sentiments between the spectator and the person principally concerned, the spectator must, first of all, endeavor as much as he can to put himself in the situation of the other, and to bring home to himself every little circumstance of distress which can possibly occur to the sufferer. He must adopt the whole case of his companion, with all its minutest incidents; and strive to render as perfect as possible that imaginary change of situation upon which his sympathy is founded.

After all this, however, the emotions of the spectator will still be very apt to fall short of the violence of what is felt by the sufferer. Mankind, though naturally sympathetic, never conceive, for what has befallen another, that degree of passion which naturally animates the person principally concerned. That imaginary change of situation, upon which their sympathy is founded, is but momentary. The thought of their own safety, the thought that they themselves are not really the sufferers, continually intrudes itself upon them; and though it does not hinder them from conceiving a passion somewhat analogous to what is felt by the sufferer, hinders them from conceiving anything that approaches to the same degree of violence. The person principally concerned is sensible of this, and at the same time passionately desires a more complete sympathy. He longs for that relief which nothing can afford him but the entire concord of the affections of the spectators with his own. To see the emotions of their hearts in every respect beat time to his own, in the violent and disagreeable passions, constitutes his sole consolation. But he can only hope to obtain this by lowering his passion to that pitch, in which the spectators are capable of going along with him. He must flatten, if I may be allowed to say so, the sharpness of its natural tone, in order to reduce it to harmony and concord with the emotions of those who are about him. What they feel will, indeed, always be in some respects different from what he feels, and compassion can never be exactly the same with original sorrow; because the secret consciousness that the change of situations, from which the sympathetic sentiment arises, is but imaginary, not only lowers it in degree, but in some measure varies it in kind, and gives it a quite different modification. These two sentiments, however, may, it is evident, have such a correspondence with one another, as is sufficient for the harmony of society. Though they will never be unisons, they may be concords, and this is all that is wanted or required.

In order to produce this concord, as nature teaches the spectators to assume the circumstances of the person principally concerned, so she teaches this last in some measure to assume those of the spectators. As they are continually placing themselves in his situation, and thence conceiving emotions similar to what he feels; so he is as constantly placing himself in theirs, and thence conceiving some degree of that coolness about his own fortune, with which he is sensible that they will view it. As they are constantly considering what they themselves would feel, if they actually were the sufferers, so he is constantly led to imagine in what manner he would be affected if he was only one of the spectators of his own situation. As their sympathy makes them look at it in some measure with his eyes, so his sympathy makes him look at it, in some measure, with theirs, especially when in their presence, and acting under their observation: and, as the reflected passion which he thus conceives is much weaker than the original one, it necessarily abates the violence of what he felt before he came into their presence, before he began to recollect in what manner they would be affected by it, and to view his situation in this candid and impartial light.

The mind, therefore, is rarely so disturbed, but that the company of a friend will restore it to some degree of tranquillity and sedateness. The beast is, in some measure, calmed and composed the moment we come into his presence. We are immediately put in mind of the light in which he will view our situation, and we begin to view it ourselves in the same light; for the effect of sympathy is instantaneous. We expect less sympathy from a common acquaintance than from a friend; we cannot open to the former all those little circumstances which we can unfold to the latter; we assume, therefore, more tranquillity before him, and endeavor to fix our thoughts upon those general outlines of our situation which he is willing to consider. We expect still less sympathy from an assembly of strangers, and we assume, therefore, still more tranquillity before them, and always endeavor to bring down our passion to that pitch, which the particular company we are in may be expected to go along with. Nor is this only an assumed appearance; for if we are at all masters of ourselves, the presence of a mere acquaintance will really compose us, still more than that of a friend; and that of an assembly of strangers, still more than that of an acquaintance.

Society and conversation, therefore, are the most powerful remedies for restoring the mind to its tranquillity, if, at any time, it has unfortunately lost it; as well as the best preservatives of that equal and happy temper, which is so necessary to self-satisfaction and enjoyment. Men of retirement and speculation, who are apt to sit brooding at home over either grief or resentment, though they may often have more humanity, more generosity, and a nicer sense of honour, yet seldom possess that equality of temper which is so common among men of the world.

CHAPTER 5: *Of the amiable and respectable Virtues.*

Upon these two different efforts, upon that of the spectator to enter into the sentiments of the person principally concerned, and upon that of the person principally concerned, to bring down his emotions to what the spectator can go along with, are founded two different sets of virtues. The soft, the gentle, the amiable virtues, the virtues of candid condescension and indulgent humanity, are founded upon the one: the great, the awful, and respectable, the virtues of self-denial, of self-government, of that command of the passions which subjects all the movements of our nature to what our own dignity and honor, and the propriety of our own conduct, require, take their origin from the other.

How amiable does he appear to be, whose sympathetic heart seems to reecho all the sentiments of those with whom he converses, who grieves for their calamities, who resents their injuries, and who rejoices at their good fortune? When we bring home to ourselves the situation of his companions, we enter into their gratitude, and feel what consolation they must derive from the tender sympathy of so affectionate a friend. And, for a contrary reason, how disagreeable does he appear to be, whose hard and obdurate heart feels for himself only, but is altogether insensible to the happiness or misery of others! We enter, in this case too, into the pain which his presence must give to every mortal with whom he converses, to those especially with whom we are most apt to sympathize, the unfortunate and the injured.

On the other hand, what noble propriety and grace do we feel in the conduct of those who, in their own case, exert that recollection and self-command which constitute the dignity of every passion, and which bring it down to what others can enter into? We are disgusted with that clamorous grief, which, without any delicacy, calls upon our compassion with sighs and tears, and importunate lamentations. But we reverence that reserved, that silent and majestic sorrow, which discovers itself only in the swelling of the eyes, in the quivering of the lips and cheeks, and in the distant, but affecting, coldness of the whole behavior. It imposes the like silence upon us. We regard it with respectful attention, and watch with anxious concern over our whole behavior, lest by any impropriety we should disturb that concerted tranquillity, which it requires so great an effort to support.

The insolence and brutality of anger, in the same manner, when we indulge its fury without check or restraint, is, of all objects, the most detestable. But we admire that noble and generous resentment which governs its pursuit of the greatest injuries, not by the rage which they are apt to excite in the breast of the sufferer, but by the indignation which they naturally call forth in that of the impartial spectator; which allows no word, no gesture, to escape it beyond what this more equitable sentiment would dictate; which never, even in thought, attempts any greater vengeance, nor desires to inflict any greater punishment, than what every indifferent person would rejoice to see executed.

And hence it is, that to feel much for others, and little for ourselves, that to restrain our selfish, and to indulge our benevolent, affections, constitutes the perfection of human nature; and can alone produce among mankind that harmony of sentiments and passions in which consists their whole grace and propriety. As to love our neighbor as we love ourselves is the great law of Christianity, so it is the great precept of nature to love ourselves only as we love our neighbor, or, what comes to the same thing, as our neighbor is capable of loving us.

As taste and good judgment, when they are considered as qualities which deserve praise and admiration, are supposed to imply a delicacy of sentiment and an acuteness of understanding not commonly to be met with; so the virtues of sensibility and self-command are not apprehended to consist in the ordinary, but in the uncommon degrees of those qualities. The amiable virtue of humanity requires, surely, a sensibility much beyond what is possessed by the rude vulgar of mankind. The great and exalted virtue of magnanimity undoubtedly demands much more than that degree of self-command, which the weakest of mortals is capable of exerting. As in the common degree of the intellectual qualities, there are no abilities; so in the common degree of the moral, there is no virtue. Virtue is excellence, something uncommonly great and beautiful, which rises far above what is vulgar and ordinary. The amiable virtues consist in that degree of sensibility which surprises by its exquisite and unexpected delicacy and tenderness. The awful and respectable, in that degree of self-command which astonishes by its amazing superiority over the most ungovernable passions of human nature.

There is, in this respect, a considerable difference between virtue and mere propriety; between those qualities and actions which deserve to be admired and celebrated, and those which simply deserve to be approved of. Upon many occasions, to act with the most perfect propriety, requires no more than that common and ordinary degree of sensibility or self-command which the most worthless of mankind are possessed of, and sometimes even that degree is not necessary. Thus, to give a very low instance, to eat when we are hungry, is certainly, upon ordinary occasions, perfectly right and proper, and cannot miss being approved of as such by everybody. Nothing, however, could be more absurd than to say it was virtuous.

On the contrary, there may frequently be a considerable degree of virtue in those actions which fall short of the most perfect propriety; because they may still approach nearer to perfection than could well be expected upon occasions in which it was so extremely difficult to attain it: and this is very often the case upon those occasions which require the greatest exertions of self-command. There are some situations which bear so hard upon human nature, that the greatest degree of self-government, which can belong to so imperfect a creature as man, is not able to stifle, altogether, the voice of human weakness, or reduce the violence of the passions to that pitch of moderation, in which the impartial spectator can entirely enter into them. Though in those cases, therefore, the behavior of the sufferer fall short of the most perfect propriety, it may still deserve some applause, and even, in a certain sense, may be denominated virtuous. It may still manifest an effort of generosity and magnanimity of which the greater part of men are incapable; and though it fails of absolute perfection, it may be a much nearer approximation toward perfection, than what, upon such trying occasions, is commonly either to be found or to be expected.

In cases of this kind, when we are determining the degree of blame or applause which seems due to any action, we very frequently make use of two different standards. The first is the idea of complete propriety and perfection, which, in those difficult situations, no human conduct ever did, or even can, come up to; and in comparison with which the actions of all men must for ever appear blameable and imperfect. The second is the idea of that degree of proximity or distance from this complete perfection, which the actions of the greater part of men commonly arrive at. Whatever goes beyond this degree, how far soever it may be removed from absolute perfection, seems to deserve applause; and whatever falls short of it, to deserve blame.

It is in the same manner that we judge of the productions of all the arts which address themselves to the imagination. When a critic examines the work of any of the great masters in poetry or painting, he may sometimes examine it by an idea of perfection, in his own mind, which neither that nor any other human work will ever come up to; and as long as he compares it with this standard, he can see nothing in it but faults and imperfections. But when he comes to consider the rank which it ought to hold among other works of the same kind, he necessarily compares it with a very different standard, the common degree of excellence which is usually attained in this particular art; and when he judges of it by this new measure, it may often appear to deserve the highest applause, upon account of its approaching much nearer to perfection than the greater part of those works which can be brought into competition with it.

Excerpts from The Public and Its Problems

John Dewey

CHAPTER IV: THE ECLIPSE OF THE PUBLIC

Optimism about democracy is today under a cloud. We are familiar with denunciation and criticism which, however, often reveal their emotional source in their peevish and undiscriminating tone. Many of them suffer from the same error into which earlier laudations fell. They assume that democracy is the product of an idea, of a single and consistent intent. Carlyle was no admirer of democracy, but in a lucid moment he said: "Invent the printing press and democracy is inevitable." Add to this: Invent the railway, the telegraph, mass manufacture and concentration of population in urban centers, and some form of democratic government is, humanly speaking, inevitable. Political democracy as it exists today calls for adverse criticism in abundance. But the criticism is only an exhibition of querulousness and spleen or of a superiority complex, unless it takes cognizance of the conditions out of which popular government has issued. All intelligent political criticism is comparative. It deals not with all-or-none situations, but with practical alternatives; an absolutistic indiscriminate attitude, whether in praise or blame, testifies to the heat of feeling rather than the light of thought.

American democratic polity was developed out of genuine community life, that is, association in local and small centers where industry was mainly agricultural and where production was carried on mainly with hand tools. It took form when English political habits and legal institutions worked under pioneer conditions. The forms of association were stable, even though their units were mobile and migratory. Pioneer conditions put a high premium upon personal work, skill, ingenuity, initiative and adaptability, and upon neighborly sociability. The township or some not much larger area was the political unit, the town meeting the political medium, and roads, schools, the peace of the community, were the political objectives. The state was a sum of such units, and the national state a federation—unless perchance a confederation—of states. The imagination of the founders did not travel far beyond what could be accomplished and understood in a congeries of self-governing communities. The machinery provided for the selection of the chief executive of the federal union is illustrative evidence. The electoral college assumed that citizens would choose men locally known for their high standing; and that these men when chosen would gather together for consultation to name some one known to them for his probity and public spirit and knowledge. The rapidity with which the scheme fell into disuse is evidence of the transitoriness of the state of affairs that was predicated. But at the outset there was no dream of the time when the very names of the presidential electors would be unknown to the mass of the voters, when they would plump for a "ticket" arranged in a more or less private caucus, and when the electoral college would be an impersonal registering machine, such that it would be treachery to employ the personal judgment which was originally contemplated as the essence of the affair.

The local conditions under which our institutions took shape is well indicated by our system, apparently so systemless, of public education. Anyone who has tried to explain it to a European will understand what is meant. One is asked, say, what method of administration is followed, what is the course of study, and what are the authorized methods of teaching. The American member to the dialogue replies that in this state, or more likely county, or town, or even some section of a town called a district, matters stand thus and thus; somewhere else, so and so. The participant from this side is perhaps thought by the foreigner to be engaged

From *The Public and Its Problems* by John Dewey. Copyright © 1927 by Ohio State University Press. This material is used by permission of Ohio University Press, www.ohioswallow.com.

in concealing his ignorance; and it would certainly take a veritable cyclopedic knowledge to state the matter in its entirety. The impossibility of making any moderately generalized reply renders it almost indispensable to resort to a historical account in order to be intelligible. A little colony, the members of which are probably mostly known to one another in advance, settle in what is almost, or quite, a wilderness. From belief in its benefits and by tradition, chiefly religious, they wish their children to know at least how to read, write, and figure. Families can only rarely provide a tutor; the neighbors over a certain area, in New England an area smaller even than the township, combine in a "school district." They get a schoolhouse built, perhaps by their own labor, and hire a teacher by means of a committee, and the teacher is paid from the taxes. Custom determines the limited course of study, and tradition the methods of the teacher, modified by whatever personal insight and skill he may bring to bear. The wilderness is gradually subdued; a network of highways, then of railways, unite the previously scattered communities. Large cities grow up; studies grow more numerous and methods more carefully scrutinized. The larger unit, the state, but not the federal state, provides schools for training teachers and their qualifications are more carefully looked into and tested. But subject to certain quite general conditions imposed by the state-legislature, but not the national state, local maintenance and control remain the rule. The community pattern is more complicated, but is not destroyed. The instance seems richly instructive as to the state of affairs under which our borrowed, English, political institutions were reshaped and forwarded.

We have inherited, in short, local town-meeting practices and ideas. But we live and act and have our being in a continental national state. We are held together by nonpolitical bonds, and the political forms are stretched and legal institutions patched in an ad hoc and improvised manner to do the work they have to do. Political structures fix the channels in which nonpolitical, industrialized currents flow. Railways, travel and transportation, commerce, the mails, telegraph and telephone, newspapers, create enough similarity of ideas and sentiments to keep the thing going as a whole, for they create interaction and interdependence. The unprecedented thing is that states, as distinguished from military empires, can exist over such a wide area. The notion of maintaining a unified state, even nominally self-governing, over a country as extended as the United States and consisting of a large and racially diversified population would once have seemed the wildest of fancies. It was assumed that such a state could be found only in territories hardly larger than a city-state and with a homogeneous population. It seemed almost self-evident to Plato—as to Rousseau later—that a genuine state could hardly be larger than the number of persons capable of personal acquaintance with one another. Our modern state unity is due to the consequences of technology employed so as to facilitate the rapid and easy circulation of opinions and information, and so as to generate constant and intricate interaction far beyond the limits of face-to-face communities. Political and legal forms have only piecemeal and haltingly, with great lag, accommodated themselves to the industrial transformation. The elimination of distance, at the base of which are physical agencies, has called into being the new form of political association.

The wonder of the performance is the greater because of the odds against which it has been achieved. The stream of immigrants which has poured in is so large and heterogeneous that under conditions which formerly obtained it would have disrupted any semblance of unity as surely as the migratory invasion of alien hordes once upset the social equilibrium of the European continent. No deliberately adopted measures could have accomplished what has actually happened. Mechanical forces have operated, and it is no cause for surprise if the effect is more mechanical than vital. The reception of new elements of population in large number from heterogeneous peoples, often hostile to one another at home, and the welding them into even an outward show of unity is an extraordinary feat. In many respects, the consolidation has occurred so rapidly and ruthlessly that much of value has been lost which different peoples might have contributed. The creation of political unity has also promoted social and intellectual uniformity, a standardization favorable to mediocrity. Opinion has been regimented as well as outward behavior. The temper and flavor of the pioneer have evaporated with extraordinary rapidity; their precipitate, as is often noted, is apparent only in the wild-west romance and the movie. What Bagehot called the cake of custom formed with increasing acceleration, and the cake is too often flat and soggy. Mass production is not confined to the factory.

The resulting political integration has confounded the expectations of earlier critics of popular government as much as it must surprise its early backers if they are gazing from on high upon the present scene. The critics predicted disintegration, instability. They foresaw the new society falling apart, dissolving into mutually repellent animated grains of sand. They, too, took seriously the theory of "Individualism" as the basis of democratic government. A stratification of society into immemorial classes within which each person performed his stated duties according to his fixed position seemed to them the only warrant of stability. They had no faith that human beings released from the pressure of this system could hold together in any unity. Hence they prophesied a flux of governmental régimes, as individuals formed factions, seized power, and then lost it as some newly improvised faction proved stronger. Had the facts conformed to the theory of Individualism, they would doubtless have been right. But, like the authors of the theory, they ignored the technological forces making for consolidation.

In spite of attained integration, or rather perhaps because of its nature, the Public seems to be lost; it is certainly bewildered.[1] The government, officials and their activities, are plainly with us. Legislatures make laws with luxurious abandon; subordinate officials engage in a losing struggle to enforce some of them; judges on the bench deal as best they can with the steadily mounting pile of disputes that come before them. But where is the public which these officials are supposed to represent ? How much more is it than geographical names and official titles? The United States, the state of Ohio or New York, the county of this and the city of that? Is the public much more than what a cynical diplomat once called Italy: a geographical expression? Just as philosophers once imputed a substance to qualities and traits in order that the latter might have something in which to inhere and thereby gain a conceptual solidity and consistency which they lacked on their face, so perhaps our political "common sense" philosophy imputes a public only to support and substantiate the behavior of officials. How can the latter be public officers, we despairingly ask, unless there is a public? If a public exists, it is surely as uncertain about its own whereabouts as philosophers since Hume have been about the residence and makeup of the self. The number of voters who take advantage of their majestic right is steadily decreasing in proportion to those who might use it. The ratio of actual to eligible voters is now about one-half. In spite of somewhat frantic appeal and organized effort, the endeavor to bring voters of a robber band may express his powers in a way consonant with belonging to that group and be directed by the interest common to its members. But he does so only at the cost of repression of those of his potentialities which can be realized only through membership in other groups. The robber band cannot interact flexibly with other groups; it can act only through isolating itself. It must prevent the operation of all interests save those which circumscribe it in its separateness. But a good citizen finds his conduct as a member of a political group enriching and enriched by his participation in family life, industry, scientific and artistic associations. There is a free give-and-take: Fullness of integrated personality is therefore possible of achievement, since the pulls and responses of different groups reinforce one another and their values accord.

Regarded as an idea, democracy is not an alternative to other principles of associated life. It is the idea of community life itself. It is an ideal in the only intelligible sense of an ideal: namely, the tendency and movement of something which exists carried to its final limit, viewed as completed, perfected. Since things do not attain such fulfillment but are in actuality distracted and interfered with, democracy in this sense is not a fact and never will be. But neither in this sense is there or has there ever been anything which is a community in its full measure, a community unalloyed by alien elements. The idea or ideal of a community presents, however, actual phases of associated life as they are freed from restrictive and disturbing elements, and are contemplated as having attained their limit of development. Wherever there is conjoint activity whose consequences are appreciated as good by all singular persons who take part in it, and where the realization of the good is such as to effect an energetic desire and effort to sustain it in being just because it is a good shared by all, there is in so far a community. The clear consciousness of a communal life, in all its implications, constitutes the idea of democracy.

Only when we start from a community as a fact, grasp the fact in thought so as to clarify and enhance its constituent elements, can we reach an idea of democracy which is not utopian. The conceptions and shibboleths which are traditionally associated with the idea of democracy take on a veridical and directive meaning only when they are construed as marks and traits of an association which realizes the defining characteristics of a community. Fraternity, liberty, and equality isolated from communal life are hopeless abstractions. Their separate assertion leads to mushy sentimentalism or else to extravagant and fanatical violence which in the end defeats its own aims. Equality then becomes a creed of mechanical identity which is false to facts and impossible of realization. Effort to attain it is divisive of the vital bonds which hold men together; as far as it puts forth issue, the outcome is a mediocrity in which good is common only in the sense of being average and vulgar. Liberty is then thought of as independence of social ties, and ends in dissolution and anarchy. It is more difficult to sever the idea of brotherhood from that of a community, and hence it is either practically ignored in the movements which identify democracy with Individualism, or else it is a sentimentally appended tag. In its just connection with communal experience, fraternity is another name for the consciously appreciated goods which accrue from an association in which all share, and which give direction to the conduct of each. Liberty is that secure release and fulfillment of personal potentialities which take place only in rich and manifold association with others: the power to be an individualized self making a distinctive contribution and enjoying in its own way the fruits of association. Equality denotes the unhampered share which each individual member of the community has in the consequences of associated action. It is equitable because it is measured only by the need and capacity to utilize, not by extraneous factors which deprive one in order that another may take and have. A baby in the family is equal with others, not because of some antecedent and structural quality which is the same as that of others, but insofar as his needs for care and development are attended to without being sacrificed to the superior strength, possessions, and matured abilities of others. Equality does not signify that kind of mathematical or physical equivalence in virtue of which any one element may be substituted for another. It denotes effective regard for whatever is distinctive and unique in each, irrespective of physical and psychological inequalities. It is not a natural possession but is a fruit of the community when its action is directed by its character as a community.

Associated or joint activity is a condition of the creation of a community. But association itself is physical and organic, while communal life is moral, that is emotionally, intellectually, consciously sustained. Human beings combine in behavior as directly and unconsciously as do atoms, stellar masses, and cells; as directly and unknowingly as they divide and repel. They do so in virtue of their own structure, as man and woman unite, as the baby seeks the breast and the breast is there to supply its need. They do so from external circumstances, pressure from without, as atoms combine or separate in the presence of an electric charge, or as sheep huddle together from the cold. Associated activity needs no explanation; things are made that way. But no amount of aggregated collective action of itself constitutes a community. For beings who observe and think, and whose ideas are absorbed by impulses and become sentiments and interests, "we" is as inevitable as "I." But "we" and "our" exist only when the consequences of combined action are perceived and become an object of desire and effort, just as "I" and "mine" appear on the scene only when a distinctive share in mutual action is consciously asserted or claimed. Human associations may be ever so organic in origin and firm in operation, but they develop into societies in a human sense only as their consequences, being known, are esteemed and sought for. Even if "society" were as much an organism as some writers have held, it would not on that account be society. Interactions, transactions, occur de facto and the results of interdependence follow. But participation in activities and sharing in results are additive concerns. They demand *communication* as a prerequisite.

Combined activity happens among human beings; but when nothing else happens it passes as inevitably into some other mode of interconnected activity as does the interplay of iron and the oxygen of water. What takes place is wholly describable in terms of energy, or, as we say in the case of human interactions, of force. Only when there exist *signs or symbols* of activities and of their outcome can the flux be viewed as from without, be arrested for consideration and esteem, and be regulated. Lightning strikes and rives a tree or rock, and the resulting fragments take up and continue the process of interaction, and so on and on. But when phases of the process are represented by signs, a new medium is interposed. As symbols are related to one another, the important relations of a course of events are recorded and are preserved as meanings. Recollection and foresight are possible; the new medium facilitates calculation, planning, and a new kind of action which intervenes in what happens to direct its course in the interest of what is foreseen and desired.

Symbols in turn depend upon and promote communication. The results of conjoint experience are considered and transmitted. Events cannot be passed from one to another, but meanings may be shared by means of signs. Wants and impulses are then attached to common meanings. They are thereby transformed into desires and purposes, which, since they implicate a common or mutually understood meaning, present new ties, converting a conjoint activity into a community of interest and endeavor. Thus there is generated what, metaphorically, may be termed a general will and social consciousness: desire and choice on the part of individuals in behalf of activities that, by means of symbols, are communicable and shared by all concerned. A community thus presents an order of energies transmuted into one of meanings which are appreciated and mutually referred by each to every other on the part of those engaged in combined action. "Force" is not eliminated but is transformed in use and direction by ideas and sentiments made possible by means of symbols.

The work of conversion of the physical and organic phase of associated behavior into a community of action saturated and regulated by mutual interest in shared meanings, consequences which are translated into ideas and desired objects by means of symbols, does not occur all at once nor completely. At any given time, it sets a problem rather than marks a settled achievement. We are born organic beings associated with others, but we are not born members of a community. The young have to be brought within the traditions, outlook, and interests which characterize a community by means of education: by unremitting instruction and by learning in connection with the phenomena of overt association. Everything which is distinctively human is learned, not native, even though it could not be learned without native structures which mark man off from other animals. To learn in a human way and to human effect is not just to acquire added skill through refinement of original capacities.

To learn to be human is to develop through the give-and-take of communication an effective sense of being an individually distinctive member of a community; one who understands and appreciates its beliefs, desires, and methods, and who contributes to a further conversion of organic powers into human resources and values. But this translation is never finished. The old Adam, the unregenerate element in human nature, persists. It shows itself wherever the method obtains of attaining results by use of force instead of by the method of communication and enlightenment. It manifests itself more subtly, pervasively, and effectually when knowledge and the instrumentalities of skill which are the product of communal life are employed in the service of wants and impulses which have not themselves been modified by reference to a shared interest. To the doctrine of "natural" economy which held that commercial exchange would bring about such an interdependence that harmony would automatically result, Rousseau gave an adequate answer in advance. He pointed out that interdependence provides just the situation which makes it possible and worthwhile for the stronger and abler to exploit others for their own ends, to keep others in a state of subjection where they can be utilized as animated tools. The remedy he suggested, a return to a condition of independence based on isolation, was hardly seriously meant. But its desperateness is evidence of the urgency of the problem. Its negative character was equivalent to surrender of any hope of solution. By contrast, it indicates the nature of the only possible solution: the perfecting of the means and ways of communication of meanings so that genuinely shared interest in the consequences of interdependent activities may inform desire and effort and thereby direct action.

This is the meaning of the statement that the problem is a moral one dependent upon intelligence and education. We have in our prior account sufficiently emphasized the role of technological and industrial factors in creating the Great Society. What was said may even have seemed to imply acceptance of the deterministic version of an economic interpretation of history and institutions. It is silly and futile to ignore and deny economic facts. They do not cease to operate because we refuse to note them, or because we smear them over with sentimental idealizations. As we have also noted, they generate as their result overt and external conditions of action and these are known with various degrees of adequacy. What actually happens in consequence of industrial forces is dependent upon the presence or absence of perception and communication of consequences, upon foresight and its effect upon desire and endeavor. Economic agencies produce one result when they are left to work themselves out on the merely physical level, or on that level modified only as the knowledge, skill, and technique which the community has accumulated are transmitted to its members unequally and by chance. They have a different outcome in the degree in which knowledge of consequences is equitably distributed, and action is animated by an informed and lively sense of a shared interest. The doctrine of economic interpretation as usually stated ignores the transformation which meanings may effect; it passes over the new medium which communication may interpose between industry and its eventual consequences. It is obsessed by the illusion which vitiated the "natural economy": an illusion due to failure to note the difference made in action by perception and publication of its consequences, actual and possible. It thinks in terms of antecedents, not of the eventual; of origins, not fruits.

We have returned, through this apparent excursion, to the question in which our earlier discussion culminated: What are the conditions under which it is possible for the Great Society to approach more closely and vitally the status of a Great Community, and thus take form in genuinely democratic societies and state? What are the conditions under which we may reasonably picture the Public emerging from its eclipse?

The study will be an intellectual or hypothetical one. There will be no attempt to state how the required conditions might come into existence, nor to prophesy that they will occur. The object of the analysis will be to show that *unless* ascertained specifications are realized, the Community cannot be organized as a democratically effective Public. It is not claimed that the conditions which will be noted will suffice, but only that at least they are indispensable. In other words, we shall endeavor to frame a hypothesis regarding the democratic state to stand in contrast with the earlier doctrine which has been nullified by the course of events.

Two essential constituents in that older theory, as will be recalled, were the notions that each individual is of himself equipped with the intelligence needed, under the operation of self-interest, to engage in political affairs; and that general suffrage, frequent elections of officials and majority rule are sufficient to ensure the responsibility of elected rulers to the desires and interests of the public. As we shall see, the second conception is logically bound up with the first and stands least render us wary of any definition of an individual which operates in terms of separateness. A *distinctive* way of behaving in conjunction and *connection* with other distinctive ways of acting, not a self-enclosed way of acting, independent of everything else, is that toward which we are pointed. Any human being is in one respect an association, consisting of a multitude of cells each living its own life. And as the activity of each cell is conditioned and directed by those with which it interacts, so the human being whom we fasten upon as individual *par excellence* is moved and regulated by his associations with others; what he does and what the consequences of his behavior are, what his experience consists of, cannot even be described, much less accounted for, in isolation.

But while associated behavior is, as we have already noted, a universal law, the fact of association does not of itself make a society. This demands, as we have also seen, perception of the consequences of a joint activity and of the distinctive share of each element in producing it. Such perception creates a common interest; that is concern on the part of each in the joint action and in the contribution of each of its members to it. Then there exists something truly social and not merely associative. But it is absurd to suppose that a society does away with the traits of its own constituents so that it can be set over against them. It can only be set over against the traits which they and their like present in some *other* combination. A molecule of oxygen in water may act in certain respects differently than it would in some other chemical union. But as a constituent of water it acts as water does as long as water is water. The only intelligible distinction which can be drawn is between the behaviors of oxygen in *its* different relations, and between those of water in *its* relations to various conditions, not between that of water and the oxygen which is conjoined with hydrogen in water.

A single man when he is joined in marriage is different in that connection to what he was as single or to what he is in some other union, as a member, say, of a club. He has new powers and immunities, new responsibilities. He can be contrasted with *himself* as he behaves in other connections. He may be compared and contrasted with his wife in their distinctive roles within the union. But as a member of the union he cannot be treated as antithetical to the union in which he belongs. As a member of the union, his traits and acts are evidently those which he possesses in virtue of it, while those of the integrated association are what they are in virtue of his status in the union. The only reason we fail to see this, or are confused by the statement of it, is because we pass so easily from the man in one connection to the man in some other connection, to the man not as husband but as businessman, scientific investigator, church member, or citizen, in which connections, his acts, and their consequences are obviously different to those due to union in wedlock.

A good example of the fact and of the current confusion as to its interpretation is found in the case of associations known as limited liability joint-stock companies. A corporation as such is an integrated collective mode of action having powers, rights, duties, and immunities different from those of its singular members *in their other connections*. Its different constituents also have diverse statuses—for example, the owners of stock from the officers and directors in certain matters. If we do not bear the facts steadily in mind, it is easy—as frequently happens—to create an artificial problem. Since the corporation can do things which its individual members, *in their many relationships outside of their connections in the corporation*, cannot do, the problem is raised as to the relation of the corporate collective union to that of individuals *as such*. It is forgotten that as members of the corporation the individuals themselves are different, have different characteristics, rights and duties, than they would possess if they were not its members and different from those which they possess in other forms of conjoint behavior. But what the individuals may do legitimately *as* members of the corporation in their respective corporate roles, the corporation does, and vice versa. A collective unity may be taken *either* distributively or collectively, but when taken collectively it is the union of its distributive constituents, and when taken distributively, it is a distribution of and within the collectivity. It makes nonsense to set up an antithesis between the distributive phase and the collective. An individual cannot be opposed to the association of which he is an integral part nor can the association be set against its integrated members.

But groups may be opposed to one another, and individuals may be opposed to one another; and an individual as a member of different groups may be divided within himself, and in a true sense have conflicting selves, or be a relatively disintegrated individual. A man may be one thing as a church member and another thing as a member of the business community. The difference may be carried as if in watertight compartments, or it may become such a division as to entail internal conflict. In these facts we have the ground of the common antithesis set up between society and the individual. Then "society" becomes an unreal abstraction and "*the* individual" an equally unreal one. Because an individual can be disassociated from this, that, and the other grouping, since he need not be married, or be a church member or a voter, or belong to a club or scientific organization, there grows up in the mind an image of a residual individual who is not a member of any association at all. From this premise, and from this only, there develops the unreal question of how individuals come to be united in societies and groups: *the* individual and *the* social are now opposed to each other, and there is the problem of "reconciling" them. Meanwhile, the genuine problem is that of adjusting groups and individuals to one another.

The unreal problem becomes particularly acute, as we have already noted in another connection, in times of rapid social change, as when a newly forming industrial grouping with its special needs and energies finds itself in conflict with old established political institutions and their demands. Then it is likely to be forgotten that the actual problem is one of reconstruction of the ways and forms in which men unite in associated activity. The scene presents itself as the struggle of the individual as such to liberate himself from society as such and to claim his inherent or "natural" self-possessed and self-sufficing rights. When the new mode of economic association has grown strong and exercises an overweening and oppressive power over other groupings, the old fallacy persists. The problem is now conceived as that of bringing individuals as such under the control of society as a collectivity. It should still be put as a problem of readjusting social relationships; or, from the distributive side, as that of securing a more equable liberation of the powers of all individual members of all groupings.

Thus our excursion has brought us back to the theme of method, in the interest of which the excursion was taken. One reason for the comparative sterility of discussion of social matters is because so much intellectual energy has gone into the supposititious problem of the relations of individualism and collectivism at large, wholesale, and because the image of the antithesis infects so many specific questions. Thereby thought is diverted from the only fruitful questions, those of investigation into factual subject matter, and becomes a discussion of concepts. The "problem" of the relation of the concept of authority to that of freedom, of personal rights to social obligations, with only a subsumptive illustrative reference to empirical facts, has been substituted for inquiry into the *consequences* of some particular distribution, under given conditions, of specific freedoms and authorities, and for inquiry into what altered distribution would yield more desirable consequences.

As we saw in our early consideration of the theme of the public, the question of what transactions should be left as far as possible to voluntary initiative and agreement and what should come under the regulation of the public is a question of time, place, and concrete conditions that can be known only by careful observation and reflective investigation. For it concerns consequences; and the nature of consequences and the ability to perceive and act upon them varies with the industrial and intellectual agencies which operate. A solution, or distributive adjustment, needed at one time is totally unfitted to another situation. That social "evolution" has been either from collectivism to individualism or the reverse is sheer superstition. It has consisted in a continuous redistribution of social integrations on the one hand and of capacities and energies of individuals on the other. Individuals find themselves cramped and depressed by absorption of...

[1]See Walter Lippmann's "The Phantom Public." To this as well as to his "Public Opinion," I wish to acknowledge my indebtedness, not only as to this particular point, but for ideas involved in my entire discussion even when it reaches conclusions diverging from his.

Three Workers

Studs Terkel

I. Terry Mason, Airline Stewardess

She has been an airline stewardess for six years. She is twenty-six-years old, recently married. The majority of airline stewardesses are from small towns. I myself am from Nebraska. It's supposed to be one of the nicest professions for a woman—if she can't be a model or in the movies. All the great benefits: flying around the world, meeting all those people. It is a nice status symbol.

"I have five older sisters and they were all married before they were twenty. The minute they got out of high school, they would end up getting married. That was the thing everybody did, was get married. When I told my parents I was going to the airlines, they got excited. They were so happy that one of the girls could go out and see the world and spend some time being single. I didn't get married until I was almost twenty-five. My mother especially thought it would be great that I could have the ambition, the nerve to go to the big city on my own and try to accomplish being a stewardess."

When people ask you what you're doing and you say stewardess, you're really proud, you think it's great. It's like a stepping stone. The first two months I started flying I had already been to London, Paris, and Rome. And me from Broken Bow, Nebraska. But after you start working, it's not as glamorous as you thought it was going to be.

They like girls that have a nice personality and that are pleasant to look at. If a woman has a problem with blemishes, they take her off. Until the appearance counselor thinks she's ready to go back on. One day this girl showed up, she had a very slight black eye. They took her off. Little things like that.

We had to go to stew school for five weeks. We'd go through a whole week of makeup and poise. I didn't like this. They make you feel like you've never been out in public. They showed you how to smoke a cigarette, when to smoke a cigarette, how to look at a man's eyes. Our teacher, she had this idea we had to be sexy. One day in class she was showing us how to accept a light for a cigarette from a man and never blow it out. When he lights it, just look in his eyes. It was really funny, all the girls laughed.

It's never proper for a woman to light her own cigarette. You hold it up and of course you're out with a guy who knows the right way to light the cigarette. You look into their eyes as they're lighting your cigarette and you're cupping his hand, but holding it just very light, so that he can feel your touch and your warmth. (Laughs.) You do not blow the match out. It used to be really great for a woman to blow the match out when she looked in his eyes, but she said now the man blows the match out.

The idea is not to be too obvious about it. They don't want you to look too forward. That's the whole thing, being a lady but still giving out that womanly appeal, like the body movement and the lips and the eyes. The guy's supposed to look in your eyes. You could be a real mean woman. You're a lady and doing all these evil things with your eyes.

Excerpt from *Working: People Talk About What They Do All Day and How They Feel About What They Do.* Copyright © 1996 by Studs Terkel. Reprinted by permission of The New Press. www.thenewpress.com

She did try to promote people smoking. She said smoking can be part of your conversation. If you don't know what to say, you can always pull out a cigarette. She says it makes you more comfortable. I started smoking when I was on the airlines.

Our airline picks the girl-next-door type. At one time they wouldn't let us wear false eyelashes and false fingernails. Now it's required that you wear false eyelashes, and if you do not have the right length nails, you wear false nails. Everything is supposed to be becoming to the passenger.

That's the whole thing: meeting all these great men that either have great business backgrounds or good looking or different. You do meet a lot of movie stars and a lot of political people, but you don't get to really visit with them that much. You never really get to go out with these men. Stewardesses are impressed only by name people. But a normal millionaire that you don't know you're not impressed about. The only thing that really thrills a stewardess is a passenger like Kennedy or movie stars or somebody political. Celebrities.

I think our average age is twenty-six. But our supervisors tell us what kind of makeup to wear, what kind of lipstick to wear, if our hair is not the right style for us, if we're not smiling enough. They even tell us how to act when you're on a pass. Like last night I met my husband. I was in plain clothes. I wanted to kiss him. But I'm not supposed to kiss anybody at the terminal. You're not supposed to walk off with a passenger, hand in hand. After you get out of the terminal, that's all yours.

The majority of passengers do make passes. The ones that do make passes are married and are business people. When I tell them I'm married, they say, "I'm married and you're married and you're away from home and so am I and nobody's gonna find out." The majority of those who make passes at you, you wouldn't accept a date if they were friends of yours at home.

After I was a stewardess for a year, and I was single, I came down to the near North Side of Chicago, which is the swinging place for singles. Stewardess, that was a dirty name. In a big city, it's an easy woman. I didn't like this at all. All these books—*Coffee, Tea and Me.*

I lived in an apartment complex where the majority there were stewardesses.[1] The other women were secretaries and teachers. They would go to our parties and they would end up being among the worst. They never had stories about these secretaries and nurses, but they sure had good ones about stewardesses.

I meet a lot of other wives or single women. The first minute they start talking to me, they're really cold. They think the majority of stewardesses are snobs or they may be jealous. These women think we have a great time, that we are playgirls, that we have the advantage to go out with every type of man we want. So when they first meet us, they really turn off on us.

When you first start flying, the majority of girls do live in apartment complexes by the airport. The men they meet are airport employees: ramp rats, cleaning airplanes and things like that, mechanics, and young pilots, not married, ones just coming in fresh.

After a year we get tired of that, so we move into the city to get involved with men that are usually young executives, like at Xerox or something. Young businessmen in the early thirties and late twenties, they really think stewardesses are the gals to go out with if they want to get so far. They wear their hats and their suits and in the winter their black gloves. The women are getting older, they're getting twenty-four, twenty-five. They get involved with bartenders too. Stewardesses and bartenders are a pair. (Laughs.)

One time I went down into the area of swinging bars with two other girls. We just didn't want anybody to know that we were stewardesses, so we had this story made up that we were going to a women's college in Colorado. That went over. We had people that were talking to us, being nice to us, being polite. Down there, they wouldn't even be polite. They'd buy you drinks but then they'd steal your stool if you got up to go to the restroom. But when they knew you weren't stewardesses, just young ladies that were going to a women's college, they were really nice to us.

They say you can spot a stewardess by the way she wears her makeup. At that time we all had short hair and everybody had it cut in stew school exactly alike. If there's two blondes that have their hair cut very short, wearing the same shade of makeup, and they get into uniform, people say, "Oh, you look like sisters." Wonder why? (Laughs.)

The majority of us were against it because they wouldn't let you say how *you'd* like your hair cut, they wouldn't let you have your own personality, *your* makeup, *your* clothes. They'd tell you what length skirts to wear. At one time they told us we couldn't wear anything one inch above the knees. And no pants at that time. It's different now.

Wigs used to be forbidden. Now it's the style. Now it's permissible for nice women to wear wigs, eyelashes, and false fingernails. Before it was the harder looking women that wore them. Women showing up in pants, it wasn't ladylike. Hot pants are in now. Most airlines change style every year.

She describes stewardess schools in the past as being like college dorms: it was forbidden to go out during the week; signing in and out on Friday and Saturday nights. "They've cut down stewardess school quite a bit. Cut down on how-to-serve-meal classes and paperwork. A lot of girls get on aircraft these days and don't know where a magazine is, where the tray tables are for passengers. . . . Every day we used to have an examination. If you missed over two questions, that was a failure. They'd ask us ten questions. If you failed two tests out of the whole five weeks, you would have to leave. Now they don't have any exams at all. Usually we get a raise every year. We haven't been getting that lately."

We have long duty hours. We can be on duty for thirteen hours. But we're not supposed to fly over eight hours. This is in a twenty-four-hour period. During the eight hours, you could be flying from Chicago to Flint, to Moline, short runs. You stop twenty minutes. So you get to New York finally, after five stops, let's say. You have an hour on your own. But you have to be on the plane thirty minutes before departure time. How many restaurants can serve you food in thirty minutes? So you've gone thirteen hours, off and on duty, having half-hours and no time to eat. This is the normal thing. If we have only thirty minutes and we don't have time to eat, it's our hard luck.

Pilots have the same thing too. They end up grabbing a sandwich and eating in the cockpit. When I first started flying we were not supposed to eat at all on the aircraft, even though there was an extra meal left over. Now we can eat in the buffet. We have to stand there with all those dirty dishes and eat our meals—if there's one left over. We cannot eat in the public eye. We cannot bring it out if there's an extra seat. You can smoke in the cockpit, in the restrooms, but not in the public's eye.

"We have a union. It's a division of the pilots union. It helps us out on duty time and working privileges. It makes sure that if we're in Cleveland and stuck because of weather and thirteen hours have gone by, we can go to bed. Before we had a union the stew office would call and say, 'You're working another seven.' I worked one time thirty-six hours straight."

The other day I had fifty-five minutes to serve 101 coach passengers, a cocktail and full-meal service. You do it fast and terrible. You're very rude. You don't mean to be rude, you just don't have time to answer questions. You smile and you just ignore it. You get three drink orders in a hurry. There's been many times when you miss the glass, pouring, and you pour it in the man's lap. You just don't say I'm sorry. You give him a cloth and you keep going. That's the bad part of the job.

Sometimes I get tired of working first class. These people think they're great, paying for more, and want more. Also I get tired of coach passengers asking for something that he thinks he's a first-class passenger. We get this attitude of difference from our airlines. They're just dividing the class of people. If we're on a first-class pass, the women are to wear a dress or a nice pants suit that has a matching jacket, and the men are to dress with suit jacket and tie and white shirt. And yet so many types of first-class passengers: some have grubby clothes, jeans and moccasins and everything. They can afford to dress the way they feel. . . .

If I want to fly first class, I pay the five dollars difference. I like the idea of getting free drinks, free champagne, free wine. In a coach, you don't. A coach passenger might say, "Could I have a pillow?" So you give him a pillow. Then he'll say, "Could you bring me a glass of water?" A step behind him there's the water fountain. In first class, if the guy says, "I want a glass of water," even if the water fountain is right by his arm, you'd bring it for him. We give him all this extra because he's first class. Which isn't fair. . . .

When you're in a coach, you feel like there's just heads and heads and heads of people. That's all you can see. In first class, being less people, you're more relaxed, you have more time. When you get on a 727, we have one coatroom. Our airline tells us you hang up first-class coats only. When a coach passenger says, "Could you hang up my coat?" most of the time I'll hang it up. Why should I hang up first class and not coach?

One girl is for first class only and there's two girls for coach. The senior girl will be first class. That first-class girl gets used to working first class. If she happens to walk through the coach, if someone asks her for something, she'll make the other girls do it. The first stew always stays at the door and welcomes everybody aboard and says good-by to everybody when they leave. That's why a lot of girls don't like to be first class.

There's an old story on the airline. The stewardess asks if he'd like something to drink, him and his wife. He says, "I'd like a martini." The stewardess asks the wife, "Would you like a drink?" She doesn't say anything, and the husband says, "I'm sorry, she's not used to talking to the help." (Laughs.) When I started flying, that was the first story I heard.

I've never had the nerve to speak up to anybody that's pinched me or said something dirty. Because I've always been afraid of these onion letters. These are bad letters. If you get a certain amount of bad letters, you're fired. When you get a bad letter you have to go in and talk to the supervisor. Other girls now, there are many of 'em that are coming around and telling them what they feel. The passenger reacts: She's telling me off! He doesn't believe it. Sometimes the passenger needs it.

One guy got his steak and he said, "This is too medium, I want mine rarer." The girl said, "I'm sorry, I don't cook the food, it's precooked." He picked up the meal and threw it on the floor. She says, "If you don't pick the meal up right now, I'll make sure the crew members come back here and make you pick it up." (With awe) She's talking right back at him and loud, right in front of everybody. He really didn't think she would yell at him. Man, he picked up the meal. . . . The younger girls don't take that guff any more, like we used to. When the passenger is giving you a bad time, you talk back to him.

It's always: the passenger is right. When a passenger says something mean, we're supposed to smile and say, "I understand." We're supposed to *really* smile because stewardesses' supervisors have been getting reports that the girls have been back-talking passengers. Even when they pinch us or say dirty things, we're supposed to smile at them. That's one thing they taught us at stew school. Like he's rubbing your body somewhere, you're supposed to just put his hand down and not say anything and smile at him. That's the main thing, smile.

When I first went to class, they told me I had a crooked smile. She showed me how to smile. She said, "Kinda press a little smile on"—which I did. "Oh, that's great," she said, "that's a *good* smile." But I couldn't do it. I didn't feel like I was doing it on my own. Even if we're sad, we're supposed to have a smile on our face.

I came in after a flight one day, my grandfather had died. Usually they call you up or meet you at the flight and say, "We have some bad news for you." I pick up this piece of paper in my mailbox and it says, "Mother called in. Your grandfather died today." It was written like, say, two cups of sugar. Was I mad! They wouldn't give me time off for the funeral. You can only have time off for your parents or somebody you have lived with. I had never lived with my grandparents. I went anyway.

A lot of our girls are teachers, nurses, everything. They do this part-time, 'cause you have enough time off for another kind of job. I personally work for conventions. I work electronic and auto shows. Companies hire me to stay in their booth and talk about products. I have this speech to tell. At others, all I do is pass out matches or candy. Nowadays every booth has a young girl in it.

People just love to drink on airplanes. They feel adventurous. So you're serving drinks and meals and there's very few times that you can sit down. If she does sit down, she's forgotten how to sit down and talk to passengers. I used to play bridge with passengers. But that doesn't happen any more. We're not supposed to be sitting down, or have a magazine or read a newspaper. If it's a flight from Boston to Los Angeles, you're supposed to have a half an hour talking to passengers. But the only time we can sit down is when we go to the cockpit. You're not supposed to spend any more than five minutes up there for a cigarette.

We could be sitting down on our jump seat and if you had a supervisor on board, she would write you up— for not mixing with the crowd. We're supposed to be told when she walks on board. Many times you don't know. They do have personnel that ride the flights that don't give their names—checking, and they don't tell you about it. Sometimes a girl gets caught smoking in the cabin. Say it's a long flight, maybe a night flight. You're playing cards with a passenger and you say, "Would it bother you if I smoke?" And he says no. She would write you up and get you fired for smoking in the airplane.

They have a limit on how far you can mix. They want you to be sociable, but if he offers you a cigarette, not to take it. When you're outside, they encourage you to take cigarettes.

You give your time to everybody, you share it, not too much with one passenger. Everybody else may be snoring away and there's three guys, maybe military, and they're awake 'cause they're going home and excited. So you're playing cards with 'em. If you have a supervisor on, that would be a no-no. They call a lot of things no-no's.

They call us professional people but they talk to us as very young, childishly. They check us all the time on appearance. They check our weight every month. Even though you've been flying twenty years, they check you and say that's a no-no. If you're not spreading yourself around passengers enough, that's a no-no. Not hanging up first-class passenger's coats, that's a no-no, even though there's no room in the coatroom. You're supposed to somehow make room. If you're a pound over, they can take you off flight until you get under.

Accidents? I've never yet been so scared that I didn't want to get in the airplane. But there've been times at takeoffs, there's been something funny. Here I am thinking, What if I die today? I've got too much to do. I can't die today. I use it as a joke.

I've had emergencies where I've had to evacuate the aircraft. I was coming back from Las Vegas and being a lively stewardess I stayed up all night, gambled. We had a load full of passengers. The captain tells me we're going to have an emergency landing in Chicago because we lost a pin out of the nose gear. When we land, the nose gear is gonna collapse. He wants me to prepare the whole cabin for the landing, but not for two more hours. And not to tell the other stewardesses, because they were new girls and would get all excited. So I had to keep this in me for two more hours, wondering, Am I gonna die today? And this is Easter Sunday. And I was serving the passengers drinks and food and this guy got mad at me because his omelet was too cold. And I was gonna say, "You just wait, buddy, you're not gonna worry about that omelet." But I was nice about it, because I didn't want to have trouble with a passenger, especially when I have to prepare him for an emergency.

I told the passengers over the intercom: "The captain says it's just a precaution, there's nothing to worry about." I'm just gonna explain how to get out of the airplane fast, how to be in a braced position. They can't wear glasses or high heels, purses, things out of aisles, under the seats. And make sure everybody's pretty quiet. We had a blind woman on with a dog. We had to get people to help her off and all this stuff.

They were fantastic. Nobody screamed, cried, or hollered. When we got on the ground, everything was fine. The captain landed perfect. But there was a little jolt, and the passengers started screaming and hollering. They held it all back and all of a sudden we got on the ground, blah.

I was great. (Laughs.) That's what was funny. I thought, I have a husband now. I don't know how he would take it, my dying on an airplane. So I thought, I can't die. When I got on the intercom, I was so calm. Also we're supposed to keep a smile on our face. Even during an emergency, you're supposed to walk through the cabin and make everybody feel comfortable with a smile. When you're on the jump seat everybody's looking at you. You're supposed to sit there, holding your ankles, in a position to get out of that airplane fast with a big fat smile on your face.

Doctors tell stewardesses two bad things about them. They're gonna get wrinkles all over their face because they smile with their mouth and their eyes. And also with the pressurization on the airplane, we're not supposed to get up while we're climbing because it causes varicose veins in our legs. So they say being a stewardess ruins your looks.

A lot of stewardesses wanted to be models. The Tanya girl used to be a stewardess on our airline. A stewardess is what they could get and a model is what they couldn't get. They weren't the type of person, they weren't that beautiful, they weren't that thin. So their second choice would be stewardess.

What did you want to be? I wanted to get out of Broken Bow, Nebraska. (Laughs.)

POSTSCRIPT: *"Everytime I go home, they all meet me at the airplane. Not one of my sisters has been on an airplane. All their children think that Terry is just fantastic, because their mom and dad—my sisters and their husbands—feel so stupid, 'Look at us. I wish I could have done that.' I know they feel bad, that they never had the chance. But they're happy I can come home and tell them about things. I send them things from Europe. They get to tell all their friends that their sister's a stewardess. They get real excited about that. The first thing they come out and say. 'One of my sisters is a stewardess.'*

"My father got a promotion with his company and they wrote in their business news that he had a family of seven, six girls and a boy, and one girl is a stewardess in Chicago. And went on to say what I did, and didn't say a word about anything else."[2]

II. Roberta Victor, Hooker

She had been a prostitute, starting at the age of fifteen. During the first five or six years, she worked as a high-priced call girl in Manhattan. Later she was a streetwalker. . . .

You never used your own name in hustling. I used a different name practically every week. If you got busted, it was more difficult for them to find out who you really were. The role one plays when hustling has nothing to do with who you are. It's only fitting and proper you take another name.

There were certain names that were in great demand. Every second hustler had the name Kim or Tracy or Stacy and a couple others that were in vogue. These were all young women from seventeen to twenty-five, and we picked these very non-ethnic-oriented WASP names, rich names.

A hustler is any woman in American society. I was the kind of hustler who received money for favors granted rather than the type of hustler who signs a lifetime contract for her trick. Or the kind of hustler who carefully reads women's magazines and learns what it is proper to give for each date, depending on how much money her date or trick spends on her.

The favors I granted were not always sexual. When I was a call girl, men were not paying for sex. They were paying for something else. They were either paying to act out a fantasy or they were paying for companionship or they were paying to be seen with a well-dressed young woman. Or they were paying for somebody to listen to them. They were paying for a *lot* of things. Some men were paying for sex that *they* felt was deviant. They were paying so that nobody would accuse them them of being perverted or dirty or nasty. A large proportion of these guys asked things that were not at all deviant. Many of them wanted oral sex. They felt they couldn't ask their wives or girl friends because they'd be repulsed. Many of them wanted somebody to talk dirty to them. Every good call girl in New York used to share her book and we all knew the same tricks.

We know a guy who used to lie in a coffin in the middle of his bedroom and he would see the girl only once. He got his kicks when the door would be open, the lights would be out, and there would be candles in the living room, and all you could see was his coffin on wheels. As you walked into the living room, he'd suddenly sit up. Of course, you screamed. He got his kicks when you screamed. Or the guy who set a table like the Last Supper and sat in a robe and sandals and wanted you to play Mary Magdalene. (Laughs.)

I was about fifteen, going on sixteen. I was sitting in a coffee shop in the Village, and a friend of mine came by. She said; "I've got a cab waiting. Hurry up. You can make fifty dollars in twenty minutes." Looking back, I wonder why I was so willing to run out of the coffee shop, get in a cab, and turn a trick. It wasn't traumatic because my training had been in how to be a hustler anyway.

I learned it from the society around me, just as a woman. We're taught how to hustle, how to attract, hold a man, and give sexual favors in return. The language that you hear all the time, "Don't sell yourself cheap." "Hold out for the highest bidder." "Is it proper to kiss a man good night on the first date?" The implication is it may not be proper on the first date, but if he takes you out to dinner on the second date, it's proper. If he brings you a bottle of perfume on the third date, you should let him touch you above the waist. And go on from here. It's a marketplace transaction.

Somehow I managed to absorb that when I was quite young. So it wasn't even a moment of truth when this woman came into the coffee shop and said; "Come on." I was back in twenty-five minutes and I felt no guilt.

She was a virgin until she was fourteen. A jazz musician, with whom she had fallen in love, avoided her. "So I went out to have sex with somebody to present him with an accomplished fact. I found it nonpleasurable. I did a lot of sleeping around before I ever took money."

A precocious child, she was already attending a high school of demanding academic standards. "I was very lonely. I didn't experience myself as being attractive. I had always felt I was too big, too fat, too awkward, didn't look like a Pepsi-Cola ad, was not anywhere near the American Dream. Guys were mostly scared of me. I was athletic, I was bright, and I didn't know how to keep my mouth shut. I didn't know how to play the games right.

"I understood very clearly they were not attracted to me for what I was, but as a sexual object. I was attractive. The year before I started hustling there were a lot of guys that wanted to go to bed with me. They didn't want to get involved emotionally, but they did want to ball. For a while I was willing to accept that. It was feeling intimacy, feeling close, feeling warm.

"The time spent in bed wasn't unpleasant. It just wasn't terribly pleasant. It was a way of feeling somebody cared about me, at least for a moment. And it mattered that I was there, that I was important. I discovered that in bed it was possible. It was one skill that I had and I was proud of my reputation as an amateur.

"I viewed all girls as being threats. That's what we were all taught. You can't be friends with another woman, she might take your man. If you tell her anything about how you really feel, she'll use it against you. You smile at other girls and you spend time with them when there is nothing better to do, but you would leave any girl sitting anywhere if you had an opportunity to go somewhere with a man. Because the most important thing in life is the way men feel about you."

How could you forget your first trick? (Laughs.) We took a cab to midtown Manhattan, we went to a penthouse. The guy up there was quite well known. What he really wanted to do was watch two women make love, and then he wanted to have sex with me. It was barely sex. He was almost finished by the time we started. He barely touched me and we were finished.

Of course, we faked it, the woman and me. The ethic was: You don't participate in a sexual act with another woman if a trick is watching. You always fake it. You're putting something over on him and he's paying for something he didn't really get. That's the only way you can keep any sense of self-respect.

The call girl ethic is very strong. You were the lowest of the low if you allowed yourself to feel anything with a trick. The bed puts you on their level. The way you maintain your integrity is by acting all the way through. It's not too far removed from what most American women do—which is to put on a big smile and act.

It was a tremendous kick. Here I was doing absolutely nothing, *feeling* nothing, and in twenty minutes I was going to walk out with fifty dollars in my pocket. That just made me feel absolutely marvelous. I came downtown. I can't believe this! I'm not changed, I'm the same as I was twenty minutes ago, except that now I have fifty dollars in my pocket. It really was tremendous status. How many people could make fifty dollars for twenty minutes' work? Folks work for eighty dollars take-home pay. I worked twenty minutes for fifty dollars clear, no taxes, nothing! I was still in school, I was smoking grass, I was shooting heroin, I wasn't hooked yet, and I had money. It was terrific.

After that, I made it my business to let my friend know that I was available for more of these situations. (Laughs.) She had good connections. Very shortly I linked up with a couple of others who had a good call book.

Books of phone numbers are passed around from call girl to call girl. They're numbers of folks who are quite respectable and with whom there is little risk. They're not liable to pull a knife on you, they're not going to cheat you out of money. Businessmen and society figures. There's three or four groups. The wealthy executive, who makes periodic trips into the city and is known to several girls. There's the social figure, whose name appears quite regularly in the society pages and who's a regular one-a-week John. Or there's the quiet, independently wealthy type. Nobody knows how they got their money. I know one of them made his money off munitions in World War II. Then there's the entertainer. There's another crowd that runs around the night spots, the 21 Club. . . .

These were the people whose names you saw in the paper almost every day. But I knew what they were really like. Any John who was obnoxious or aggressive was just crossed out of your book. You passed the word around that this person was not somebody other people should call.

We used to share numbers—standard procedure. The book I had I got from a guy who got it from a very good call girl. We kept a copy of that book in a safe deposit box. The standard procedure was that somebody new gave half of what they got the first time for each number. You'd tell them: "Call so-and-so, that's a fifty-dollar trick." They would give you twenty-five dollars. Then the number was theirs. My first book, I paid half of each trick to the person who gave it to me. After that, it was my book.

The book had the name and phone number coded, the price, what the person wants, and the contact name. For four years I didn't turn a trick for less than fifty dollars. They were all fifty to one hundred dollars and up for twenty minutes, an hour. The understanding is: it doesn't get conducted as a business transaction. The myth is that it's a social occasion.

You're expected to be well dressed, well made up, appear glad to see the man. I would get a book from somebody and I would call and say, "I'm a friend of so-and-so's, and she thought it would be nice if we got together." The next move was his. Invariably he'd say, "Why don't we do that? Tonight or tomorrow night. Why don't you come over for a drink?" I would get very carefully dressed and made up. . . .

There's a given way of dressing in that league—that's to dress well but not ostentatiously. You have to pass doormen, cabdrivers. You have to look as if you belong in those buildings on Park Avenue or Central Park West. You're expected not to look cheap, not to look hard. Youth is the premium. I was quite young, but I looked older, so I had to work very hard at looking my age. Most men want girls who are eighteen. They really want girls who are younger, but they're afraid of trouble.

Preparations are very elaborate. It has to do with beauty parlors and shopping for clothes and taking long baths and spending money on preserving the kind of front that gives you a respectable address and telephone and being seen at the right clubs and drinking at the right bars. And being able to read the newspapers faithfully, so that not only can you talk about current events, you can talk about the society columns as well.

It's a social ritual. Being able to talk about what is happening and learn from this great master, and be properly respectful and know the names that he mentions. They always drop names of their friends, their contacts, and their clients. You should recognize these. Playing a role.. . . .

At the beginning I was very excited. But in order to continue I had to turn myself off. I had to disassociate who I was from what I was doing.

It's a process of numbing yourself. I couldn't associate with people who were not in the life—either the drug life or the hustling life. I found I couldn't turn myself back on when I finished working. When I turned myself off, I was numb—emotionally, sexually numb.

At first I felt like I was putting one over on all the other poor slobs that would go to work at eight-thirty in the morning and come home at five. I was coming home at four in the morning and I could sleep all day. I really thought a lot of people would change places with me because of the romantic image: being able to spend two hours out, riding cabs, and coming home with a hundred dollars. I could spend my mornings doing my nails, going to the beauty parlor, taking long baths, going shopping. . . .

It was usually two tricks a night. That was easily a hundred, a hundred and a quarter. I always had money in my pocket. I didn't know what the inside of a subway smelled like. Nobody traveled any other way except by cab. I ate in all the best restaurants and I drank in all the best clubs. A lot of people wanted you to go out to dinner with them. All you had to do was be an ornament.

Almost all the call girls I knew were involved in drugs. The fast life, the night hours. At after-hours dubs, if you're not a big drinker, you usually find somebody who has cocaine, 'cause that's the big drug in those places. You wake up at noon, there's not very much to do till nine or ten that night. Everybody else is at work, so you shoot heroin. After a while the work became a means of supplying drugs, rather than drugs being something we took when we were bored.

The work becomes boring because you're not part of the life. You're the part that's always hidden. The doormen smirk when you come in, 'cause they know what's going on. The cabdriver, when you give him a certain address—he knows exactly where you're going when you're riding up Park Avenue at ten o'clock at night, for Christ sake. You leave there and go back—to what? Really, to what? To an emptiness. You've got all this money in your pocket and nobody you care about.

When I was a call girl I looked down on streetwalkers. I couldn't understand why anybody would put themselves in that position. It seemed to me to be hard work and very dangerous. What I was doing was basically riskless. You never had to worry about disease. These were folks who you know took care of themselves and saw the doctor regularly. Their apartments were always immaculate and the liquor was always good. They were always polite. You didn't have to ask them for money first. It was always implicit: when you were ready to leave, there would be an envelope under the lamp or there'd be something in your pocketbook. It never had to be discussed.

I had to work an awful lot harder for the same money when I was a streetwalker. I remember having knives pulled on me, broken bottles held over my head, being raped, having my money stolen back from me, having to jump out of a second-story window, having a gun pointed at me.

As a call girl, I had lunch at the same places society women had lunch. There was no way of telling me apart from anybody else in the upper tax bracket. I made my own hours, no more than three or so hours of work an evening. I didn't have to accept calls. All I had to do was play a role.

As a streetwalker, I didn't have to act. I let myself show the contempt I felt for the tricks. They weren't paying enough to make it worth performing for them. As a call girl, I pretended I enjoyed it sexually. You have to act as if you had an orgasm. As a streetwalker, I didn't. I used to lie there with my hands behind my head and do mathematics equations in my head or memorize the keyboard typewriter.

It was strictly a transaction. No conversation, no acting, no myth around it, no romanticism. It was purely a business transaction. You always asked for your money in front. If you could get away without undressing totally, you did that.

It's not too different than the distinction between an executive secretary and somebody in the typing pool. As an executive secretary you really identify with your boss. When you're part of the typing pool, you're a body, you're hired labor, a set of hands on the typewriter. You have nothing to do with whoever is passing the work down to you. You do it as quickly as you can.

What led you to the streets?

My drug habit. It got a lot larger. I started looking bad. All my money was going for drugs. I didn't have any money to spend on keeping myself up and going to beauty parlors and having a decent address and telephone.

If you can't keep yourself up, you can't call on your old tricks. You drop out of circulation. As a call girl, you have to maintain a whole image. The trick wants to know he can call you at a certain number and you have to have a stable address. You must look presentable, not like death on a soda cracker.

I looked terrible. When I hit the streets, I tried to stick to at least twenty dollars and folks would laugh. I needed a hundred dollars a night to maintain a drug habit and keep a room somewhere. It meant turning seven or eight tricks a night. I was out on the street from nine o'clock at night till four in the morning. I was taking subways and eating in hamburger stands.

For the first time I ran the risk of being busted. I was never arrested as a call girl. Every once in a while a cop would get hold of somebody's book. They would call one of the girls and say, "I'm a friend of so-and-so's." They would try to trap them. I never took calls from people I didn't know. But on the streets, how do you know who you're gonna pick up?

As a call girl, some of my tricks were upper echelon cops, not patrolmen. Priests, financiers, garment industry folks, bigtimers. On the street, they ranged from junior executive types, blue-collar workers, upwardly striving postal workers, college kids, suburban white collars who were in the city for the big night, restaurant workers.. . .

You walk a cerain area, usually five or six blocks. It has a couple of restaurants, a couple of bars. There's the step in-between: hanging out in a given bar, where people come to you. I did that briefly.

You'd walk very slowly, you'd stop and look in the window. Somebody would come up to you. There was a ritual here too. The law says in order to arrest a woman for prostitution, she has to mention money and she has to tell you what she'll do for the money. We would keep within the letter of the law, even though the cops never did.

Somebody would come up and say, "It's a nice night, isn't it?" "Yes." They'd say, "Are you busy?" I'd say, "Not particularly." "Would you like to come with me and have a drink?" You start walking and they say, "I have fifteen dollars or twelve dollars and I'm very lonely." Something to preserve the myth. Then they want you to spell out exactly what you're willing to do for the money.

I never approached anybody on the street. That was the ultimate risk. Even if he weren't a cop, he could be some kind of supersquare, who would call a cop. I was trapped by cops several times.

The first one didn't even trap me as a trick. It was three in the morning. I was in Chinatown. I ran into a trick I knew. We made contact in a restaurant. He went home and I followed him a few minutes later. I knew the address. I remember passing a banana truck. It didn't dawn on me that it was strange for somebody to be selling bananas at three in the morning. I spent about twenty minutes with my friend. He paid me. I put the money in my shoe. I opened the door and got thrown back against the wall. The banana salesman was a vice squad cop. He'd stood on the garbage can to peer in the window. I got three years for that one.

I was under age. I was four months short of twenty-one. They sent me to what was then called Girls' Term Court. They wouldn't allow me a lawyer because I wasn't an adult, so it wasn't really a criminal charge. The judge said I was rehabilitable. Instead of giving me thirty days, he gave me three years in the reformatory. It was very friendly of him. I was out on parole a couple of times before I'd get caught and sent back.

I once really got trapped. It was about midnight and a guy came down the street. He said he was a postal worker who just got off the shift. He told me how much money he had and what he wanted. I took him to my room. The cop isn't supposed to undress. If you can describe the color of his shorts, it's an invalid arrest. Not only did he show me the color of his shorts, he went to bed with me. Then he pulled a badge and a gun and busted me.

He lied to me. He told me he was a narc and didn't want to bust me for hustling. If I would tell him who was dealing in the neighborhood, he'd cut me loose. I lied to him, but he won. He got me to walk out of the building past all my friends and when we got to the car, he threw me in. (Laughs.) It was great fun. I did time for that—close to four years.

What's the status of the streetwalker in prison?

It's fine. Everybody there has been hustling. It's status in reverse. Anybody who comes in saying things like they could never hustle is looked down on as being somewhat crazy.

She speaks of a profound love she had for a woman who she's met in prison; of her nursing her lover after the woman had become blind.

"I was out of the country for a couple of years. I worked a house in Mexico. It had heavy velour curtains—a Mexican version of a French whorehouse. There was a reception area, where the men would come and we'd parade in front of them.

"The Mexicans wanted American girls. The Americans wanted Mexican girls. So I didn't get any American tricks. I had to give a certain amount to the house for each trick I turned and anything I negotiated over that amount was mine. It was far less than anything I had taken in the States.

"I was in great demand even though I wasn't a blonde. A girl friend of mine worked there two nights. She was Norwegian and very blonde. Every trick who came in wanted her. Her head couldn't handle it all. She quit after two nights. So I was the only American.

"That was really hard work. The Mexicans would play macho. *American tricks will come as quickly as they can. Mexicans will hold back and make me work for my money. I swear to God they were doing multiplication tables in their heads to keep from having an orgasm. I would use every trick I knew to get them to finish. It was crazy!*

I was teaching school at the same time. I used Alice in Wonderland *as the text in my English class. During the day I tutored English for fifth- and sixth-grade kids. In the evening, I worked in the call house.*

"The junk down there was quite cheap and quite good. My habit was quite large. I loved dope more than anything else around. After a while I couldn't differentiate between working and not working. All men were tricks, all relationships were acting. I was completely turned off."

She quit shooting dope the moment she was slugged, brutally beaten by a dealer who wanted her. This was her revelatory experience. "It was the final indignity. I'd had tricks pulling broken bottles on me, I'd been in razor fights, but nobody had ever hit *me." It was a threat to her status. "I was strong. I could handle myself. A tough broad. This was threatened, so. . ."*

I can't talk for women who were involved with pimps. That was where I always drew the line. I always thought pimps were lower than pregnant cockroaches. I didn't want anything to do with them. I was involved from time to time with some men. They were either selling dope or stealing, but they were not depending on my income. Nor were they telling me to get my ass out on the street. I never supported a man.

As a call girl I got satisfaction, an unbelievable joy—perhaps perverted—in knowing what these reputable folks were really like. Being able to open a newspaper every morning, read about this pillar of society, and know what a pig he really was. The tremendous kick in knowing that I didn't feel anything, that I was acting and they weren't. It's sick, but no sicker than what every woman is taught, all right?

I was in *control* with every one of those relationships. You're vulnerable if you allow yourself to be involved sexually. I wasn't. They were. I called it. Being able to manipulate somebody sexually, I could determine when I wanted that particular transaction to end. 'Cause I could make the guy come. I could play all kinds of games. See? It was a tremendous sense of power.

What I did was no different from what ninety-nine percent of American women are taught to do. I took the money from under the lamp instead of in Arpege. What would I do with 150 bottles of Arpege a week?

You become your job. I became what I did. I became a hustler. I became cold, I became hard, I became turned off, I became numb. Even when I wasn't hustling, I was a hustler. I don't think it's terribly different from somebody who works on the assembly line forty hours a week and comes home cut off, numb, dehumanized. People aren't built to switch on and off like water faucets.

What was really horrifying about jail is that it really isn't horrifying. You adjust very easily. The same thing with hustling. It became my life. It was too much of an effort to try to make contact with another human being, to force myself to care, to feel.

I didn't care about me. It didn't matter whether I got up or didn't get up. I got high as soon as I awoke. The first thing I'd reach for, with my eyes half-closed, was my dope. I didn't like my work. It was messy. That was the biggest feeling about it. Here's all these guys slobbering over you all night long. I'm lying there, doing math or conjugations or Spanish poetry in my head. (Laughs.) And they're slobbering. God! God! What enabled me to do it was being high—high and numb.

The overt hustling society is the microcosm of the rest of the society. The power relationships are the same and the games are the same. Only this one I was in control of. The greater one I wasn't. In the outside society, if I tried to be me, I wasn't in control of anything. As a bright, assertive woman, I had no power. As a cold, manipulative hustler, I had a lot. I knew I was playing a role. Most women are taught to become what they act. All I did was act out the reality of American womanhood.[3]

III. Maggie Holmes, Domestic

What bugs me now, since I'm on welfare, is people saying they give you the money for nothin'. When I think back what we had to come through, up from the South, comin' here. The hard work we had to do. It really gets me, when I hear people . . . It do somethin' to me. I think violence.

I think what we had to work for. I used to work for $1.50 a week. This is five days a week, sometimes six. If you live in the servant quarter, your time is never off, because if they decide to have a party at night, you gotta come out. My grandmother, I remember when she used to work, we'd get milk and a pound of butter. I mean this was pay. I'm thinkin' about what my poor parents worked for, gettin' nothing. What do the white think about when they think? Do they ever think about what *they* would do?

She had worked as a domestic, hotel chambermaid, and as "kitchen help in cafés" for the past twenty-five years, up North and down South. She lives with her four children.

When it come to housework, I can't do it now. I can't stand it, cause it do somethin' to my mind. They want you to clean the house, want you to wash, even the windows, want you to iron. You not supposed to wash no dishes. You ain't supposed to make no beds up. Lots of 'em try to sneak it in on you, think you don't know that. So the doorbell rings and I didn't answer to. The bell's ringin' and I'm still doin' my work. She ask me why I don't answer the bell. I say; "Do I come here to be a butler?" And I don't see myself to be no doormaid. I came to do some work and I'm gonna do my work. When you end up, you's nursemaid, you's cook. They put all this on you. If you want a job to cleanin', you ask for just cleanin'. She wants you to do in one day what she hasn't did all year.

Now this bugs me: the first thing she gonna do is pull out this damn rubber thing—just fittin' for your knees. Knee pads—like you're workin' in the fields, like people pickin' cotton. No mop or nothin'. That's why you find so many black women here got rheumatism in their legs, knees. When you get on that cold floor, I don't care how warm the house is, you can feel the cold on the floor, the water and stuff. I never see nobody on their knees until I come North. In the South, they had mops. Most times, if they had real heavy work, they always had a man to come in. Washin' windows, that's a man's job. They don't think nothin' about askin' you to do that here. They don't have no feeling that that's what bothers you. I think to myself; My God, if I had somebody come and do my floors, clean up for me, I'd appreciate it. They don't say nothin' about it. Act like you haven't even done anything. They has no feelin's.

I worked for one old hen on Lake Shore Drive. You remember that big snow they had there?[4] Remember when you couldn't get there? When I get to work she says: "Call the office." She complained to the lady where I got the job, said I was late to work. So I called. So I said, in the phone (Shouts), *What do you want with me? I got home four black, beautiful kids. Before I go to anybody's job in the morning I see that my kids are at school. I gonna see that they have warm clothes on and they fed.* I'm lookin' right at the woman I'm workin' for. (Laughs.) When I get through the phone I tell this employer: "That goes for you too. The only thing I live for is my kids. There's nothin', you and nobody else." The expression on her face: What is this? (Laughs.) She thought I was gonna be like (mimics "Aunt Jemima"): "Yes ma'am, I'll try to get here a little early." But it wasn't like that. (Laughs.)

When I come in the door that day she told me pull my shoes off. I said, "For what? I can wipe my feet at the door here, but I'm not gettin' out of my shoes, it's cold." She looked at me and said: Oh my God, what I got here? (Laughs.) I'm knowin' I ain't gonna make no eight hours here. I can't take it.

She had everything in there snow white. And that means work, believe me. In the dining room she had a blue set, she had sky-blue chairs. They had a bedroom with pink and blue. I look and say, "I know what this means." It means sho' 'nough—knees. I said, "I'm gonna try and make it today, *if* I can make it." Usually when they're so bad, you have to leave.

I ask her where the mop is. She say she don't have no mop. I said, "Don't tell me you mop the floor on your knees. I know you don't." They usually hid these mops in the clothes closet. I go out behind all these clothes and get the mop out. (Laughs.) They don't get on their knees, but they don't think nothin' about askin' a black woman. She says, "All you—you girls. . . ." She stop. I say, "All you *niggers,* is that what you want to say?" She gives me this stupid look. I say, "I'm glad you tellin' me that there's more like me." (Laughs.) I told her, "You better give me my money and let me go, 'cause I'm gettin' angry." So I made her give me my carfare and what I had worked that day.

Most when you find decent work is when you find one that work themselves. They know what it's like to get up in the morning and go to work. In the suburbs they ain't got nothin' to do. They has nothin' else to think about. Their mind's just about blowed.

It's just like they're talkin' about mental health. Poor people's mental health is different than the rich white. Mine could come from a job or not havin' enough money for my kids. Mine is from me being poor. That don't mean you're sick. His sickness is from money, graftin' where he want more. I don't have *any.* You live like that day to day, penny to penny.

I worked for a woman, her husband's a judge. I cleaned the whole house. When it was time for me to go home, she decided she wants some ironing. She goes in the basement, she turns on the air conditioner. She said, "I think you can go down in the basement and finish your day out. It's air conditioned." I said, "I don't care what you got down there, I'm not ironing. You look at that slip, it says cleanin'. Don't say no ironin'. She wanted me to wash the walls in the bathroom. I said, "If you look at that telephone book they got all kinds of ads there under house cleanin'". She said the same thing as the other one, "All you girls—" I said same thing I said to the other one; "You mean niggers." (Laughs.)

They ever call you by your last name?

Oh God, they wouldn't do that. (Laughs.)

Do you call her by her last name?

Most time I don't call her, period. I don't say anything to her. I don't talk nasty to nobody, but when I go to work I don't talk to people. Most time they don't like what you're gonna say. So I keep quiet.

Most of her jobs were "way out in the suburbs. You get a bus and you ride till you get a subway. After you get to Howard,[5] you gets the El. If you get to the end of the line and there's no bus, they pick you up. I don't like to work in the city, 'cause they don't pay you nothin'. And these old buildings are so nasty. It takes so much time to clean 'em. They are not kept up so good, like suburbs. Most of the new homes out there, it's easier to clean."

A commonly observed phenomenon: during the early evening hour, trains, crowded, predominantly by young white men carrying attaché cases, pass trains headed in the opposite direction, crowded, predominantly by middle-aged black women carrying brown paper bags. Neither group, it appears, glances at the other.

"We spend most of the time ridin'. You get caught goin' out from the suburbs at nighttime, man, you're really sittin' there for hours. There's nothin' movin'. You got a certain hour to meet trains. You get a transfer, you have to get that train. It's a shuffle to get in and out of the job. If you miss that train at five o'clock, what time you gonna get out that end? Sometime you don't get home till eight o'clock.. . . "

You don't feel like washin' your own window when you come from out there, scrubbin'. If you work in one of them houses eight hours, you gotta come home do the same thing over . . . you don't feel like . . . (sighs softly) . . . tired. You gotta come home, take care of your kids, you gotta cook, you gotta wash. Most of the time, you gotta wash for the kids for somethin' to wear to school. You gotta clean up, 'cause you didn't have time in the morning. You gotta wash and iron and whatever you do, nights. You be so tired, until you don't feel like even doin' nothin'.

You get up at six, you fix breakfast for the kids, you get them ready to go on to school. Leave home about eight. Most of the time I make biscuits for my kids, cornbread you gotta make. I don't mean the canned kind. This I don't call cookin', when you go in that refrigerator and get some beans and drop 'em in a pot. And TV dinners, they go stick 'em in the stove and she say she cooked. This is not cookin'.

And *she's* tired. Tired from doin' what? You got a washing dryer, you got an electric sweeper, anything at fingertips. All she gotta do is unfroze 'em, dump 'em in the pot, and she's tired! I go to the store, I get my vegetables, greens, I wash 'em. I gotta pick 'em first. I don't eat none of that stuff, like in the cans. She don't do that, and she says she's tired.

When you work for them, when you get in that house in the morning, boy, they got one arm in their coat and a scarf on their head. And when you open that door, she shoots by you, she's gone. Know what I mean?

They want you to come there and keep the kids and let them get out. What she think about how am I gonna do? Like I gets tired of my kids too. I'd like to go out too. It bugs you to think that they don't have no feelin's about that.

Most of the time I work for them and they be out. I don't like to work for 'em when they be in the house so much. They don't have no work to do. All they do is get on the telephone and talk about one another. Make you sick. I'll go and close the door. They're all the same, everybody's house is the same. You think they rehearse it . . .

When I work, only thing I be worryin' about is my kids. I just don't like to leave 'em too long. When they get out of school, you wonder if they are out on the street. The only thing I worry is if they had a place to play in easy. I always call two, three times. When she don't like you to call, I'm in a hurry to get out of there. (Laughs.) My mind is gettin' home, what are you gonna find to cook before the stores close.

This Nixon was sayin' he don't see nothin' wrong with people doin' scrubbin'. For generations that's all we done. He should know we want to be doctors and teachers and lawyers like him. I don't want my kids to come up and do domestic work. It's degrading. You can't see no tomorrow there. We done this for generation and generation—cooks and butlers all your life. They want their kids to be lawyers, doctors, and things. You don't want 'em in no cafés workin'. . . .

When they say about the neighborhood we live in is dirty, why do they ask me to come and clean their house? We, the people in the slums, the same nasty women they have come to their house in the suburbs every day. If these women are so filthy, why you want them to clean for you? They don't go and clean for us. We go and clean for them.

I worked one day where this white person did some housework. I'm lookin' at the difference how she with me and her. She had a guilt feeling toward that lady. They feel they shouldn't ask them to do this type of work, but they don't mind askin' me.

They want you to get in a uniform. You take me and my mother, she work in what she wear. She tells you, "If that place so dirty where I can't wear my dress, I won't do the job." You can't go to work dressed like they do, 'cause they think you're not working—like you should get dirty, at least. They don't say what kind of uniform, just say uniform. This is in case anybody come in, the black be workin'. They don't want you walkin' around dressed up, lookin' like them. They asks you sometimes, "Don't you have somethin' else to put on?" I say, "No, 'cause I'm not gettin' on my knees."

They move with caution now, believe me. They want to know, "What should I call you?" I say, "Don't call me a Negro, I'm black." So they say, "Okay, I don't want to make you angry with me." (Laughs.) The old-timers, a lot of 'em was real religious. "Lord'll make a way." I say, "I'm makin' my own way." I'm not anti-Bible or anti-God, but I just let 'em know I don't think that way.

The younger women, they don't pay you too much attention. Most of 'em work. The older women, they behind you, wiping. I don't like nobody checkin' behind me. When you go to work, they want to show you how to clean. That really gets me, somebody showin' me how to clean. I have been doin' it all my life. They come and get the rag and show you how to do it. (Laughs.) I stand there, look at 'em. Lotta times I ask her, "You finished?" I say, "If there's anything you gotta go and do, I wish you'd go." I don't need nobody to show me how to clean.

I had them put money down and pretend they can't find it and have me look for it. I worked for one, she had dropped ten dollars on the floor, and I was sweepin' and I'm glad I seen it, because if I had put that sweeper on it, she coulda said I got it. I had to push the couch back and the ten dollars was there. Oh, I had 'em, when you go to dust, they put something . . . to test you.

I worked at a hotel. A hotel's the same thing. You makin' beds, scrubbin' toilets, and things. You gotta put in linens and towels. You still cleanin'. When people come in the room—that's what bugs me—they give you that look: You just a maid. It do somethin' to me. It really gets into me.

Some of the guests are nice. The only thing you try to do is to hurry up and get this bed made and get outa here, 'cause they'll get you to do somethin' else. If they take that room, they want everything they paid for. (Laughs.) They get so many towels, they can't use 'em all. But you gotta put up all those towels. They want that pillow, they want that blanket. You gotta be trottin' back and forth and gettin' all those things.

In the meantime, when they have the hotel full, we put in extra beds—the little foldin' things. They say they didn't order the bed. They stand and look at you like you crazy. Now you gotta take this bed back all the way from the twelfth floor to the second. The guy at the desk, he got the wrong room. He doesn't say, "I made a mistake." You take the blame.

And you get some guys . . . you can't work with afightin' 'em. He'll call down and say he wants some towels. When you knock, he says, "Come in." He's standing there without a stitch of clothes on, buck naked. You're not goin' in there. You only throw those towels and go back. Most of the time you wait till he got out of there.

When somethin's missin', it's always the maid took it. If we find one of those type people, we tell the house lady, "You have to go in there and clean it yourself." If I crack that door, and nobody's in, I wouldn't go in there. If a girl had been in there, they would call and tell you, "Did you see something?" They won't say you got it. It's the same thing. You say no. They say, "It *musta* been in there."

Last summer I worked at a place and she missed a purse. I didn't work on that floor that day. She called the office, "Did you see that lady's purse?" I said, "No, I haven't been in the room." He asked me again, Did I . . . ? I had to stay till twelve o'clock. She found it. It was under some papers. I quit, 'cause they end up sayin' you stole somethin'.

You know what I wanted to do all my life? I wanted to play piano. And I'd want to write songs and things, that's what I really wanted to do. If I could just get myself enough to buy a piano. . . . And I'd like to write about my life, if I could sit long enough: How I growed up in the South and my grandparents and my father—I'd like to do that. I would like to dig up more of black history, too. I would love to for my kids.

Lotta times I'm tellin' 'em about things, they'll be sayin', "Mom, that's olden days." (Laughs.) They don't understand, because it's so far from what's happening now. Mighty few young black women are doin' domestic work. And I'm glad. That's why I want my kids to go to school. This one lady told me, "All you people are gettin' like that." I said, "I'm glad." There's no more gettin' on their knees.

Studs Terkel was born Louis Terkel in New York City in 1912. He was brought up in Chicago, and graduated from the University of Chicago. Terkel has been an actor, playwright, columnist, and disc jockey, but he is best known as the man who makes books out of tape recordings of people he gets to talk. These oral histories are Division Street: America (1966), Hard Times (1970), and Working (1974).

Mary Church Terrell vs. Thomas Nelson Page: Gender, Race, and Class in Anti-Lynching Rhetoric

Martha Solomon Watson

Martha Solomon Watson is Sanford Berman Professor and founding Dean of the Greenspun College of Urban Affairs. Currently, she is a seminarian and postulant for Holy Orders at the Episcopal Theological Seminary of the Southwest in Austin, Texas.

Examining the exchange between Thomas Nelson Page and Mary Church Terrell about lynching in the 1904 North American Review, *this essay considers how her ideological position, which emerged from her gender, race, and class, shaped her response. Although these factors enabled her response and built identification with her audience, the essay argues that they created a "trained incapacity" that led her to reaffirm damaging racial stereotypes and to accentuate class cleavages within her race. Rather than responding to Page's "scurrilous attacks on colored men," Church Terrell reinforced the prejudices she sought to dismantle.*

In January 1904, the *North American Review* published "The Lynching of Negroes: Its Causes and Prevention," by Thomas Nelson Page, a prominent Southern apologist. The essay was one in his series on Southern race relations that appeared later that year as *The Negro: The Southerner's Problem*. Although typical of defenses of lynching in that era, Page's analysis of the problem and his solution outraged Mary Church Terrell, a prominent African American spokeswoman. In her autobiography, Church Terrell recalled Page's essay as "one of the most scurrilous attacks on colored men of this country which has ever appeared in print." Alleging it to be "full of misleading statements from beginning to end," she insisted, "I thought I could not survive if something were not done to correct the impressions that Mr. Page's article had made."[2]

As was common for African Americans in the era, Church Terrell besieged the editor to no avail.[3] But the intervention of her friend William Dean Howells led the editor to reply that he would consider a response, predicating ultimate publication on whether he liked her essay.[4] Apparently, he approved her submission because it appeared in the June issue under the title "Lynching From a Negro's Point of View."[5] Her success in gaining the editor's acquiescence was, in itself, remarkable. Other Page essays had appeared in *McClure's* but, despite a meeting with a magazine representative, Church Terrell was unable to gain access to those pages. As she noted in her daybook, "They wanted nothing controversial."[6]

Page's work reflected white Americans' efforts to rationalize and excuse racial problems, especially lynching. In particular, his essay iterates the prevalent sexual mythology that surrounded the topic: lynchings follow from the rapes of white women by brutal black men. His essay was the sort of casuistry Church Terrell continuously sought to expose in her public advocacy. As Karlyn Kohrs Campbell observes: "She had an unshakable belief that if whites, particularly northern whites, knew and understood the plight of African-Americans, they would act to reaffirm the nation's fundamental values, to remove obstacles to

Republished with permission of Michigan State University Press, from *Rhetoric and Public Affairs, Volume 1, Issue 1* by Martha Solomon Watson. Copyright © 2009 by Michigan State University Press; permission conveyed through Copyright Clearance Center, Inc.

African-American achievement, and to create conditions offering equality of opportunity to all."[7] Church Terrell's comment in her autobiography suggests that her focus would be exploding the mythology Page was exploiting. Her intention to counter his "scurrilous attacks on colored men of this country" triggers this essay. Countering the mythology that incorporated images of African American men as violent sexual predators was the greatest challenge of antilynching activists of her time; thus, her success or failure in dismantling that narrative can shed light on the rhetorical barriers marginalized groups faced and, in many instances, continue to face in public advocacy.

Although several scholars have examined Church Terrell's writings from various perspectives, only Elizabeth McHenry and Karlyn Kohrs Campbell have explored the Page-Church Terrell exchange in some detail.[8] Their foci differ, but they agree about certain aspects of Church Terrell's essay. First, gaining access to the pages of the *NAR* depended on her ability to avoid upsetting both the editors and potential readers. As Kohrs Campbell concludes, "First and foremost, she had to avoid offending editors and Northern, much less Southern, readers, which meant the highly confrontational but perceptive arguments about the economic bases for mob violence and the sexual relationships that lynchings were used to hide, which had been articulated by Ida B. Wells Barnett, were off limits."[9]

Second, as McHenry notes, "Page had the upper hand. He had defined the terms of the argument … try as she might to subtly shift its focus to issues that were of more pressing interest to the African-American community, the topics Page initiated and his perspective were inescapable."[10] In short, both Kohrs Campbell and McHenry agree that to secure publication, Church Terrell had to position her essay as a response; she was not free to craft a statement without regard for his arguments.

McHenry and Kohrs Campbell also concur that Page's depiction of rape as a proximate cause for lynchings presented a compelling narrative. According to Kohrs Campbell, "Page offered a dramatic scenario to engage his readers, a scenario that obscured and overwhelmed those boring *Chicago Tribune* statistics."[11] McHenry characterizes Page's efforts as an "extreme portrayal of southern women as frail, frightened, and fragile victims who needed to be protected by southern white chivalry." Such portrayals, she suggests, served as "a sort of acceptable folk pornography" in the South.[12] Moreover, as Kohrs Campbell notes, Page focuses on "a common scourge that threatens 'their women,' a threat he dramatizes in extreme terms and with detailed examples," a move that both obscures other factors about lynching and unites white Americans.[13]

These analyses of Church Terrell's writings make clear the external challenges she faced as an African-American in getting access to a journal controlled by white Americans and suggest the constraints she as an African-American woman faced writing a response to Page on this topic. And these scholars are clear about the difficulty she encountered in crafting an effective response to Page's "absorbing scenarios of sexual promiscuity, bestiality, and brutality."[14]

Yet, in their efforts to explain Church Terrell's relative impotence in responding to Page—McHenry labels her response "lifeless"—these scholars elide attention to other salient features in Church Terrell's essay that actually reinforced the depictions Page provided.[15] Focusing on the external constraints to her discourse, they fail to consider how her ideology and her commitment to particular gender roles influenced her response.

Church Terrell's response to Page was inevitably situated in the discourse in the African-American community about how best to advance the race and the role women were to play in that progress. The controversy between Booker T. Washington and William E. B. Du Bois is well documented and much discussed. Although impressed with Washington's accomplishments, Church Terrell was an adherent of Du Bois's notions about the importance of the Talented Tenth. Her commitment was to the advancement of her race through and by elite leadership, particularly by women, capable of providing the moral uplift their downtrodden sisters and brothers needed. Her allegiance to this ideology informed her response to Nelson in important ways.

This essay revisits Church Terrell's essay with an eye to understanding how her ideological position, which grew out of her social class, gender, and race, shaped her response in ways that reaffirmed certain scenarios that were compelling to contemporary audiences. Briefly, I will contend that as her gender, race, and social class enabled her response and helped her build identification with her target audience, they also created what Kenneth Burke calls a "trained incapacity" in her public advocacy on this topic.[16] Because her gender and class biases pervade the response to Page, Church Terrell in the end reaffirms the mythology and stereotypes that excused lynching and accentuates class cleavages within her own race. I will argue that her essay, rather than responding to the "scurrilous attacks on colored men," as she had aspired to do, instead reinforced the negative stereotypes to which Page had appealed and that animated resistance to antilynching efforts. In effect, the interplay of gender, race, and class in Church Terrell's essay lent weight to the narrative that dominated public perceptions of lynching rather than dismantling it.

My argument will unfold in several stages. First, I will briefly discuss "lynching" as a social and political trope in post–Civil War America, suggesting the stereotypes and mythology that surrounded it. Then I will consider Page's essay to highlight the play of race, gender, and class issues within it. Next, I will turn to Church Terrell's essay to demonstrate how her class bias informed her refutation of his arguments. Finally, I will discuss the rhetorical implications of my analyses.

LYNCHING IN THE AFTERMATH OF THE CIVIL WAR

Although all statistics are questionable because many lynchings went unreported and definitions of the term varied, scholars estimate that between 1882 and 1930 "there were 2,018 separate incidents of lynching in which at least 2,462 African-American men, women and children met their deaths in the grasp of southern mobs, comprised mostly of whites."[17] Lynchings of other groups were not unknown, but lynching as a topic of public discourse during the last decades of the nineteenth century and the first decades of the twentieth referred to the white-on-black violence that was most common in the South. Between 1880 and 1920 lynching reached its zenith, with the bloodiest years being 1892 and 1893 when more than 90 African-Americans died annually at the hands of mobs.[18] Because of its prevalence, by the dawn of the twentieth century lynching had become a metaphor for the dynamics of racial conflict in the South.[19] African-American leaders saw the issue as so problematic that, from its inception, the National Association for the Advancement of Colored People (NAACP) included passing a national antilynching law among its priorities.[20]

Understanding lynching as a social construct in post–Civil War America requires an appreciation of its economic and political roots as well as an understanding of its public face. Stuart Tolnay and E. M. Beck observe that the prevalence of lynching during this period had its source in the intersection of race and economics in the South. Dismissing claims that lynchings grew out of frustrations with a slow jurisprudential system, they aver that Southern whites "used lynchings as a tool for maintaining dominance in a society that was forced to accept a revolutionary change in the status of blacks—from slaves to freedmen."[21] Jonathan

Markovitz sees a similar function: "More generally, lynching worked to ensure that African Americans were aware that the color bar was still firmly in place and that 'integrated spaces could prove deadly.'"[22]

Because the new status of African-Americans posed threats to the prevailing social structure, Tolnay and Beck contend that "economic forces were clearly the most important undercurrent that carried southern society to such outrageous extremes of brutality. ... Blacks were most vulnerable to the rope and faggot when lynching had the potential to benefit most white society, for example, during periods of economic distress."[23] Such dominance extended to the legal, political, social, and economic spheres.[24]

As African-Americans began to expose the horrors of lynching, spokesmen in the South rhetorically defended the practice in an effort to shift attention from its economic and social roots. Bolstered by prevalent racial stereotypes of African-Americans as inferior, a mythology about lynching began to emerge. Discussing a local incident, an editorial in the August 1, 1906, *Atlanta Constitution* articulated the myth succinctly:

> He [the black man] grows more bumptious on the street. More impudent in his dealings with white men; and then, when he cannot achieve social equality as he wishes, with the instinct of the barbarian to destroy what he cannot attain to, he lies in wait, as that dastardly brute did yesterday near this city, and assaults the fair young girlhood of the south.[25]

This rationalization of lynching as a way to punish and perhaps prevent such rapes of white women by black men became a dominant narrative in Southern apologies for the practice although, in fact, only a small percentage of lynchings were linked to that crime.

As images of the ignorant, docile slave faded, a set of depictions emerged centering around "the threatening black 'beast'—a coarse caricature ripe with animalistic violence. Through the mythology of racial retrogression, African-American males were widely portrayed as sexually driven 'brutes' with a special affinity for white women, and many whites were convinced that these atavistic threats could be controlled only through extralegal sanctioning."[26] A proposed letter to the *Reader's Digest* in the files of the Association of Southern Women for the Prevention of Lynching presented a common viewpoint. Speaking directly to African-Americans, the writer insists: "As long as your negroe [sic] men violate white women, no hope of real emancipation may be shown you by the white race. This animal characteristic of negroes as is shown almost daily in the newspapers, will forever stamp a stigma on your race." The hope for the advancement of the race, according to this letter writer, depended on the acknowledgment of and the ability to deal with this issue: "You know as well as I that as long as white men lynch blacks for sex crimes, the negroe [sic] has no hope of gaining Caucasian respect. Now instead of trying to get laws to prevent lynchings (which are just punishments for the vicious crimes of the black rapers), why not reform your own race?"[27] As late as the 1921–22 debates about the Dyer Anti-Lynching Bill, Representative Thomas Sisson from Mississippi reiterated this mythology when he insisted he "would rather the whole black race of this world were lynched than for one of the fair daughters of the South to be ravished and torn by one of these black brutes."[28]

In her study of narratives of mob violence in the South between 1880 and 1940, Susan Jean contends that the Southern press in particular participated in a societal effort "to bound the definition and representation of the phenomenon."[29] Supporters "drew distinctions among lynchings and, when lynchings fell out of the bounds of propriety, they often expressed their disapproval." But press depictions of lynching provided key elements: "a black man committing a crime against a white woman (or, less frequently, an esteemed white man), public expression of outrage over the incident, and communal execution of 'justice.'" As one scholar notes, this portrayal was "like a text that white southerners read to themselves about themselves," and whites found in it a confirmation of the "honorable," "redemptive" nature of lynching. Many lynching reports in white newspapers served to bolster this image, thereby legitimizing the practice.[30]

Within the context of contemporary Southern culture, lynching served other social purposes, among them the reaffirmation of gender stereotypes and the obscuring of class divisions. As Martha Hodes observes, lynching "not only terrorized black men and women, but it also subordinated white women. White women's fear was in fact a favorite theme of lynching apologists. ... The construction of white female purity in the post-Reconstruction South was dependent upon images of black men as bestial, and a white woman's innocence was contingent upon assault by a black man rather than a white man."[31] In an era when some were challenging traditional gender roles, lynchings served to highlight female vulnerability and reiterate prevalent stereotypes about women. Further, lynchings worked to reinscribe white men as powerful agents in a changing social culture. Jonathan Markovitz points out that "lynch mobs ... wanted to reinforce images of white men as chivalrous protectors of white women."[32]

Particularly important for the Page-Church Terrell exchange, lynching served to diminish social class boundaries among whites, subsuming those differences under the mantle of males protecting women's purity. Markovitz continues: "The culture of segregation presented a stark picture of a world divided into distinct races, but this image glossed over intraracial social divisions. By providing lessons about the power of segregation, lynching also worked to forge common bonds of 'whiteness' between working-class and poor whites and white elites."[33] As we will see, Church Terrell's response accentuated social cleavages within the African-American community.

Clearly, then, as understood in the era from 1870 onward, lynching was fraught with stereotypes about race, gender, and class. Regardless of statistical evidence, lynching continued to be depicted as a reaction to the sexual violence of black men against white women. Often implicit in such discussions was the suggestion of class differences between the perpetrators and the victims: the black men were bestial, brutish, ignorant, and scarcely human, whereas the women were represented as "fair daughters" and "the fair young girlhood" of the genteel South.

As lynching proliferated, African-Americans began to respond. Often they acceded to the mythology that lynching was the result of sexual violence; their appeal was for legal processes rather than mob violence to allot punishment. Still many agreed with the analysis offered in 1892 by Ida B. Wells, who was to become the best known and most controversial antilynching crusader: "the whole matter is explained by the well-known opposition growing out of slavery to the progress of the race."[34] At the time of the Page-Church Terrell exchange, Wells had become the most notable African-American antilynching advocate, and her discourse provided a backdrop for their essays.

Interestingly, the two women were motivated to speak out against lynching by the same incident: the lynching of Thomas Moss, a mutual friend and a respectable Memphis businessman.[35] The murder of their prosperous friend, who was not accused of rape, proved to them that economics and power were behind lynchings, not sexual violence. Prompted by the incident, Wells, as a journalist, sought to discover the facts about the relationships between lynching and rapes. That research led her to explore the permutations of illicit sexuality: black men assaulting white women, white men assaulting black women, and most controversially, the possibility of consensual relationships between white women and black men.

In debunking the alleged link between rapes and lynchings, Wells willingly confronted the sexual and gender dimensions of the issue. Her sometimes abrasive approach breached the bounds of sexual decorum by emphasizing not only the possibility of consensual relationships between white women and black men but also the essential hypocrisy of Southern apologists who ignored the rape of African-American women and girls. She pointed out that "the miscegenation laws of the South only operate against the legitimate union of the races; they leave the white man free to seduce all the colored girls he can but it is death to the colored man who yields to the force and advances of a similar attraction in white women."[36] "White men lynch the offending Afro-American," she contended, "not because he is a despoiler of virtue, but because he succumbs to the smiles of white women."[37] As Linda McMurry observes in her biography of Wells, "while white men proclaimed themselves the protectors of their women's purity, a woman emerged as the defender of black men's honor and lives. This role reversal caused controversy, and Wells provoked animosity as well as admiration."[38] Thus, although the two women became vocal about lynching because of the same issue, and although both sought to dispute the alleged causal relationship between rapes and lynchings, their style and approach differed radically. As we shall see, class influenced Church Terrell's interpretation of the gender and sexual aspects of lynching.

THOMAS NELSON PAGE: THE CAUSE AND PREVENTION OF LYNCHING

Although Page's viewpoint is repugnant to modern readers, his essay reveals his rhetorical adroitness. First, in responding to concerns about lynching, Page positions himself as a socially responsible citizen, seeking to remedy a growing problem. For him, the brutality of lynching is significant not because of the injustice to the victim, but rather because it undermines social order. His concern, then, is to address lynching to preserve social stability. At the same time, by drawing distinctions between the men who commit the rapes that spur lynchings and other responsible African-Americans, he avoids being seen as a blatant racist. Second, he organizes his essay in a problem/solution format. Featuring lynching as an issue of concern to society as a whole because it disrupts social order, Page outlines actions that other concerned citizens can take to alleviate the problem. Third, within his discussion he crafts two compelling narratives for his audience. Making careful, but sustained use of racial stereotypes, he reiterates the well-established mythology of lynching. Further, in discussing solutions to the problem, he provides another narrative that points his readers to the path of action to preserve the social order by working to end lynchings.

First, noting the spread of lynching and the increasing brutality of the incidents, Page enacts the role of a concerned, responsible citizen as he avers: "the time appears to be ripe … to eradicate what is recognized by cool heads as a serious menace to our civilization."[39] Deploring "several revolting instances of lynching of negroes in its most dreadful form," he focuses on "the means to put an end to this barbarity."[40] Indeed, the very barbarity of the recent incidents leads him to claim that "there must be some imperative cause" to stir "thoughtful," "reasonable," and "rational" men to "the pitch where the law is trampled under foot, the officers of the law are attacked, and their prisoner taken from them and executed."[41]

While admitting that most lynchings are not connected to rape and that most occur in the South, Page insists that "ravishing" of white women by black men has served as the catalyst for increasing racial violence and observes "the murders in the South partake somewhat of the nature of race-conflicts." Later, after an allusion to rapes that were so brutal that the details could not be published, he combines a condemnation of lynching with a defense of lynch mobs:

It is these unnamable horrors which have outraged the mind of those who live in regions where they have occurred, and where they may at any time occur again, and upsetting reason, have swept from their bearings cool men and changed them into madmen, drunk with the lust of revenge.[42]

Deploring its impact on society as a whole, he concedes: "Lynching as a remedy [to alleged rapes] is a ghastly failure; and its brutalizing effect on the community is incalculable. ... The real injury is to the perpetrators of the crime of destroying the law, and to the community in which the law is slain."[43] The social repercussions of lynching, rather the injustice of the act itself, become the problem confronting thoughtful citizens.

Throughout the essay, Page alludes to powerful and prevalent social stereotypes. Although he acknowledges that the majority of lynchings are not attributable to cases of rape, he highlights the mythology that makes that linkage at least nine times in his essay. For example, lynchings, he avers, reflect "the determination to put an end to the ravishing of their women by an inferior race, no matter what the consequence."[44] Later, he returns to this theme, noting that in the last 20 years "hundreds of women and a number of children have been ravished and slain."[45]

His depictions of the perpetrators of rape reduce them to brutes. At one point he opines: "In the first place, the negro does not generally believe in the virtue of women. It is beyond his experience. He does not generally believe in the existence of actual assault. It is beyond his comprehension."[46] These African-American males are not only intoxicated with the allure of "social equality," they are also oblivious to core values of the society.

Avoiding charges of blatant racism, Page insists he is not speaking "of the respectable and law-abiding-element among the Negroes, who unfortunately are so often confounded with the body of the race from which come most of the malefactors."[47] He observes, however, that the "many negroes who are law-abiding and whose influence is for good ... are not generally among the leaders."[48] To his mind, the "negro orators and preachers" are not among this group "of sound minded" African-Americans for "their sympathy is generally with the 'victim' of the mob, and not with his victim."[49] Indeed, he faults the preaching of "social equality" by such leaders as a source for the change in formerly docile African-Americans.[50] He concludes that, having followed public discussion of the issue by African-Americans, he has come to "the painful realization that even the leaders of the negro race—at least those prominent enough to hold conventions and write papers on the subject—have rarely, by act or word, shown a true appreciation of the enormity of the crime of ravishing and murdering women. ... Underlying most of their protests is the suggestion, that the victim of the mob is innocent and a martyr."[51] In Page's world, then, African-Americans are divided into three distinct social groups: the perpetrators of rape, the "leaders" who sympathize with them, and the "right thinking" who have limited influence.

Page also draws class distinctions within his own race, observing that "since the assaults began again, they have been chiefly directed against the plainer order of people, instances of attacks on women of the upper class, though not unknown, being of rare occurrence."[52] In his view, then, rape, the reputed cause for lynch mobs, is implicitly enmeshed in issues of class: women of a certain "class" are largely insulated from the threat of physical assault, while African-Americans of that same class largely defend the attackers and do little to solve the problem.[53] Apparently, "whiteness" trumps class as an issue for Page, because he deprecates violence against women in a class different than his own.

Page's solution to the problem focuses on constructive action by right thinking people of both races. Faced with the social problems lynching creates, all concerned citizens must act to preserve the social order.

Certainly, he insists, justice needs to move more rapidly. In addition, right thinking African-Americans must "take charge of the crime of ravishing and firmly put it away from them." They must control the alleged crimes that are the catalysts for the lynch mobs. For their part, whites must assume responsibility for ending acts of lynching.[54] So, despite his earlier castigation of their indifference, Page returns to a plea to middle- and upper-class African-Americans to assist in stamping out the horrors of lynching, apparently by intervening to stop the "ravishings" to which he objects.

If Page's viewpoint offends modern readers, his rhetorical skills are nonetheless notable. He has crafted an appealing rhetorical persona as a concerned citizen while avoiding being dismissed as a blatant racist. Significantly, he portrays lynching not as a problem of justice or the violated civil rights of the victims; rather, his concern is that the spirit that fuels lynching leads to broader threats to social order. Through examples and allusions, he has drawn on the powerful and prevalent stereotypes around lynching that ground the act in retribution for sexual crimes. And he has offered solutions that require other concerned citizens to assume responsibility for protecting civil stability.

From a larger perspective, Page crafted two narratives for his audience. The first narrative repeats the mythology that underlay lynching at the time: bestial black men rape innocent white women; this appropriately enrages white men who recklessly rush to avenge the crime, regrettably disrupting the social order. This narrative gained added appeal from its reliance on the gendered stereotypes of white women and black men, its affirmation of white men as powerful agents, and its simultaneous condemnation and excusing of a heinous crime. In short, as McHenry notes, Page advanced "a narrative of black bestiality and white victimization that was in keeping with the images of African Americans commonly circulated in the media."[55]

Within the scene provided by the first narrative, the second scenario urges concerned citizens of both races to assume responsibility for doing their part to resolve this problem. African-American leaders should work diligently to control the troublesome elements in their own race, while white citizens should assure swift jurisprudence. Within this scenario, white citizens could both view lynching as deplorable and provide leadership, albeit not taxing leadership, to solve the problem. Of course, within this scenario, the major onus for solving the problem lay with African-American leaders. From a dramatistic perspective, this scenario highlighted agent and purpose, idealism and mysticism, an emphasis on his readers' ability to make change and their noble purpose in pursuing it.[56] Taken together, these two narratives were compelling in that they described a problem in terms that were widely accepted, and then they offered a solution that urged concerned citizens to act responsibly for a significant social good.

"LYNCHING FROM A NEGRO'S POINT OF VIEW"

In crafting a response to Page, Church Terrell confronted not only the substance of his arguments but also his rhetorical persona and tone. Since she was writing as an African-American woman to a largely white audience, building credibility was essential. Further, because Page supplemented his concern for social order with adroit allusions to dominant racial mythologies and stereotypes, Church Terrell faced the larger public perception of lynching. For her audience, her response would inevitably be situated in the larger social conversation about lynching, a conversation rife with gender and racial stereotypes. Wells's mode of confronting those stereotypes created the stir Church Terrell needed to avoid. Because Page had developed such compelling narratives, Church Terrell needed to provide an alternative analysis that was equally compelling.

A seasoned advocate, Church Terrell draws on her considerable rhetorical skills to craft her response to Page. First, realizing her challenges, she takes pains to build identification with her audience through her tone, rhetorical stance, and stylistic choices. To a large extent, her identification with her audience derives from her social position; she speaks as an educated, upper-class citizen to her counterparts in the largely white audience. Although her response reveals flashes of her anger and lapses into sarcasm, it also demonstrates her competence and intelligence to the readers. Second, relying on her skills in argument, she refutes Page's arguments systematically without mentioning his name or disparaging him. By avoiding a focus on Page, Church Terrell rhetorically shifts her attention to the social prejudices he represents. She avoids personalizing the argument and risking a perception that she is attacking him.

This approach leads her to challenge the linkage he has created between lynching and sexual violence, using his own data to her advantage. In so doing, she also reiterates and affirms the damaging stereotypes of African-American men that underlay public perceptions of lynching. Her elitism leads her to defend her social class at the expense of other members of her race. Finally, her alter- native analysis of the problem is far less compelling and more accusatory than the one Page has provided.

She begins with a stark recital of the scope and immediacy of the problem:

31 lynched in the first three months of 1904, with 15 murdered in a single week in Arkansas.[57] Page's insistence that prominent African-Americans ignore lynching is inaccurate, for her comment indicates she is well aware of the scope of the problem. Drawing on shared patriotic values reinforces her identification with the audience: "Those who are jealous of their country's fair name feel keenly the necessity of extirpating this lawlessness, which is so widespread and has taken such deep root. But means of prevention can never be devised, until the cause of lynching is more generally understood." While her syntax and her diction here clearly mark her as the social equal of her readers, her rational approach builds her ethos. These rhetorical techniques continue throughout the essay, enhancing her credibility.

Never directly linking her rebuttal to Page's essay, Church Terrell then moves to her discussion of the four "commonly made" mistakes, which are the arguments he has advanced but which also represent widespread beliefs she hopes to dispel. She first refutes the claim that rape is related to lynching: "it is a great mistake to suppose that rape is the real cause of lynching in the South. … It is easy to prove that rape is simply the pretext and not the cause of lynching."[58]

Citing statistics drawn from Page's essay without reference to him, she asserts that "men who admit the accuracy of the figures gravely tell the country that lynching can never be suppressed, until negroes cease to commit a crime with which less than one-fourth of those murdered by mobs are charged."[59]

Perhaps to counter Page's dramatic references to "unnamable horrors" and "ravishing of their women by an inferior race," she augments her rebuttal with a vivid example of an especially brutal lynching of a man and wife for an alleged murder, clear evidence that rape is often not the cause of lynching brutality.[60]

She concludes: "But since three-fourths of the negroes who have met a violent death at the hands of Southern mobs have not been accused of this crime, it is evident that, instead of being the 'usual' crime, rape is the most unusual of all the crimes for which negroes are shot, hanged and burned."[61] Church Terrell buttresses her refutation by citing information from two apparently white citizens, Prof. Andrew Sledd, who lost his job for speaking out against lynching, and Bishop Candler of Georgia, who "made a strong protest against lynching, and called attention to the fact that, out of 128 negroes who had been done to death in 1902, only 16 were even accused of rape."[62] Church Terrell's attention to this point is undoubtedly more an effort to educate the public than to answer Page, who had already admitted that only the minority of lynchings were linked directly to rape.

Still without mentioning Page, Church Terrell counters his claim that aspirations for "social equality" have been the impetus for rapes. This topic leads her into drawing sharp class distinctions within her race that reinforce the common stereotypes about African-American men. One would be mistaken, she contends, "to suppose that the negro's desire for social equality sustains any relation whatsoever to the crime of rape." Citing eyewitnesses, she suggests that "the negroes who are known to have been guilty of assault have, as a rule, been ignorant, repulsive in appearance and as near the brute creation as it is possible for a human being to be." Those who have "been guilty of ravishing white women" know nothing of "social equality" and even if aware of the concept, would have "no clearer conception of its meaning than he had of the principle of the binomial theorem." From her own experience with a "number of ignorant negroes" she reports she has "never found one who seemed to have any idea of what social equality means, or who expressed a desire to put this theory into practice when it was explained to him."[63]

In the next paragraph, she defends her own class, contrasting it with other less fortunate African-Americans. "Negroes who have been educated in Northern institutions of learning with white men and women, and who for that reason might have learned the meaning of social equality and have acquired a taste for the same, neither assault white women nor commit other crimes, as a rule."[64] She holds that such people do not belong to "the criminal class." Rather it is "illiterate negroes, who are the only ones contributing largely to the criminal class" that are "coddled and caressed by the South." Further, the "dear old 'mammy' or a faithful old 'uncle' who can neither read nor write and who assure their white friends that they would not, if they could" are held up as models of appropriate behavior.[65]

Other texts reveal the pervasiveness of this condescending and divisive class bias. For example, in her 1896 "First Presidential Address to the National Association of Colored Women," Church Terrell calls on her sisters to join her in efforts to elevate their race and urges a focus on "Homes, more homes, purer homes, better homes." As she deplored the conditions in which many of her race lived, she described their dwellings as places in which "the air is foul, the manners bad and the morals worse," noting that such a "so called home" was "a menace to health, a breeder of vice, and the abode of crime."[66] She urged her compatriots to support efforts to educate the uneducated in how to sweep, dust, cook, and wash as well as "how to clothe children neatly, how to make and especially mend garments, how to manage their household economically." She alleges that the children of these homes are "fairly drinking in the permissible example of their elders, coming in contact with nothing but ignorance and vice."[67]

The title of an essay published in *Twentieth Century Negro Literature* reflects her gender and class biases: "What Role is the Educated Negro Woman to Play in Uplifting Her Race?" She mentions the progress of one branch of the NACW in Tuskegee in spreading "the light of knowledge and the gospel of cleanliness to their poor benighted sisters."[68] Throughout these essays, Church Terrell equates poverty and lack of hygiene with inferiority and even immorality. Undoubtedly, her depictions of the living conditions for many of her race were accurate; still her assumption that ignorance and poverty are linked to immorality reveals her strong class bias.

Moving on through Page's argument, Church Terrell defends her own social class against his allegations of their indifference to lynching: "The third error on the subject of lynching consists of the widely circulated statement that the moral sensibilities of the best negroes in the United States are so stunted and dull, and the standard of morality even among the leaders of the race is so low, that they do not appreciate the enormity and heinousness of rape."[69] Later she mentions these leaders as representing "the intelligence and decency" of their race as she asserts that they frequently express their horror at the crime and do all in their power to exhort against it.

Having refuted Page's arguments point by point, Church Terrell offers her analysis of the causes of lynching, which contrasts markedly with his. In the first place, she asserts it is grounded in "race hatred, the hatred of a stronger people toward a weaker who were once held as slaves." In her view, lynching stems from "the same spirit of intolerance and of hatred" that gave rise to the Ku Klux Klan and the Jim Crow laws.[70]

The second cause of lynching is "the lawlessness prevalent in the section where nine-tenths of the lynchings occur." Like Page she deplores the social disruption produced by lynching, but she sees the social climate in the South as the cause, not rape. "Lynching is," she insists, "the aftermath of slavery. The white men who shoot negroes to death and flay them alive, and the white women who apply flaming torches to their oil-soaked bodies today, are the sons and daughters of women who had but little, if any, compassion on the race when it was enslaved." Citing press coverage, she notes that lynch mobs are allegedly composed of the "best citizens" of an area, who disperse quickly when their work is done.[71]

However, even if one discredits such claims and assumes that lynchings are the product of the lower socioeconomic classes, she still holds that the social environment produced their propensity to violence. Even if one is willing to agree that "the children of poor whites" in the South are responsible for the lynchings, "it is because their ancestors were brutalized by their slaveholding environment." She concludes: "It is too much to expect, perhaps, that the children of women who for generations looked upon the hardships and the degradation of their sisters of a darker hue with few if any protests, should have mercy and compassion upon the children of that oppressed race now."[72] Evidence of the race hatred and general lawlessness of the South goes beyond lynchings. Church Terrell points to the "peonage system" in Alabama and Mississippi as well as efforts to oppose education for freed slaves as further proof of the "spirit of vengeance and intolerance in its ugliest and most brutal form."[73]

Page had urged the "better" classes of African-Americans to condemn actively the "ravishings" that allegedly stimulated lynchings as he observed the need for members of his own race to be more systematic and prompt in administering appropriate justice. In contrast, once again accentuating class divisions, Church Terrell points to the need for "the masses of ignorant white people in that section" to be "educated and lifted to a higher moral plane. It is difficult," she continues, "for one who has not seen these people to comprehend the density of their ignorance and the depth of their degradation."[74] She reinforces her point by citing an unnamed "well-known white author who lives in the South" and the *Atlanta Constitution,* which remarks on the level of illiteracy in the South.[75]

A second, vital solution is for "all classes of white people" in the South to "respect the rights of other human beings, no matter what may be the color of their skin, become merciful and just enough to cease their persecution of a weaker race and learn a holy reverence for the law."[76] She concludes with a call for a "renaissance of popular belief in the principles of liberty and equality upon which this government was founded." Only such a rekindling of fundamental principles can remove the "stain" on "the fair name of the United States" which lynching creates.[77]

Clearly, Church Terrell counters Page's arguments, leaving no point unchallenged. But her response fails to address the more compelling aspects of his essay. In particular, not only does she fail to challenge the narrative he provides about lynching, but she also accedes to the negative characterizations of her race that underlie that narrative. Further, her response accentuates class divisions among African Americans. If lynching served to unify the white community because it portrayed all white men as chivalrous defenders of white women, Church Terrell insisted that her own social class was superior to the "ignorant" masses, which produced the brutish men who raped white women.

Page had artfully constructed his argument in problem/solution format and had developed two compelling narratives. On this narrative level, Church Terrell's response was much less effective than her rebuttal of his arguments. First, while she insisted that lynching was a significant problem, she located the source of the problem in widespread racism. Had racism been localized in the South, this analysis might have been compelling. But racial stereotypes were widespread and deep-rooted; the racism she deplored was a factor in the broader social climate. Moreover, if Northern readers could agree with some aspects of her depictions of the culture in the South, acting on her judgments required creating cleavages within the white community. As we have seen, however, the racial and gender stereotypes that supported Page's narratives created cohesion, not divisions, within white society. Finally, her solution to the problem, the massive reeducation of Southern whites and the reshaping of Southern culture, was far more demanding on the readers and far less appealing rhetorically than Page's admonitions toward being responsible citizens. In essence, Church Terrell's response failed to address the most compelling aspects of Page's essay.

Although Church Terrell had pursued a response because of her desire to answer Page's "scurrilous" attacks on African-American men, this close reading of her text demonstrates how she actually reiterated those attacks. In so seasoned an advocate, this inconsistency seems surprising. An explanation lies in considering the role social class and gender played in Church Terrell's thinking and, consequently, in her advocacy.

NEGOTIATING THE INTERSECTIONS OF GENDER, CLASS, AND RACE

If her autobiography is indicative, Church Terrell was inured to and often oblivious to the privileges that inhered in her social class. One incident reported in her autobiography is representative and suggestive. As a child studying in Ohio, where her parents had sent her to assure she would receive the quality of education unavailable to her race in the South, she was stunned when she realized her connection to the slaves her class was studying. She reports that she felt "humiliated and disgraced." Recovering her composure, she "resolved that so far as this descendant of slaves was concerned, she would show those white girls and boys whose forefathers had always been free that she was their equal in every respect. At that time I was the only colored girl in the class, and I felt I must hold high the banner of my race."[78] Here Church Terrell's reaction to her connection with less fortunate members of her race and her clear sense of her difference from them—a difference created by class privilege—is significant. Further, this episode indicates the perspective she would adopt throughout her life: she would work to elevate the backwardness of her race.

The details of her life, including her excellent education, extensive travel abroad, and her marriage to Robert Terrell, the first African-American graduate of Harvard Law School, confirm the unusual status she enjoyed. Indeed, one of her most famous works, "What It Means to Be Colored in the Capitol of the United States," based largely on her own experiences, is a litany of the frustrations and even humiliations that middle- and upper-class African-Americans faced in Washington, D.C.

Throughout her autobiography Church Terrell offers no clue that she perceived how her class affected her experiences, her public life, or her viewpoints. Indeed, the title she chose for her autobiography, *A Colored Woman in a White World,* reflects her angle of vision. She has clear ideas about how her gender and her race affect her life; she conveys no sense that her social class skewed her vision. Interestingly, in his introduction to her autobiography, H. G. Wells hinted at the issue of class as a factor in human lives when he wrote, "Mrs. Church Terrell has lived her life through a storm of burning injustices; but if she had been born a sensitive and impressionable white girl in a village on some English estate, destined normally to be an under-housemaid and marry an under-gardener, she would have had almost the same story to tell, if not in flamboyant colors then in aquatint."[79] Wells's clear understanding of how social class bounded opportunities also suggested that class privilege created insensitivities. Church Terrell's political ideology was clearly grounded in class distinctions.

Although Church Terrell was impressed by the work of Booker T. Washington and although her husband probably owed his judgeship to Washington's influence, she preferred a different approach in working for the advancement of her race. A disciple of William E. B. Du Bois's philosophy of the Talented Tenth, Church Terrell saw the future of her race as being in the hands of the elite. Her faith was in an educated elite rather than the "well-trained laboring class" that Washington hoped to create.[80] Thus, she sometimes drew sharp lines between herself and others of her race in disparaging ways. A passage from a message to the National Association of Colored Women reflects this tendency. Church Terrell avers: "Even though we wish to shun them [the masses], and hold ourselves entirely aloof from them, we cannot escape the consequences of their acts." She continues by insisting that aside from duty, concerns for policy and self preservation "would demand that we do go down among the lowly, the illiterate, and even the vicious to whom we are bound by the ties of race and sex."[81] As Beverly Washington Jones observes, this rhetoric reveals the "class biases" and paternalism of the women elites who made up the NACW.[82] Kevin K. Gaines notes the prevalence of this attitude among the black elite: "black elites made uplift the basis for a racialized elite identity claiming Negro improvement through class stratification as race progress, which entailed an attenuated conception of bourgeois qualifications for rights and citizenship." Further, he notes, "black opinion leaders deemed the promotion of bourgeois morality, patriarchal authority, and a culture of self-improvement ... as necessary to their recognition, enfranchisement, and survival as a class."[83]

Church Terrell's commitment to the concept of the Talented Tenth also led her to assume a distinctive role as a woman in advancing her race. In her public advocacy Church Terrell adhered to the motto of the National Association of Colored Women: "Lifting as we climb," a goal that clearly iterated her sense of her own superiority. Historian Audrey Thomas McCluskey identifies Church Terrell as part of a generation whose "goal was to set a 'racial standard' by demonstrating achievement, respectability, race pride, and moral certitude."[84] A charter member of the NAACP, she embraced the responsibility of using her resources to work for the advancement of her race. She saw herself as a leader in the African-American community. McCluskey describes this attitude: "The women of this class acknowledged a special calling to 'set the standard' for the race in the struggle for equality. They believed that the fate of the race rested on the shoulders of its 'best women.'"[85] She was able, as were other women of her social class and race, to serve, in McCluskey's phrase, "as racial ambassadors and liaisons to the white establishment."[86] She was an acceptable colleague in the struggle for woman suffrage, an appropriate respondent for the *North American Review,* and an ideal leader for the National Association of Colored Women. As McCluskey indicates, "Terrell's values were those of the first and second generation of free blacks who wanted to redeem the race through enlightened class-conscious leadership."[87]

Together, her social class and her gender generated a particular orientation, one that McCluskey terms "progressive conservatism." Inherent in this viewpoint was a sense of "noblesse oblige toward the poor." Church Terrell and others accepted the responsibility of setting a "racial standard" by highlighting the achievements of their race, demonstrating their respectability in embracing solidly middle-class values, asserting their pride in their race, and claiming the moral high ground in their beneficent works.[88]

Further, as a woman, Church Terrell felt a particular need to set a moral tone, as her work with the NACW reveals. Acquiescing to the stereotypes of African-American men who allegedly raped white women seemed natural to Church Terrell. The ignorant, the poor, the socially disprivileged were "different" from her and they needed African-American women like her to lead them in new directions.

Church Terrell's orientation toward gender issues also constrained her discussion of lynching. An ardent supporter of suffrage, she was nonetheless somewhat conservative about women's roles. Certainly, she encouraged women to pursue careers and to exercise their political power.[89] At the same time, however, she perceived the primary influence of women to be moral uplift and focused many of the efforts of the NACW on improvements in the home. As I observe elsewhere, "the venues in which Church Terrell initially pursued her efforts to improve her race were ones suitable for a 'respectable' middle-class woman of her day."[90] Beverly Washington Jones notes, "The NACW was conservative in that it aimed not to alter the domestic nature of the social position of its members, but to make them better wives and mothers."[91] In her speeches to the members of the NACW, Church Terrell emphasizes that "our peculiar status" makes women better equipped to undertake the projects of moral reform within the lower reaches of African-American culture and to create bonds with their less fortunate sisters through "heart to heart talks."[92]

Church Terrell's model for responsible womanhood, then, involved commitment to homes and families. In her response to Page, for example, she calls on Southern white women to "arise in the purity and power of their womanhood" to help squelch mob violence.[93]

Church Terrell's sense of the moral superiority of women and their special responsibilities undoubtedly made it difficult for her to explore the illicit sexual liaisons between white women and African-American men that Wells exposed. Even so, that same gender conservatism permitted her to acknowledge and decry the sexual violence toward African-American women that was commonplace, particularly in the South. As she explains, "Throughout their entire period of bondage colored women were debauched by their masters. From the day they were liberated … prepossessing young colored girls have been considered the rightful prey of white gentlemen in the South."[94] In essence, Church Terrell could understand the victimization of women, black or white, by men. The very idea of illicit consensual relationships between white women and African-American men violated her social boundaries.

From a theoretical perspective, Church Terrell's gender and class created a "trained incapacity" for her when addressing lynching. According to Kenneth Burke, because we are forced, like other animals, to "interpret the signs" about us, gradually we develop an orientation, a set of characteristic frames that help us understand our world.[95] Some frames prove more reliable, more usable than others. Indeed, Burke suggests we develop a "trained incapacity … whereby one's very abilities can function as blindnesses."[96] Succinctly put, "A way of seeing is also a way of not seeing."[97] If Church Terrell's background experiences as an elite African- American woman made her keenly aware of the challenges to her race, her gender and social class skewed her angle of vision. They constituted a "trained incapacity" that frustrated her efforts to respond fully to Page because she assented to the class distinctions he emphasized.

Simply claiming the leadership in her community that was vital to her political agenda created other rhetorical dilemmas in this context. Ella Shohat and Robert Stam argue that negative stereotypes such as those Church Terrell confronted are particularly problematic. On the one hand, "any negative behavior by any member of the oppressed community is instantly generalized as typical, as pointing a perpetual backsliding toward some presumed negative essence. … [E]ach negative image of an underrepresented group becomes, within the hermeneutics of domination, sorely overcharged with allegorical meaning." In other words, although members of dominant groups can defuse negative judgments because of their social position, destructive stereotypes about nondominant groups tend to grow in force and strength.[98]

Because stereotypes about her race were so negative and so pervasive, to be effective as an advocate in the larger society, Church Terrell had to dissociate herself and others of her social milieu from lower-class members of their race. Distancing herself from the prevalent racial stereotypes that characterized African-Americans as illiterate, uneducated, and debased was essential for Church Terrell to gain credibility with the broader public. Chaim Perelman and Lucie Olbrechts-Tyteca describe this rhetorical move as dissociation. It always involves "breaking connecting links" by "affirming that elements which should remain separate and independent have been improperly associated."[99] Through dissociation, Church Terrell sought to undermine the negative linkages that were crystallized in the prevalent racial stereotypes and to establish herself as a leader within her community through and because of her social class. However, to the extent she succeeded in that task, she also capitulated to prevalent social stereotypes about her race at least as they applied to the less fortunate.

Thus, despite her rhetorical skill, Church Terrell's social class colored her attitudes toward others of her race. At the same time, her aspirations as a female leader and her agenda for change demanded that she dissociate herself and her compatriots from the prevalent stereotypes. Both of these factors propelled her to respond to Page in ways that reaffirmed the very stereotypes she hoped to disparage.

CONCLUSION

Engaging Page in the *North American Review*, Church Terrell entered a rhetorical space fraught with stereotypes about gender, race, and class. By her own report she was motivated by a desire to respond to Page's "scurrilous" attacks on African-American men, one featuring a mythology that sanctioned lynching. These stereotypes had resisted the attempts of the African-American community to defuse them because they were deeply embedded in the social fabric of the South and had gained currency with Northern audiences. Further, medical science and even evolutionary theory were educed to support the notion that African-Americans were a more primitive, less advanced race.

For her own part, Church Terrell had assailed the white press for its perpetuation of such stereotypes. As Jinx Coleman Broussard reports, "Race was an early and constant theme of Terrell's journalism career; therefore, she devoted considerable attention to the white press's propensity to misrepresent her race in the United States and abroad."[100] But as we have seen, factors in her own life and thinking caused her to affirm some of the same depictions she deplored.

The reaffirmation of particular racial stereotypes and the mythology surrounding lynching by an African-American woman of her stature was powerful. On the one hand, the identification she built so carefully with her audience added weight to her views. She spoke to readers as a peer. Further, because of both her gender and her race, her depiction of certain members of her race as ignorant and of some African-American men as brutish was particularly forceful. If Page could be dismissed as an apologist for lynching, Church Terrell rhetorically reinforced his damaging and appealing scenario and narratives.

Like all African-American advocates of her generation, Church Terrell faced the conundrum of how to gain access to the public sphere controlled by the dominant class and how to work most effectively to overcome the barriers, often embedded in stereotypes, that confronted her race. This essay offers one perspective on how she tried to confront, and in this case failed to meet, those dual challenges. In her response to Page, Church Terrell presented a rhetorical persona that was both acceptable to the mostly white readers and an implicit repudiation of their biases concerning her race. At the same time, she explicitly reiterated and affirmed the stereotypes that were so damaging to those African-Americans less privileged than she. One cannot deny the importance and power of Church Terrell's advocacy. Her work in drawing attention to the accomplishments of her race, both to educate the public and to provide role models for African American children, was commendable.[101]

Her ability to help white audiences understand the issues confronting her race undoubtedly helped change public perceptions. But in this specific case, Church Terrell's orientation toward racial issues reiterated and reinforced the negative stereotypes that haunted her race and exacerbated class cleavages within her own community.

NOTES

1. Thomas Nelson Page, "The Lynching of Negroes: Its Causes and Prevention," *North American Review* 178 (January 1904): 33–48.
2. Mary Church Terrell, *A Colored Woman in a White World* (1940; rpt., New York: Arno Press, 1980), 224–25.
3. See Jinx Coleman Broussard, *Giving Voice to the Voiceless: Four Pioneering Black Women Journalists* (New York: Routlege, 2003), especially 62–64 for the challenges Church Terrell faced in getting access to publications other than those controlled by African Americans. Karlyn Kohrs Campbell makes a similar point in "The Power of Hegemony: Capitalism and Racism in the 'Nadir of Negro History,'" in *Rhetoric and Community: Studies in Unity and Fragmentation*, ed. J. Michael Hogan (Columbia: University of South Carolina Press, 1998), especially 38–40. Hereafter cited as "Nadir."
4. Church Terrell, *Colored Woman*, 225.
5. Mary Church Terrell, "Lynching from a Negro's Point of View," *North American Review* 178 (June 1904): 853–68. Reprinted in Beverly Washington Jones, *Quest for Equality: The Life and Writings of Mary Eliza Church Terrell, 1863-1954* (Brooklyn, NY: Carlson Publishing, 1990), 167–81. Further citations to this article will reference the page numbers in the Quest reprint. Elizabeth McHenry indicates that the editors compelled Church Terrell to substitute "Negro" for the original "Colored Woman" in her title, a small but significant change: "Toward a History of Access: The Case of Mary Church Terrell," *American Literary History* 19 (2007): 389.
6. February 14, 1905, Mary Church Terrell Papers, Library of Congress. Quoted in Karlyn Kohrs Campbell, "Mary Church Terrell (1863–1945), a voice for African Americans," in *Women Public Speakers in the United States, 1925-1993: A Bio-Critical Sourcebook*, ed. Karlyn Kohrs Campbell (Westport, CT: Greenwood Press, 1994), 112.
7. Campbell, "Mary Church Terrell," 109.
8. Other scholars have examined Church Terrell's contributions from various perspectives. See Jinx C. Broussard, *Giving Voice to the Voiceless,* 55–82, and "Mary Church Terrell: A Black Woman Journalist Seeks to Elevate Her Race," *American Journalism* 19 (2002): 13–35, for a description of Church Terrell's position as a journalist. For a consideration of the performative aspects of Church Terrell's

autobiography, see Eileen C. Cherry, "Mule of the World: The Embodiment of Mary Church Terrell," in *Voices Made Flesh: Performing Women's Autobiography*, ed. Lynn C. Miller, Jacqueline Taylor, and M. Heather Carverer (Madison: University of Wisconsin Press, 2003), 66–83. Finally, Kohrs Campbell has done much to highlight Church Terrell's rhetorical career. In addition to the material cited above, see: "Style and Content in the Rhetoric of Early Afro-American Feminists," *Quarterly Journal of Speech* 72 (1986): 434–45, for a treatment of Church Terrell and other prominent spokeswomen, and *Man Cannot Speak for Her: A Critical Study of Early Feminist Rhetoric* (Westport, CT: Greenwood Press, 1989), 1:150–55, for an overview of her work as it relates to suffrage.

9. Campbell, "Nadir," 43.
10. McHenry, "Toward a History of Access," 389.
11. Campbell, "Nadir," 42.
12. McHenry, "Toward a History of Access," 388.
13. Campbell, "Nadir," 42.
14. McHenry, "Toward a History of Access," 389.
15. McHenry, "Toward a History of Access," 389.
16. Kenneth Burke, *Permanence and Change: An Anatomy of Purpose*, 3rd ed. (Berkeley: University of California Press, 1984), 7.
17. Stewart E. Tolnay and E. M. Beck, *A Festival of Violence: An Analysis of Southern Lynchings, 1882–1930* (Urbana: University of Illinois Press, 1995), 17.
18. Tolnay and Beck, *A Festival of Violence*, 29.
19. Jonathan Markovitz, *Legacies of Lynching: Racial Violence and Memory* (Minneapolis: University of Minnesota Press, 2004), xvii–xix.
20. See Robert L. ZanGrando, *The NAACP Crusade Against Lynching, 1909–1950* (Philadelphia: Temple University Press, 1980), for a detailed history of their efforts.
21. Tolnay and Beck, *A Festival of Violence*, 256.
22. Markovitz, *Legacies of Lynching*, xxviii.
23. Tolnay and Beck, *A Festival of Violence*, 256–57.
24. See Peter Ehrenhaus and A. Susan Owen, "Race Lynching and Christian Evangelicalism: Performance of Faith," *Text and Performance Quarterly* 24 (2004): 276–301, for an intriguing discussion of the relationship of lynching to religious practices and traditions.
25. Quoted in Tolnay and Beck, *Festival of Violence*, 18.
26. Tolnay and Beck, *Festival of Violence*, 14.
27. Quoted in Markovitz, *Legacies of Lynching*, 8. This letter exists in the Claude Neal Papers of the Association for Southern Women to Prevent Lynching. There is no evidence about whether it was ever published.
28. Quoted in Markovitz, *Legacies of Lynching*, xv.
29. Susan Jean, "'Warranted' Lynchings: Narratives of Mob Violence in White Southern Newspapers, 1880–1940," *American Nineteenth Century History* 6 (2005): 353.
30. Jean, "'Warranted' Lynchings," 355. Quotation in the original is from W. Fitzhugh Brundage, *Lynching in the New South: Georgia and Virginia, 1890–1930* (Chicago: University of Illinois Press, 1993), 17.
31. Martha Hodes, *White Women, Black Men: Illicit Sex in the Nineteenth-Century South* (New Haven, CT: Yale University Press, 1993), 200, 198.
32. Markovitz, *Legacies of Lynching*, xvi.
33. Markovitz, *Legacies of Lynching*, xxviii.

34. Ida B. Wells, "Southern Horrors: Lynch Law in All its Phases," *Man Cannot Speak For Her: Key Texts of the Early Feminists*, ed. Karlyn Kohrs Campbell (New York: Praeger, 1989), 2:401.

35. See Hodes, *White Women, Black Men*, 204–5, for this incident in relation to Wells Barnett. See *Colored Woman*, 105–6, for Church Terrell's narrative of the lynching.

36. Wells, "Southern Horrors," 392–93.

37. Wells, "Southern Horrors," 393.

38. Linda O. McMurry, *To Keep the Waters Troubled: The Life of Ida B. Wells* (Cary, NC: Oxford University Press, 2000), xv.

39. Page, "The Lynching of Negroes," 34.

40. Page, "The Lynching of Negroes," 34.

41. Page, "The Lynching of Negroes," 34.

42. Page, "The Lynching of Negroes," 38.

43. Page, "The Lynching of Negroes," 43.

44. Page, "The Lynching of Negroes," 39. The use of the possessive "their women" rather than simply "women" is noteworthy in its suggestion of the gender dynamics and stereotypes in this discourse.

45. Page, "The Lynching of Negroes," 42.

46. Page, "The Lynching of Negroes," 44.

47. Page, "The Lynching of Negroes," 33.

48. Page, "The Lynching of Negroes," 44, 46.

49. Page, "The Lynching of Negroes," 46.

50. Page, "The Lynching of Negroes," 36–37.

51. Page, "The Lynching of Negroes," 45.

52. Page, "The Lynching of Negroes," 37.

53. To my knowledge, no evidence is available to support Page's claim about the class of rape victims. Social circumstances may, indeed, have offered some protection to certain groups of white women. However, his depiction seems to correspond to persistent stereotypes about the types of women who are rape victims. Ida Wells-Barnett seeks to disrupt this preconception by noting that women of a genteel class often willingly seek black partners. See "Southern Horrors," 393.

54. Page, "The Lynching of Negroes," 46.

55. McHenry, "Toward a History of Access," 387.

56. Kenneth Burke, *A Grammar of Motives* (1945; rpt., Berkeley: University of California Press, 1969), 3–20.

57. Church Terrell, "Lynching from a Negro's Point of View," 167.

58. Church Terrell, "Lynching from a Negro's Point of View," 167–68.

59. Church Terrell, "Lynching from a Negro's Point of View," 168.

60. Page, "The Lynching of Negroes," 38, 39.

61. Church Terrell, "Lynching from a Negro's Point of View," 168–69.

62. Church Terrell, "Lynching from a Negro's Point of View," 169.

63. Church Terrell, "Lynching from a Negro's Point of View," 169.

64. Church Terrell, "Lynching from a Negro's Point of View," 170.

65. Church Terrell, "Lynching from a Negro's Point of View," 170.

66. Mary Church Terrell, "First Presidential Address to the National Association of Colored Women," *Quest*, 135.

67. Church Terrell, "First Presidential Address," 136.

68. Mary Church Terrell, "What Role is the Educated Negro Woman to Play in the Uplifting of Her Race?" *Quest*, 152.

69. Church Terrell, "Lynching from a Negro's Point of View," 171.

70. Church Terrell, "Lynching from a Negro's Point of View," 174.

71. Church Terrell, "Lynching from a Negro's Point of View," 174–75.

72. Church Terrell, "Lynching from a Negro's Point of View," 175.

73. Church Terrell, "Lynching from a Negro's Point of View," 177.

74. Church Terrell, "Lynching from a Negro's Point of View," 179–80.

75. Church Terrell, "Lynching from a Negro's Point of View," 180.

76. Church Terrell, "Lynching from a Negro's Point of View," 180.

77. Church Terrell, "Lynching from a Negro's Point of View," 181.

78. Church Terrell, *Colored Woman*, 20–21.

79. Church Terrell, "Preface," *Colored Woman*, n.p.

80. Church Terrell, *Colored Woman*, 191.

81. Mary Church Terrell, "The Duty of the NACW to the Race," *Quest*, 144.

82. Beverly Washington Jones, "The Woman's Club Movement," *Quest*, 26.

83. Kevin K. Gaines, *Uplifting the Race: Black Leadership, Politics, and Culture in the Twentieth Century* (Chapel Hill: University of North Carolina Press, 1996), xv, 3.

84. Audrey Thomas McCluskey, "Setting the Standard: Mary Church Terrell's Last Campaign for Social Justice," *The Black Scholar* 29 (Summer 1999): 47–48.

85. McCluskey, "Setting the Standard," 47.

86. McCluskey, "Setting the Standard," 48.

87. McCluskey, "Setting the Standard," 48.

88. McCluskey, "Setting the Standard," 48.

89. See for example, her call for women to become lawyers: "Needed: Women Lawyers," *Negro Digest*, September 1943, 57–59. Reprinted in *Quest*, 327–29.

90. Martha Solomon Watson, *Lives of Their Own: Rhetorical Dimensions in Autobiographies of Women Activists* (Columbia: University of South Carolina Press, 1999), 98.

91. Jones, "The Women's Club Movement," 21.

92. Church Terrell, "First Presidential Address," 137.

93. Church Terrell, "Lynching from a Negro's Point of View," 175.

94. Church Terrell, "Lynching from a Negro's Point of View," 178.

95. Kenneth Burke, *Permanence and Change: An Anatomy of Purpose* (1935; rpt., Indianapolis: Bobbs-Merrill, 1965), 5.

96. Burke, *Permanence and Change*, 7.

97. Burke, *Permanence and Change*, 49.

98. Ella Shohat and Robert Stam, *Unthinking Eurocentrism: Multiculturalism and the Media* (New York: Routledge, 1994), 183.

99. Chaim Perelman and Lucie Olbrechts-Tyteca, *The New Rhetoric: A Treatise on Argumentation*, trans. John Wilkinson and Purcell Weaver (Notre Dame, IN: University of Notre Dame Press, 1969), 190, 411–12.

100. Broussard, "Mary Church Terrell," 65.

101. Broussard, "Mary Church Terrell," 21–22.

Language Teaching: New Worlds/New Words

bell hooks

Like desire, language disrupts, refuses to be contained within boundaries. It speaks itself against our will, in words and thoughts that intrude, even violate the most private spaces of mind and body. It was in my first year of college that I read Adrienne Rich's poem, "The Burning of Paper Instead of Children." That poem, speaking against domination, against racism and class oppression, attempts to illustrate graphically that stopping the political persecution and torture of living beings is a more vital issue than censorship, than burning books. One line of this poem that moved and disturbed something within me: "This is the oppressor's language yet I need it to talk to you." I've never forgotten it. Perhaps I could not have forgotten it even if I tried to erase it from memory. Words impose themselves, take root in our memory against our will. The words of this poem began a life in my memory that I could not abort or change.

When I find myself thinking about language now, these words are there, as if they were always waiting to challenge and assist me. I find myself silently speaking them over and over again with the intensity of a chant. They startle me, shaking me into an awareness of the link between languages and domination. Initially, I resist the idea of the "oppressor's language," certain that this construct has the potential to disempower those of us who are just learning to speak, who are just learning to claim language as a place where we make ourselves subject. "This is the oppressor's language yet I need it to talk to you" (Adrienne Rich). Then, when I first read these words, and now, they make me think of standard English, of learning to speak against black vernacular, against the ruptured and broken speech of a dispossessed and displaced people. Standard English is not the speech of exile. It is the language of conquest and domination; in the United States, it is the mask which hides the loss of so many tongues—all those sounds of diverse, native communities we will never hear, the speech of the Gullah, Yiddish, and so many other unremembered tongues.

Reflecting on Adrienne Rich's words, I know that it is not the English language that hurts me, but what the oppressors do with it, how they shape it to become a territory that limits and defines, how they make it a weapon that can shame, humiliate, colonize. Gloria Anzaldúa reminds us of this pain in *Borderlands/La Frontera* when she asserts, "So, if you want to really hurt me, talk badly about my language." We have so little knowledge of how displaced, enslaved, or free Africans who came or were brought against their will to the United States felt about the loss of language, about learning English. Only as a woman did I begin to think about these black people in relation to language, to think about their trauma as they were compelled to witness their language rendered meaningless with a colonizing European culture, where voices deemed foreign could not be spoken, were outlawed tongues, renegade speech. When I realize how long it has taken for white Americans to acknowledge diverse languages of Native Americans, to accept that the speech their ancestral colonizers declared was merely grunts or gibberish was indeed *language,* it is difficult not to hear in standard English always the sound of slaughter and conquest. I think now of the grief of displaced "homeless" Africans, forced to inhabit a world where they saw folks like themselves, inhabiting the same skin, the same condition, but who had no shared language to talk with one another, who needed "the oppressor's language." *This is the oppressor's language yet I need it to talk to you.* When I imagine the terror of Africans on board slave ships, on auction blocks, inhabiting the unfamiliar architecture of plantations, I consider that this terror extended beyond fear of punishment, that it resided also in the anguish of hearing

From *Teaching to Transgress: Education as the Practice of Freedom* by bell hooks. Copyright © 1994 by Taylor & Francis Group LLC - Books. Reprinted by permission.

a language they could not comprehend. The very sound of English had to terrify. I think of black people meeting one another in a space away from the diverse cultures and languages that distinguished them from one another, compelled by circumstance to find ways to speak with one another in a "new world" where blackness or the darkness of one's skin and not language would become the space of bonding. How to remember, to reinvoke this terror. How to describe what it must have been like for Africans whose deepest bonds were historically forged in the place of shared speech to be transported abruptly to a world where the very sound of one's mother tongue had no meaning.

I imagine them hearing spoken English as the oppressor's language, yet I imagine them also realizing that this language would need to be possessed, taken, claimed as a space of resistance. I imagine that the moment they realized the oppressor's language, seized and spoken by the tongues of the colonized, could be a space of bonding was joyous. For in that recognition was the understanding that intimacy could be restored, that a culture of resistance could be formed that would make recovery from the trauma of enslavement possible. I imagine, then, Africans first hearing English as "the oppressor's language" and then rehearing it as a potential site of resistance. Learning English, learning to speak the alien tongue, was one way enslaved Africans began to reclaim their personal power within a context of domination. Possessing a shared language, black folks could find again a way to make community, and a means to create the political solidarity necessary to resist.

Needing the oppressor's language to speak with one another they nevertheless also reinvented, remade that language so that it would speak beyond the boundaries of conquest and domination. In the mouths of black Africans in the so-called "New World," English was altered, transformed, and became a different speech. Enslaved black people took broken bits of English and made of them a counter-language. They put together their words in such a way that the colonizer had to rethink the meaning of English language. Though it has become common in contemporary culture to talk about the messages of resistance that emerged in the music created by slaves, particularly spirituals, less is said about the grammatical construction of sentences in these songs. Often, the English used in the song reflected the broken, ruptured world of the slave. When the slaves sang "nobody knows de trouble I see—" their use of the word "nobody" adds a richer meaning than if they had used the phrase "no one," for it was the slave's *body* that was the concrete site of suffering. And even as emancipated black people sang spirituals, they did not change the language, the sentence structure, of our ancestors. For in the incorrect usage of words, in the incorrect placement of words, was a spirit of rebellion that claimed language as a site of resistance. Using English in a way that ruptured standard usage and meaning, so that white folks could often not understand black speech, made English into more than the oppressor's language.

An unbroken connection exists between the broken English of the displaced, enslaved African and the diverse black vernacular speech black folks use today. In both cases, the rupture of standard English enabled and enables rebellion and resistance. By transforming the oppressor's language, making a culture of resistance, black people created an intimate speech that could say far more than was permissible within the boundaries of standard English. The power of this speech is not simply that it enables resistance to white supremacy, but that it also forges a space for alternative cultural production and alternative epistemologies—different ways of thinking and knowing that were crucial to creating a counter-hegemonic worldview. It is absolutely essential that the revolutionary power of black vernacular speech not be lost in contemporary culture. That power resides in the capacity of black vernacular to intervene on the boundaries and limitations of standard English.

In contemporary black popular culture, rap music has become one of the spaces where black vernacular speech is used in a manner that invites dominant mainstream culture to listen—to hear—and, to some extent, be transformed. However, one of the risks of this attempt at cultural translation is that it will trivialize black vernacular speech. When young white kids imitate this speech in ways that suggest it is the speech of those who are stupid or who are only interested in entertaining or being funny, then the subversive power of this speech is undermined. In academic circles, both in the sphere of teaching and that of writing, there has been little effort made to utilize black vernacular—or, for that matter, any language other than standard English. When I asked an ethnically diverse group of students in a course I was teaching on black women writers why we only heard standard English spoken in the classroom, they were momentarily rendered speechless. Though many of them were individuals for whom standard English was a second or third language, it had simply never occurred to them that it was possible to say something in another language, in another way. No wonder, then, that we continue to think, "This is the oppressor's language yet I need it to talk to you."

I have realized that I was in danger of losing my relationship to black vernacular speech because I too rarely use it in the predominantly white settings that I am most often in, both professionally and socially. And so I have begun to work at integrating into a variety of settings the particular Southern black vernacular speech I grew up hearing and speaking. It has been hardest to integrate black vernacular in writing, particularly for academic journals. When I first began to incorporate black vernacular in critical essays, editors would send the work back to me in standard English. Using the vernacular means that translation into standard English may be needed if one wishes to reach a more inclusive audience. In the classroom setting, I encourage students to use their first language and translate it so they do not feel that seeking higher education will necessarily estrange them from that language and culture they know most intimately. Not surprisingly, when students in my Black Women Writers class began to speak using diverse language and speech, white students often complained. This seemed to be particularly the case with black vernacular. It was particularly disturbing to the white students because they could hear the words that were said but could not comprehend their meaning. Pedagogically, I encouraged them to think of the moment of not understanding what someone says as a space to learn. Such a space provides not only the opportunity to listen without "mastery," without owning or possessing speech through interpretation, but also the experience of hearing non-English words. These lessons seem particularly crucial in a multicultural society that remains white supremacist, that uses standard English as a weapon to silence and censor. June Jordan reminds us of this in *On Call* when she declares:

> I am talking about majority problems of language in a democratic state, problems of a currency that someone has stolen and hidden away and then homogenized into an official "English" language that can only express nonevents involving nobody responsible, or lies. If we lived in a democratic state our language would have to hurtle, fly, curse, and sing, in all the common American names, all the undeniable and representative participating voices of everybody here. We would not tolerate the language of the powerful and, thereby, lose all respect for words, per se. We would make our language conform to the truth of our many selves and we would make our language lead us into the equality of power that a democratic state must represent.

That the students in the course on black women writers were repressing all longing to speak in tongues other than standard English without seeing this repression as political was an indication of the way we act unconsciously, in complicity with a culture of domination.

Recent discussions of diversity and multiculturalism tend to downplay or ignore the question of language. Critical feminist writings focused on issues of difference and voice have made important theoretical interventions, calling for a recognition of the primacy of voices that are often silenced, censored, or marginalized. This call for the acknowledgment and celebration of diverse voices, and consequently of diverse language and speech, necessarily disrupts the primacy of standard English. When advocates of feminism first spoke about the desire for diverse participation in women's movement, there was no discussion of language. It was simply assumed that standard English would remain the primary vehicle for the transmission of feminist thought. Now that the audience for feminist writing and speaking has become more diverse, it is evident that we must change conventional ways of thinking about language, creating spaces where diverse voices can speak in words other than English or in broken, vernacular speech. This means that at a lecture or even in a written work there will be fragments of speech that may or may not be accessible to every individual. Shifting how we think about language and how we use it necessarily alters how we know what we know. At a lecture where I might use Southern black vernacular, the particular patois of my region, or where I might use very abstract thought in conjunction with plain speech, responding to a diverse audience, I suggest that we do not necessarily need to hear and know what is stated in its entirety, that we do not need to "master" or conquer the narrative as a whole, that we may know in fragments. I suggest that we may learn from spaces of silence as well as spaces of speech, that in the patient act of listening to another tongue we may subvert that culture of capitalist frenzy and consumption that demands all desire must be satisfied immediately, or we may disrupt that cultural imperialism that suggests one is worthy of being heard only if one speaks in standard English.

Adrienne Rich concludes her poem with this statement:

> I am composing on the typewriter late at night, thinking of today. How well we all spoke. A language is a map of our failures. Frederick Douglass write an English purer than Milton's. People suffer highly in poverty. There are methods but we do not use them. Joan, who could not read, spoke some peasant form of French. Some of the suffering are: it is hard to tell the truth; this is America; I cannot touch you now. In America we have only the present tense. I am in danger. You are in danger. The burning of a book arouses no sensation in me. I know it hurts to burn. There are flames of napalm in Cantonsville, Maryland. I know it hurts to burn. The typewriter is overheated, my mouth is burning, I cannot touch you and this is the oppressor's language.

To recognize that we touch one another in language seems particularly difficult in a society that would have us believe that there is no dignity in the experience of passion, that to feel deeply is to be inferior, for within the dualism of Western metaphysical thought, ideas are always more important than language. To heal the splitting of mind and body, we marginalized and oppressed people attempt to recover ourselves and our experiences in language. We seek to make a place for intimacy. Unable to find such a place in standard English, we create the ruptured, broken, unruly speech of the vernacular. When I need to say words that do more than simply mirror or address the dominant reality, I speak black vernacular. There, in that location, we make English do what we want it to do. We take the oppressor's language and turn it against itself. We make our words a counter-hegemonic speech, liberating ourselves in language.

The Master's Tools Will Never Dismantle the Master's House

Audre Lorde

I agreed to take part in a New York University Institute for the Humanities conference a year ago, with the understanding that I would be commenting upon papers dealing with the role of difference within the lives of American women: difference of race, sexuality, class, and age. The absence of these considerations weakens any feminist discussion of the personal and the political.

It is a particular academic arrogance to assume any discussion of feminist theory without examining our many differences, and without a significant input from poor women, Black and Third World women, and lesbians. And yet, I stand here as a Black lesbian feminist, having been invited to comment within the only panel at this conference where the input of Black feminists and lesbians is represented. What this says about the vision of this conference is sad, in a country where racism, sexism, and homophobia are inseparable.

To read this program is to assume that lesbian and Black women have nothing to say about existentialism, the erotic, women's culture and silence, developing feminist theory, or heterosexuality and power. And what does it mean in personal and political terms when even the two Black women who did present here were literally found at the last hour? What does it mean when the tools of a racist patriarchy are used to examine the fruits of that same patriarchy? It means that only the most narrow parameters of change are possible and allowable.

The absence of any consideration of lesbian consciousness or the consciousness of Third World women leaves a serious gap within this conference and within the papers presented here. For example, in a paper on material relationships between women, I was conscious of an either/or model of nurturing which totally dismissed my knowledge as a Black lesbian. In this paper there was no examination of mutuality between women, no systems of shared support, no interdependence as exists between lesbians and women-identified women. Yet it is only in the patriarchal model of nurturance that women "who attempt to emancipate themselves ay perhaps too high a price for the results," as this paper states.

For women, the need and desire to nurture each other is not pathological but redemptive, and it is within that knowledge that our real power I rediscovered. It is this real connection which is so feared by a patriarchal world. Only within a patriarchal structure is maternity the only social power open to women.

Interdependency between women is the way to a freedom which allows the I to be, not in order to be used, but in order to be creative. This is a difference between the passive be and the active being.

Advocating the mere tolerance of difference between women is the grossest reformism. It is a total denial of the creative function of difference in our lives. Difference must be not merely tolerated, but seen as a fund of necessary polarities between which our creativity can spark like a dialectic. Only then does the necessity for interdependency become unthreatening. Only within that interdependency of difference strengths, acknowledged and equal, can the power to seek new ways of being in the world generate, as well as the courage and sustenance to act where there are no charters.

From *Sister Outsider* published by Crossing Press, Random House Inc. Copyright © 1984, 2007 by Audre Lorde. Used herein by permission of the Charlotte Sheedy Literary Agency, Inc.

Within the interdependence of mutual (nondominant) differences lies that security which enables us to descend into the chaos of knowledge and return with true visions of our future, along with the concomitant power to effect those changes which can bring that future into being. Difference is that raw and powerful connection from which our personal power is forged.

As women, we have been taught either to ignore our differences, or to view them as causes for separation and suspicion rather than as forces for change. Without community there is no liberation, only the most vulnerable and temporary armistice between an individual and her oppression. But community must not mean a shedding of our differences, nor the pathetic pretense that these differences do not exist.

Those of us who stand outside the circle of this society's definition of acceptable women; those of us who have been forged in the crucibles of difference—those of us who are poor, who are lesbians, who are Black, who are older—know that survival is not an academic skill. It is learning how to take our differences and make them strengths. For the master's tools will never dismantle the master's house. They may allow us temporarily to beat him at his own game, but they will never enable us to bring about genuine change. And this fact is only threatening to those women who still define the master's house as their only source of support.

Poor women and women of Color know there is a difference between the daily manifestations of marital slavery and prostitution because it is our daughters who line 42nd Street. If white American feminist theory need not deal with the differences between us, and the resulting difference in our oppressions, then how do you deal with the fact that the women who clean your houses and tend your children while you attend conferences on feminist theory are, for the most part, poor women and women of Color? What is the theory behind racist feminism?

In a world of possibility for us all, our personal visions help lay the groundwork for political action. The failure of academic feminists to recognize difference as a crucial strength is a failure to reach beyond the first patriarchal lesson. In our world, divide and conquer must become define and empower.

Why weren't other women of Color found to participate in this conference? Why were two phone calls to me considered a consultation? Am I the only possible source of names of Black feminists? And although the Black panelist's paper ends on an important and powerful connection of love between women, what about interracial cooperation between feminists who don't love each other?

In academic feminist circles, the answer to these questions is often, "We do not know who to ask." But that is the same evasion of responsibility, the same cop-out, that keeps Black women's art out of women's exhibitions, Black women's work out of most feminist publications except for the occasional "Special Third World Women's Issue," and Black women's texts off your reading lists. But as Adrienne Rich pointed out in a recent talk, which feminists have educated themselves about such an enormous amount over the past ten years, how come you haven't also educated yourselves about Black women and the differences between us —white and Black—when it is key to our survival as a movement?

Women of today are still being called upon to stretch across the gap of male ignorance and to educated men as to our existence and our needs. This is an old and primary tool of all oppressors to keep the oppressed occupied with the master's concerns. Now we hear that it is the task of women of Color to educate white women—in the face of tremendous resistance—as to our existence, our differences, our relative roles in our joint survival. This is a diversion of energies and a tragic repetition of racist patriarchal thought.

Simone de Beauvoir once said: "It is in the knowledge of the genuine conditions of our lives that we must draw our strength to live and our reasons for acting."

Racism and homophobia are real conditions of all our lives in this place and time. I urge each one of us here to reach down into that deep place of knowledge inside herself and touch that terror and loathing of any difference that lives there. See whose face it wears. Then the personal as the political can begin to illuminate all our choices

> *Prospero, you are the master of illusion.*
> *Lying is your trademark.*
> *And you have lied so much to me*
> *(Lied about the world, lied about me)*
> *That you have ended by imposing on me*
> *An image of myself.*
> *Underdeveloped, you brand me, inferior,*
> *That's the way you have forced me to see myself*
> *I detest that image! What's more, it's a lie!*
> *But now I know you, you old cancer,*
> *And I know myself as well.*

~ Caliban, in Aime Cesaire's <u>A Tempest</u>

Lorde, Audre. "The Master's Tools Will Never Dismantle the Master's House." 1984. *Sister Outsider: Essays and Speeches*. Ed. Berkeley, CA: Crossing Press. 110-114. 2007. Print.

Unit 3: Placing Texts in Contexts

Rhetoric, Emotion, and Places of Persuasion

Susan Miller

INTRODUCTION

> If names are not properly defined and used, the speech can never sound agreeable. If the speech jars, nothing can be accomplished. This means that there would be no proper observance of ritual and ceremonial activities, the legal system would collapse, and people would no longer know how correctly to behave themselves.
>
> —*Zhu Zi Ji Cheng*

RHETORICS, PEDAGOGIES, AND METHODS

It is obvious to many who focus on rhetoric's history that there is no longer one entity that fits that term, and some think that there never was, that no unified rhetorical tradition ever existed. The ways we refer to rhetoric make it for once easy to agree with Gorgias that nothing exists that this word refers to. One frequent response to this situation is to claim that the way I use the term *rhetoric* is right and that others' uses are wrong. But outside an interplay of definitions, which postpones some discussions forever, we might turn to different historical methods and consider emphases in various schools outside the still active view of rhetoric as types of Aristotelian argument. Rather than define it, we might ask, "What versions of rhetoric are going to be of use to us in particular situations?"

Answering that question may allow us to uncover a history of choice itself. At the least, it would create an overview of many culturally constitutive discourses among which shared definitions are but one condition of trust. There are, we quickly see, others.

My use of the word *rhetoric* thus understands it as a plurality—multiple metadiscourses derived from ritual, imaginative, and affiliative discursive practices that we trust for their well-supported and reasoned statements, but also because they participate in infrastructures of trustworthiness we are schooled to recognize,

From *Trust in Texts: A Different History of Rhetoric* by Susan Miller. Copyright © 2008 by Board of Trustees, Southern Illinois University. Reprinted by permission.

sometimes by lessons and habits we cannot name. Those infrastructures vary according to the time when a specialized plane of understanding and its consequences emerges in specific cultures—political, religious, social, technological, even meteorological impact on what we know and how we can know it. But the purpose of these prescriptive networks remains constant: to endow a discursive practice with precedent trustworthiness. These rhetorics organize our emotional receptivity to statements on which we can depend for answers to speculative questions. They thereby guide us to choices that may not produce the best outcome but that we trust to be the "right thing," not in a shallow morality but because we are persuaded of their source's share in our best interests.

From the discrete perspective on discourse that modern intertextuality permits, we feel that way because we recognize various hierarchies that more than one oratorical rhetoric contains. We base this disposition to trust on what Mary Hamilton in *Situated Literacies: Readings and Writing in Context* calls "structured routines and pathways that facilitate and regulate actions, the rules of appropriateness and eligibility" (17). Those rules differ markedly among discourses that unevenly change over time. Contemporary cultures, for instance, have medical and epistolary discourses whose phenomenologies of trust determine how any interaction with them may succeed, or not, depending on their interlocutors' schooled view of "appropriateness and eligibility." Thus, we accept a letter as authentic automatically, or reject it with equal speed, because we have at least tacit training to sense its relation to a long history of forgeries, as M. T. Clanchy explains in *From Memory to Written Record: England 1066-1307*.[1] We learn epistolary rhetoric, as we do routines of medical communication, as cultural pedagogies under one rubric: they are metadiscourses that organize persuasion around specific conditions of trust.

Pedagogy is of course yet another term we think of as having a discrete tradition. It is rarely recognized as the name of historically diffused formal schooling and self-instruction in temporally, regionally, and otherwise situated conditions of trust in language itself. From infancy, we learn an absolute difference between words that are "right" and "wrong." But we are then differentially encultured to identify reliable ways of thinking and talking, especially those organized around imaginary, speculative, yet crucial decisions. Such discourses emerge from antique civilizations and their precedents, offering separately framed ways to consider choices we make despite our ignorance of the knowledge on which they must be based within areas we have neither mastered nor enact, and often that no one has. That is, we trust discourse we perceive to contain unknowns—undisclosed if not secret content that inevitably intimates that more than we know might be known. Such persuasion tells us as well that we already know more because we learn by precept and example about a metadiscourse whose very formulation promises that the unknown is not unknowable. This is to say that many mechanisms around uncertainty function symbolically and charismatically, not logically or analytically.

A chief benefit of this approach to rhetoric is to highlight its culturally constitutive nature and thereby to set aside arguments about its conceptual definitions. Conceptual definitions never connect ideas to the circumstances that produce them; their treatments most often downplay the interested uses to which they have been put; and they by nature separate one metadiscourse from another. They do not link their inevitably overlapped results for people, for sociability, and ultimately for institutions. But a pedagogic definition of rhetoric also renovates the historiography usually applied to it, well after we jettison Hegelian chronologies of canons formed around concepts rather than situated uses. Obviously, we add content to rhetoric's history by emphasizing that its multiple forms constitute a plurality of instructive, variously situated lessons in language and in aesthetic, formal, and ordinary discourses that create contexts for choice.

But this awareness also allows us to rethink methods after the telling anecdotes of New History, which reverts to traditional omniscience about progress; after Sponge-Histories, which absorb overlooked, marginal participants into dominant discourses they rightfully have had doubts about joining; and after myriad other ways of manipulating time, which portray it as a product of totalizing concepts. As research about multiplicities of literacies has done, this emphasis also uncovers the egoism of rhetoric's own "autonomous model," the essentialist view of literacy that New Literacy Studies critiques for its abstractions of civilized smartness. That criticism thus shows that New History reproduces formal categories despite its narrations of "actual" moments. It especially admits that neither discourse practices nor speaking subjects are singular, logical, or consistent. As Albert Einstein reminds historians, time itself is multiple interrelated levels, not neat past/present/future categories. We can only construct and control the past and the future in an emergent present. Thus, another benefit of making cultural teachings the shared purpose of many rhetorics is that doing so insists that a multiplicity of lessons will change relative to the view of its observers as a present emerges.

Of course, it is also obvious that an autonomous model of rhetoric treated as a singular, historical oratory imagines it as a conceptual tradition constituted by carefully formulated teachings. But that model also transmits an abstract if always locally exemplified code. In this context, variations in lessons about public speech are taken to fragment a unified whole, not to demonstrate that oratory appears, is superseded, and is finally de-emphasized in relation to other rhetorics that have been recruited to build a particular cultural imaginary. Nonetheless, the forms and genres most closely associated with oratory all stimulate admirable imitation exercises, but never only admiration. That is, handbooks, style guides, transferred instructions in preaching, ongoing declamatory performances, treatises that define universal taste as a quality of readers, and Aristotle's and Early Modern French poetics all realize discrete metadiscourses as direct instruction in named techniques. We might generalize John Ward's comment on later uses of classical rhetoric in epistolography to that instruction: "Classical rhetorical theory, prose composition and epistolography responded to distinct market niches which appeared from time to time in different places as a consequence of social and political changes" (175).

These instructions all describe processes that determine credibility and more—the infrastructures of our choices to believe. We remember Peter Ramus for textbooks and Augustine and Richard Whately for lessons in preaching and even Socrates for worry over how to create the best speech. But we may nonetheless fit each figure and treatise into conceptual histories whose methods lift their skirts at the thought of real teaching.

Yet variations within these lessons fit more than "market niches." For instance, Renaissance English style guides participate in attempts to create a vernacular as authoritative and as trustworthy as Latin in an emergent post-Latinate literacy, not in the fragmentation of a never unified rhetoric. And considering that Book III of Aristotle's *Rhetoric* may have been a transposed work from his early teaching—and that scholars continue to disagree about the dates and sources of the composition of parts of the whole as we have it (Kennedy, *Aristotle* 304)—it is likely that its third chapter about style is part of an attempt to bring disparate elements of composition together, not part of a unified theory that falls apart toward the end. But in any case, Renaissance style handbooks and a new philology devoted to vocabulary respond to new, national interests.

These examples also point out the ambiguity of naming rhetorical "theory" of any sort, historically and now. With few but quickly canonized exceptions, the most commonly conceptualized rhetoric is a practice, specifically a teaching practice. Thus, much we call rhetorical theory presents how-to's of production. They might be interpreted as how-to's of textual analysis but are not intended to be so, at least in their composition before the twentieth century. In almost all cases, the work we call rhetorical theory is not so effective a meta-analysis of practice as the *Symposium*'s critique of poetic representation. Apart from that persuasive Realist dissection of how a poet's mediated imitations cannot convey universal truths, theories of metadiscourse are thin on the ground before the eighteenth century and remain relatively rare outside literary theory.

However, when we treat rhetorics as pedagogies, we more easily notice how they form, inflect, and disseminate their content in ways that connect it to local circumstance. For instance, Jay Fliegelman's *Declaring Independence: Jefferson, Natural Language, and the Culture of Performance*, which analyzes both American nationalist language and rhetorically performed political aims, notes John Witherspoon's late-eighteenth-century "great rule of sincerity." Witherspoon recommends self-revelation in speeches aimed to dismantle ranked hierarchy in new democracies, a suggestion that captures the spirit of American rebellion against monarchic control and aristocratic ranks (Fliegelman 119). Later, after the American Civil War, school rhetorics pointedly perform what Jean Ferguson Carr, Stephen L. Carr, and Lucille M. Schultz's *Archives of Instruction: Nineteenth-Century Rhetorics, Readers, and Composition Books in the United States* calls a "subversive reverence." That is, they gather the discrete, detailed prescriptions of earlier rhetorics into general principles that smooth over their distinctness from each other. The resulting simplified systems teach new mass education's enlarged student population, who are hereby trained to trust and to aim for a national character, to replace divisive regionalism (47). Through this work, American rhetorics also promote idealized life narratives of citizenship, a plot of participation by fundamentally Calvinist, self-monitorial actors who learn from these modified lessons in rhetoric to avoid further civic disorder.

To respond effectively to various cultural exigencies requires that such pressures also remain familiar. Their frameworks must assure the continuing legibility and status of a discursive response to shifting cultural needs in literary, religious, dramatic, poetic, political, and other discourses whose practices merge in systematic lessons. Repetitive exercises that require using conventional figures and naming taxonomies of argumentation certainly inculcate rhetoric's Hudibrastic "tools."[2] But repetition also characterizes histories of a unified rhetoric's recurring novel debuts. That is, even a limited history of metadiscursive teaching practices compressed into one oratorical tradition shows how those practices circulate and recirculate across cultures. They deliver seemingly pure prescriptions for appropriate motives, speakable topics, and a conventional range of discursive actions in various present circumstances. But such repetition is also crucial to monitoring, reprocessing, and delivering the lineaments of trust.

This is obviously to say that multiple dull lessons alter historically to conserve dominant social structures and cooperation with them in fresh circumstances. These unfamiliar conditions sometimes include war, new forms of government, challenges to economic relations, inventions that disturb established social relations and patterns of communication, and other events perceived to require rearticulating principles and thus also require revising linguistic and discursive conventions that sustain their credibility. This process shifts spoken and graphic conventions, rewrites the implications of specific words, and highlights new or newly elastic genres. A variety of metadiscursive lessons reorganize trust in religious, philosophical, political, aesthetic, and practical reconstructions of reality.

In such moments of cultural slippage, interruption, and self-interrogation, shifted circumstances also turn up discourse pedagogy's extremely durable power to recuperate limits on what may be said. Roland Barthes calls those limits our "Aristotelian vulgate."[3] Paolo Valesio argues that "the content of man's vision has always been expressible only through a set of ready-made simplifying forms whose recognition . . . requires only a long, cold look at the underlying similarity of all acts of human communication, where it is always the same mechanisms, always the same frames that keep reappearing" (31–34). Insofar as both critics willingly privilege conventional expression in these ways, they imply that the metadiscursive teachings that become prominent in any era will be rewritten explanations of discursive processes that nonetheless immediately become authoritative. We accept them even as they are recomposed because they conform to structures they may otherwise be expected to replace. This is also to note again that even oblique historical claims that the authority of rhetoric derives from conceptual alliances with philosophy efface the powers of discourse networks. Metadiscourses control what to say and how to say it, not knowing what it is or how it came to be.

Thus, with Gorgias again in mind, we might note that critics invested in language, literature, and philosophy prefer interpretation along hermeneutic lines to analyses of how discourse is produced and deployed in material circumstances. That preferred focus on singular texts also ignores how these discourses and theories of their production accomplish the power of cultural reproduction. But not even an interpretative turn in rhetoric—much less the cultural and linguistic turns that have followed it—has forestalled the need for detailed discussions of that production in the protected third space that postcolonial critics name as a way to suspend fixed, often stereotyped identity. By extension, third spaces also remove professional conversations from fixed methods and worn paradigms for understanding their appropriate objects of study. Yet the freedoms of spaces that suspend surety also allow us to be deserted by once comforting traditions. In this rhetorical case, without foundational certainty that speakers and writers interchangeably control the meanings that emerge from interpretive technologies, we already wander into ambivalence. Rhetoricians are simultaneously strategically essentialized scholars and critics who know not only what they mean but what Cicero surely did, and also new media participants in a linguistic turn in which *meaning*, now a word *only* in quotation marks, depends on operations within language.

In this rhetorical culture, as always, what we do not see and cannot know attracts and repels us in almost identical measure. The ways of thinking and talking that mediate between apprehension about the unknown and attraction to it always require creating trust, a nonce confidence that unevenly collapses troublesome distances between a symptom and a diagnosis, death and its aftermath, heroes and their destinies, and especially our likely control of responses to community puzzles. Insofar as cultures school their constituents to rely on community experience and individual perceptions more than they do on guesses, fantasy, self-interested advice, and even the combined data and enchantment that constitute supposedly rational argumentation, those cultures define insight as *emotional* agreement, no matter how provisional or temporary.

These propositions are not meant to suggest that one original, archetypical, explanatory discourse first combined with a hardwired trusting human response to allay unevolved human insecurity. Nor do they indicate that systematic address to such uncertainties inevitably fragments into the disseminated conventions of such an impossible archetype. Neither do these hypotheses involve more or less enduring trust in the original purposes of those conventions. Narratives of progress that tell how developed rationalist minds eventually forgo primitive magic to become "scientific" are certainly belied by current political decision-making, as they are by the operatic if fulfilling results of romance. Yet historical accounts of discourse production easily produce such narratives when they turn up progress and decline or imagine time itself as a series of this-then-that absolute changes. The result is to apply the same explanatory metaphors to any materialized social process, to thereby foster the view that cultures can erase or irrevocably transform any such process. Such method totalizes even the most particular local views and circumstances into one abstraction—The State, The Speech, The Speaker. These constructs are not only theoretical, for the State, Speech, and Speaker they produce behave precisely as they are hereby taught, as totally impenetrable performances, not responses to exigent circumstances.

Such models in common histories of rhetoric overwhelm the possibility that the discourse of "history" could narrate accumulating options—in this case, accrued ways to address fairly stable human and social discourses that will be redeployed in new models in recurring human situations. That is, in this alternative to a historiography built from concepts, competitions, and belief in absolute change, one or more common discourses of intercession that address a specific community vexation may become the most prominent model for addressing that collective issue. But obviously, other models will also supply conventional ways to contain anxiety and inspire useful responses to experience. Such means remain differently active and multiply differentially, largely in thrall to material and political possibilities for their production and reproduction. For instance, we now invite representatives of religious discourses to preside at weddings and at many state events. But their modern presence collects other mythic representatives of solemn surety in many rituals; it neither critiques nor obliterates them.

Retained historical models also can disallow interest in the relative credibility of mediating discourses, at least apart from their embedment in uneven power relations. That is, when specific ways of forming, talking about, and performing linguistic conventions are imagined to result from contests of social strength, but not actually to constitute those contests, their relative credibility and thus their uses appear to be enforced in absolute ways. The loss is that they are not then treated as acceptable or not in proportion to their fit to a specific conventional audience's responses. Nonetheless, relations of power never *essentially* define a discourse of mediation, nor do they evenly sustain its perceived place among others. For instance, drama, oratory, medical persuasion, and other trusted interpretations in specific cultures may become less easily staged and less willingly received at any time. They will thus disproportionately contribute to conventional subject positions that are trusted as "normal." But obstacles to their production, dissemination, or reception never entirely erase their persuasive force nor our shared willingness to use these agreed-upon frameworks to make experience available to memory and reflection. Despite claims to the contrary, e-mail never replaces what appear in its wake to be cumbersome handwritten notes. Electronic writing allows us to contrast still active ways of writing in terms of available time and different expectations of temporary immediacy in relationships.

My claims that persuasion is always a matter of trust that precedes any form of its expression and that its worthiness for that trust will be verified against multiple discursive conventions obviously revise the possibility of one rhetorical tradition. Like many other historiographies, this view questions the reliability of origin stories—here, an Athena-like birth of oratory in classical Greece. It also moots the possibility that systematic rhetoric is or may be made obsolete by forces outside it. No abstracted "philosophy" can dismantle multiply realized lessons about discourse production, no matter how poor their reputation among Idealistic essentialists. Outside patriarchal histories, which insist on dialectically enacted wins, losses, and syntheses, rhetorical performance is only one among many systematic ways of encouraging comfort with uncertainty. Defined here as one discourse about discourse, rhetoric is identified with the singular spirit claimed by sophistic Socrates, with the orator who embodies conventional responses to events that assure emotional assent to any well-argued position, with the scribe who transmits documents to renew the displaced authority of these early cultural icons, with the vernacular stylist, and, in recent circumstances, with the circulated post print text whose source is impossible to distinguish from its publicity. In this current case, rhetoric portrays credibility as a reputation without exemplary cases.

TOPICS: SIMULTANEOUS AND CONSECUTIVE

To make these suggestions at all credible and thematically manageable from the specific angles of incidence I sketch below, this study describes a decentered, always mobile relation between texts and their acceptance as trusted cultural resources. To do so, it simultaneously follows the chronological canon that constitutes one familiar rhetorical tradition and injects into it topics and perspectives rarely used to qualify its singularity. Classical oratory occupies chapter 1, "Decentering Rhetoric," as the master text of rhetoric studies now under revision by new political and social histories of antique worlds, especially by relatively recent discoveries of sophisticated uses of texts that occur millennia before the invention of the alphabet. My critical return to commonly accepted wisdoms about Athenian oratory does not question the superiority of the classical Greek texts that we do have as against others that we cannot know of. But it does refer to work that reveals, for instance, highly specialized and sometimes secreted writing systems used only within discrete vocations, as impressed stamps were used on small clay envelopes that contained cargo records read by merchant ship captains along the Mediterranean coast. In addition to using this information to suggest that neither the media nor the messages of oratory are likely to have been singular, the chapter takes up the extraordinary sophistication of ancient links among character, convention, and style.

The chapters that follow in turn address early modern technologies of trust in print, rhetorics, and texts, especially the emblematic phenomenology of uncertainty that enables epistolary rhetorics and that underlies the standardized language and consciousness sought in eighteenth-century moral philosophy (see chapter 3). The conclusion returns to the antique bifurcation of selves identified as "real" versus "emotional." This last chapter provides a retrospective context for the earlier propositions of the book, an ending that results from wanting to show that linear chronologies inevitably downplay how ever-emerging futures will reinvent any enduring tension in a new emergent present.

Chapter 2, "Trusting Texts," revisits the suppositions of many histories of classical rhetoric to show that print, often glorified as another alphabet, caused neither cultural revolutions nor a very direct intervention in common communicative practices. That is, overlaid print/manuscript practices result in print imitations of existing literacies. Coteries shared manuscript poetry; rural communities received holographic newsletters reporting royal acts and important legislation. Thus, handwritten texts stimulated the invention of print by exposing its potential economic advantages to literary and political cultures.

But print documents also imitate the manuscripts they transcribe. For instance, early printed plays might be authored by typesetters who, like medieval scribes, capture many versions of one text and introduce to it variations and errors as they edit to accommodate the space, time, and political danger attached to language. Across these traditionally demarcated eras, and still today, the letter and its treatments in various epistolary rhetorics also access the phenomenology of trust that may or may not attach to any written text. I suggest that such assent is always at stake in letters, which mediate between experience and unknowable circumstances around them, between a supposed direct statement and its absent source. Correspondence is thus a theoretical touchstone for issues around the multiplicity of rhetorics: the genre comments on the medieval theoretical sophistication that required minuscule details about how to fictionalize textual authenticity. And unlike other preprint genres, it cannot be thought of as an imitation of somehow direct spoken communication. Nonetheless, discrete epistolary rhetorics prescribe how to maintain the illusion of a writer's physical presence to verify the intentions of unavailable individuals and offices.

Chapter 3, "The Mobility of Trust," argues that eighteenth-century European postrevolutionary cultures rework much of the metadiscursive grounding of trusted texts. The period's rhetorical treatises articulate a Lockean version of the Cartesian individual, whose consciousness becomes the source of credible perception in the period's novels, political sermons, scientific papers, and other emergent genres. This consciousness is partially constructed from classical literary actors and philosophical characters in highly stylized public self-presentations. In toto, this move to consciousness requires a general reconception of trust, just when status and ecclesiastical probity are made broadly available, even to women, insofar as both of those human markers emerge from control of particular styles.

This is to say that conventional language had earlier indicated prior entitlements, indications that gradually become valued for their own sake, apart from their actual signification of class standing, high or low. Particular preferences are labeled "Taste," which becomes more abstract than an individual's preferred objects, acts, and surroundings as it is increasingly used to designate a standard applied to individual understanding. Just when differential access to truth and tradition in these societies becomes a secular social problem, not a result of God-given ranks, that standing is also devalued in favor of the standard of thoughtful, thus trusted, deliberation. The newly interiorized identities of republican citizens render ancient oratorical conventions less persuasive as sensitivity and sincerity come to certify authors. They become self-supported writers, members of a demarcated profession, just as they more often advertise their access to secrets of the heart by staged withdrawals from society. Shakespeare's sociability, which Samuel Johnson stresses in the preface to his edition of Shakespeare's plays, becomes less a marker of poet s' perceptivity than is the unfortunate self-absorption displayed in Johnson's biography of Richard Savage. Savage is one of the first widely known nonfictional English characters who attributes the cause of events to psychological trauma he shares with his family.

Chapter 3 ends by arguing that eighteenth-century political and social changes have discursive results in the trans-European revival of elocutionary rhetoric. That topic, eagerly avoided in most rhetoric studies communities, centers the chapter's consideration of nationalism and language standardization. These lessons contribute to the longer, ongoing project of creating stable and publishable vernaculars precisely by articulating—if in two senses—a linguistic and vocal norm meant to replace both local dialects and Latin as the medium of consequential discourses. Its teaching also enacts a symbolic oligarchy insofar as elocutionary precision excludes most speakers and those with no elementary education in writing or only rudimentary practice.

This survey is not meant to predict a progressive chronology. As the title of the conclusion suggests ("Centering Rhetoric—The Psychology of Anxious Moments and Solemn Occasions"), the book ends by returning to questions raised at least tacitly here and in the first chapter. The conclusion addresses the human character again, especially its constructed historical division into opposed rational and irrational/emotional forces. This section's brief picture of antique practices of the self in Mediterranean prehistory explains the creation of the rational/irrational self along the lines of E.R. Dodds's *The Greeks and the Irrational*. He describes shamanistic customs that entered Mediterranean cultures and were incorporated into human identities as sources of the impulses of a split individual. That split, identified on notice of different perceptions in waking and sleeping states, defines the Greek word *thumos* not as "anger" but as "spirit," the force of intrinsic emotion that causes energized human acts and insights that were privileged over experience.

This source helps frame the principal thematic of this study, the significance in the West of conflicts between the seen and the unseen, the known and the unknowable. These antique practices help explain how it becomes normal to imagine that "mind" is a reality rather than a metaphor equivalent to the mathematical equations that constitute almost all we know of wormholes. Their persistence asserts that mind is not feeling, that material realities are ontologically different from their transcendent counterparts, and that the human body contains a hidden interior spirit. The concrete historical intervention of shamanism closes the theoretical circle of this book's topics by returning to their first focus on the tentative yet always hopeful trust with which we endow any site of crafted explanation. But this assertion is not exactly equal to providing access to the thinking and sources that support it, which I sketch below.

The Trouble with Emotion, and Rhetoric

We all claim expertise about the feelings that we have, or do not have, and about our reasons for expressing them, or not. We own feelings as properties that constitute our images of a self and, in particular, easily assert that we feel ourselves and others trustworthy, or not, depending on an exchanged "I know how you feel." Despite competition with supposedly primal tendencies, we most frequently experience trust or its absence as an often preconscious dis/comfort with ourselves, our circumstances, and others. As a verb, it is often understood without an object; some of us are by nature "trusting." Yet this and other emotional dispositions have until recently been unmentionable topics in positivist knowledge-making. As recently as the 1950s and 1960s, scientist Michael Polanyi's differences with positivism were circulated with cultlike enthusiasm as a surrogate for many scholars' irritation about the scientism that recognized neither the uses of his unarticulated "tacit knowledge" nor his view that human creativity creates science. In the humanities, his *Personal Knowledge: Towards a Post-Critical Philosophy* allowed the word "personal" some respectability and with it a wary possibility that (a feeling of) satisfaction creates assent

Of course, Polanyi is one of many such place-markers. But it is still likely that we may be very well schooled without thinking emotion is a plausible topic for investigation. With the exception of various studies of particular, usually unpleasant and sinful emotions (envy, anger, humiliation, and the like), emotion has been acknowledged as a universal human attribute, sometimes an attribute of animals that are equally endowed with feeling or at least with the evolutionary sources of our sophisticated expressions. Since the philosophical phenomenon "Descartes," emotion is a collectible we all keep without pride, an indiscreet counterpart to valued reason. Within a long antique medical history, we usually treat *pathos* as the unfortunate third persuasive appeal in Aristotle's *Rhetoric*, subordinate to reason in explanations of ancient rhetorical schemata. As Donald Bryant puts it in a seminal article calling for further research to distinguish rhetoric, "Rhetoric is thus closely involved with logical and psychological studies [and] employs imagination and emotion not to supplant but to support reason" (420). Here and elsewhere after Homer's more realistic understanding of motives, emotion comes in last, at its best a (gendered) handmaid of reason.

Until recently, praise from psychologists for Book II of Aristotle's *Rhetoric* as their discipline's founding document has not meant that they take emotion to be an appropriate object of study. As Magda B. Arnold's preface to *Feelings and Emotions: The Loyola Symposium* says, "Before 1927 [at the first Wittenburg Symposium on the topic], emotion was viewed with suspicion because its value for scientific psychology appeared doubtful" (x). In his study *Emotion: A Comprehensive Phenomenology of Theories and Their Meaning for Therapy*, James Hillman notes the 1955 *Encyclopedia Britannica* entry on this topic: "Our knowledge of the topic emotion is much less complete than our knowledge of the other topics in the field of psychology." Hillman is exasperated about this gap: "When we come home to systematic (academic or theoretical) psychology to inquire quite naively: 'What is emotion, how is it defined, what is its origin, nature, purpose, what are its properties and laws, everyone uses this concept "emotion"—what are we speaking about?', we find a curious and overwhelming confusion" (7). Hillman recruits René Descartes as well, citing, "There is nothing in which the defective nature of the sciences which we have received from the ancients appears more clearly than in what they have written on the passions" (7). The same might be said of the topic in later social-scientific approaches to rhetoric.

Of course, histories of rhetoric include excellent studies of the appeal to emotion as pathos, often in attention to Aristotle's treatment of it, and writing studies has focused attention on its pedagogic relation to composing. Examples include W. W. Fortenbaugh's comprehensive *Aristotle on Emotion: A Contribution to Philosophical Psychology, Rhetoric, Poetics, Politics, and Ethics*[4]; Jakob Wisse's *Ethos and Pathos from Aristotle to Cicero*; William Grimaldi's exposition in *Aristotle*, Rhetoric II: *A Commentary*; Douglas N. Walton's *The Place of Emotion in Argument*; Elizabeth Belfiore's *Tragic Pleasures: Aristotle on Plot and Emotion*; Lawrence D. Greene's "Aristotle's *Rhetoric* and Renaissance Views of the Emotions"; and two essays by Lynn Worsham: "Going Postal: Pedagogic Violence and the Schooling of Emotion" and "Eating History, Purging Memory, Killing Rhetoric," the latter of which appears in *Writing Histories of Rhetoric*. That collection also includes Takis Poulakos's "Human Agency in the History of Rhetoric: Gorgias's Encomium of Helen," which equates emotion with the power of language over Helen and her appropriate, a-rational response. Unpublished papers include Lance Stockwell's "Appealing through Logic and Emotion: Logos, Pathos, and OJ [Simpson]"; Grant Boswell's "Language and Emotion in 17th-Century Rhetorics"; Laura Micciche's "Emoting for a Change: Feminism and the Rhetoric of Anger," which became (with co-author Dale Jacobs) *A Way to Move: Rhetorics of Emotion and Composition Studies*; and John Hell's "The 'Appearance' of Emotion in *Republic*."

Increasing numbers of theorists in writing studies take up the place of emotion in composing, as does Alice G. Brand in "The Why of Cognition: Emotion and the Writing Process" and "Social Cognition, Emotions, and the Psychology of Writing," and Cynthia Haynes in "pathos@play.prosthetic.emotion." Kia Jane Richmond's "Repositioning Emotions in Composition Studies" notes Susan McLeod's *Notes on the Heart: Affective Issues in the Writing Classroom* and Bruce McPhearson and Nancy Fowler's "Making Connections: Writing and Emotion." Jennifer Edbauer's "(Meta) Physical Graffiti: 'Getting Up' as Affective Wanting Model" exemplifies more recent work that links writing and emotion outside the academy. It cites similar approaches to emotion and writing by Worsham (above), Christa Albrecht-Crane, Anna Gibbs. Fred Kemp, Nedra Reynolds, and cultural critics Eve Sedgwick and Lawrence Grossberg.

Treatises that link emotional "suasion" to "moral philosophy" are legion, as are references to emotion training in vast numbers of educational programs, from sophistic philosophy through the very different aims and audiences of mass education. Copious attention to emotion by contemporary philosophers is represented in relatively recent collections like Amélie Oksenberg Rorty's *Essays on Aristotle's* Rhetoric; Juha Sihvola and Troels Engberg-Pedersen's *The Emotions in Hellenistic Philosophy*; Martha Nussbaum's *Love's Knowledge: Essays on Philosophy and Literature, The Therapy of Desire: Theory and Practice in Hellenistic Ethics*, and other studies; and Paul E. Griffiths's *What Emotions Really Are: The Problem of Psychological Categories*. Nonetheless, insiders in rhetoric have generally set this topic aside. It is taken up elsewhere more frequently, especially by those who turn to emotion to guide academic composition studies from its current focus on epistemology or to guide rhetoric from its parallel emphasis on hermeneutics. Perhaps most important in relation to this study is Daniel Gross's 2006 *The Secret History of Emotion: From Aristotle's* Rhetoric *to Modern Brain Science*, which critiques "a generalized psychology . . . and passions that were once overtly rhetorical . . . [that] now quietly gird the Western . . . belief that emotion is hardwired to the human nature we all share equally" (8). His is the landmark study of rhetoric and emotion from a contemporary perspective.

Of course, myriad accepted sources in countless forms link the definition of rhetoric with emotion itself. Some include "emotional appeal" among logical fallacies; some are media and political descriptions of lies, of obfuscation, and of "what I do not agree with" as "just a lot of rhetoric." Exemplary interdisciplinary approaches that theorize the diverse historical activities contained in the word "rhetoric" still appear squeamish about emotion as an important topic. Brian Vickers's earlier belief that to revitalize rhetoric studies "we must first re-think our conception of the relation between language, feelings, and the codes of expression" has not been realized in work that might claim to support it (16). For instance, Walton's *The Place of Emotion in Argument* clings to the view that logic is equal to valid persuasion, not a part of it. It concedes that emotion can supply "good and reasonable argument [if it] contributes to the proper goals of the dialogue" (29), which it firmly qualifies by making a "problem" of emotions' positive valence. They must "be treated with caution because they can also be used fallaciously. . . . [C]ertain types of emotional appeals are very powerful as arguments in themselves, and they may have a much greater impact on an audience than is warranted" (3).

A subtler, more disappointing yet informative example is an outline of the "Rhetoric Culture" project, a collection of essays edited and written by an international group of anthropologists. It acknowledges a "very real turn toward rhetoric in almost all the human sciences." It includes topics in general and basic anthropology, linguistics, rhetoric, literature, psychology, and philosophy. Its editors plan to gloss "the interaction of rhetoric and culture." They list seven categories of diversely addressed topics, which I arrange in order of the number of essays devoted to them: general theory (18); linguistics (17); social relations (12); religion (10); economics, law, and politics (11); creativity (9); and emotion (5). As the least frequently addressed topic, emotion receives less attention than the similarly "soft" creativity.[5]

This example invites appropriate complaints from two groups of theorists. Many historians of rhetoric emphasize emotion as a feature of pedagogic history in studies of individual rhetoricians (for example, Augustine) or imagined groups (for example, the Sophists). And many cited here and later give painstaking attention to emotion in ways that might have already renewed rhetoric's typical historiography. But avoiding the topic of emotion is more likely, for compelling reasons we see in the relative dispositions of interests of the "Rhetoric Culture" project. Thus, precisely named "rationalizations" of rhetoric respond to its generally poor reputation and its intensification by a perceived early modern turn to strictly demarcated categories of learning. Despite their habitual vehemence, Sir Francis Bacon and Peter Ramus do not befriend the topic. Among rhetoricians, no matter how differently situated, emotion may be a specifically unpleasant topic with a specific bad reputation that is fully articulated in post-Cartesian claims for reason over emotion, for mind over matter, for substance over style. In our time, for instance, this feeling is still frequently expressed—in subtle reversals that assert that "reason is rhetorical" or that demur by saying the rhetoric of inquiry is not "unreasonable or unempirical."[6]

As Gross and others also note, Descartes' focus in *The Passions of the Soul* (1649) itself may best exemplify the contests portrayed in these pairs. *The Passions* follows many earlier associations between the body and feelings, a common trope that varies across historical definitions of "science," which then still needed quotation marks. But Descartes also unfolds a prescient description that links formerly separated elements of human nature. Unlike earlier physical science that argues that human "faculties" occupy places in the brain, stomach, heart, and bowels, *The Passions* connects feeling to the body through a "little gland" (the pineal gland) in the middle of the brain, supposed to orient "animal spirits" through nerves to muscles (xxii). This description imagines a physical circuit that contemporary brain science now also identifies as the almond-shaped amygdala, a twentieth-century discovery of a part of the human limbic system in the brain's temporal lobe. This site of affective response and memory is said to stimulate fear and probably most purely negative and positive feelings, which after their formation continue to generate messages to the body throughout life.[7] Mind and body interact under secular auspices, then and now.

Post-Renaissance theories hereby remedy emotional disturbances through the mind, not the spirit Descartes does so with confidence, believing that those mired in emotion can be helped to "transcend their bodily dispositions" to "achieve the conquest of the 'habitus' which defines virtue" (xxiv). More than a century later in new rhetorics of consciousness, Bishop Richard Whately describes the logic of religion by bracketing feeling as "faith" in it; Hugh Blair connects feeling to the Taste of the universal individual's preferences; David Hume and Henry Home, Lord Kames, obliquely remind us that Aristotle's treatment of style is a consequential entrée to affect, a perception that I rely on as well. George Campbell, the hero of this quick survey, follows John Locke in his assertion that descriptive images stimulate imagination, a recipient's involvement in persuasion. Conviction is thus a matter of feeling. In Locke's words:

> To conclude[:] when persuasion is the end, passion also must be engaged. If it is fancy which bestows brilliancy on our ideas, if it is memory which gives them stability, passion doth more, it images them. Hence they derive spirit and energy. . . . So far therefore it is from being an unfair method of persuasion to move the passions, that there is no persuasion without moving them. (VII.IV, qtd, in Campbell, *Philosophy* 77)

Casting persuasion as a result of individual consciousness thus becomes the remedy for emotional errors, for it brings Mind to bear on feeling. But a general devaluation of the body includes a distaste for feeling that still allows arguments to be made and accepted as conceptual projects, apart from their always local, situated, and material content. That is, the rationalist critique of rhetoric is not precisely the conventional criticism of Plato's *Symposium*. There, epistemology is at stake for a cultural figure, a poet, who is cast as unable to translate perceptual experience of an object, whether actual or imagined, into its Form. Insight overcomes a poet's experience. However, Socrates' critique of rhetoric in the *Gorgias* and *Phaedrus* differently pits the pedagogic performance habits of philosophy against those of oratory in a directly opposing view of how we come to Knowledge and Enlightenment through interactive experience. These dialogues stage contests that importantly enact Socrates' objections to any persuasion that does not result from interlocutory exchanges. As G. B. Hereford's *The Sophistic Movement* says, Socrates rejects any conventional discourse that does not examine a conversant (33).[8] Both dialogues thus dramatize how a soul apprehends Truth through interactions that change perceptions *by virtue of* relationships. Enlightenment, which is not always limited to a knowledge of facts, results from cooperative, face-to-face interactions, however strictly Socrates manages them. As both dialogues also emphasize, neither passive, immobile auditors nor isolated composers of oratorical set speeches can reach Truth. Its apprehension results from the interplay of conversation, which in the Aristotelian sense of "discovery" invents situated ideas, not Ideas. Thus, the long speeches Socrates ridicules in the *Gorgias* and the scroll of Lysias's speech under Phaedrus's robe are unreliable guides, orphaned "writing" that is made meaningless by its fixity, as many have noted. But when we focus on the epistemological faults of rhetoric rather than its erroneous polemical methods, we see a critique of writing enacted, not merely stated, in these texts. That is, writing represses emotional relationships that Socrates' gradual dissections of fixed opinion do enact—young lover and mentor, youth and tutor, fan and performer, acolyte and priest.

The trouble with rhetoric is not that it is "emotional," not "relational," insofar as emotions are not evaluations but experiences in the relationships needed to reach Truth. Instead, the trouble is that oratorical realizations of rhetoric are not so effective as vehicles for that journey as the myths, conversations, friendly if bickering exchanges, and love of chic alternative rhetorics. Oratory, Plato claims, becomes trivial *doxa,* what everyone knows yet knows apart from the relational context needed to verify anyone's logic. No matter how ironically engaging Socrates' tone, the dialogues express ancient fear of losing control of discourse precisely by imposing on it the "due process" of a system—a writing system—that can produce unsituated performances.

Thus ancient, early modern, and later fears of emotion are not precisely the continuing philosophical problem with rhetoric as oratory, nor precisely equal to each other. Especially early treatments outside the often unnoticed but absolute influence of later Stoicism treat emotion as a process, not as a series of named moods, and do so in more positive light than current rhetoric studies take note of. Thus, Athenian worry about losing elite control of a mob of impassioned citizens is also distinct from the early modern fear that an individualized, upstart "self" will disorient the established social force of convention. This post-Cartesian and postrevolutionary fear has more to do with the possibility that social secularization will unloose the chaos of equity as it provides unmediated access both to spiritualism and to education. In addition, print conduct books teach both discursive conventions and successfully moral character habits apart from traditionally sanctioned formal and informal education. They allow anyone to acquire an individually earned property right in otherwise hierarchically distributed salvation, status, and wealth. The emotion portrayed negatively in ancient renditions and later Augustinian and other Christian views, while severely tainted in all settings, is not impossible in rational beings. Emotion is capable of a positive value in itself, well beyond its recaptured worth in reevaluations of positivism in many human sciences.

Such reevaluations of emotion now also take place in cultural studies. Once recognized by psychology, the positive valence of emotion as a social practice has been taken up in work that acknowledges its situated nature, often in the interest of defining how Western and Eastern expressions of emotion differ and thus impinge on business interactions. But a survey of this work might note how its own constitutive emotional tenor sustains nineteenth-century attitudes expressed as ranked categories of human and extra-human behaviors. With at least financially ecumenicist purposes, many evaluative studies of emotion undertaken in the 1980s and 1990s acknowledge that discussions *of* emotion are also "socially and culturally embedded" (Irvine 252).

For instance, in "The Cultural Construction of Self and Emotion: Implications for Social Behavior," Hazel Rose Markus and Shinobu Kitayama assert that "[b]y definition, an emotional event requires another person for its evocation, experience, and expression" (103). However, when this constitutive interaction crosses cultures, misunderstandings result. Like many others who ignore class differences in describing emotion, these authors argue that (the display of?) anger is more acceptable in the West than in Japan because it reveals valued Western independence (101). That contrast is extended in their view that Chinese children are encouraged to see the world as a "network of relationships of which they are a part." "Chinese mothers explicitly stress fostering a happy, close, harmonious relationship with the child, as opposed to [the evidently Western value of] building self-esteem, as a goal of child-rearing" (103). Anna Wierzbicka, in "Everyday Conceptions of Emotion: A Semantic Perspective," describes "universal conceptual primitives" that are retained and placed in discourse differently from place to place, even within supposedly total "Western" or "European" cultures. For instance, in Russia, "the absence of 'emotions' indicates a deadening of a person's *dusa* (heart/soul)" (22). Alan Macfarlane, in "Individualism and the Ideology of Romantic Love," takes issue with social historians who identify companionate marriages as relatively recent results of early modern economies, arguing that the biology of sexuality, if not necessarily expressed, is encouraged in societies whose kinship systems are weakened for various situated reasons (129). This view also appears in Victor S. Johnston's *Why We Feel: The Science of Human Emotion*, which argues that "blocks of meaning can arise only from learned associations between environmental events and the evolved emergent feeling states of conscious biological organisms. A child's developing semantic memory depends upon learning the relationship between those feelings, its behavior, and the world around it" (99).

These views tacitly define emotion as individually evaluative, intentional, and self-interested. Robert C. Solomon's "The Politics of Emotion," an account of gendered manipulative behaviors, notes that "many emotions are about power, persuasion, manipulation, and intimidation" (11). Keith Tester agrees with Hannah Arendt that "compassion is an emotional extension of the individual into the world" and claims that without its better work, people may feel "deeply" without attending to the needs or situations of those who have stimulated that deep feeling (68). In a useful summary, Dinesh Sharma and Kurt W. Fischer portray culturally aware views of such individualized emotion as follows: "From a cultural standpoint, even the most basic emotions and certainly self-conscious emotions can be seen as related to complex clusters of culturally meaningful behaviors and meanings, a 'flow of emotion' . . . consisting of culture-specific embodiments, symbolic meaning, display rules, and interpersonal scripts" (9–10).

Of course, liberally intended cultural studies of emotion in the later twentieth century may also trace the colonizing relation of Western to other cultures. They embed a desire for economic cooperation to occur under Western auspices in normalizing studies that suggest a payoff for cross-culturalism. For instance, one study identifies a different and supposedly only Japanese male emotion, *amae,* a strong desire to be petted and otherwise allowed to be dependent on others. Apart from the obvious universality of this feeling among Westerners across sexes and equal entitlements to express it, the study makes clear my point that cultural studies of emotion unintentionally display chauvinism. This one closes its description with the claim that Western men, who are more "independent" and "manly," could "bring themselves to *amaeru* more if they wanted to" (Morsbach and Tyler 141, 144).

This research paradigm has been significantly altered immediately following worldwide awareness of Mid-Eastern motives to intervene in Western and Far Eastern economic and religious traditions. What was taken to be a previously unexpressed primitivism created anxiety about emotion that had been infrequently expressed in research contexts after the late nineteenth century except as Orientalism.[9]

But recent comments make explicit two agendas that require further qualification of this paradigm's directive tendencies. First, some recent commentary emphasizes that Islamic, Jewish, and other Mid-Eastern populations actually *have* emotions, much as nineteenth-century abolitionists used that claim to win sympathy for African-American slaves. A review cited in advertising a documentary account of Palestinian/Israeli conflict in the Gaza Strip, the 2002 Ram Loevy film *Close, Closed, Closure,* claims that "a wide range of views . . . stresses the importance of reminding the world that the Palestinians are not merely casualties, . . . but *human beings* with *dreams, emotions, and a persevering sense of humor.* The film contributes to our understanding of *the average Palestinian family*" (Rogers 4, emphasis added). Assigning emotion and family life to a highlighted Other perhaps is here less a result of colonialism than of a worldwide anxiety about motives unfamiliar in idealized Western experience.

Thus, a second desire assimilates what are cast as impenetrable motives, specifically of terrorists. In particular, recent Western schooling omits Judeo-Christian idealizations of martyrdom and thus offers no preparation that sanctions aggressive, religiously justified suicide. Terri Toles Patkin's 2004 article "Explosive Baggage:

Female Palestinian Suicide Bombers and the Rhetoric of Emotion" critiques Western media for concerted efforts to mystify the feelings of female suicide bombers while accepting that their male counterparts act out of what are taken to be comprehensible ideological motives. Yet she also says it is impossible to know these women's "emotional and cognitive responses to engaging in terror" (80).

Of course, it is also universally ordinary to portray female motives as beyond the male pale. In this unfortunately familiar instance, their sacrifice is less honored than accused—as extreme feminism, as a product of relationships with male terrorists, as mental ineptitude, as lack of femininity, and as any other quality that excludes women from being "political animals," which is Patkin's telling alternative (82). Male terrorists are called "living weapons," a label that divorces their ideological constitution from a female emotional makeup, evidently to find a "comprehensible explanation" in the purity attributed to doctrinaire male political actors (85). Summarizing this prejudicial interpretative framework, Patkin says that despite its opacity to most, the actual motive is found in "the lessons of the Palestinian culture of martyrdom that both sexes absorb. . . . [M]artyrs attain the status of celebrities," religious leaders justify martyrdom in elaborate theological interpretations, and "young people, female and male, eagerly line up for a one-way ticket to Paradise" (87).

My point is not to belabor the gender-coding that dogs descriptions of both male and female emotions, motives, and susceptibilities and thus writes tediously predictable scripts like this one within a larger stereotyping crusade. But here, this extremely consequential emotional opacity verifies that feeling arises from cultural scripts that are never entirely outside the ken of others, as male and female Christian martyrs might remind Westerners, but that are nonetheless invisible to those unschooled to trust them.

EMOTIONAL EDUCATIONS

Paideia, a formal curriculum in liberal arts, has since classical Greece tied its usually male recipients to history, to each other, and, if less often noted, to a particular range of emotional responses. Werner Jaeger's *Paideia: The Ideals of Greek Culture* calls these connections "one unbroken line of thought from early critics of Homer's heaven to the Christian fathers" (213), But paideia is more importantly the standard example of a broadly conceived emotional education that is woven from shared sessions of rigorous attention to oral and written texts. This is primarily a literary education. Its graduates internalize guidance from heavenly Muses and a shared spirituality, a tacit power most visible in its uses as a socializing imprimatur. Theologian Diana Swancutt explains this circuit:

> *Paideia* was simultaneously the type or system of primary education in the Hellenistic and Roman periods and a civilizing influence that provided national stability throughout the Greek and Roman empires by educating their citizens and subjects about the virtues of their cultures. In other words, *paideia* was an education in civilization that taught as virtuous the societal standards of empire. The "system" of primary education (called *enkyklios paideia*) supported those standards in part by embracing its own set of traditional texts. Dominated . . . by the poetic epics of Homer, young boys—Greek and non-Greek alike—came to identify with Greek heroes and ideals as they recited, learned, and occasionally wrote lines from the stories of the *Iliad* and *Odyssey*. (n.p.)

Thus, as a civilizing force, paideia is a conceptual frame around the lessons it teaches its elite recipients about a shared emotional code. It bonds them as a class demarcated because it shares the emotional range demonstrated in the texts its members have parsed, read, recited, and taken as models for their compositions. They hereby also share this education's ideas about standards of credible behavior, a mobile judgment of fitting responses to specific situations and appropriate ways of talking about them. In archaic Greece, Christian Rome, and later, the result is a sense of belonging among those who have been supervised together in physical, linguistic, compositional, and interpersonal exercises.

One hero of this educational process is Lollianus the grammarian, whose third-century petition from Egypt to Rome asking emperors Gallenus and Valerian for his back pay is exemplary. In it, he evokes precisely this thread of trust. He appeals to both their "heavenly magnanimity" and "*your fellowship* with the Muses (for *Paideia* sits beside you on the throne)" (Brown 35, emphasis added). As Peter Robert Lamont Brown's *Power and Persuasion in Late Antiquity: Towards a Christian Empire* says of Lollianus and indirectly of legions of others, many hope "to cling to the great through the delicate osmosis of shared culture" (35). And as this petition demonstrates, that literary culture's heroic ideals result not only from actual friendships that are cemented by shared physical and academic performances in classes but also by justifiably assumed trust among any whose similar experience is known. Of course, Greek athletic and military contests forge links to differently stringent drill and practice in grammar and rhetorical exercises. From this combination, a certain disposition also emerges, one whose education is well worth its length and expense. But insofar as the method of this curriculum is primarily repetition and imitation, another paideia is available outside elite groups. Since the standard of manly and gentlemanly behaviors is displayed, observed, and regularly emulated, dedicated onlookers can assimilate it—women, slaves, the poor, and unsophisticated rural groups are also its common foils. With varying entitlement across that range, it is a cultural signature.

To demonstrate the powers of that signatory experience, Brown takes expressions of anger as an example. But the feeling he discusses is not a primal, biologically encoded anger portrayed as a product of the brain's renamed "little gland" of the limbic system. Nor is it a psychological response derived from a negative rationalist evaluation of feelings. Among late-empire politicians who share this education, anger is less personal than either of those views imagines. It is constituted by decorous mediations of literary allusions like those Lollianus writes, which convey that writer and reader share values about the proper response, paying what is due.

Yet this anger is also potentially much more dangerous than its explosions in psychologized counterparts who are differently educated. That is, among the educated elite of the Christian empire, anger and political power relations are identical; this anger *is* power. The cultural glue of training in the Muses manufactures shared attitudes toward the *uses* of anger, not a refined conceptual fit of degree to cause. Thus, if anger is inappropriately demonstrated, it of and in itself destroys the social place of those it thereby marks as unacceptable. Modern analyses of anger, whether scientific and behavioral, philosophical, or psychological, all fall far short of explaining this emotion as it was understood as an action, not a cause.

As Brown explains, the empire's far-flung educational identity politics could bring down the imperial governor of a city or province who might unfortunately exercise anger in a violent prerogative of publicly flogging a member of a local elite. To do so was taken to show disdain for class friendship, to reject the bonds that otherwise maintained a shared interest in orderly governance.[10] As Brown says:

> "Anger" was the antithesis to a harmonious and controlled mode of public action. Anger, indeed, emerged as a central component in the language of late Roman politics. It meant . . . the sudden, shameful collapse of self-restraint, associated with a public outburst of rage. But it more usually denoted the morose resentment of a man who would not allow the claims of friendship and esteem, [which] linked one "servant of the Muses" to another, to take effect. Either form of anger was held to constitute a serious breach of decorum. (54)

Brown also realigns the modern assumption that regretting one's anger results from a psychologically motivated change of heart, or that second thoughts and "working through" an outburst lead to interpersonal resolutions. He stresses that in the emotional tuition of a preconsciousness world, anger that breached decorum was in some measure a reversible act. Men of paideia could repent: a governor or emperor might treat breaking the bonds of shared paideia as a normal human lapse, "In this way, emphasis on anger formed part of the late Roman language of amnesty. The counterpart of anger was clemency" (55). There, anger is a matter of persuasion. It is based on mutual trust derived from a shared code, and its restraint, expression, or repentance maintains that code as well. This is to say that it is neither individual emotional property nor reacted to as though it were. Any form of its manifestation—public expression or repentance—launches a public transaction that is visible as violent action or as the "resentment" Brown acutely notes. In such frameworks, plainly repressed anger might be a strategic way to maintain a bargaining position, not a different psychological repression.

Despite the cultural differences I emphasize, contemporary students are not without such uses of feeling. For instance, we read of the righteous wrath of Achilles, or of Superman, which results from an enduring honor code that equalizes rewards to successful warriors. In the *Iliad*, uneven rewards evoke direct action, create and undo alliances, and reshape a world—all after an obviously staged oratorical debate. And as Bryan Register demonstrates, in Gorgias's *Encomium to Helen* a generalized manly lust for Helen creates the circumstance of Achilles' wrath. The insult to his honor and his responding wrath are nonetheless political communications among men, as the *Iliad*'s public debate about it demonstrates. In addition, Gorgias defends Helen's susceptibility to language with a relevant pun: "With a single body she brought together many bodies of men who had great pride for great reasons . . . and they all came because of a love which wished to conquer" (Register 4).[11] That is, anger and lust are both consequential acts whose social and political motives and results have quite ironically become invisible to many who claim for the post-Freudian individual an acute consciousness of feelings and of how they work.

The equivalences among emotion, a literary education, and persuasion thus explain more than the results of calling some ancient literary and legal behaviors "irrational." That equality also uncovers a more textured rhetorical history. For instance, well apart from formal and theoretical treatment of emotional appropriateness in Book II of Aristotle's *Rhetoric* and elsewhere, the instrumentality *of philia* in Athenian society grounds exemplary legal narratives about trust from speakers like Demosthenes (48.14–15) and Lysias (1: 6–7). In Demosthenes, a trusted slave is blamed for cheating a household advisor, a deed especially unacceptable because their positions imply their friendship. In Lysias, a wife who betrays her husband had been thought to be trustworthy—affiliated to her husband's interests—through affection for her new child, Both cases illustrate what Lin Foxhall's study of the Athenian "politics of affection" calls a dubious yet expected "generalized reciprocity" (55). Thus, these examples of unexpected individual limits on that reciprocity occasion significant anxieties among a class trained to expectations of trust.[12] Lynette G.M. Mitchell's *Greeks Bearing Gifts: The Public Use of Private Relationships in the Greek World, 435-323 B.C.* emphasizes Foxhall's points on affection. For instance, Mitchell there argues that ancient affiliations depended primarily on exchanges among personal friends in Athens whose relationships supported the *polis*. Philia, she says, expressed the relation between an individual and society and thus was "a series of complex obligations, duties and claims" larger than interpersonal affection (7).

This view of friendship as a social exchange, not interpersonal goodwill, follows Aristotle's philia of "utility" (*Nicomachean Ethics [NE]* 8, II56aI4–30). He says, "The *philiai* of citizens and tribesmen and fellow-sailors" is like the "*philiai* between associates . . . 'according to some agreement'" (*NE* 8, II6IbII). In all these accounts, friendship involves a more or less regulated association (*NE* II6IbII and II59b31–2). It is always conventional, either by virtue of a formal agreement or "naturally," as an expectation of family, kin, and lovers whose social bonds exist in relation to long histories of law and custom. Thus, trust, gifting, expectations of friendship, and biological relationships all make primarily rhetorical statements. As with the third-century empire's anger, unconventional means of handling such expectations occasion consequential social anxiety but, so far as we know, especially for Achilles, not low self-esteem.

These sources are not, however, origin stories. Antique emotional pedagogies are so commonplace as to be invisible after a long history of equally prepsychological definitions of appropriate relationships in which feeling is a transaction, specifically an action that indicates standing among others. For instance, the thirteenth-century BCE Ten Commandments not only address a specific community but also define its sins as offenses to social order. The commandments in turn prescribe the appropriate relationship to God (acknowledging primacy, speaking respectfully, worshiping with devotion), then how to regulate the conduct of the primary family unit and five additional ways to maintain order by avoiding specific disruptive acts: murder, adultery, theft, false accusations, and covetousness. We might assume the last item on this list controls a private, ultimately self-critical passion—envy. But covetousness here implies scheming to acquire items that the commandments portray as belonging to a neighbor.[13] Many foundational lists of commandments, rules, and strictures predate and follow the Decalogue that establishes this one community's relation to God as a matter of its mutuality.

In his "Story—List—Sanction: A Cross-Cultural Strategy of Ancient Persuasion," James W. Watts points out that ancient Near East and eastern Mediterranean royal inscriptions form similar three-part lists that "specify the contents of [the king's] decrees" (199). Recovered from several Kassite kings of Babylon who ruled in the middle of the second millennium BCE, these lists show congruence among such social rules. Athenian Solon's sixth-century BCE commandments include "Honor the gods," "Have regard for your parents," and, in first place, "Trust good character more than promises." These prescriptive codes guide the emotional tone of credible interactions, as in Solon's "When giving advice, do not recommend what is most pleasing, but what is most useful." But well before Solon legislates exile as punishment for murder, that deed evokes the same penalty in numerous epochs: "Homicide disturbs civic or community order, and this threat is addressed by sending the murderer directly into exile. . . . The time frame and the route of exile were carefully prescribed; even the unintentional killer must keep out of Attica and away from games and festivals attended by all Greeks. If he returned, he could be killed" (Dougherty 33).

Later forms of punishment suggest even more frightening narratives that disallow the possibility that crimes against a community's peace are consequential only to their perpetrators and victims. For instance, as Pope Gregory the Great's sixth-century version of the Seven Deadly Sins enumerates, they disrupt relations to God and to others, not a flow of interiorized probity. Pre-Reformation Christianity judges pride, avarice (greed), envy, wrath, lust, gluttony, and sloth to damage the body of the church, not the psyche of their sources. Thus, in addition to the obviously transactional nature of sins against God and neighbors, gluttony implies taking more than one's share. Sloth, first defined as laziness in regard to spiritual work, also bespeaks failure to provide for one's dependents. Later sixteenth-century punishments for these sins are appropriate metaphorical responses to consequential damage to Christian relationships.

But schooled literary sensibility is also at work in these responses to sin: pride evokes torture on a stone wheel; greed is repaid with boiling in oil; envy results in immersion in freezing water; anger is repaid with dismemberment; lust matches being burned alive; gluttony requires eating rats, toads, and snakes; and sloth is tossed into a snake pit. Commandments, transgressions, corresponding virtues, and similar lists across Western cultures share a socializing purpose in concert with ancient ethical philosophy and the well-wrought rhetoric of Pauline epistolary sermons. All prescribe and prohibit implied emotional environments. All assume that feeling is a behavior toward others, a sustaining force that motivates, controls, and evaluates community interactions.

Of course, emotional education is also the obvious goal in much of Aristotle and Plato. They disagree in some measure about whether schooling can overcome, develop, or actually erase an already inherited disposition, the chemistry that later is individualized to one psycho-logic. The *Nicomachean Ethics* explains why private schooling is superior in shaping character: "For as in cities, laws and *prevailing types of character* have force, so in households do the injunctions and *the habits of the father*" (10.9, emphasis added). Among later philosophers, Galen, Seneca, and others treat education as a way to infuse passion with rational controls.[14] It is obvious as well that when the Roman Empire is dismantled, Christian Augustine's *De Doctrina* teaches a rhetoric to preachers that stresses clear speaking to uneducated converts. But it also stresses the exercise of compassion, the disposition that becomes the overriding emotional tenor of pastoral care before and well after fearsome Puritanism.

Brown argues that the early Christian church's success was also largely a rhetorical production of its character, which depended in great measure on attaching this constructed compassion to one trope, paradox. That is, the obvious wealth of the earliest church leaders and the poverty of their followers are absorbed into the paradox of *sacrifice*: gain requires a loss that is impossible without possessing something to lose. Brown says of wealthy bishops and cooperative local notables that "the theme of 'love of the poor' exercised a gravitational pull [to join the church] quite disproportionate to the actual working of Christian charity . . . [drawing] into its orbit the two closely related issues of who, in fact, were the most effective protectors . . . of the lower classes of the cities and of how wealth was best spent by the rich" (78). Compassion vies with the strength of empire. In contradiction to traditional Christian care of only its own indigent newcomers, widows, and orphans, fourth-century Christianity expands charity to create a dedicated emotional politics. Supplementing the traditional elite paideia, this Christian bonding derives from a different entitlement in which members of the early Christian church programmatically identify with a massive constituency of nonelites. The unentitled are to be included in a religious access to shared love and compassion, the emotional/political expression of the Christian establishment's identification with their circumstances. Much later, a similarly strategic promise of freedom allows emergent republican "citizens" without material resources to identify with power on the basis of a secular equality among "all men [who] are created equal." Submitting to the paradox of democratic governance by elites in the early American colonies and other revolutionary states, republican citizens are included in a precisely named identity politics. Its founding dynamics are repeated as they spawn state institutions of many sorts—and, of course, in many repetitions of its founding dynamics, in a precisely named identity politics.

The Trouble with Rhetoric, and Emotion

The different history of rhetoric implied by these and other examples of how emotions constitute cultures is of little value without evidence that many discrete discourses about discourse signal their recognition of such agendas. It is easily said that emotion is a still denigrated topic, one associated with either hidden human motives or transparent results of clearly moral, chemical, or judgmental forces. It is also arguable that rhetoric studies have already evinced many of the theoretical and disciplinary troubles that regularly come up throughout this study, for instance, questionable Hegelian historical models and the American compression of many rhetorics into one oratorical origin that is mistaken for universal access to equitable political participation. As the synapse of culture, metadiscursive education sensitively but unobtrusively responds to changing circumstance. It makes needed repairs to the emotional infrastructures that permit such misrecognitions, to maintain legible interactions within interested groups. But in these cases, the interests served by upholding transhistorical spins on history need reevaluation in light of their continuing resonance across classes and discrete yet globally interactive cultures.

That project of reevaluation is not accomplished by changes in the methods of any branch of discourse theory, nor by applying already worn approaches to overlooked texts. The issue at stake is emotional and thus a matter of redefining the project to hand. For instance, as Seth L. Schein describes the need to introduce cultural circumstances into that project, he outlines the construction needed to imagine one classical rhetoric as follows:

> The most important lesson Classics can learn from Cultural Studies is that cultures, including classical cultures, consist not of a single, authoritative tradition but of multiple, competing discourses, practices, and values. . . . The construction of a classical tradition is not only a matter of simplistically misreading or decontextualizing complex, historically conditioned texts. It involves a kind of censorship, whether inadvertent or deliberate, that includes some works in a canon and excludes others, or else deflects attention from admittedly canonical works that seem methodologically or ideologically problematic. (294).

Obviously, I would take his suggestions beyond "works" by adding attention to pedagogy to any list of censored cultural voices that nonetheless hold absolute power over reproduction. But neither overlooked works nor teachings that introduce to histories of rhetoric its multiple cultural settings and varied metadiscursive tasks will direct historical attention only to leftovers from a main meal. The well-taught emotional force of many situated forms of persuasion accounts for shifted emphases in the systematic theories now included in legitimate rhetoric. The traditional, reversed narrative that begins with legitimacy as a given condition of interest omits cultural history. For instance, systematic handbook treatments of rhetoric since Aristotle and before might not be dismissed or treated only as formalist outlines were they taken up as simultaneously comprising descriptions of practice and prescriptions for placing their users in specific societies of the educated, as many treatments of later conduct books by cultural historians argue. Directions for producing disembodied speeches and other texts, which both genres make available, teach how to behave in language in ways that allow disparate readers to acquire signs of the emotional codes that legible discourse affirms.

These resources—handbooks and other supposedly untheorized guides—are the supplement Jacques Derrida and Georges Bataille call a cultural "excess," "underbelly," "subtext" or "static electricity that holds the system intact."[15] Any textbook fits that definition, but those that manage language have special consequence because their examples embody values—even at the level of the sentence to be diagrammed. They teach appropriate gestures and responses that rarely acknowledge difference.

Consequently, the vaguely realized formality of rhetoric's treatises and their sometimes combative or defensive tenor might also be cast as a background—the primer on which paintings appear—that enables stating new cases about persuasion. The return of a repressed rhetorical center might involve following Brown's lead to focus on the circumstances around discourses whose result has been to regulate emotions, especially by directing their situated displays in conventional discursive interactions like appeals to the Muses and repentance for anger itself. Pedagogy that determines the consequences of these and other appeals to emotion foregrounds the culturally honored dispositions I have sketched. It manages identities, in undiminished but now widely disseminated importance, as what "holds the system intact."

In addition to many educational studies, these propositions allude to Louis Althusser's "Ideology and Ideological State Apparatuses (Notes towards an Investigation)." It names ideological apparatuses, chief among them schooling, as invasions of private realms, especially a classed self, by state-sanctioned institutional practices. But Althusser also defines ideology not as a set of beliefs but a process of assent necessary to form what he terms an "imaginary relation to the real" (164). That move does not entirely uncover the power of teaching that holds a system intact through seemingly only informative lessons that suggest such relations by teaching literature, history, and other cross-cultural narratives. But if we explain his model as rhetorical, a metadiscourse that applies to many ways of reproducing culturally sanctioned identities, its uses become less deterministic. For instance, paideia is neither a state institution nor a centralized system equivalent to a titled ideological apparatus. But its diffusion among a class, not only in one nation-state, expanded its power. Its students draw on trust that can be called into play provisionally, to erase or modify official differences and ultimately to create precisely countercultural associations. If shared elite access to the Muses becomes elite solidarity, it also operates independently of local standing and uneven power relations like those Brown describes in Roman provinces. More importantly, solidarity endures as a discourse, a relational rhetoric, among others whose powers are not determined by articulated class structures.

This exemplary theoretical limit demonstrates that the trouble with rhetoric *and* emotion is different from and greater than issues I attach to either member of that pair. If we hope to theorize that relationship as correlative, its incapacity to reward straightforward investigations that produce predictable outcomes, however theoretical, becomes visible after only a glance at the messy nature of human interaction. Histories of emotion, their separate definitions, and empirical studies aimed to expose their singular causes and matched results emulate similar treatments in contemporary rhetoric studies. In its treatment of specific emotions, what counts as either an essential or a disciplinary definition of rhetoric tells how to measure the effects of persuasive moves. Rhetoric studies adds to these parallel cases a history that places its vehemence in unseen consciousness that it treats as an always to-be-interpreted phenomenon, not as a result of custom, schooling, and overlayered cultural scripts. Both its theories and its histories also remain distant from the often overlooked subtextual energies that mark interactions with what we do not know and may decide. In this view, modern dispositions are rhetorically layered results of variously nuanced instruction from many sources, including religious and political institutions. They may be imagined within the rhetoric George Kennedy recently defined as a "form of emotional energy" (*Comparative* 3).

To take one instance that clarifies these relations among trust, cultural dispositions, and discourse: As Socrates took trouble to show, knowledge of rhetoric is not knowledge of medicine. But neither is it knowledge of nothing. The metadiscursive processes that medical discourses realize show how mutual trust and authority work in particular cultures and, specifically in this case, how medical discourses persuade us to act in ways that on their face require peculiar leaps of faith. As we know from perhaps the oldest extant medical document, written circa 2100 BCE, the Mesopotamian scientist-*ashipu*, evidently referred to earlier as a sorcerer-doctor, who read signs to determine the sin, heredity, or other extrinsic cause of illness differs from his cooperating peer, the physician-*asu*, who diagnoses on the basis of physical symptoms and precedent cases to prescribe a drug, tonic, or washes, bandages, and plasters for a sore spot. Educated patients trust both and might also visit the Temple of Gula for a diagnosis.

Yet so far as we know, none found a palm reader a safe source of treatment. Given the qualities of our own medical practitioners, this example vividly reminds us that trust is culturally educated to move us to act or not. And from our perspective on discourse, that feeling obviously derives from recognizing hierarchies that the subtexts of various rhetorics create and verify, dispositions based on Hamilton's "routines and pathways . . . the rules of appropriateness and eligibility." A rhetorically encultured patient recognizes the logic and aesthetics of hierarchic eligibility, which are inculcated, never memorized for a test.

These hierarchies also inform trustworthy self-presentations, where the same conditions apply. It does not matter if we go to a seminary to learn pastoral care, or to a university to absorb the terms used in postmodernism, or to medical school to learn how to wield a stethoscope with authority. Our credibility in these cases is not derived from directly taught information, nor from credentials, nor from practice exercises, nor even from personable projected personalities. But those preparatory settings allow us to access systems that require trust, especially in their secret knowledge. That enculturation, not into knowledge but into knowledge *of* knowledge systems, allows us to occupy expectations: we grasp symbolic significations of holding and of being held within various forms of unverifiable knowledge.

Another way to say this is that accounts of persuasion need to consider the emotional effects of charisma. A later doctor in an expensive suit whose educated speech is familiar to us projects a whole range of charismatic signifiers that makes some of us think she will be a trustworthy clinician. But others might infer from these signs that she is a slick upper-class jerk who has ripped off the working class to afford that suit. In either case, choices between faith healers and doctors, and choices by them, will result from comfort within a particular unverifiable code, emotional ways that we trust, or not, different purveyors of knowledge to which we have no access.

These cases suggest consequences for teaching rhetoric. All differently assert that we are not persuaded by argumentative proofs, nor by signs of expertise, knowledge, and fairness in their sources. We trust discourse we perceive to contain unknown, secreted if not secret content, when we feel that there is more to be known, yet that we already know more by virtue of our teachers' access to a metadiscourse whose very existence promises that the unknown is not unknowable. This is to say that many mechanisms around uncertainty function symbolically and charismatically, not logically or analytically.

It follows, logically, that in addition to the demands we impose on theory when we recognize many rhetorics, full accounts of a unified oratorical rhetoric and Aristotelian argumentation cannot be only logical and coherent. Often neatly categorized but inchoate nonetheless, our self-contradictory, overdetermined, and certainly culturally taught feelings recognize more to be said. Emotion has had little systematic attention until recently, as I have said. But despite a great deal of current notice, emotion is still usually treated as a singular creature of rationalism. Only a few articulate an aesthetics of emotion as a way to explain our personal theories of life and choice, our ways of imagining ourselves as occupants of good or bad stories. But in any version of rhetoric, that self-aestheticizing result of modernism—like style, our illusion of control—invites attention. Here, I ground that consideration in only a nonce definition of reality: as Catullus had it, I hate and I love. In that overdetermined multiplicity of feeling, which in Poem 85 includes the poet's tortured curious awareness,[16] we individually join a history like the one I have been suggesting. Its logic is self-contradictory, and its chronologies are obvious projections of our own emerging present. We form and trust these narratives individually, precisely until, as we do and do not use conceptual definitions of rhetoric, we do not.

Instrumental and Constitutive Rhetoric in Martin Luther King Jr.'s "Letter from Birmingham Jail"

Michael Leff and Ebony A. Utley

Traditional conceptions of rhetorical ethos treat character exclusively as an instrument of persuasion, but the persona of the rhetor often functions as a means of constituting the self in relation to a complex network of social and cultural relationships. This generative function of character becomes especially important in cases where suppressed groups attempt to find rhetorical means to alter their circumstances. Using Martin Luther King Jr.'s "Letter from Birmingham Jail" as a case study, we argue that the text develops a complex and nuanced construction of King's character. This construct allows King to criticize his target audience without alienating himself from it and also allows the "eavesdropping" black audience to discover a model for reconstructing their own sense of agency. This constitutive dimension of character occurs simultaneously and in intimate connection with its use as an instrument of persuasion concerning specific issues. Based on this case, we argue that rigid distinctions between instrumental and constitutive functions of rhetoric are misleading and that rhetorical critics should regard the constitution of self and the instrumental uses of character as a fluid relationship.

Almost 30 years ago, in an essay devoted to the *Autobiography of Malcolm X*, Thomas W. Benson commented that rhetoric is, among other things, a way of constituting the self within a scene composed of "exigencies, constraints, others and the self," and it is also a resource for "exercising control over self, others, and by extension the scene."[1] Thus Benson assigns rhetoric a dual function. It is simultaneously generative and instrumental, because it helps to constitute the identity of self, other, and scene, while it also pulls these identities within the orbit of situated interests. Moreover, once this duality is acknowledged, it virtually forces the critic to expand and complicate the conventional interest in "ethical proof," because the persona of the rhetor emerges not just as an instrument of persuasion but also as something constituted within the rhetorical medium.

Viewed from our current vantage point, Benson's observations seem prescient. He anticipates a set of pivotal issues associated with recent interest in constitutive rhetoric and with the emergence of "interpretive" or "conceptual" criticism.[2] He also locates a subject—Malcolm X in particular and African-American protest rhetoric in general—where these problems arise with special clarity and urgency. In Malcolm's texts, we encounter a persona that, as Benson says, sometimes takes on the aspect of "a magnificent anti-hero, an existentialist saint, or a mythic witness to America's oppressive racism," but that also sometimes seems to display the qualities of a hustler, an opportunist, or a cynical manipulator of words and audiences.[3] Thus, a tension between the constitutive and instrumental functions surfaces almost immediately when examining Malcolm's rhetoric, and although it is generally less obtrusive in other African-American rhetors during the civil rights revolution of the 1960s, it is still a prominent feature of their discourse—and for good reason. Their efforts to overcome a system that repressed and demeaned them required rhetorical instruments sufficient not only to serve immediate political ends but also to constitute a new conception of themselves and their fellow African-Americans.

Republished with permission of Michigan State University Press, from *Rhetoric and Public Affairs, Volume 7, Issue 1* by Michael Leff and Ebony A. Utley. Copyright © 2004 by Michigan State University Press; permission conveyed through Copyright Clearance Center, Inc.

In this essay, we concentrate upon Martin Luther King Jr.'s "Letter from Birmingham Jail" and argue that it displays a subtle and complex interrelationship between construction of self and instrumental appeals through character. On our reading of the text, the "Letter" harmonizes aspects of its author's persona by blending and balancing the representation of the self in relation to what Benson calls "the exigencies, constraints, and others" connected with the scene. King's effort to move through a tangle of events and ideas toward a decorous sense of order contrasts notably with the confrontational rhetoric of Malcolm X,[4] but we hope to demonstrate that in constructing an effective persona, King shares the burden and opportunity of crossing between instrumental and constitutive concerns. Before turning to the text of the "Letter," however, we need to consider the context in which it appeared and some of the circumstances of its composition.

1. The Background

Early in 1963, the Southern Christian Leadership Conference (SCLC) targeted Birmingham, Alabama, for a nonviolent direct action campaign designed to force the city to modify or eliminate its segregation laws. For a variety of reasons, the campaign was delayed until April 3, and when it did begin, it encountered serious problems. Only a handful of protestors proved willing to subject themselves to arrest, and so the effort to force concessions by filling the city's jails was failing. Moreover, white moderates, and even some blacks, thought the campaign ill timed, since the newly elected city government had been given no opportunity to deal with the segregation issue. Worse yet, the city's attorneys obtained a federal injunction forbidding King and other SCLC leaders from sponsoring, encouraging, or participating in a demonstration unless they obtained a permit from the city. In effect, this meant that SCLC either had to abandon the campaign or violate federal court orders.

King decided that it was necessary to violate the injunction and that he himself would lead a march and submit to arrest. This "faith act," he hoped, would invigorate the campaign, and on April 12, 1963 (Good Friday, a day chosen for its symbolic importance), King headed a protest demonstration through the streets of Birmingham and was arrested. Refusing to post bail until April 19, he remained in jail for eight days.[5]

On the morning of the 13th, the day after King was imprisoned, the *Birmingham News* printed a short open letter signed by eight local clergymen. The clergy criticized the direct action campaign as an untimely and unwise effort "led in part by outsiders" and urged the black residents of Birmingham to obey the law, withdraw support from the demonstrations, and resolve their grievances through the courts and the negotiation process.[6] King's "Letter from Birmingham Jail" was a direct response to the clergymen's statement.

The history of the "Letter"'s composition is a matter of some interest. According to the conventional story, King began writing his response on the margins of the newspaper that published the clergymen's letter, then on odd scraps of paper provided by a sympathetic prison guard, and finally on a legal tablet provided by King's attorney. While King was engaged in composition, his visitors carried the marginalia, scraps, and pages to SCLC headquarters where a secretary typed the individual bits until the text was completed.

There is no reason to doubt the truth of this story as far as it goes, but it does not seem to be the whole story. Although the "Letter" is dated April 16, no version of it circulated in public until after the first week of May, and internal evidence rather clearly indicates that the published version of the work could not have been completed until after April 19. Thus, at least some parts of the "Letter" likely were composed and/or revised after King left prison.[7] The tone and content of the document, however, create the impression that the author wrote it from within a prison cell, and as we will note later, this impression greatly contributes to King's self-representation and to the persuasive impact of the "Letter" as a whole.

2. KING'S "LETTER": THE RHETORIC OF THE TEXT

With this background in mind, we can turn to the text itself and to the construction and representation of agency within it. This interpretative inquiry has an affinity with the neoclassical concern for the rhetor's ethos, but in the neoclassical approach, the tendency is to designate character as a mode of proof, to locate instances where it is invoked, and to isolate it as a discrete element in the persuasive process. In the interpretative frame, the agency of the rhetor refers not just to the use of character appeals but also to the way that rhetors place themselves within a network of communicative relationships. At a minimum, the explication of this process demands attention to: (1) the rhetor's construction of self, (2) the rhetor's construction of the audience (what Edwin Black calls the "second persona"),[8] and (3) the enactment within the text of the relationship between rhetor and audience. In what follows, we will try to explain how King's "Letter" works along all three of these lines and to indicate how they converge to create and represent an identity for King both as writer and as social/political actor.

One of the most prominent features of the text is its extensive use of direct address. Whereas the clergymen's letter is addressed to no one in particular, King begins with the salutation "My Dear Fellow Clergymen," and the first paragraph continues in this vein as King's "I" speaks in response to the "you" who composed the earlier letter. And the dialogic relationship is underscored by the wording of the paragraph's final sentence: "But since I feel that you are men of genuine good will and your criticisms are sincerely set forth, I would like to answer your statement in what I hope will be patient and reasonable terms."[9] This pattern is sustained through the body of the "Letter" as King organizes its content into a seriatim response to claims attributed to the eight clergymen. The following schema indicates this structure:

A. Introduction
B. Refutation
    1. That King is an outsider
    2. That King and his supporters should negotiate rather than demonstrate
    3. That the demonstrations are ill timed
       (First confession: King's disappointment with white moderates)
    4. That nonviolent direct action precipitates violence
    5. That racial problems will resolve themselves over time
    6. That King and his supporters are extremists
       (Second confession: King's disappointment with white clergy)
    7. That the Birmingham police deserve praise
C. Conclusion

Save for the fifth point on the list, King introduces every one of his refutations with the use of the second-person pronoun, and most often he fashions a direct response in the first person. (For example, discussion of the second claim begins: "You deplore the demonstrations that are presently taking place in Birmingham. But I am sorry that your statement did not express a similar concern for the conditions that brought the demonstrations into being" [85].) At times, King enhances this interactive sensibility by means of rhetorical questions. (For example, "You may well ask: 'Why direct action? Why sit-ins, marches, etc.? Isn't negotiation a better path?' You are exactly right in your call for negotiation" [86].) In short, King exploits the form of the "Letter" to localize, personalize, and dramatize the issues in the civil rights debate.

Although King's "Letter" literally and directly addressed the eight Birmingham clergymen, it was never delivered to them, nor were they, in fact, his intended audience. The clergymen functioned rhetorically as a synecdoche, as a representation of the larger audience King wanted to reach, and his decision to respond to their statement and his manner of doing so were both strategic. The success of the Birmingham campaign, and of SCLC efforts in general, depended heavily on support from white moderates—Americans already inclined to oppose racial segregation in principle and to feel uncomfortable about the discrepancy between their basic values and the discriminatory policies then practiced in the South, but who were also fearful about direct action campaigns and the threat they posed to public order. When the eight clergymen published their statement, they offered King an opportunity to embody this target audience (and hence to use it as a rhetorical construct) without appearing to manufacture an artificial situation. Equally important, as Richard P. Fulkerson has noted, the invocation of specific individuals as an ostensible audience allowed King to cultivate a personal tone and to project his personality in ways that would have been impossible in a document addressed to no one in particular.[10] The "Letter," then, effectively used an actual event to construct a personalized version of both writer and audience through a double synecdoche. Just as the eight clergy stood for white moderates, so also did King stand for the SCLC and the African-Americans engaged in nonviolent direct action campaigns.

While the "Letter"'s external structure proceeds in a point-by-point linear order, the rhetoric of the text also develops recurrent themes—repeated ideas, images, and arguments that work through the linear sequence of refutational arguments. These themes represent King as an agent of change who embodies the basic values of his white moderate audience and who acts with restraint and respect even as he attempts to reform glaring injustices. This development, an example of what Kenneth Burke calls repetitive form,[11] allows King to disagree with his audience while still remaining consubstantial with it. His dissent thereby seems to arise from within the *habitus* of his interlocutors.

From the opening salutation, King repeatedly emphasizes his status as a Christian minister and his unwavering commitment to the church. This point achieves its most notable articulation in the course of King's "second confession," where he expresses disappointment with white clergymen who "remain silent behind the anesthetizing security of stained-glass windows," and with white churches that stand on the sideline and preach an otherworldly religion. This is strong criticism, but King explains that it comes from a person firmly embedded in the Christian tradition: "In deep disappointment, I have wept over the laxity of the church. Be assured that my tears have been tears of love . . . Yes, I love the church; I love her sacred walls. How could I do otherwise? I am in the rather unique position of being the son, the grandson, and great-grandson of preachers" (97). Here King's figuration overlaps at three levels of embodiment: Christianity is made physical through representation of the church as a walled, physical space; King, coming from a lineage domiciled within those walls, assumes an identity connected with that Christian space, and from this inside position his disappointment with the church can manifest itself only as tears of love. All this figurative work presents King as someone who has the appropriate credentials to criticize the church from within and to recall it to its own ideals.

More generally, King embodies his solidarity with mainstream American values through the use of appeals to authority. The text is peppered with references to venerated figures from American history, Judeo-Christian lore, and the Western intellectual tradition. These include Paul, Socrates, Reinhold Niebuhr, Thomas Aquinas, Martin Buber, Paul Tillich, Jesus, Amos, Martin Luther, John Bunyan, Abraham Lincoln, Thomas Jefferson, and T. S. Eliot, and King invokes these references to vindicate and explain his own actions. For example, in response to the charge that he is "an outsider," King cites scriptural precedent for his activity: "Beyond this, I am in Birmingham because injustice is here. Just as the eighth-century prophets left their little villages and carried their 'thus saith the Lord' far beyond the boundaries of their hometowns; and just as the apostle Paul left his little village of Tarsus and carried the gospel of Jesus Christ to practically every hamlet and city of the Graeco-Roman world, I too am compelled to carry the gospel of freedom beyond my particular hometown" (84–85).

King is obviously concerned to dispel the perception that he is an outsider in Birmingham and a radical who adheres to positions that fall outside the orbit of respectable American opinion. The appeals to authority counter this image at two levels. First, by citing icons of accepted belief and faith, King associates himself with figures who command unquestioned respect from his target audience, and this helps to establish commonality with it. Second, the words and deeds of these respected individuals, insofar as they appear to be the same as or similar to King's words and deeds, become exemplars that sanction King's position and open space for it within the conceptual horizons of his audience. If Amos, Paul, Socrates, and even Jesus behaved as agitators, then it follows that agitation to expose and overcome injustice is no threat to the common tradition, but is instead something needed to renew and sustain its integrity.

King not only constructs his persona through strategies of embodiment, but he also uses the text to enact the kind of agency that he wants to have associated with himself and his movement. By enactment, we are referring not just to what the text says, but to what it does, and throughout the "Letter" King's verbal action as writer and advocate presents a complex but consistent representation of his character. The manner of his argument and his style of arguing combine to depict the man as energetic, active, committed to principles, and committed to act in accordance with those principles but to do so in a poised, balanced, reasonable, and restrained manner. The dominant image is one of restrained energy, and this image is well calculated to diffuse the accusation that King is a dangerous radical who lacks prudent judgment and acts without due regard for practical consequence.

Throughout the sequence of refutations, the text enacts balanced judgment through what Fulkerson calls a "dual pattern."[12] King responds to the allegations against him first on an immediate practical level and then on the level of principle, and as this pattern unfolds, the reader witnesses King exercising the kind of judgment most appropriate to deliberation—judgment that simultaneously encompasses particulars and principles and that engages questions both of expediency and honor. The first of King's refutations provides a clear illustration of this strategy. In responding to the charge that he is an "outsider," King begins by explaining that the Birmingham affiliate of the SCLC asked for his assistance, and so he is "here, along with several members of my staff, because we were invited here." But this is not the end of the matter, since beyond such particular concerns there is also a moral imperative that leads King to confront injustice just as the Hebrew prophets and the apostle Paul did. And, to place the issue on an even broader ground, King recognizes "the interrelatedness of all countries and states. . . . Injustice anywhere is a threat to justice everywhere. We are caught in an inescapable network of mutuality, tied in a single garment of destiny. Whatever affects one directly affects all indirectly" (85). Thus, whether judgment rests on the concrete particulars of the case or on sweeping ethical principle, King should not be regarded as an outsider; his presence in Birmingham is both appropriate and right.

The second, third, and fourth refutational sections also employ this double structure, but it is in the sixth section, where King addresses the charge of extremism, that the technique achieves its most powerful articulation.

He begins his response by expressing surprise that anyone would label him as an extremist, since in actuality he stands "in the middle of two opposing forces in the Negro community." On one side, there are those who simply acquiesce to injustice and do nothing, and on the other there are the black nationalists who react to injustice with hatred and bitterness and come "perilously close to advocating violence." Between these extremes of complacency and angry despair, King offers the "more excellent way" of nonviolent protest, and he acknowledges disappointment that this position would be regarded as extremist. King, however, has a second thought on the matter, and he "gradually gained a bit of satisfaction from being considered an extremist. Was not Jesus an extremist in love—'Love your enemies, bless them that curse you, pray for them that despitefully use you.'" This appeal to authority continues through a long list of heroic figures (including Amos, Paul, Martin Luther, John Bunyan, Abraham Lincoln, and Thomas Jefferson) who are also linked to famous quotations expressing extreme ideas. And King concludes that the question is not whether "we will be extremists" but whether we will be extremists for love and justice or extremists for hate and injustice (92–94).

As other commentators have noted, this passage distinguishes between extremism understood as placement along a spectrum of existing positions and extremism understood in terms of intensity of conviction.[13] By the first standard, King is not an extremist but rather a dialectically tempered moderate, since his position comes between and constructively synthesizes the antithetical forces of apathy and violence. By the second standard, however, King is an extremist because he is passionately committed in principle to act against and eradicate injustice, and as King's historical witnesses demonstrate, extremism of this type supports the fundamental values of the society. This passage, then, combines restrained practical judgment with a passionate determination to overcome injustice, and the passion, however strongly it is expressed, still moves along constructive lines, because faith, justice, and love channel its energy.

Another notable feature of this passage is King's restraint in choosing the words he uses to address his critics. When labeled as an extremist, King reacts not with an expression of anger or indignity but disappointment. This sort of verbal control recurs throughout the "Letter." Thus, in the two sections that digress from the sequence of refutations, King makes his most critical comments about the inaction of the white community, but he studiously avoids the language of accusation. Instead, he "confesses" his disappointment with them. This restraint not only characterizes King's choice of words, but also, and more powerfully, it is enacted in the structure of some of his sentences.

In one of the most memorable parts of the text, King offers a carefully modulated response to the charge that the demonstrations are untimely. African-Americans, he reminds his readers, already have had to wait for 340 years for their rights, and it is no wonder that they are growing impatient. "Perhaps it easy for those who have never felt the stinging darts of segregation to say, 'Wait'":

> But when you have seen vicious mobs lynch your mothers and fathers at will and drown your sisters and brothers at whim; when you have seen hate-filled policemen curse, kick, brutalize, and even kill your black brothers and sisters with impunity; when you see the vast majority of your twenty million Negro brothers smothering in an airtight cage of poverty in the midst of an affluent society; when you suddenly find your tongue twisted and your speech stammering as you seek to explain to your six-year-old daughter why she can't go to the public amusement park that has just been advertised on television, and see tears welling up in her little eyes when she is told that Funtown is closed to colored children, and see the depressing clouds of inferiority begin to form in her little mental sky, and see her begin to distort her little personality by uncon-

sciously developing bitterness toward white people; when you have to concoct an answer for a five-year-old son asking in agonizing pathos: "Daddy, why do white people treat colored people so mean?"; when you take a cross-country trip and find it necessary to sleep night after night in the uncomfortable corners of your automobile because no motel will accept you; when you are humiliated day in and day out by nagging signs reading "white" and "colored"; when your first name becomes "nigger" and your middle name becomes "boy" (however old you are) and your last name becomes "John," and when your wife and mother are never given the respected title "Mrs.," when you are harried by day and haunted by night by the fact that you are a Negro, living constantly at tiptoe stance never quite knowing what to expect next, and plagued with inner fears and outer resentments; when you are forever fighting a degenerating sense of nobodiness; then you will understand why we find it difficult to wait. (88–89)

The most obviously remarkable feature of this sentence is its length—331 words, which makes it by far the longest sentence in the text and probably one of the longest sentences in contemporary English prose. But the syntax of the sentence also deserves attention. Because it is structured in left-branching or periodic form, the syntactic complexity of the sentence develops through the accretion of dependent clauses that occur before the main clause. This arrangement suspends the completion of the sentence as a meaningful unit until the end, and so, to understand the sentence, the reader must wait until the final 11 words provide closure. Moreover, since the dependent clauses narrate a series of injuries, insults, and outrages, the whole development iconically represents the plight of the African-American.[14] The white readers, who have never directly suffered from the "stinging darts of segregation," must wait while this long list of grievances continues to assault their sensibilities, and so they vicariously experience the frustration of the African-American. The sentence enacts and transmits that experience in a way that no propositional argument could accomplish.

Given the length of the sentence, the tension that mounts through it, and the vivacity with which it represents the effects of injustice, we might expect it to end on a strong note of outrage and anger, perhaps even with an accusation against those who ask African-Americans to wait. Instead, however, the climax comes in the form of an understated address to the white audience: "Then you will understand why we find it difficult to wait." The understatement may work to heighten the emotional impact of the sentence, but it is also a striking enactment of King's restraint, and it is difficult to imagine a more appropriate textual representation of King's pledge to proceed in reasonable and patient terms.

Toward the end of the "Letter," when he questions the clergyman's praise of the police, King uses this same verbal technique for building and containing emotional energy:

I don't believe that you would have so warmly commended the police force if you had seen its angry violent dogs literally biting six unarmed Negroes. I don't believe you would so quickly commend the policemen if you would observe their ugly inhuman treatment of Negroes here in the city jail; if you would watch them push and curse old Negro women and young Negro girls; if you would see them slap and kick old Negro men and young boys; if you will observe them, as they did on two occasions, refuse to give us food because we want to sing our grace together. I'm sorry that I can't join you in your praise for the police department. (98–99)

The loose or right branching construction of the long sentence does not suspend meaning as does the periodic sentence King uses earlier, and partially for this reason, this passage does not have quite the same dramatic impact. Nevertheless, the pattern of energy and restraint is apparent. The long sentence accumulates grievances through its many clauses, and the short sentence that follows offers a controlled, understated response addressed directly to the ostensible audience.

To sum up, in the "Letter from Birmingham Jail" King attempts to reach his target audience by dispelling the perception that he is a radical given to intemperate action and committed to views that fall outside the mainstream of American society. The text consistently works to represent King in a different light, and it does so not just by direct statement, but also by demonstrating balanced, temperate forms of judgment as it engages key issues and by the enactment of restrained energy in the very structure of the prose. At the end of the "Letter," King articulates this theme in two nicely balanced sentences that sum up the position he occupies throughout the text:

> If I have said anything in this letter that is an overstatement of the truth and is indicative of unreasonable impatience, I beg you to forgive me. If I have said anything in this letter that is an understatement of the truth and is indicative of my having a patience that makes me patient with anything less than brotherhood, I beg God to forgive me. (100)

3. Persona and Audience in King's "Letter"

Readers of the "Letter from Birmingham Jail" often testify to its powerfully evocative effect. For many Americans, the "Letter" produced an immediate, unified response that restructured and reframed their perception of a complex situation, and E. Culpepper Clark has offered a plausible account for this response. King, he maintains, gathered together an ambiguous set of cultural experiences and expectations and transformed them "into the controlling metaphor for interpreting nonviolent civil disobedience." Writing from the confinement in a prison, King could exercise a prophetic voice that recalled his people to their better selves and that resonated "with the Judeo-Christian struggle against human bondage."[15]

King's actual imprisonment in Birmingham Jail is a necessary condition for the metaphor to work, but the image of a man writing in a cramped, isolated prison cell is in large part constructed by the text itself. And it was not enough simply for King to construct a prisoner's voice, since not all prisoners are prophets. King also faced the more difficult task of embedding himself within a culture that segregated people of his race. The prophetic voice does not come from the outside; it must arise from within the people whom it criticizes. It must incarnate what is highest and best in the culture of that people and summon them to act on standards the prophet embodies and the audience shares.[16] The prophet is a member of the tribe, and so, to be a prophet among the Hebrews, one must be a Hebrew. And what is required to be a prophet among white Americans? That is a role King neither inherits by birth nor gains through any other easy access. He must argue himself into it, and the "Letter" is wonderfully designed to achieve just this purpose. It constructs King as an agent who grounds his identity in the religious, intellectual, and political values of the American tribe, and it enacts a form of agency that sustains connection between author and reader even in the presence of disagreement. King emerges from the "Letter" not just as someone who can argue with a white audience on its own terms but as an agent who can elevate that audience by forcing it to acknowledge its sins of omission and by demanding consistency between its actions and its highest values.

To this point, our reading of the text has followed the writer-audience ratio that is central to its explicit argument. But while the white moderate surely is the ostensible target audience, King must have known that the text would also circulate among African-American readers. A systematic study of the coexistence of this black audience requires more attention than we can give to it in this essay, but we can offer a sketch of how shifting focus to the text's other audience enhances our understanding of the constitutive function of rhetoric.

The black audience for King's "Letter" has a status similar to what James L. Golden and Richard D. Rieke call the eavesdropping audience for the rhetoric of Malcolm X and other militant African-American rhetors. While these militants usually speak directly and specifically to a black audience, they are also quite aware of white "eavesdroppers" who are listening even though they are not addressed, and it seems clear that their discourse is intended to have an impact on the whites who "overhear" what is said. This concern about the eavesdropping audience, Golden and Rieke argue, arises from its association with the existing power structure, and so the eavesdropping audience is constructed as an effort to induce people in power to effect change.[17]

As we have shown, King's commitment to writing himself inside the values of mainstream American society enables him to make a direct appeal to the audience of white moderates, but it is the black readers of the text who must be persuaded to risk their bodies. Without their active involvement, nonviolent civil disobedience cannot work, since blacks must exercise their power to protest if they are to force whites to align their professed beliefs with their actions. Thus, even though King places the white audience at the center of his text, his effort to persuade it results from and consequently is constrained by black action. By analogy with the white eavesdroppers on the rhetoric of Malcolm and other militant blacks, we can think of black readers of King's "Letter" as eavesdroppers who are being urged to exercise power to effect change. In this case, the black audience is instructed about how to adopt personae that will make them more effective agents for change and about the means for implementing this agency.[18] If we regard the "Letter" as an appeal to power and conscience and the proper alignment between the two, we must consider it as an appeal not just to the ostensible white audience but also to the collective power and conscience of black people.

Viewed from this angle, the "Letter" constructs a model for African-Americans to adopt and enact. In the opening paragraph, King represents himself in a way that reveals key features of that model. The salutation, "My Dear Fellow Clergymen," sets King on equal footing with the white men he is addressing, and in the sentence that follows, we learn that although King is confined in jail, he is an important and busy man who generally does not have time to answer criticism. In this instance, however, since he thinks the eight clerics are sincere men of good will, he elects to respond to them and to do so in patient and reasonable terms. Thus, even though confined physically, King remains an active agent who exercises choice about when and how to respond to others.

King's immediate situation—his imprisonment—corresponds to the imagery he uses later in the text to characterize the general condition of African-Americans. He depicts them as "smothering in an airtight cage of poverty," as forced to sleep "in the uncomfortable corners" of their automobiles, as threatened by the "quicksand of racial injustice," and as prone to fall into the "dark dungeons of complacency." Yet, like King himself, African-Americans are beginning to break through these restraints. They are experiencing a new militancy, and they carry the "gospel of freedom," create constructive tension, stride toward freedom, move with "a cosmic energy" toward racial justice, and rise out of the "dark dungeons" to the "hills of creative protest."

By contrast, the white moderates are inert and immobile even though they face no restraints imposed from the outside. They have become, in King's words, stumbling blocks to freedom, dams blocking social progress, silent witnesses of injustice, anesthetized behind stained glass windows, and paralyzed by the chains of conformity. White moderates, then, are passive, while the once passive blacks are becoming agents of change. No longer willing to accept stolid indifference, they demand their rights as American citizens and insist that sincere people of good faith lend them their support. But morally and practically, they are best advised to make these demands in the spirit of King's example. In breaking out of restraints imposed upon them, they should accept a measure of self-restraint. Although white moderates often fail to exercise proper judgment, they can be called to their better selves through actions that force injustice to their attention and through discourse that addresses them in patient and reasonable terms.

For black readers, then, King's "Letter" offers an invitation to adopt a rather specific conception of themselves as they struggle to attain equal rights, and King's placement of himself within the African-American community appears in quite a different light than it does when the text is read from the perspective of a white moderate audience. For the white reader, King's assertion that he "stands between" the "'do-nothingism' of the complacent" and "hatred and despair of the black nationalist" (93) appears as a strategy designed to blunt the accusation that he is an intemperate radical, and it thus functions to help unify the writer and the audience. On the other hand, for the black "eavesdroppers," this placement suggests points of differentiation as well as identity; King's position represents an option that some may accept as the "more excellent way" and others may reject. The black audience, in effect, is instructed about how to distinguish the attitudes of its members and invited to make a positive choice in favor of one of the alternatives.

In sum, "Letter from Birmingham Jail" constructs the persona of an author who is critical of his white audience but not alienated from it. He shares its Christian and democratic values, and recognizes its concern about practical matters, but he also calls upon that audience to acknowledge and act in accordance with its own principles. By insinuating himself within the lifeworld of his auditors, King can deploy his ethos instrumentally as a means of allaying fears about the immediate scene of social protest, but he can also establish a model of restrained energy that encourages the white audience to reaffirm its basic values as it reconsiders its view of African-Americans. At the same time, the text constructs a persona that black readers can use as a model for becoming effective actors on the American scene. Like King, they can view themselves as agents who need not and will not suffer the indifference of white moderates, who can break free of external restraints without losing self-restraint, and who can work from within American society to make fundamental changes in the way they conceive themselves and are conceived by others. Thus at several levels and in respect to different audiences, King's text functions both as an instrument that uses constructions of self to alter attitudes and as a medium for constituting self within a scene composed of "exigencies, constraints, others, and self."

Notes

1. Thomas W. Benson, "Rhetoric and Autobiography: The Case of Malcolm X," *Quarterly Journal of Speech* 60 (1974): 1.
2. The terms "interpretive" and "conceptual" are used by James Jasinski to describe what he calls the most important development in rhetorical criticism during the past two decades. This approach, already suggested in Benson's essay, concentrates on providing "thick descriptions" of particular cases rather than the construction or verification of abstract theoretical principles. See James Jasinski, "The Status of Theory and Method in Rhetorical Criticism," *Western Journal of Communication* 65 (2001): 249–70; and also the entry entitled "Criticism in Contemporary Rhetorical Studies," in James Jasinski, *Sourcebook on Rhetoric: Key Concepts in Contemporary Rhetorical Studies* (Thousand Oaks, Calif.: Sage, 2001), 124–44.

3. Benson, "Rhetoric and Autobiography," 6.

4. On the indecorous nature of Malcolm's rhetoric, see Robert E. Terrill, "Protest, Prophecy, and Prudence in the Rhetoric of Malcolm X," *Rhetoric & Public Affairs* 4 (2001): 34. Terrill's reading of Malcolm's "The Ballot or the Bullet" provides an interesting counterpoint to our interpretation of King's "Letter" presented in this paper.

5. Detailed accounts of these events are provided in Taylor Branch, *Parting the Waters: America in the King Years, 1954–63* (New York: Simon and Schuster, 1988), 673–802; and David Garrow, *Bearing the Cross: Martin Luther King, Jr. and the Southern Christian Leadership Conference* (New York: Vintage, 1986), 231–64.

6. The text of this letter is reprinted in S. Jonathan Bass, *Blessed Are the Peacemakers: Martin Luther King Jr., Eight White Religious Leaders, and the "Letter from Birmingham Jail"* (Baton Rouge: Louisiana State University Press, 2001), 235–36.

7. Concerning the composition and circulation of the "Letter," see Bass, *Blessed Are the Peacemakers*, 110–62; E. Culpepper Clark, "An American Dilemma in King's 'Letter from Birmingham Jail,'" in *Martin Luther King and the Sermonic Power of Discourse*, ed. Carolyn Calloway-Thomas and John Louis Lucaites (Tuscaloosa: University of Alabama Press, 1993), 34–49; and Martha Solomon Watson's essay in this issue of *Rhetoric & Public Affairs*.

8. Edwin Black, "The Second Persona," *Quarterly Journal of Speech* 56 (1970): 109–19. For reasons that will become apparent later in this essay, we think it would be better to consider the rhetor's construction of *audiences* rather than of *the audience*, and so we are introducing an amendment to Black's well-known concept.

9. All references to the "Letter" are from Martin Luther King Jr., *I Have a Dream: Speeches and Writings that Changed the World*, ed. J. M. Washington (San Francisco: Harper, 1986), 83–100. Specific page references to this edition are indicated parenthetically in the text of the paper.

10. Richard P. Fulkerson, "The Public Letter as Rhetorical Form: Structure, Logic, and Style in King's 'Letter from Birmingham Jail,'" *Quarterly Journal of Speech* 65 (1979): 124. Fulkerson's essay, in our judgment, remains the most systematic guide to the rhetoric of the "Letter," and we have relied upon it throughout our reading of the text.

11. Kenneth Burke, *Counterstatement* (Los Altos, Calif.: Hermes, 1931), 125.

12. Fulkerson, "The Public Letter as Rhetorical Form," 127.

13. See Fulkerson, "The Public Letter as Rhetorical Form," 128.

14. On the structure and rhetorical impact of the sentence, see Mia Klein, "The Other Beauty of Martin Luther King's 'Letter from Birmingham Jail,'" *College Composition and Communication* 32 (1981): 30–37.

15. Clark, "An American Dilemma," 48–49.

16. On the immanent role of prophetic discourse, see Michael Walzer, *Interpretation and Social Criticism* (Cambridge, Mass.: Harvard University Press, 1987), 64–94. James Darsey (*The Prophetic Tradition and Radical Rhetoric in America* [New York: New York University Press, 1997], 111) puts the point somewhat differently when he says that the prophet is "simultaneously insider and outsider." But Darsey's point is fundamentally the same as Walzer's—the prophet must be inside the culture but must have achieved sufficient conceptual distance from existing practices to be able to note and criticize discrepancies between those practices and the ideals of the culture. On "rhetorical distance," see Michael Osborn's essay in this issue of *Rhetoric & Public Affairs*.

17. James L. Golden and Richard D. Rieke, *The Rhetoric of Black Americans* (Columbus, Ohio: Charles E. Merrill, 1971), 18–19.

18. There is no doubt that King regarded a positive change in black self-esteem as a vital and necessary part of the movement. In other speeches and writings of this period, he maintains that nonviolent direct action precipitated psychological change—it contributed to "something revolutionary" that was occurring in the "mind, heart, and soul of Negroes all over America" (*Why We Can't Wait* [New York: Harper and Row, 1964], 64). Nonviolent direct action, he maintained, challenged stereotypes about blacks, often unconsciously accepted by blacks themselves, that they were inferior and unable to act independently because it gave them a means for peaceful action directed toward their own liberation and for connecting local communities into a national network.

Rhetorical Distance in
"Letter from Birmingham Jail"

Michael Osborn

Michael Osborn is Professor Emeritus of Communication at the University of Memphis in Memphis, Tennessee.

This essay explores the concept of rhetorical distance as the counterpart of esthetic distance. Rhetorical distance functions as a critical lens through which one may view Martin Luther King Jr.'s "Letter from Birmingham Jail." It reveals King's artistry in controlling an array of implied symbolic spatial relationships to achieve rhetorical ends. Chief among these relationships are those that divided King from his ostensible audience, his ostensible audience from his actual audience, his actual audience from that level of illumination required for them to grasp the issues agitated by King's movement, and the chasm that separated African-Americans from the heritage promised them by mythic America. The essay revisits more precisely the contrasts between rhetoric and poetic, and explores a tragic ethical flaw that may lie at the heart of the human communication condition. The essay concludes by considering how the "Letter"'s rhetoric served the prevailing journalistic melodrama and by connecting its work to the functions of rhetorical depiction.

King's "Letter from Birmingham Jail" reminds one of the recurring importance of symbolic space in his rhetoric. His affinity for space appears most obviously in his final Memphis speech, in which the vertical metaphor functions along with the Children of Israel parable as the key figurative components of his rhetoric.[1] As that speech begins, King imagines himself alone on an implied promontory, talking with God. As the speech concludes, King, again upon his mountain, can see the Promised Land in the distance. But as he and his listeners share the exultation of this prospect and his triumph over the fear of impending martyrdom, his "I" becomes a "we," and his listeners, enlarged by the vision of the speech, are lifted rhetorically to his side.

This signature metaphor of the mountaintop draws upon two dialectically opposed traditions in the history of rhetorical practice. In the first, vertical metaphors are expressions of established, conventional power. As they stand upon symbolic mountains, speakers in effect celebrate their superior positions with respect to others. For them, the sense of spatial elevation expresses graphically their sense of their own power, their triumphant self-esteem. In the second tradition, space represents oppression and cultural confinement. For those who are dominated and exploited, elevation represents the vastness of power that looms over them, presses them down, and limits them to life within a sphere or place.[2]

King reconciles and then exploits the tension between these traditions. On the one hand, he repeats the pattern of assumed superiority to the point of audacity. He opens his speech on a peak of perspective where only he and God can stand. But King must stand so high because his listeners have been reduced to such low position, bent down by generations and traditions of oppression. He must assume the heroic stance because they have been so degraded. Because they are identified with him and he with them, he embodies, foretells,

Republished with permission of Michigan State University Press, from *Rhetoric and Public Affairs, Volume 7, Issue 1* by Michael Osborn. Copyright © 2004 by Michigan State University Press; permission conveyed through Copyright Clearance Center, Inc.

and enacts their transformation. Only from such an exalted stance can he exert the moral leverage needed to lift them into asserting their humanity and self-respect. Thus King's spatial metaphor catches and accelerates the wind of the rising race.

Richard P. Fulkerson has already observed how the "Letter from Birmingham Jail" also reflects this preoccupation with depth and height, amplified by its entanglement with the archetypal metaphor of darkness and light. In his words:

> Two archetypal patterns are dominant, that of depth versus height and dark versus light. The present system and segregation are repeatedly characterized as being down and dark, while the hope for the future involves rising and coming into the light. The Negroes live in a "dark shadow" and must "rise from the dark depths." They are "plunged into an abyss of injustice where they experience the bleakness of corroding despair." Policy must be lifted from "quicksand" to "rock," and "we have fallen below our environment"; Negroes are in a "dark dungeon"; in the emphatic and optimistic final paragraph . . . America now suffers under the "dark clouds of racial prejudice" in a "deep fog of misunderstanding," but "tomorrow the radiant stars of love and brotherhood will shine."[3]

As vital as the vertical metaphor may be in King's rhetorical vision, especially when amplified by the powerful pattern of darkness and light, "Letter from Birmingham Jail" also reminds one that figurative space is but part of a larger galaxy of symbolic power, which we shall call "rhetorical distance." Here we draw a contrast with that effect identified by art critics as "esthetic distance." In what Clement Greenberg calls the "classic essay" on the subject,[4] psychologist Edward Bullough spoke of esthetic distance as a kind of psychic separation between our cognitive and our vital or engaged selves.[5] Our normal state of cognition, Bullough argues, is practical and selective; art offers us the "sudden revelation" of what we do not normally observe, constrained as we are by our personal interest in situations. As Greenberg has described the effect:

> "Distance" here means detachment from practical reality . . . Esthetic distance lets you watch, behold, experience anything whatsoever without relating it to yourself as a particular human being with your particular hopes and fears, interests and concerns. You detach yourself from yourself. (Schopenhauer)[6]

Thus art enlarges our constricted awareness, awakens in us a greater understanding. The function of art is to balance two contradictory pulls: first, to absorb us into the story of a work so that we may feel and share its intensity; second and simultaneously, to find that ideal distance from the story so that we may contemplate the larger vistas of meaning it engages. Some works, Bullough notices, achieve artistic status only with the passage of time, which gradually dulls and subdues our practical interests in situations and opens us to the esthetic potential within the works. This might explain how speeches such as Lincoln's "Gettysburg Address" or "Second Inaugural" might emerge over time as part of the literary as well as rhetorical heritage of a people.

In its original signification, "esthetic distance" seemed to be one of those rich but vague concepts that augment our appreciation for *what* art can accomplish without telling us a great deal about *how* it works.[7] As reformulated by Wayne C. Booth, however, "esthetic distance" invites a greater understanding of artistic technique and becomes more useful to the critic.[8] For Booth, "esthetic distance" describes the artist's effort to control the perception of art objects to enhance their appreciation. In fictional literature, for example, the writer must manage the multiple senses of distance that can simultaneously join or separate the author, the narrator, fictional characters, and assumed readers. Booth concludes: "Every literary work of any power—whether or not its author composed it with his audience in mind—is in fact an elaborate system of controls over the reader's involvement and detachment along various lines of interest."[9] Critics can ponder (and elucidate) how (and how well) the author constructs this "system of controls" and confronts the artistic challenge.

Rhetorical distance, I argue, can also be rich and useful as an analogous concept in rhetorical criticism. On the one hand, working as the counterpart to that general function identified by Bullough, rhetorical distance obliterates rather than establishes the distance we may feel between ourselves and the world that impinges upon us. The rhetorician desires typically to engage the auditor with a particular case or to enhance engagement as an inducement to judgment and action. Rhetorical distance completes itself not in esthetic contemplation, but in passionate affirmation of the rhetor's intent.

Interpreted differently, more on that level of understanding provided by Booth, rhetorical distance invites a greater understanding of rhetorical artistry. Here we view rhetorical distance as the manipulation of specific symbolic spatial relationships to advance rhetorical ends. Key points on this grid of relationships can include the positioning of the rhetorician and the audience with respect to each other, controlling auditors' sense of space and time so that rhetorical subjects may seem closer or more remote from their interests,[10] and enlarging, reducing, arranging, and rearranging material points of focus such that the world presented to auditors coheres with the rhetorician's vision and purpose.

"Rhetorical distance" may seem a novel concept, but as usual there is really little new under the rhetorical sun. Aristotle had already written of magnification and minification, the strategic enlargement or suppression of character and events.[11] Francis Bacon described the rhetorical function as the convergence of reason and the imagination, in effect telescoping time and distance to achieve "the better moving of the will."[12] And Kenneth Burke featured the concepts of identification and division, a striking but somewhat limited two-valued expression of the importance of controlling and manipulating the distance between speaker and audience, audience and adversaries, policies and practices.[13] Nevertheless, rhetorical distance may be one of those fresh ways of conceiving and expressing these phenomena of symbolic space, a novel lens that can reveal new detail.

KING'S JAIL THROUGH THE LENS OF RHETORICAL DISTANCE

The possible importance of rhetorical distance occurs as one studies "Letter from Birmingham Jail," and the reading offered here may serve to suggest its possible utility as a critical perspective. As usual in rhetorical texts, what happens first can be quite significant in revealing less obvious agendas. "My Dear Fellow Clergymen," the opening salutation of the "Letter," may seem "warm [and] tactful," as Fulkerson suggests,[14] but it functions already as an implied rebuke. The statement to which King was responding, signed by eight leaders representing various religious faiths, had in fact not even mentioned him or acknowledged his identity as a pastor, certainly not as an equal. They had denied him space: he was not even visible on their horizon. As Malinda Snow has observed, "King achieved for himself the legitimacy that the eight had denied him by failing to name him in their statement. . . . The salutation . . . makes King a colleague, an equal."[15] Thus, from the outset, King asserts his identity and claims his seat at their table, whether welcome or not. From that point on, ironies abound. King finds himself "confined here in the Birmingham city jail," certainly a lowly posture from which to address anyone. Yet Snow is certainly correct in suggesting that "[l]ike Paul, he shrewdly used his prison cell as an ironic pulpit."[16] Despite his situation, King implies an executive stance with respect to the eight critics: "If I sought to answer all the criticisms that cross my desk, my secretaries would have little time for anything other than such correspondence in the course of the day." His manner suggests that it is they who are asking audience of him, not he of them, but he grants their supposed request in a manner that is graceful, yet rather royal, perhaps even condescending: "Since I feel that you are men of genuine good will and that your criticisms are sincerely set forth, I want to try to answer your statements in what I hope will be patient and reasonable terms." This ironic tension between the lowly and the elevated continues in the narrative of the origination of the "Letter": In an author's note introducing the document in his *Why We Can't Wait*, King makes a big point of how this eloquent and majestic statement was first penned "on the margins of the newspaper . . . [and] on scraps of writing paper supplied by a friendly Negro trusty."[17] From humble beginnings rises this lofty document. And again, as we suggested in the analysis of his final speech, if all this seems just a bit pompous, the pomposity itself functions as a corrective for the degradation of the race for which King must serve as synecdoche.

If King's account implies that his "Letter" was a spontaneous reaction to an unwelcome provocation, S. Jonathan Bass indicates that the possibility of such a letter, written in the spirit of a Pauline episde, had been contemplated for some time by Southern Christian Leadership Conference (SCLC) strategists. The function of such a letter would be to articulate the meaning of the movement to a wider audience, hopefully encouraging both spiritual and material support for it. The ministers' letter and the circumstances of King's imprisonment provided the dramatic opportunity for such a letter, which was written, Bass suggests, with an "eye for media consumption."

> For the accomplished public relations strategists in the SCLC, this seemed a golden opportunity for publicity: an entire media crusade centered on the biblical image of a lone apostolic leader, confined to a jail cell, writing a letter of admonishment and love to his accusers and fellow churchmen.[18]

Moreover, the "Letter" was carefully edited, refined, and completed in the weeks *after* King's actual jail time. It functioned more to celebrate the resolution of the Birmingham crisis than to somehow convince the eight ministers, many of whom thought the "Letter" to be singularly unfair.[19]

Beyond these first implied positionings in King's "Letter," the first topic expressly addressed again concerns rhetorical distance: the ministers' statement has implied that King is an "outsider," that he is not even a legitimate participant in the Birmingham crisis. The point is a critical one, for as Fulkerson observes, "If the argument about "outsiders" has any validity . . . then King has no right to discuss circumstances in Birmingham. He must earn the right to talk."[20] King rejects this marginalized placement and closes the distance by responding on several levels of increasing sophistication: (1) the SCLC has a chapter in Birmingham, and he is there as a legitimate leader of that association. (2) Tapping into his religious identity, he is there "because injustice is here." Like the biblical prophets and the apostle Paul, he must carry "the gospel of freedom" where it is needed. (3) Finally, he is there to acknowledge his moral responsibility as part of the overarching human family: "Injustice anywhere is a threat to justice everywhere. We are caught in an inescapable network of mutuality, tied in a single garment of destiny." He is there because he must be there.

Not only is he "of" them, as a fellow clergyman, and legitimately present "in" the situation, he is also "above" them. Later he would credit his very presence in jail for the mind-set that would allow him to conceive his moral elevation: "Jail helps you to rise above the miasma of everyday life. You can think about things. You can meditate a little."[21] Nevertheless, this implied positioning is also surely an instance of the "transcendence" strategy Judith D. Hoover finds at work in the document, as she applies the model of political apologia developed by B. L. Ware and Wil A. Linkugel.[22] Of the four key strategies of apologia, two of these, *differentiation* and *transcendence,* constitute specific strategic forms of rhetorical distance. In this instance King transcends both the context of the present struggle and his listeners. Unlike them, he understands the historical situation. But he instructs them in the grand strategy of the Birmingham movement, just as any kindly teacher might attempt to cure the ignorance and elevate the understanding of novice students. He informs them that his purpose there is not to bring peace, but to create tension "that will help men rise from the dark depths of prejudice and racism to the majestic heights of understanding and brotherhood." The implication is breathtaking: not only is King attempting to lift a degraded race, but he is also trying to purify and elevate the society that has degraded them. It is, especially in retrospect, a gigantic and dangerous feat of moral engineering.

Again, as he confronts the claim that they should "wait," be patient, he appeals to his listeners on the existential basis of what it means to be black within a racist society. Most Negroes, he says, are "smothering in an airtight cage of poverty in the midst of an affluent society." They cannot go certain places because they are black, and so they must watch "ominous clouds of inferiority" develop in the minds of their sons and daughters as they learn that "Funtown" is closed to colored children. As a Negro traveler, you often discover that you must "sleep night after night in the uncomfortable corners of your automobile because no motel will accept you." In the celebrated, over three-hundred-word sentence that details these many humiliations, the use of the second-person plural pronoun ("you") invites the white reader especially to enact a ritual of identification: in effect, to cross the boundaries of race to realize what it means to be black in a racist society. In an even larger sense, the Negro is captured within what Buber described as an "I-it" relationship, in which persons are relegated to the status of things. King cites Paul Tillich's view that "sin is separation," and asks: "[I]s not segregation an existential expression of man's tragic separation, his awful estrangement, his terrible sinfulness?" The sense of both actual and spiritual spatial restriction is overpowering: "a series of suffocating images"[23] magnifies the longing to break out, not just from the Birmingham jail, but from the American prison.

King again deals with the implication that his nonviolent movement is extremist. He answers by repositioning both the movement and himself between those in the Negro community who counsel timid acceptance of their fate and others who occupy the battlements of black nationalism. The tactic represents strategic *differentiation,* reassuring both the cautious (King is not a militant revolutionary) and the impatient (King is no Uncle Tom, either). "I have tried to stand between these two forces, saying that we need emulate neither the 'do-nothingism' of the complacent nor the hatred and despair of the black nationalist." This moderation is dynamic, for it redirects discontent "into the creative outlet of nonviolent direct action." It propels King and his followers "toward the promised land of racial justice." Thus this deliberate effort at readjusting rhetorical distance not only fixes King and his followers between two extremes, but also pictures them as "moving with a sense of great urgency" toward desirable social and moral goals.

The risk of such repositioning is that it might invite the dangerous conclusion that King is a moderate. Therefore, having redefined his political position on the grid of symbolic space and having seized the middle ground, King instantly blurs the picture through an additional strategy of *transcendence.* He is willing to accept the label of "extremist," if it can be redefined in sacred and idealized political terms. "Was not Jesus an extremist for love? . . . Was not Amos an extremist for justice? . . . Was not Paul an extremist for the Christian gospel?" The litany continues through Martin Luther, John Bunyan, Abraham Lincoln, and Thomas Jefferson, and concludes: Perhaps the South, the nation and the world are in dire need of creative extremists." He names a number of well-known southern intellectuals who have joined the movement, then chides these religious leaders who have signed the statement for not having also accepted identification with movement goals and values. Southern churches are beautiful, wealthy, imposing parts of the landscape, but they have been largely silent on these great issues of the human family. They have shrunk into irrelevancy and have disappeared from the moral landscape. He prefers the early church, much more humble in size, but made enormous by its courage and martyrdom in the face of political intimidation.

He concludes by expressing his great optimism about the movement. It will triumph because of its vital identification both with America and with the will of God: "Our destiny is tied up with America's destiny. . . . We will win our freedom because the sacred heritage of our nation and the eternal will of God are embodied in our echoing demands." Thus King asserts his faith that what Gunnar Myrdal had described as an "American Dilemma"—the distance between the nation's creed and its actual practice—would be closed in an eventual triumph of ideals.[24] This identification allows him to rise above the scene of discord, to reconceive the American scene as a nation that would recognize new heroes, the dedicated martyrs of the civil rights movement, and to imagine for himself a new ethos within these new spiritual parameters. In this other, later time, transformed by love and redeemed by sacrifice, he will greet them "not as an integrationist or a civil rights leader but as a fellow clergyman and a Christian brother."[25] They will embrace within a scene in which "the radiant stars of love and brotherhood will shine over our great nation with all their scintillating beauty."

Let us now step back from the fine text of the document so that we can see the larger pattern of positionings and repositionings effected by King's control of rhetorical distance. The overall theme of this pattern is that King's "Letter," so mild and loving in tone, functions as profound refutation.[26] It refuses to accept the marginality and invisibility thrust upon King by the ministers' statement. Instead, it projects his ethos in large and luminous outline, and elevates him vis-à-vis his critics into moral authority. It asserts his legitimate place at the center and foreground of the civil rights struggle. At the same time it subverts the implied moral authority of the ministers. Like modern pharisees, they make a great show of their faith, but the heart of Christ is not in their splendid temples. Instead, they are profoundly ignorant of the Gospel as constituting a design for Godly living, and of this movement to apply Christian precepts to a world deeply stained with cultural and political sin. Or perhaps they refuse to acknowledge the existential realities of segregation. Either way, the document reduces their stature to that of moral pygmies, while it projects the image of King and his followers in heroic terms.[27] As Rabbi Milton Grafman, one of the infamous eight, would later acknowledge somewhat ruefully, "He made us look ridiculous."[28] But again, it is King's persona that is especially at issue here: In the symbolic logic of this document, if he is granted respect, so also will be the race that he represents.

Beyond repositioning King and his critics with respect to each other, the document also counters an implied presumption concerning the segregated lifestyle in southern society. The doctrine of gradualism with its accompanying advice to wait patiently for small increments of change assumes that such racial positioning, while perhaps regrettable, is nevertheless tolerable for an unspecified time. King's graphic summary of what it means to be black in a racist society answers eloquently this implication: injustice, humiliation, the denial of personhood, these are all intolerable. The race must no longer be denied its place at the table of the human family; the symbolic space that tolerates segregation must undergo profound and immediate revision. The Christian doctrine requires no less than societal conversion.

LARGER MEANINGS OF RHETORICAL DISTANCE

Considered in the context of recent rhetorical study, the contrast suggested here between rhetorical and esthetic distance revisits in a more precise way the general topic of the relationships between rhetoric and poetic.[29] Clearly that topic implies not different forms of discourse, but rather different impulses, the one leading to strategic disengagement, the other to engagement, the one to a larger compass of understanding and appreciation, the other to commitment and action, the one to an exhilarating expansion of the mind, the other to intense focus upon some urgent and compelling cause.[30] To achieve its ends, rhetorical distance manipulates symbolic space to establish tactical relationships between rhetor and auditors, auditors and their sense of themselves, and auditors and the time/space continuum in which they exist. Rhetorical distance arranges perceptions so that certain features of this surrounding symbolic environment loom large in consciousness, while others fade into insignificance.

While the two impulses that manifest themselves in rhetorical and esthetic distance may differ, they may also be complementary, and may interplay within a discourse production. We acknowledged this possibility earlier, when we spoke of the passage of time affecting the transformation of Lincoln's speeches into the literary and esthetic heritage of the West. In like manner, an eloquent work like "Letter from Birmingham Jail" can manifest poetic as well as rhetorical features. While overwhelmingly rhetorical both in intent and effect, the work also aims to reveal a larger moral horizon to its readers. Earlier critics have observed that there actually are two audiences for the "Letter," the ostensible and the actual. The ostensible audience, the eight unfortunate clergy whom it addresses directly, serve as King's foil.[31] Whether they were converted or affronted by the "Letter" may have been of little moment to him.[32] His goal was to use their perceived moral shortcomings as leverage to lift his actual audience—that larger group of readers who would encounter the "Letter"—to a moment of revelation concerning the profound moral and religious issues that were engaged by the movement. The strategic distance King created between the ostensible and actual audiences of his work represents its central dynamic, and it makes little difference whether we call this distance "esthetic" or "rhetorical," or conclude finally that it represents some sort of rhetorical/esthetic fusion.

The symbolic work performed by rhetorical distance does remind us, however, of a tragic ethical flaw that may lie at the heart of the human communication condition. All communication is partial, in that it focuses and emphasizes certain topics and is silent on others. But rhetorical communication exacerbates this tendency by constructing strategically selected accounts of situations that will induce listeners to respond and act. No matter how eloquent and spiritually elevated these accounts may seem, they also run the risk of oversimplifying the situations they depict and maligning the character and motives of perceived adversaries. Rhetoric can mislead us by distorting reality and can mutilate the memories of those caught up in conflict. A reader of King's "Letter" might never know that the eight clergy pilloried in its pages had actually issued a courageous public rebuke some months earlier to Governor George Wallace for his rhetoric of hatred, defiance, and resistance to court-ordered integration.[33] These eight ministers, all leaders of various denominations in Alabama, themselves differed in their degree of commitment to racial change in Alabama. Nevertheless, even the most conservative among them were willing to take a public stand in condemning Wallace's rhetoric of defying the courts. They knew that if they spoke together, they might have a better chance of being heard. They did not have to step into the glare of this bitter arena, knowing that at best they would be answered with insult and opprobrium, and that at worst they would invite attention to themselves, their families, and churches from some violent and vicious elements. But step they did, and King's caricature offers little credit for the part they attempted to play in the cause of human dignity.

In striking their unpopular position in the earlier admonition to Wallace, the eight clergy did unknowingly reduce their rhetorical options in dealing later with King and his movement. To be consistent, they also had to urge the advocates of civil rights to press their case in the courts and not in the streets. In the end, we may find their support of the gradualist position refuted so brilliantly by King to be a timid move in the direction of brotherhood, but at that time in Alabama any such move by men of their position was momentous and magnified. One of their number, Rabbi Milton Grafman, always resented those of his cloth who made "cameo" appearances in the South in favor of civil rights, then returned to the safety of northern pulpits as "heroes of a fanciful crusade." He accused them of "homiletical heroics at a safe distance" and emphasized the importance of staying in Alabama and working quietly from inside the state to expand its horizons of tolerance.[34] In this case we know, as King could not know at the time, that many of these men would lose their positions, be endangered in their homes and churches, and eventually be run out of the state for the sympathy they expressed for civil rights objectives. It is perhaps tragic that they must go down in history as King depicted them, and also ironic: had King not been so eloquent, they would not be thus remembered. But such again may be the cruel and inescapable nature of the human communication condition. They had a larger role to play as foils for King's magnificent rhetoric and for the greater moral goals he envisioned.

As he depicted the eight ministers, King prepared their characterizations to fit within a prevailing pattern of journalistic mentality. Bass identifies the pattern by quoting reporters of the time:

> "We wrote our stories like western movie scenarios," remembered one veteran reporter. . . ." There's the good guys, there's the courthouse, there's the bad sheriff," observed another. "Just change the names and the name of the town and the story was already written because this had become a ritual kind of reporting."[35]

We recognize this pattern as melodrama, the most rhetorical of the forms of drama.[36] The characters of melodrama are drawn so that they represent simplistic, opposing moral absolutes. These characters cannot grow or change, because they must express a dialectic of stable relationships that structures the melodrama: the hero is and forever shall be the hero, the villains are dependably evil. Again, the characters depict representative class or group portraits rather than individuals. These portraits justify arguments, because they imply that people drive historical process rather than the other way around. As they deny the deterministic idea that process controls people, they magnify the importance of personal sacrifice and privilege emotional proofs.

If we apply this template to particulars in the Birmingham situation, we note that King and his followers represent the principle of ethical change, while the ministers are positioned to represent resistance. While the "Letter" invites its ostensible audience to learn and change, the power of its appeal to its actual audience depends on depicting the ministers as agents of the forces of reaction. This adamantine division powers King's appeal to his actual audience to identify with movement goals. To make the melodrama work, King and his followers must do the work of angels, while the eight ministers must somehow represent the forces of evasion and delay, if not outright opposition. And because these characters are what they are, King's arguments are supported by extremes of ethos: the transcendent morality of the one group contrasted with the self-evident immorality of the other. Finally, the effectiveness of King's nonviolent strategy depends upon the irresistible power of victimage: righteous suffering authenticates and vindicates the movement, and the power of pathos as it forms vivid pictures of that suffering animates King's arguments.

All of which leads us to conclude that rhetorical distance, in the work that it performs, also contributes to the process we have elsewhere called *rhetorical depiction*,[37] in that it attempts to control how the participants in rhetorical transactions see themselves and the world that beckons them to action. In particular, the rhetor controlling rhetorical distance can shape the *presentation* of subjects, establishing a template for experience that helps auditors make sense of their lives. Manipulating symbolic space, the rhetor can augment or diminish appropriate *feelings*, enhance *identification*, bestir *action*, and *celebrate* values and the icons that personify them.

Looking through the lens of rhetorical distance permits one to see more clearly the many dimensions of meaning in the "Letter from Birmingham Jail." Rhetorical distance is surely not the whole of rhetorical artistry, but it does encompass considerable scope. Perhaps this exercise in application to King's magnificent "Letter" may encourage us to explore the concept in greater detail.

NOTES

1. Michael Osborn, "'I've Been to the Mountaintop': The Critic as Participant," in *Texts in Context: Dialogue on Significant Episodes in American Political Rhetoric,* ed. Michael Leff and Fred Kauffeld (Davis, Calif.: Hermagoras Press, 1989), 149–66; Malinda Snow, "Martin Luther King's 'Letter from Birmingham Jail' as Pauline Epistle," *Quarterly Journal of Speech* 71 (1985): 318–34.
2. Michael Osborn, "Patterns of Metaphor among Early Feminist Orators," in *Rhetoric and Community: Studies in Unity and Fragmentation,* ed. J. Michael Hogan (Columbia: University of South Carolina Press, 1998), 10–13.
3. Richard P. Fulkerson, "The Public Letter as Rhetorical Form: Structure, Logic, and Style in King's 'Letter from Birmingham Jail,'" *Quarterly Journal of Speech* 65 (1979): 131.
4. Clement Greenberg, *Homemade Esthetics: Observations on Art and Taste* (New York: Oxford University Press, 1999), 74.
5. Edward Bullough, "Psychical Distance as a Factor in Art and an Aesthetic Principle," *British Journal of Psychology* 5 (1912): 87–98.
6. Greenberg, *Homemade Esthetics,* 73.
7. John Hospers is especially critical of the ambiguities that flaw Bullough's formulation of the concept: "The Esthetic Attitude," in *A Modern Book of Esthetics: An Anthology,* ed. Melvin Rader, 4th ed. (New York: Holt, Rinehart and Winston, 1973), 400.
8. Wayne C. Booth, *The Rhetoric of Fiction,* 2d ed. (Chicago: University of Chicago Press, 1983).
9. Booth, *Rhetoric of Fiction,* 123.
10. *The Rhetoric of Aristotle,* trans. Lane Cooper (New York: Appleton-Century-Crofts, 1932), 1:7, 1:9, 1:14 (34–44, 46–55, 78–79).
11. It is this sense of rhetorical distance, actual geographical distance that metamorphoses into a cultural symbol, that Michael J. Hostetler traces in his "Washington's Farewell Address: Distance as Bane and Blessing," *Rhetoric & Public Affairs* 5 (2002): 393–407.
12. Francis Bacon, *Advancement of Learning,* in *Great Books of the Western World,* 54 vols. (Chicago: Benton, 1952), 30:66–67 (Bk. 2, 18:2–5).
13. Kenneth Burke, *A Rhetoric of Motives* (Berkeley: University of California Press, 1969), 3–43.
14. Fulkerson, "Public Letter," 125.
15. Snow, "Pauline Epistle," 322.
16. Snow, "Pauline Epistle," 319.
17. *Why We Can't Wait* (New York: New American Library, 2000), 64. E. Culpepper Clark wrestles with the question of textual authenticity and the complicated context in which the "Letter" was produced in his "The American Dilemma in King's 'Letter from Birmingham Jail,'" in *Martin Luther King, Jr., and the Sermonic Power of Public Discourse,* ed. Carolyn Calloway-Thomas and John Louis Lucaites (Tuscaloosa: University of Alabama Press, 1993), 33–49.
18. S. Jonathan Bass, *Blessed Are the Peacemakers: Martin Luther King Jr., Eight White Religious Leaders, and the "Letter from Birmingham Jail"* (Baton Rouge: Louisiana State University Press, 2001), 115–16.
19. Bass chronicles their various reactions in *Blessed Are the Peacemakers.*
20. Fulkerson, "Public Letter," 125.

21. Cited by Judith D. Hoover, "Reconstruction of the Rhetorical Situation in 'Letter from Birmingham Jail'" in *Sermonic Power of Public Discourse,* ed. Calloway-Thomas and Lucaites, 57. The quotation is from King's "Speech to the Alabama Christian Movement for Human Rights," May 3, 1963. Audio tape recording, Birmingham Public Library Archives.

22. Hoover, "Reconstruction," 50–65; B. L. Ware and Wil A. Linkugel, "They Spoke in Defense of Themselves: On Generic Criticism of Apologia," *Quarterly Journal of Speech* 59 (1973): 273–83.

23. Ronald E. Lee, "The Rhetorical Construction of Time in Martin Luther King, Jr.'s 'Letter from Birmingham Jail,'" *Southern Communication Journal* 56 (1991): 280.

24. James A. Colaiaco, *Martin Luther King, Jr.: Apostle of Militant Nonviolence* (New York: St. Martin's Press, 1993), 93.

25. Snow argues that this vision of a scene transformed by brotherhood resembled the "greeting" that often came at the close of Pauline and other Greek letters. It was a "distinct literary form which was intended to establish a bond of friendship." In the context of the Birmingham situation, she describes King's inclusion of it in his "Letter" as "audacious" ("Pauline Epistle," 322).

26. Here we affirm the conclusion reached by Fulkerson, "Public Letter," 121–36, and by Haig A. Bosmajian, "The Rhetoric of Martin Luther King's 'Letter from the Birmingham Jail,'" *Midwest Quarterly* 21 (1967): 127–43.

27. Bass paints a far more sympathetic picture of the eight ministers in his *Blessed Are the Peacemakers.*

28. Diane McWhorter, *Carry Me Home: Birmingham, Alabama: the Climactic Battle of the Civil Rights Revolution* (New York: Simon and Schuster, 2001), 537.

29. Some representative works on this theme are Gordon E. Bigelow, "Distinguishing Rhetoric from Poetic Discourse," *Southern Speech Journal* 19 (1953): 83–97; Kenneth Burke, "Rhetoric and Poetic," *Language as Symbolic Action: Essays on Life, Literature, and Method* (Berkeley: University of California Press, 1966), 295–307; W. S. Howell, "Literature as an Enterprise in Communication," *Quarterly Journal of Speech* 33 (1947): 417–26; Hoyt H. Hudson, "Rhetoric and Poetry," *Quarterly Journal of Speech* 10 (1924): 143–54; August W. Staub, "Rhetoric and Poetic: The Rhetor as Poet-Plot-Maker," *Southern Speech Journal* 26 (1961): 285–90; and August W. Staub and Gerald P. Mohrmann, "Rhetoric and Poetic: A New Critique," *Southern Speech Journal* 28 (1962): 131–41.

30. For an especially rich explanation of the esthetic impulse, see Harold Osborne, *The Art of Appreciation* (London: Oxford University Press, 1970), 201–21.

31. This use of the eight clergymen as rhetorical foil had the effect of grouping them as though they were of one mind. Bass points out the considerable variation among their racial attitudes, noting in particular that the four youngest members of the group were the most progressive and receptive to change.

32. Here I risk underestimating King, his motives, and the power of his rhetoric. As James Findlay has observed, Bass provides evidence that King's moral arguments "deeply affected at least some of the eight clergy who had opposed him. . . . Especially revealing . . . [is] the transforming impact of King's work on the leader of Birmingham's Catholics, Bishop Joseph Durick" (Review of Bass. *Blessed Are the Peacemakers,* in *Journal of American History* 89 [2002]: 722–23). See Bass, *Blessed Are the Peacemakers,* 188, 198.

33. Bass, *Blessed Are the Peacemakers,* 17–23.

34. Bass, *Blessed Are the Peacemakers,* 177–78.

35. Bass, *Blessed Are the Peacemakers,* 95.

36. Michael Osborn and John Bakke, "The Melodramas of Memphis: Contending Narratives during the Sanitation Strike of 1968," *Southern Communication Journal* 63 (1998): 220–34.

37. Michael Osborn, "Rhetorical Depiction," in *Form, Genre, and the Study of Political Discourse,* ed. Herbert W. Simons and Aram A. Aghazarian (Columbia: University of South Carolina Press, 1986), 79–107.

Martin Luther King's "Letter from Birmingham Jail" as Pauline Epistle

Malinda Snow

MARTIN LUTHER KING'S "Letter from Birmingham Jail" was published in 1963. Since then, it has been widely read, admired, and reprinted as an eloquent expression of the philosophy of the American civil rights movement of the fifties and sixties.[1] Yet it has generated surprisingly little critical discussion. Only three essays examine the "Letter" as a literary document.[2] The earliest, by Haig A. Bosmajian, was written while King was still alive and a figure of controversy. Bosmajian's chief goal was to set King outside the crowd of polemicists and demagogues who raised their voices at the time, and also to set him, as a master rhetorician, above the other well-meaning civil rights activists who spoke or wrote for the cause. Comparing King to such public letter writers as Thomas Mann and Emile Zola, Bosmajian analyzed the "Letter" paragraph by paragraph, commenting on its logical structure, rhetorical appeals, and style. Richard P. Fulkerson, while noting the similarity between Zola's Dreyfus letter and King's "Letter," focused on a rhetorical analysis of King's argumentative techniques, particularly refutation. He also considered King's effective use of references to theological writers, his choice of similes, and his management of tone. Fulkerson discussed King's appeal to his complex audience: the eight clergymen named in the salutation and the members of the general public who read the published letter. Mia Klein concentrated on the emotional appeals in the "Letter," particularly rhythm in sentence structure.

These essays analyze King's work in classical, Aristotelian-Ciceronian terms. While such analyses are worthwhile, they do not consider principles or models outside classical rhetoric. Although both Bosmajian and Fulkerson describe King's "Letter" as a public letter, neither mentions St. Paul's letters and their possible influence upon King. Bosmajian, Fulkerson, and Klein praise King's diction and figurative language but do not consider how the diction and imagery of the English Bible affected his style.

Similarities between the "Letter" and Paul's writings have not gone entirely unnoticed, however. Soon after its publication, a reader wrote to the *Christian Century* to point out that King's work should be seen "in the best tradition of Pauline prison letters."[3] No scholar, however, has pursued the relationships between King's "Letter" and Paul's letters or biblical literature generally.

My purpose is to show the ways in which biblical literature informs King's "Letter." I will argue that, in Paul, King discovered a model or *type* for himself and that from the English Bible he garnered images that contributed notably to its rhetorical success. My argument has three major propositions: first that, following the homiletic traditions of black American Protestantism, King assumed both a Pauline role and a Pauline literary form in the "Letter from Birmingham Jail"; second, that this role was only the most prominent of many scriptural allusions that King used; and, third, that the "Letter," like many of Paul's epistles, was not merely a letter but also sermon. Like Paul, King was separated from those to whom he would have spoken. Like Paul, he shrewdly used his prison cell as an ironic pulpit and the letter as a means to reach his audience. Like Paul, King meant his letter not only for those named in the salutation but also for a larger, more general

"Martin Luther King's 'Letter from Birmingham Jail' as Pauline Epistle" by Malinda Snow from *Quarterly Journal of Speech,* Vol. 71, No. 3, August 1, 1985. Copyright © 1985 The National Communication Association, reprinted by permission of Taylor & Francis Ltd., www.tandfonline.com on behalf of The National Communication Association

group. Finally, like Paul, King declared his own apostleship so that he might present himself as one possessed of religious truth and able to define moral action in light of **that truth.**

TYPE AND ANTITYPE IN RELIGIOUS DISCOURSE

A preacher sets out to discover in biblical texts symbolic lessons applicable to human experience. Similarly, in traditional biblical exegesis, one searches for (or discovers) *types:* people or events in sacred history, usually in the Old Testament, that anticipate or foreshadow people or events, usually in the New Testament. For example, Moses may be seen as a type of Christ, the tree of Eden as a type of the "tree" of Calvary, and so on (the second item in these and similar pairs is the *antitype*). Both the homiletic scriptural example and the type depend upon a correspondence between a biblical occurrence or person and something to be explained—whether an event in one's life or another biblical circumstance.[4]

Before the reformation, Christian typology usually concentrated upon the prefigurative relationship of the Old Testament to the New. With the reformation came "the new Protestant emphasis upon the application of Scripture to the self, that is, the discovery of scriptural paradigms and of the workings of Divine Providence, in one's own life."[5] This change meant that biblical situations became types of, not merely examples for, modern life.[6] English Puritans, particularly the Puritan settlers of New England, who saw themselves as Israel, the Chosen People, offer striking examples of Protestant typology.[7]

The general Protestant inclination to discover contemporary antitypes for biblical types influenced black American Protestantism. When the slaves embraced Christianity, they found in biblical narratives a way to express their own experience profoundly and metaphorically. Biblical stories of suffering prefigured their suffering; biblical stories of victory over impossible odds prefigured their hopes. In the story of the Children of Israel in Egypt, they discovered the central type of their experience, which prefigured their own deliverance from slavery. They merged biblical and contemporary time. As Henry H. Mitchell observed, a black preacher tends to speak of a biblical character "as one who might have known him."[8] The singer who asks, "Were you there?" is presuming at least the possibility of "Yes" as an answer. The merging of biblical and contemporary time still marks black Protestant theology and homiletics: the slaves' descendants often still treat biblical narrative as current event.

As a theologian, King understood the applications of typology and spoke of types and antitypes in his sermons. And, following the tradition of the black church, he found biblical types for modern antitypes. For instance, in one sermon he treated Mahatma Gandhi as an antitype of Moses and the British leaders as antitypes of the Pharaohs.[9] In another sermon he used St. Paul as a type for those who do not reach all their goals; he told his hearers: "One of the most agonizing problems within our human experience is that few, if any, of us live to see our fondest hopes fulfilled" (p. 78). The biblical analogue is Paul's unrealized hope—described in the Letter to the Romans—to visit Spain.

On another occasion, Paul became King's type and persona. The sermon entitled "Paul's Letter to American Christians" is in the form of a Pauline letter, which King pretended to have received. In it King imitated the New Testament letter form and style, speaking as "Paul" against racial segregation in the American church. By identifying with Paul and adopting the form of the Pauline letter, King not only made vivid reference to the apostle's teaching and made ancient texts pertinent to modern affairs, he also lent authority and force to his own argument against racial prejudice.

In the "Letter from Birmingham Jail," written seven years after "Paul's Letter to American Christians," King did not imitate the Pauline epistle as explicitly as in his earlier sermon. In the "Letter," he wrote as himself and closed with his own name. Nevertheless, the "Letter" exploits the form and scope of the Pauline letter, and it is worth noting that King did not hesitate to compare himself to Paul. Early in it he argued:

> I am in Birmingham because injustice is here. . . . Just as the Apostle Paul left his village of Tarsus and carried the gospel of Jesus Christ to the far corners of the Greco-Roman world, so I am compelled to carry the gospel of freedom beyond my own home town. Like Paul, I must constantly respond to the Macedonian call for aid. (p. 78)

A crucial word here is *apostle.* Paul opened many letters with a formula; the opening of the Epistle to the Romans serves as an example: "Paul, a servant of Jesus Christ, called to be an apostle, separated unto the gospel of God (which he had promised afore by his prophets in the holy scriptures) . . ." (Romans 1:1-2). The word ἀπόστολος, *apostolos,* "one who is sent," becomes a rhetorical device through which Paul asserted that he belonged, that he had authority and was not an outsider.[10] King not only compared himself to Paul but he also insisted upon his own position as apostle, one *sent* to Birmingham, not an outsider there. The "Macedonian call for aid" refers to a message that Paul received in a vision while at Troas: "There stood a man of Macedonia, and prayed him, saying, 'Come over into Macedonia and help us'" (Acts 16:9). This incident became for later missionaries a type of their own call and an affirmation that no one called to preach the gospel in a distant place is an intruder or outsider.

Paul's position as apostle, as a stranger but not an outsider, exemplifies the irony manifested in his career. Paul was an enemy of Christians turned Christian, a persecutor persecuted, an imprisoned preacher using his cell as a platform. He was quite aware of the irony of his own situation and, indeed, the irony of the Christian gospel: "But hath God chosen the foolish things of the world to confound the wise; and hath God chosen the weak things of the world to confound the things which are mighty" (I Corinthians 1:27). The "Letter from Birmingham Jail" is a masterly work whose author recognized both the irony of the gospel and the parallels between his own life and Paul's that could be rhetorically exploited.

King's life also manifested its ironies and, like Paul, King capitalized on them. The "Letter" depends upon a series of ironies: the prisoner boldly writes of freedom, the lawbreaker confidently defines justice, the white community's attempt to shut away and ignore the black leader enhances that leader's public recognition and humiliates his opponents.

To examine King's "Letter" as a Pauline epistle and sermon, it is helpful to recall the occasion that prompted it. With other marchers, King was arrested in Birmingham in April 1963 after violating an injunction forbidding further demonstrations.[11] Jailed on Friday, April 12, he found in the Saturday Birmingham *Post Herald* a statement by eight clergymen who called the demonstrations "unwise" and "untimely." Because that statement is not readily accessible and may be unfamiliar to King's readers, I quote it in full:

> We the undersigned clergymen are among those who, in January, issued "An Appeal for Law and Order and Common Sense," in dealing with racial problems in Alabama. We expressed understanding that honest convictions in racial matters could properly be pursued in the courts, but urged that decisions of those courts should in the meantime be peacefully obeyed.

Since that time there had been some evidence of increased forbearance and a willingness to face facts. Responsible citizens have undertaken to work on various problems which cause racial friction and unrest. In Birmingham, recent public events have given indication that we all have opportunity for a new constructive and realistic approach to racial problems.

However, we are now confronted by a series of demonstrations by some of our Negro citizens, directed and led in part by outsiders. We recognize the natural impatience of people who feel that their hopes are slow in being realized. But we are convinced that these demonstrations are unwise and untimely.

We agree with certain local Negro leadership which has called for honest and open negotiations of racial issues in our area. And we believe this kind of facing of issues can best be accomplished by citizens of our town metropolitan area, white and Negro, meeting with their knowledge and experience of the local situation. All of us need to face that responsibility and find proper channels for its accomplishment.

Just as we formerly pointed out that "hatred and violence have no sanction in our religious and political traditions," we also point out that such actions as incitement to hatred and violence, however technically peaceful actions may be, have not contributed to the resolution of our local problems. We do not believe that these days of new hope are days when extreme measures are justified in Birmingham.

We commend the community as a whole, and the local news media and law enforcement officials in particular, on the calm manner in which these demonstrations have been handled. We urge the public to continue to show restraint should the demonstrations continue, and the law enforcement officials to remain calm and continue to protect our city from violence.

We further strongly urge our own Negro community to withdraw support from these demonstrations, and to unite locally in working peacefully for a better Birmingham. When rights are consistently denied, a cause should be pressed in the courts and in negotiations among local leaders, and not in the streets. We appeal to both our white and Negro citizenry to observe the principles of law and order and common sense. (Birmingham *Post Herald,* April 13, 1963, p. 10)

Writing first on the margins of his newspaper, then on paper brought to him, King composed the "Letter" in answer to this statement.[12]

When he responded to the statement, King made four rhetorically astute choices: to respond at all; to respond at length to each proposition in the statement; to adopt a tone of patience and goodwill; and to cast his message in the form of a Pauline letter. The second and third choices have been discussed at length by Bosmajian, Fulkerson, and Klein. I shall concentrate on the first and fourth choices.

RHETORICAL STRATEGIES

The Assumption of Equality

As civil rights leader and as rhetor, King, like Paul, knew how to seize an opportunity. Plainly, the clergymen expected no answer to their statement. By answering, however, King achieved for himself the legitimacy that the eight had denied him by failing to name him in their statement and suggesting that mere "outsiders" came to cause trouble.[13] The salutation, "My Dear Fellow Clergymen," makes King a colleague, an equal. If King is a colleague or "brother," his response is not only appropriate but also obligatory—one's brothers deserve an answer. The conclusion of the "Letter" tells us that King meant to maintain the position of brother and equal: "I also hope that circumstances will soon make it possible for me to meet each of you, not as an integrationist or a civil-rights leader, but as a fellow clergyman and a Christian brother" (p. 100). This sentence resembles the "greeting" that often came at the close of Pauline and other Greek letters. "The greeting was a distinct literary form which was intended to establish a bond of friendship. It was essentially one of those gestures which has emotional expression as its main purpose."[14] In King's case, the expressed hope of a meeting was both irreproachably natural, on the one hand, and notably audacious, on the other.

The Assumption of a Pauline Persona

King achieved authority and power by using the apostolic letter form along with biblically grounded imagery and syntax. Although the eight clergymen used their positions as religious leaders to gain a hearing, they employed virtually no religious references (except for the statement that "hatred and violence have no sanction in our religious and political traditions"). Rather than avoiding religious forms, allusions, and diction, King embraced them and used them extensively. The churchmen, on the other hand, simply signed their names, as if to invest their statement with religious authority by implication. This, of course, they could not do. As Kenneth Burke has said, "If you want to operate, like a theologian, with a terminology that includes 'God' as its key term, the only sure way to do it is to put in the term, and that's that."[15] King used the key term and transformed the discussion into a religious dialogue.

When King chose the Pauline model, he took on not the Hellenized Jew of the Greek texts but the Paul of the English translators, notably the 1611 translators. The "Letter" contains many significant passages where King's style clearly echoes the Pauline epistles of the Authorized Version. Furthermore, additional images and syntactic patterns in the "Letter" may be traced to other biblical books. Like Paul's epistles themselves, King's "Letter" is a complex allusive structure, reflecting the author's grasp of scriptural literature.[16]

The "Letter" contains a number of straightforward references to St. Paul's letters. Most obvious is the quotation in King's response to the charge of extremism: "Was not Paul an extremist for the Christian gospel: 'I bear in my body the marks of the Lord Jesus'" (p. 92; the reference is to Galatians 6:17). Discussing the middle way between complacency and black nationalism, King observed, "there is the more excellent way of love and nonviolent protest" (p. 90). Paul wrote to the Corinthians, "and yet shew I unto you a more excellent way. Though I speak with the tongues of men and of angels, and have not charity, I am become as sounding brass. . . " (I Corinthians 12:31-13:1). Through the phrase "a more excellent way," King associated his *love,* for which nonviolent action is a medium, and the love ("charity") of St. Paul's famous meditation. After having brought Paul's meditation into his reader's mind, King recalled the passage again a few pages later, as he confessed disappointment with the church. "There can be no disappointment where there is not deep love. Yes, I love the church" (p. 95). St. Paul asserted that despite spiritual gifts, one was nothing without love (I Corinthians 13:1-3). In his "Letter," King broadened the power of love, arguing that it is a necessary condition for disappointment and thus for the nonviolent protest that arises from disappointment. Like Paul, he placed love at the foundation of constructive action.

King alluded to Paul's characterization of the church as the body of Christ: "Yes, I see the church as the body of Christ. But, oh! How we have blemished and scarred that body . . ." (p. 95). The point made by Paul and developed by King is that the church is a whole: "For as the body is one, and hath many members, and all the members of that one body, being many, are one body: so also is Christ" (I Corinthians 12:12). If the church is a whole, then segregation and other racist practices unnaturally divide that whole.

Among the exponents of divisive behavior, King cited as the worst "not the White Citizen's Counciler or the Ku Klux Klanner, but the white moderate, who is more devoted to 'order' than to justice . . . ." He is "the Negro's great stumbling block in his stride toward freedom . . . " (p. 87). St. Paul warned the Romans, "Let us not therefore judge one another any more: but judge this rather, that no man put a stumbling block or an occasion to fall in his brother's way" (Romans 14:13). To those at Corinth, Paul wrote: "But take heed lest by any means this liberty of yours become a stumbling block to them that are weak" (I Corinthinans 8:9). In both these uses, the apostle urged a sense of responsibility upon his audience. More particularly, the passages are interesting because Paul argued for a consideration of one's fellows over a narrow concern for what is "legal." These Pauline allusions highlight two thematically important ideas in the "Letter": first, King's love for the church and reliance on that love to provide integrity to his protest, and, second, his disappointment with the white moderate churchman.

During the course of his letters, Paul often addressed his audience directly. A few examples will illustrate the style: "Nevertheless, brethren, I have written the more boldly unto you . . ." (Romans 15:15). "Now concerning spiritual gifts, brethren, I would not have you ignorant" (I Corinthians 12:1). "I marvel that ye are so soon removed from him that called you into the grace of Christ . . ." (Galatians 1:6). King used a similar technique. Examples are not so much allusions to particular statements by Paul as evidence that King was using the same epistolarly technique. "I must make two honest confessions to you, my Christian and Jewish brothers" (p. 87). "I commend you, Reverend Stallings, for your Christian stand on this past Sunday . . ." (p. 93). These and similar passages maintain a dialectic rhythm in the "Letter," giving it the immediacy and vigor of a dialogue—the same immediacy and vigor one senses in Paul's letters.

The last paragraph of King's "Letter" expresses a wish: "I hope this letter finds you strong in the faith" (p. 100). To his converts Paul also spoke of such strength. For example, he praised Abraham, who "staggered not at the promise of God through unbelief, but was strong in faith, giving glory to God" (Romans 4:20). In closing his first letter to Corinth, he admonished: "Watch ye, stand fast in the faith quit you like men, be strong" (I Corinthians 16:13). King did not admonish; he merely expressed a hope. Nevertheless, that expression reminds us that he, like Paul, although more subtly, offered spiritual advice to his audience. Through a gently expressed hope, King exhorted them to be strong in faith. His strategy was to appeal to his audience as a traditional theologian and preacher, not as a rabble-rouser or as a dangerous outsider. His Pauline allusions, like his more obvious—indeed deliberately obvious—references to Augustine, Aquinas, Tillich, Buber, Jefferson, Eliot, Socrates, and others, help cast him in this role of the theologian, advisor, and preacher. Like Paul, King used the scriptures as a quarry for proofs, examples, and phraseology.

A stylistic habit that strengthens the link between the "Letter" and the English Bible is King's use of a prepositional phrase to express a metaphor, in which the headword of the phrase is a concrete noun, and the object of the preposition is an abstract noun. Examples include "garment of destiny" (p. 79), "darts of segregation" (p. 83), and "cup of endurance" (p. 84). In such phrases the headword establishes a lexical connection to a metaphor in the Bible. King was not simply quoting, however. He modified his use of the headword either by changing the object of the preposition or adding a prepositional phrase. For instance, Isaiah wrote of exchanging "the garment of praise for the spirit of heaviness" (61:3). King wrote, "We are caught in an inescapable network of mutuality, tied in a single garment of destiny" (p. 79).

In a significant phrase, King's headword is *cup*. The word appears metaphorically several times in the Bible, as in the image of Psalm 23, "my cup runneth over." The Psalmist wrote, "I will take the cup of salvation, and call upon the name of the Lord" (116:13). Paul, perhaps recalling the Psalmist's usage, wrote of the eucharist: "The cup of blessing which we bless, is it not the communion of which we speak?" (I Corinthians 10:16). In the gospels the word *cup* takes on a somber meaning. Jesus asked James and John, "Are ye able to drink of the cup that I shall drink of. . . ?" (Matthew 20:22). In Gethsemane just before his arrest, he prayed, "Take away this cup from me" (Mark 14:36; see also Luke 22:42). King's usage carries the dark connotation of the gospels, with an ironic recollection of the cheerful image of Psalm 23. King wrote: "There comes a time when the cup of endurance runs over, and men are no longer willing to be plunged into the abyss of despair" (p. 84). In the rhetoric of Christian literature, *cup* signifies the redemptive suffering of the innocent. King's reference to the suffering of America's black population recalls biblical uses and ties the black Americans to previous innocent sufferers.

In fact, King used the prepositional phrase with the biblically significant headword several times when he described the victims of racial prejudice. As examples, consider the headwords *shadow, dart,* and *chain.*

The headword *shadow* appears in the image of the broken promises and failed negotiations in Birmingham. "As in so many past experiences," King said, "our hopes had been blasted, and the shadow of deep disappointment settled upon us (p. 80). "Shadow of disappointment" calls to mind the image of Psalm 23, "the valley of the shadow of death." Actually "the shadow of death," a proverbial phrase used to describe death and despair, also appeared in Psalm 44:19, "covered us with the shadow of death," and in Job 3:5 and 10:21-22. King's usage rhetorically joins the suffering of contemporary black Americans to that of biblical speakers who are both faithful and (at least in Job's case) plainly innocent.

Like *shadow, dart* appears in a description of suffering. To the charge that his march was "untimely," King responded with a diatribe against those who would cry, "Wait!" "For years now I have heard the word 'Wait!' It rings in the ear of every Negro with piercing familiarity" (p. 83). The word *piercing* echoes uncomfortably as the reader proceeds several sentences further: "Perhaps," wrote King, "it is easy for those who have never felt the stinging darts of segregation to say, 'Wait'" (p. 83).[17] In the Bible, *dart* may refer to a literal weapon: "The sword of him that layeth at him cannot hold: the spear, the dart, nor the habergeon" (Job 41:26). I Likewise in Proverbs: "Till a dart strike through his liver. . ." (7:23). But a dart I may also be a metaphoric danger. Paul used it thus in his famous passage on "the whole armor of God": "Above all, taking the shield of faith, wherewith ye shall be I able to quench all the fiery darts of the wicked" (Ephesians 6:16).

Just as King used *dart* to represent an inward pain, he used *chains* to describe inward restraints. As he despaired of the church, he wrote, "But again I am thankful to God that some noble souls from the ranks of organized religion have broken loose from the paralyzing chains of conformity and joined us. . ." (p. 97). Biblical writers spoke of chains, both literal and figurative. The author of II Peter described the fallen angels, who were "delivered into chains of darkness" (2:4). The Psalmist wrote of those whose "pride compasseth them about as a chain" (73:6). Presumably they, like the fallen angels, deserved their suffering, but in the following use from Lamentations one cannot know whether the sufferer is guilty. The author spoke as one afflicted by an enemy: "He hath hedged me about, that I cannot get out: he hath made my chain heavy" (3:7). Chains are metaphors of punishment and despair. None of the writers suggested that such chains can be broken. On one occasion, however, a literal chain was broken. Peter, imprisoned by Herod, was miraculously set free: "And his chains fell off from his hands" (Acts 12:7). In King's usage, "the chains of conformity" would appear to have been forged, like the Psalmist's chain of pride, by the wearers themselves. But King suggested even those chains can be broken, like Peter's.

As he used *cup, shadow, dart,* and *chain* to summon up biblical accounts of suffering, King used the metaphors of *rock* and *quicksand* to recall biblical characterizations of stability and instability. Arguing that his audience must cease waiting and act, King urged: "Now is the time to lift our national policy from the quicksand of racial injustice to the solid rock of human dignity" (p. 90). Old Testament people frequently used *rock* as an image for God. For example, in Deuteronomy: "He is the Rock his work is perfect" (32:4). Hannah declared: "neither is there any rock like our God" (I Samuel 2:2). A rock may also symbolize any heroic figure; Isaiah foretold the coming of a king who would be "as the shadow of a great rock in a weary land" (32:2). Jesus, punning on Peter's name, announced, "Thou art Peter, and upon this rock I will build my church" (Matthew 16:18). Quicksands are a variation on the sand foundation in the parable of the men who built houses: "The wise man, which built his house upon a rock. . ." and the "foolish man, which built his house upon the sand: and the rain descended, and the floods came, and the winds blew, and beat upon that house; and it fell: and great was the fall of it" (Matthew 7:24–27). King may also have had in mind a couplet from a popular hymn:

On Christ the solid rock I stand,
All other ground is sinking sand.[18]

Treacherous, sinking quicksand typifies racial injustice. The rock, an image of righteousness, stability, and dignity, resonates with its Old Testament associations with God and the godly.

These and similar images in the "Letter" exist on at least two figurative levels. At the first level is simple metaphor, making the abstract not merely concrete but felt. One feels the weight of the garment, the sinking into the quicksand, the coldness of the shadow, the piercing of the darts, and the impediment of the chains. King made his audience literally feel the burden of racial bigotry. At the second level, each headword—*shadow, dart,* and so on— brings with it its biblical associations. King's image of the shadow or the dart stimulates the reader to recall other shadows or darts, much as one infers a meaning for a painting in which iconographically significant objects appear. These images become the keys to a meaning that the reader works out, usually subconsciously.

It is easy to see how nouns can function in this iconographic manner, but verbs may also have iconographic significance. The "Letter from Birmingham Jail" includes some biblical images contained not in prepositional phrases but in verbs or verbal constructions. Consider two examples: *root out* and *walk.* Discussing the need for "creative extremists" (p. 92) to take action where white moderates had failed. King observed, "Few members of the oppressor race can understand the yearnings of the oppressed, and still fewer have the vision to see that injustice must be rooted out by strong, persistent, and determined action" (p. 93). Whatever must be rooted out is, naturally, *rooted* and well established. It must be dug up, with no fragment left to take root again. The Deuteronomist characterized the treatment of those who worshipped false gods: "And the Lord rooted them out of their land in anger. . ." (29:28). Bildad, Job's "comforter," promised that the wicked man's "confidence shall be rooted out of his tabernacle" (Job 18:14). The Psalmist addressed a similar threat to boastful deceivers: "God shall likewise destroy thee for ever, he shall take thee away, and pluck thee out of thy dwelling place, and root thee out of the land of the living" (52:5). The biblical use of *root out* appears either in statements of what has occurred or in promises (threats) of what will occur. And furthermore, it is often a person or persons who will be rooted out. By contrast, King's usage, applied to an abstraction (injustice) seems mild. King is only observing what *should* be done. Yet even in the "Letter," *root out* retains some of the violence of the biblical usage: the thing to be rooted out will be manhandled and tossed aside as worthless and malignant. *Rooting out* is an "extreme" action, and King bound his usage to biblical images of the same sort of extreme conduct.

At first glance, the verb *to walk* seems entirely free of biblical associations and not likely to operate as a biblical image. Yet, King praised the few whites who have broken from convention and joined in his cause: "They have left their secure congregations and walked the streets of Albany, Georgia, with us" (p. 97). In fact, in the English Bible one may find *walk* as a metonymy standing for a series of actions that might be conveyed in the phrases "to conduct oneself," "to pass through life, "to live one's life," or more simply "to live" or "to exist." Biblical writers often modified *walk,* so as to mean "the righteous person's safe passage through life. There are exceptions: danger may also walk, as in the Psalmist's description of "the pestilence that walketh in darkness' (91:6); but in the majority of cases, one who walks is both righteous and protected. The biblical examples are so numerous that a few selections must suffice:

> But as for me, I will walk in mine integrity: redeem me, and be merciful unto me. (Psalm 26:11)

> Better is the poor that walketh in his uprightness, than he that is perverse in his ways, though he be rich. (Proverbs 28:6)

> . . . as ye have received of us how ye ought to walk and to please God, so ye would abound more and more. (I Thessalonians 4:1)[19]

For King, to walk was as morally significant an action as to go to jail. His career saw him do both often and lead others in them. He used the phrase "stride toward freedom" ("Letter," p. 87) as a book title. Those who walked with him in Albany and in Birmingham performed an action of magnitude and moral significance. To walk was an act expressing personal courage, a faith in the rightness of one's action, and a trust of those walking along with oneself. All these meanings have their source in the biblical image *to walk*. In his marches, King took the biblical metaphor of "walking uprightly" and made it literal. In the "Letter" his use of the verb *to walk* summons up a biblical context for the civil rights marches.

THE "LETTER" AS SERMON

The "Letter from Birmingham Jail" is both an epistle in the Pauline style and also a sermon. Among modern students of Paul, it is not unusual to find the contention that the Pauline epistles themselves are sermons.[20] Despite the private queries, messages, and asides appearing here and there, Paul's letters were essentially public documents, composed and delivered orally. Beda Rigaux argued that Paul's letters "are official acts in his capacity of being an Apostle." He added, "In many instances, the letters seem to be nothing more than a literary prolongation of a previous sermon text which had been delivered orally."[21] Bo Reicke explains that "Most New Testament epistles are not literary substitutes for conversation, like private letters, but ways of speaking publicly to congregations that could not be addressed in person."[22] Furthermore, following the practice of the day, Paul dictated to an amanuensis,[23] usually writing only a sentence or two of greeting in his own hand (see, for instance, I Corinthians 16:21 and Colossians 4:18). He spoke the text of the letter aloud and in doing so might easily have used specific passages from sermons previously delivered.[24]

Like Paul, King had well-established habits of delivery that characterized his sermons and marked his writing. King's habits of composition were those of the extempore preacher. Despite the fact that some of his sermons were written down and later published, he grew up in a tradition where the preacher was expected to compose as he delivered the sermon. Much of what he said the preacher drew from a mental storehouse stocked from the Bible. For the extempore preacher, the Bible became a resource similar to the stock of phrases and images retained by the Homeric rhapsode.[25] Thus, like Homeric epic, the "extempore" sermon may be less spontaneous and more conventional than would first appear. King successfully used the methods of extempore preaching as he composed the "Letter"; he had read widely and his mental storehouse was well stocked. He took advantage of his uncommon skill and knowledge, avoiding the pitfalls (e.g., redundancy, shapelessness, illogicalness) that people of less skill might have stumbled into.

A good deal of the beauty of the "Letter" comes from King's skillful use of the extempore preacher's techniques.[26] His references and allusions, for example, sound natural rather than bookish because they did not come directly from books. In jail without notes or books, King had only his memory to consult. He could recall the gist of Martin Buber's "I and Thou" relationship and summarize it easily. The reader is not obliged to plow through lengthy quotations from Tillich or Aquinas, but in these and other cases King has given us the kernel of their thought.

Memory is developed and honed by the extempore preacher. He is able to remember short passages and to use key phrases to summarize longer passages. King quoted Amos from memory, not quite accurately, but upon revision he left the sentence as he recalled it, because pendantic correctness of detail was not his stylistic goal. The imagery and diction that we have traced to biblical usages came into the "Letter" through King's memory, not simply a lexical memory but a capacity to remember rhythm, tone, and context as well.

Parallel structure, effectively managed throughout the "Letter," frequently marks King's sermons and speeches. Speakers within many traditions, of course, use parallel structure, but the elaborate repetition King used to build to a climax is particularly popular in the tradition of black pulpit oratory. In the "Letter" the best example of such a device is the remarkable sentence—more than a page long—composed of "when" clauses in parallel, building to a conclusion. The sentence comes when King dismissed the urging of white Americans that blacks wait to let justice be done rather than seek to bring it about by direct action:

> But when you have seen vicious mobs . . .;
> when you have seen hate-filled policemen . . .;
> when you see the vast majority . . .;
> when you suddenly find your tongue twisted . . .;
>   and see tears welling up . . .;
>   and see ominous clouds of inferiority . . .;
>   and see her beginning to distort . . .;
> when you have to concoct an answer . . .;
> when you take a cross-country drive . . .;
> when you are humiliated day in and day out . . .;
> when your first name becomes "nigger" . . .;
> when you are harried by day and haunted by night . . .;
> when you are forever fighting . . .;
> then you will understand why we find it difficult to wait.
> (pp. 83–84)

The effect of such passages is to transform King's readers into auditors.[27]

To grant that King's oral style influenced the "Letter" is not to grant that the "Letter" is itself a sermon, however. Modern readers, accustomed to thinking of sermons as discourses occurring only in fixed services of worship, might object that to be a sermon, a message must be *spoken* from a pulpit to a congregation. These readers would certainly point out that King had no pulpit, did not speak, and had no congregation.[28]

All these objections are accurate. King did not deliver the "Letter from Birmingham Jail" from a pulpit or even a church; he did not address a body of listeners seated before him. And yet in the "Letter" he performed one of a preacher's major tasks—that of prophecy. The Hebrew word for preaching is related to that for prophecy.[29] The prophets, proclaiming the message of God, were preachers, not writers.[30] Walter Russell Bowie reminded his modern-day readers of the preacher's role: preaching "must be prophetic." He went on to explain the prophet's task: "The prophet first of all will be helping his people remember the everlasting reality of God, the moral accountability of man, the sacredness of personality, and the seriousness of life."[31] Here Bowie described in general terms the task and the topics King set for himself in the "Letter."

Defending himself against the implied charge of being an outsider, King compared himself not only to Paul but also to the prophets: "Just as the prophets of the eighth-century B.C. left their villages and carried their 'thus saith the Lord' far beyond the boundaries of their home towns . . . so I am compelled to carry the gospel of freedom . . ." (p. 78). Later, calling Amos an "extremist for justice," King quoted him: "Let justice roll like waters and righteousness like an ever-flowing stream" (p. 92; the reference is to Amos 5:24). The biblical prophets did not call for justice or righteousness in the abstract; they spoke of particular contemporary injustices and transgressions. They wept at the wrongdoing and suffering around them. Isaiah lamented: "Look away from me; I will weep bitterly, labor not to comfort me . . ." (22:4). Likewise Jeremiah said: "Oh, that my head were waters, and mine eyes a fountain of tears . . ." (9:11). The author of Nehemiah confessed: "I sat down and wept . . ." (1:4). King admitted: "I have wept over the laxity of the church" (p. 95).

Although prophets weep, they also pronounce judgment. For example, Isaiah: "thus saith the Lord God. . . . Judgment also will I lay to the line. . ." (28:16-17). King boldly echoed the prophets, speaking out against the contemporary church: "But the judgment of God is upon the church as never before" (p. 96). Like the biblical prophets, King saw wrongdoing and was moved to tears; he was also spurred to denounce the injustice he saw.

King's "Letter," then, is by no means a sermon in any limited, modern sense. On the other hand, in it King performed the preacher's traditional role as prophet, as one who sees clearly and speaks the truth plainly. Moreover, when one recalls what truth King spoke and why he was separated from a potential congregation, one comes closer to understanding how the "Letter from Birmingham Jail" can be seen as a sermon.

One of the major themes of the "Letter" is the failure of the white church to promote racial justice. King accused white churchmen of not doing what they should have done and of not seeing what they should have seen:

> Some have been outright opponents, refusing to understand the freedom movement and misrepresenting its leaders; all too many others have . . . remained silent behind the anesthetizing security of stained-glass windows. (p. 94)

White American churchgoers, blinded by the religious clichés and prejudices that the stained-glass windows symbolize in King's text, are the major audience of the "Letter." They are the congregation: to them King is really speaking, despite his ostensible address to the eight clergymen.[32] Thus the fact that the "Letter" was not delivered in a church before a congregation should not be seen as proof that it is not a sermon.

CONCLUSION

At the outset of this essay, I introduced three propositions: that Martin Luther King, in the "Letter from Birmingham Jail," used the Apostle Paul as a type for himself and the Pauline epistle as a model for the "Letter"; that he took from the English Bible not just a literary form but also a series of iconographically signficant words and images; and that he shaped his material into a text that, like Paul's letters, should be seen as a sermon. It is appropriate to examine a few of the implications of this argument.

One clear implication is that for King the Bible was heuristic. In the constrained circumstances under which the "Letter" was composed, his heuristic devices consisted largely of the clergymen's statement and the biblical images, word-clusters, literary forms, and *personae* that he carried in his memory. Using these devices, he constructed his text. For the reader, the Bible may also be heuristic. When we see his allusions and recall their biblical contexts, we find King's text more accessible, more readable. In recognizing his allusions, we are in a sense inventing the text for ourselves rather than reading something invented according to a system we do not understand. An extensive discussion of the relationships between memory and invention, on the one hand, and memory and readability, on the other, is far beyond the scope of my essay, but one cannot investigate biblical allusion in the "Letter" without recognizing those relationships.

Clearly, King identified with Paul. A reader might well ask, "Why Paul?" King's career, like Paul's, developed in such a way that his ministry extended beyond the traditional institutions of the day. Having left the conservative Jewish community, Paul moved on the fringes of Roman society, never again settling down as one rooted in a particular place. Of the various congregations he founded or visited, none was his special home. King, although officially pastor of several churches, did not limit himself to ministering only to those congregations. Like Paul, he spoke not *for* one church or *to* one church. More and more, he moved impatiently beyond the bounds set by institutional religion.

Of all bibilical personages, Paul perhaps best stands for the destruction of barriers. Had King chosen an Old Testament type or model, as many seventeenth-century New England Puritan preachers did, he might have created various implications of a Chosen People, of insiders and outsiders. This is precisely what he could not do. His message was against division or separation and all the social institutions, including jails and segregated churches, that can be used to promote division or segregation.

More important than any historical similarities between King and Paul, however, is the rhetorical opportunity that King seized when he borrowed Paul's literary form. The epistle as written by Paul has not been widely used outside the New Testament. He and his contemporaries invented it; it flourished for several generations but died away in the second century.[33] By reviving this ancient form, King was able to take advantage of its particular rhetorical conventions: its dialectic rhythm of statement and response, its use of scriptural texts and imagery, and—perhaps most important for King at the moment of writing—its author-audience relationship. The very composing of an epistle (as a proxy sermon) defines one's audience as people who are to be advised, guided, and convinced, but who, more significantly, are to be persuaded of certain conclusions not merely because they are logical or appealing but because they are in accord with the audience's own beliefs. Paul did not try to convert his audience with his letters. Presumably he and his fellow missionaries accomplished conversions through more direct and intimate means. Paul's letters aimed to strengthen the belief of the converted, to show them how to conduct themselves in light of their belief, and to teach them the implications of their belief.

Like Paul, King assumed the common ground of belief between himself and his audience. The rhetorical prominence of the Bible in the "Letter" is one sign of this assumption. King's overall rhetorical strategy in the "Letter" was the strategy of Pauline epistle. He said, in effect, "If you believe in these truths, then you must act in a certain way." The eight clergymen could not deny their beliefs, nor can the white moderate public whom King sought to reach in his larger audience. King used the beliefs of his audience urging them that civil order and routine must, according to those beliefs, be subordinate to the freedom and welfare of their fellow human beings.

"All real living is meeting," wrote Martin Buber.[34] In the "Letter from Birmingham Jail" King closes, as we have seen, with a wish to meet the eight clergymen. Paul also wished to be with those to whom he wrote. As Amos Wilder has observed, "Paul writes always as one thwarted by absence and eagerly anticipating meeting or reunion."[35] Early in his letter to the Romans, for example, he confessed that he prayed, "making request, if by any means now at length I might have a prosperous journey by the will of God to come unto you" (1:10). Paul's letters are the written substitutes for a face-to-face meeting.

The New Testament scholar Robert W. Funk has argued that such a passage in a Pauline letter should be called the "apostolic *parousia*," after the Greek word for "presence."[36] In these sections Paul expresses his hopes to visit the recipients. For Paul, writing was not the best means of reaching his audience and manifesting his authority as an apostle: "Since Paul gives precedence to the oral word, the written word will not function as a primary medium of his own apostleship."[37] Nevertheless, Paul used all his literary abilities to make his letters effective. Like Paul, King used a language that encouraged a meeting of people. The success of his biblically founded language may be seen immediately when one compares his "Letter" to the clergymen's statement: their dry, secular prose conveys only self-satisfaction and the demand that others fit their preconceptions. No meeting with their readers is sought. Their language is civil rather than pastoral; it expresses little human concern. King's language, on the other hand, is pastoral in that the writer shows genuine care for a well-defined audience whom he sought to guide and teach.

The rhetoric of Paul's letters (and of much biblical literature) is not the rhetoric of the classical oration. Argument was not Paul's major goal, nor is it King's, no matter how effectively each man could argue specific issues. Paul's and King's rhetoric is closer to that of liturgy than to that of argument. It is a commonplace of rhetorical instruction that argument begins not with disagreement but with doubt.[38] One might say that liturgy begins with faith: It is the acting out of the premises one accepts as truths. All the components of liturgy, including its language, are intended to move an audience to become participants. Liturgy, that is to say, facilitates *meeting*, in the sense that Buber used the term. Liturgy may be written but it cannot be read in the way that an argument can be read, alone and silently. To exist, liturgy depends upon the presence and participation of a group, or at least of "two or three."

Like liturgy, King's activities in Birmingham were belief acted out. Those who marched with him joined his action as believers join in a liturgy. In traditional Christianity, liturgy recreates the events in Jesus's life taken as central to the faith—notably, the Last Supper as recreated in the Eucharist. In the typology of black American Protestantism, biblical events have a significance that may be expressed liturgically. King's going to jail and composing the epistle/sermon in jail recreated Paul's action, in the manner of liturgical re-creation. The "Letter" seeks to reach its audience (both the eight clergymen and the moderate white public) and to unite them in action with King. Speaking in 1962 to the National Press Club, King explained his methods (as practiced most recently in Albany): "I feel that this way of nonviolence is vital because it is the only way to reestablish the broken community."[39] His activities in Birmingham the next year had the same goal.

With its Pauline form and its extensive biblical imagery, the "Letter from Birmingham Jail" appeals to an audience familiar with Judeo-Christian literature and who accept the ethical teachings of the Bible. Using the resources of the preacher, King urged his audience to enter into a liturgical acting out of their belief, as in all liturgy, with the goal of meeting; for without the brotherhood and respect generated through meeting, no true justice can be done. King's apostolic mission in Birmingham was to bring about union and seek justice. His arrest was planned to act out the separation and injustice he opposed. The longer-than-planned stay in jail and the clergymen's statement provided opportunity to create unity and bring about justice. It is through the active, liturgical rhetoric of the Pauline letter that he accomplished his mission.

NOTES

[1] Under the title of *Letter from Birmingham City Jail,* it was published in 1963 by the American Friends Service Committee and also by the Division of Christian Social Concern. In *Why We Can't Wait* (New York: Harper & Row, 1964), King published a slightly revised version, which I refer to here.

[2] Haig A. Bosmajian, "The Rhetoric of Martin Luther King's Letter from Birmingham Jail," *Midwestern Quarterly,* 8 (1967), 127–43; Richard P. Fulkerson, "The Public Letter as Rhetorical Form: Structure, Logic, and Style in King's 'Letter from Birmingham Jail,'" *Quarterly Journal of Speech,* 65 (1979), 121–34; and Mia Klein, "The *Other* Beauty of Martin Luther King's 'Letter from Birmingham Jail,'" *College Composition and Communication,* 32 (1981), 30–37. See also Lucy A.M. Keele, "A Burkeian Analysis of the Rhetorical Strategies of Martin Luther King," Diss. University of Oregon, 1972; and Hortense J. Spillers, "Martin Luther King and the Style of the Black Sermon," *The Black Scholar,* 3, No. 1 (1971), 14–37.

[3] Glen V. Wiberg, Letter to Editor, *Christian Century,* 80 (1963), 986.

[4] Readers will find useful discussions of typology in Erich Auerbach, *Mimesis: The Representation of Reality in Western Literature* (Garden City, NY: Anchor-Doubleday, 1957), p. 170.; and in Northrup Frye, *The Great Code: The Bible and Literature* (New York and London: Harcourt Brace Jovanovich, 1982), *passim.*

[5] Barbara Lewalski, "Typological Symbolism and the 'Progress of the Soul' in Seventeenth-Century Literature," in *Literary Uses of Typology from the Late Middle Ages to the Present,* ed. Earl Miner (Princeton: Princeton University Press, 1977), p. 81.

[6] For further discussion of the change in typological exegesis brought by the Reformation, see Paul Korshin. *Typologies in England 1650–1820* (Princeton: Princeton University Press, 1982), p. 31.

[7] See Emory Elliott, "From Father to Son: The Evalution of Typology in Puritan New England," in Miner, pp. 204–27.

[8] Henry H. Mitchell, *Black Preaching,* rev. ed. (New York: Harper and Row, 1979), p. 123. See also Benjamin Mays and J.W. Nicholson, *The Negro's Church* (1933; rpt. New York: Negro Universities Press, 1969), p. 67.

[9] Martin Luther King, "The Death of Evil Upon the Seashore," in *Strength to Love* (New York: Harper & Row 1963), p. 61. Subsequent references to King's sermons are to this source.

[10] Karl Barth says of Romans 1:1 that in it Paul, as apostle, "dares to approach others and to demand a hearing without fear either of exalting himself or of approximating too closely to his audience. He appeals only to the authority of God. This is the ground of his authority. There is no other." *The Epistle to the Romans,* 6th ed., trans Edwyn C. Hoskyns (London: Oxford University Press, 1933), p. 28.

[11] The marchers deliberately violated the injunction, and King meant to be arrested. He spent longer in jail than planned because bail money had been used up and more had to be raised. See *Why We Can't Wait*, pp. 69–70.

[12] Ibid., pp. 77–78n. David Levering Lewis is wrong to suggest that the "Letter" responded to a statement of January 1963. See *King: A Biography*, 2nd ed. (Urbana: University of Illinois Press, 1978), pp. 186–87.

[13] Fulkerson is not being precise when he says, "The clergymen *accuse King* and his followers" (p. 122, my italics).

[14] Terence Y. Mullins, "Greeting as a New Testament Form," *Journal of Biblical Literature*, 87 (1968), 425 and 418.

[15] *Language as Symbolic Action* (Berkeley and Los Angeles: University of California Press, 1966), p. 46.

[16] To list Paul's scriptural allusions and citations would be a monumental task. For selected examples, readers may see I Corinthianans 8:6; 9:9; 10:5–10, 26; 14:36; and 15:32–33. For a discussion of Paul's homiletic use of scripture, see Robin Scroggs, "Paul as Rhetorician: Two Homilies in Romans 1–11," in *Jews, Greeks, and Christians: Essays in Honor of Willian David Davies*, ed. Robert Hamerton-Kelly and Robin Scroggs (Leiden: E.J. Brill, 1976), pp. 278ff.

[17] Klein discusses the emotional effect of the word *dart*; see pp. 36–37.

[18] The text of the hymn, "The Solid Rock," is by Edward Mote. It may be found in several collections, including *The Broadman Hymnal* (Nashville: Broadman, 1940), p. 96.

[19] See also Psalms 23:4; 56:13; 84:11, 116:9; 119:45; 138:7; Proverbs 28:18; Isaiah 2:5; 30:21; Jeremiah 6:16; Micah 6:8; Romans 4:11–12; 6:4; 8:1; 14:15; and Galatians 6:16.

[20] For instance, Robin Scroggs says, "He is first of all a preacher, a rhetorician" (p. 273).

[21] Beda Rigaux, *The letters of St. Paul*, trans. Stephen Yonic, O.F.M., S.S.L. (Chicago: Franciscan Herald Press, 1968), pp. 119 and 128.

[22] Reicke explains that the models for the New Testament letters are homiletic:
The central parts of the New Testament epistles do not reflect the influence of Jewish and Greek letter traditions in the way that the salutation and conclusion do. The heart of the epistles is generally a doctrinal section followed by a series of admonitions. These may be regarded as following the forms of Jewish, Greek, and Christian preaching.
See Bo Reicke, Introduction, *The Epistles of James, Peter, and Jude*, The Anchor Bible (Garden City, NY: Doubleday, 1964), p. xxxi.

[23] Martin R.P. McGuire, "Letters and Letter Carriers in Christian Antiquity," *Classical World*, 53 (1960), 150.

[24] In addition, it was the custom that letters received were read aloud, even if the recipient was alone (Ibid). On the composition of Paul's letters, see Martin Dibelius, *A Fresh Approach to the New Testament and Early Christian Literature* (New York: Scribner's, 1936), pp. 145 f.; and Wayne A. Meeks, notes on I Thessalonians 1:2–3:13 in *The Writings of St. Paul*, Norton Critical Edition (New York: W.W. Norton, 1972), p. 7.

[25] A discussion of oral composition among ancient Greek rhapsodes may be found in Milman Parry, *The Making of Homeric Verse: Collected Papers*, ed. Adam Parry (Oxford: Clarendon, 1971).

[26] King spent the first days of April 1963 speaking in Birmingham on many of the same issues to be addressed in the "Letter"; he had, for instance, rehearsed the defense against the "outsider" charge. See *Why We Can't Wait*, pp. 62-65, for his account of speeches made in preparation for the march.

[27] Parallel structure appears often in Paul's letters. Rigaux notes the influence of parallelism in Hebrew poetry (p. 127). Modern preachers, including King and others in the black homiletic tradition, might feel the same influence, of course.

[28] King did not hesitate to preach outside churches; James H. Thurber and John L. Petelle point out that "the Negro minister appears not to consider his church alone as his pulpit": "The Negro Pulpit and Civil Rights," *Central States Speech Journal,* 19 (1968), 275.

[29] Hartwig Hirschfield, "Preaching (Jewish)," in *Encyclopedia of Religion and Ethics,* ed. James Hastings (New York: Scribner's, 1951), p. 220.

[30] Amos Wilder points out the prophets' reluctance to write: "In Israel's tradition God's servants the prophets did not write unless they were ordered to . . . "; see *Early Christian Rhetoric* (Cambridge: Harvard University Press, 1971), p. 13.

[31] *Preaching* (New York and Nashville: Abingdon, 1954), pp. 54 and 56.

[32] The clergymen, whom King steadily addresses as *you,* are only the secondary audience. Their statement is a convenient summary of a widely held set of attitudes. King did not need to follow Paul's occasional practice of making up opponents. In the clergymen's statement he has an actual text to oppose, but this fact does not in itself make its authors his principal audience. Despite pride of leadership, the clergymen are too few to effect the changes desired by King.

[33] Readers may find accounts of the literary use of the epistle after Paul in William G. Doty, *Letters in Primitive Christianity* (Philadelphia: Fortress Press, 1973), pp. 65ff; and Alfred E. Barnett, *Paul Becomes a Literary Influence* (Chicago: University of Chicago Press, 1941), *passim.*

[34] Martin Buber, *I and Thou,* 2nd ed., trans. Ronald Gregor Smith (New York: Scribner's, 1958), p. 11.

[35] Wilder, p. 14.

[36] Robert W. Funk, "The Apostolic *Parousia:* Form and Significance," in *Christian History and Interpretation: Studies Presented to John Knox,* ed. W.R. Farmer, *et al.* (Cambrige: Cambridge University Press, 1967), p. 258.

[37] Funk, p. 269.

[38] For example see Cleanth Brooks and Robert Penn Warren, *Modem Rhetoric,* 4th ed. (New York: Harcourt Brace Jovanovich, 1979), pp. 129ff.

[39] Address to the National Press Club, Washington, D.C., July 19,1962; rpt. in *The Congressional Record,* July 20,1962, p. 14248.